Walter Walsh

The Secret History of the Oxford Movement

Fourth Edition

Walter Walsh

The Secret History of the Oxford Movement
Fourth Edition

ISBN/EAN: 9783744660976

Printed in Europe, USA, Canada, Australia, Japan

Cover: Foto ©ninafisch / pixelio.de

More available books at **www.hansebooks.com**

THE SECRET HISTORY

OF

THE OXFORD MOVEMENT

THE SECRET HISTORY

OF

THE OXFORD MOVEMENT

BY

WALTER WALSH

FOURTH EDITION. TWENTY-SECOND THOUSAND

LONDON
SWAN SONNENSCHEIN & CO., Ltd.
PATERNOSTER SQUARE, E.C.
1898

PREFACE.

I HAVE written this book at the request of an eminent Dignitary of the Church of England, noted for the liberality and breadth of his views of religion. He represented to me the need of a work which might be the means, in God's hands, of opening the eyes of loyal Churchmen to what is going on underneath the surface; and, as I have had exceptional opportunities for studying this aspect of the Ritualistic question, I have, though with not a little anxiety, complied with his request. I have written in no narrow-minded or party spirit. There is not, I believe, a single expression of my own opinion in the volume which will give offence either to Evangelical Churchmen, Broad Churchmen, or old-fashioned High Churchmen of the school of the late Bishop Samuel Wilberforce and Dean Burgon. I have little doubt that men of all these parties will agree with what I have written. Ritualists and Romanizers will, of course, not agree with me at all. Those who work in the dark do not love the man who seeks to drag them forth into the light of day.

I have taken every pains to be fair towards those whose conduct and teaching I criticize. I would not willingly misrepresent them in any way whatever. It was my anxiety to be fair and accurate, which induced me to adopt the plan of allowing these secret workers to tell their story *in their own words*. And, therefore, I have given full references and proofs for everything, taken from the writings of the Ritualists themselves. All my authorities are Ritualistic, with the exception of, perhaps, a score, whose testimonies were necessary for my purpose. The italics in the quotations are, with a very few exceptions, my own, not those of the persons quoted.

It is a significant fact that secrecy has largely characterized the Ritualistic Movement, even from the first year of its existence, when it was known by another name. Abundant proofs of this fact will be found in the following pages. Secret Ritualistic Societies have now come into existence, and they are increasing in number every year. At present the Church of England is literally honeycombed with Secret Societies, all working in the interests of the scheme for the Corporate Reunion of the Church of England with the Church of Rome. These secret plotters are the real wire-pullers of the Ritualistic Movement.

A great deal of that which was strictly secret in the early days of the Oxford Movement has now been made public by means of the Biographies and Letters of some of the principal actors. I have endeavoured to utilize the revelations made in those publications in the following pages. They are scattered here and there through many volumes, and no attempt has hitherto been made to bring them together in one book. But my principal authorities have been the secret and privately printed documents of the Ritualists themselves. From these I have been able to give reports of speeches delivered in the secret meetings of

Secret Societies, and of Semi-Secret Societies, several of them by men who have since risen to positions of eminence within the Church of England. In these secret gatherings they expressed themselves with a freedom which they have never adopted in their public utterances.

The Secret History of the *Priest in Absolution* is here given for the first time. Lord Redesdale's exposure in the House of Lords, in 1877, of that very indecent Confessional book for the use of Ritualistic Father Confessors, raised a great storm of indignation throughout the country. His lordship was not an Evangelical, but—as the present Bishop of Winchester informs us in his *Life of Archbishop Tait*— "a sober and trusted High Churchman of the earlier sort." Of course, the exposure produced a terrible commotion in the ranks of the Secret Society of the Holy Cross, which was held responsible for the book. The Brethren of that Society held many occult meetings to consider what they should do under such adverse circumstances. I have given full reports of these secret gatherings, as printed for the use of the Brethren only. I think most sober-minded Churchmen will admit, after reading the speeches delivered by prominent Ritualistic clergymen on those occasions, that the proceedings of the Society were by no means characterized by straightforward dealing, but that, on the contrary, they were decidedly cunning and Jesuitical. In this connection I have necessarily had to comment largely on the Ritualistic Confessional; but I have carefully abstained from writing anything which would offend the modesty of any Christian man or woman.

Of necessity much has been left out of this volume which I should have been glad to insert. There are intervals in the Secret History of the Oxford Movement which have yet to be filled up, when the documents necessary for the purpose are forthcoming.

It is hoped that this volume may be the means of proving to many Churchmen, who have hitherto taken no interest in the Ritualistic question, that the contest now going on within the Church of England, and which, unhappily, threatens to rend her asunder, is not one about trifles. There are many men and women who love to hear the best music sung in our Churches, and wish to have the services conducted with the utmost possible reverence, who do not wish to surrender the priceless privileges of the Reformation, including freedom from Papal tyranny, in order that their Church, and the Church of their forefathers, shall, instead of going forward, return to the corruptions of the Dark Ages. It is hoped that this volume may enable many to see that behind the Ritual, and the outward pomp and grandeur of Ritualistic services, are the unscriptural doctrines which that Ritual is designed to teach, and which our forefathers found unendurable. All loyal Churchmen, by whatever name they call themselves, should unite in ejecting the lawless from their ranks, after an effort has been made to secure their obedience. Things are rapidly drifting towards a state of Ecclesiastical Anarchy. Indeed, in thousands of parishes, Anarchy already prevails, where Ritualistic priests persist in making their own whims and fancies their supreme law, and in doing only that which is right in their own eyes. I think it was Sydney Smith who said, of the Tractarian clergyman of his own time, that "He is only for the Bishop, when the Bishop is for him." It is so still; but with this unfortunate difference,—as a rule, the Bishop "*is* for him." Episcopal smiles and favours are heaped on the secret plotters whose work is described in this volume; and the leaders of the State vie with the Bishops in promoting those who are systematically lawbreakers.

The influence of public opinion needs to be brought to bear upon this question. Compromise is out of the question. Either our Rulers in Church and State must unite together in maintaining law and order, or the Church of England will cease to be the Established Church of the nation. I am not pleading in any way for the narrowing of the existing boundaries of the Church of England, as defined in her formularies and laws. No considerable body, at present, wishes for anything of the kind. But I do maintain that law and order ought to be *supreme* in the Church, as much as in the State, and at present this, unfortunately, is not the case. At present the extreme Ritualists are a law unto themselves. There is not in existence a tribunal to whose Judgments they will yield obedience, when they come into collision with their own superior judgments. Reasonable men would say that it is better to have even imperfect tribunals than no tribunal at all; and that it is wise to obey those which exist until efforts for their reformation are successful. But this does not appear to be the opinion of the Ritualists. Better that all English Church law and order shall go down than they should cease to do as they like. Bearing in mind their wholehearted efforts for Corporate Reunion with Rome, as described in the two last chapters of this volume, when a state of loyalty and obedience to the Pope would again come into existence in the Church of England, does it not

CONTENTS.

PAGE

CHAPTER I.—THE SECRET HISTORY OF THE OXFORD MOVEMENT - - - - - - - 1

    Birth of the Movement—Its Secret Teaching—Promoters dislike their names being known to the Public—Tract "On Reserve"—Newman writes against Popery—"Eats his dirty words"—Ward on Equivocation—Newman Establishes a Monastery—Pusey gives his approval—Newman's double dealing about it—Lockhart's experience in this Monastery—Mark Pattison's experience—" Stealing to Mass at the Catholic Church "—Faber's visit to Rome—Faber kisses the Pope's foot—Desanctis on Jesuits in Disguise—Midnight secret Meetings at Elton—Dr. Pusey privately orders a "Discipline with five knots"—Dr. Pusey secretly wears hair shirts—Ritualistic Sisters of Mercy to take the "Discipline"—A Ritualistic Sister whipped most cruelly—Romanists sell articles of "Discipline" to Ritualists—Maskell's Testimony as to Tractarian evasions and trickery.

CHAPTER II.—THE SOCIETY OF THE HOLY CROSS - - 46

    Its secret birth in 1855—Brethren forbidden to mention its existence—Its secret Statutes—Its secret signs—Its mysterious "Committee of Clergy"—The Roll of sworn Celibates—Their Oath—Its secret Synods and Chapters—Brethren must push the Confessional amongst young and old—Its Confessional Book for little children—Its secret Confessional Committee—Issues the *Priest in Absolution*—Secret birth of the Retreat Movement—First secret Retreat in Dr. Pusey's rooms—Starts the "St. George's Mission" at St. Peter's, London Docks—Dr. Pusey a member of the Mission—The Bishop of Lebombo a member of the Society of the Holy Cross—Sensational letter from him—Ritualistic Holy Water—Brethren alarmed at publicity—The Society establish an Oratory at Carlisle—Its secret history—Organizes a Petition for Licensed Confessors—Reports of speeches at its secret Synods—Their dark plottings exposed.

CHAPTER III.—THE SECRECY OF THE RITUALISTIC CONFESSIONAL - - - - - - 80

> The Confessional always a secret thing—Abuse of the Ritualistic Confessional at Leeds—Dr. Pusey on the Seal of the Confessional—Ritualistic Sisters teach girls how to confess to priests—Secret Confessional books for penitents—Dr. Pusey revives the Confessional—Four years later writes against it—He hears Confessions in private houses—"His penitent's burning sense of shame and deceitfulness"—Bishop Wilberforce's opinion of Dr. Pusey—A Ritualistic priest's extraordinary letter to a young lady—How Archdeacon Manning hears Confessions on the sly, "a hole and corner affair."

CHAPTER IV.—THE SECRET HISTORY OF "THE PRIEST IN ABSOLUTION" - - - - - - 93

> Part I. of the *Priest in Absolution*—Praised by the Ritualistic Press—Part II. secretly circulated amongst "Catholic" priests only—Lord Redesdale's exposure of the book in the House of Lords—Archbishop Tait says it is "a disgrace to the community"—Secret letter from the Master of the Society of the Holy Cross—Statement of the S. S. C.—Special secret Chapter of the Society to consider the *Priest in Absolution*—Full report of its proceedings, with speeches of the Brethren—Refuse to condemn the book—Discussion in Canterbury Convocation—Severe Episcopal Censures—Immoral Ritualistic Confessors ruin women; Testimony of Archdeacon Allen—Dr. Pusey's acknowledgments of the dangers of the Confessional; It is the road by which a number of Christians go down to hell—Another secret meeting of the Society of the Holy Cross—Reports of the speeches and resolutions—Some Bishops secretly friendly to the Society—Canon Knox-Little's connection with the Society of the Holy Cross—Strange and Jesuitical Proceedings at the Society's Synod.

CHAPTER V.—THE ORDER OF CORPORATE REUNION - 147

> Origin of Order of Corporate Reunion shrouded in mystery—Its first "Pastoral"—It professes "loyalty" to the Pope—Prays for the Pope in its secret Synod—Its Bishops secretly consecrated by foreign Bishops—Who were they? "Bishop" Lee and "Bishop" Mossman—"Bishop" Mossman professes belief in the Pope's Infallibility—Birth of the Order rejoices the Romanists—Its proceedings discussed by the Society of the Holy Cross—Some secret documents—Eight hundred Church of England clergy secretly ordained by a bishop of the Order.

CONTENTS. xiii

CHAPTER VI.—RITUALISTIC SISTERHOODS . . . 162

Ritualistic Sisterhoods formed on Roman models—Dr. Pusey visits Romish Convents in Ireland—Borrows Rules from English and Continental Nunneries—Hislop on the Pagan origin of Convents—Dr. Pusey's first Sister visits Foreign Convents—Miss Goodman's experience of Dr. Pusey's Sisterhood—Rule of Obedience—Shameful tyranny over the Sisters—The Sister must obey the Superior "yielding herself as wax to be moulded unresistingly" —The mercenary Rule of Holy Poverty—Are Ritualistic Convents Jails?—The Vow of Poverty at St. Margaret's, East Grinstead—A secret Convent Book quoted—Life Vows—Is it easy to embezzle the Sister's money?—The secret Statutes of All Saints' Sisterhood, Margaret Street; and the Clewer Sisterhood—Sisters and their Wills—Evidence before the Select Committee—Bishop Samuel Wilberforce on Conventual Vows—Archbishop Tait on Conventual Vows—Ritualistic Nuns Enclosed for Life—" Father Ignatius'" Nuns—Whipping Ritualistic Nuns—Miss Cusack's experience of Dr. Pusey's Sisterhood, "a Hell upon earth"—Cases of Cruelty in Dr. Pusey's Sisterhood—Hungry Sisters Tempted—Private Burial Grounds in Ritualistic Convents—Secret Popish Service in a Ritualistic Convent Chapel; a Mass "in Latin from the Roman Missal"—Superstitious Convent Services—Extracts from a secret book for Dr. Pusey's Sisterhood—Sisterhoods and Education: A Warning to Protestant Parents.

CHAPTER VII.—THE CONFRATERNITY OF THE BLESSED SACRAMENT - - - - - - 202

Protestant Martyrs and the Mass—Latimer's testimony—Restoration of the Mass by the Ritualists—Birth of the Confraternity of the blessed Sacrament—Its objects and work—Its secret *Intercession Paper*, ordered to be "destroyed" when done with—Its "medal" may be buried with deceased members—First exposure of an *Intercession Paper* at Plymouth—Great excitement—How the *Rock* found an *Intercession Paper*—Secret proceedings at New York—The secret "Roll of Priests-Associate"—Dread lest it should fall into Protestant hands—Curious letter from a Priest-Associate—Extracts from the papers of the C. B. S.—Requiem Masses for Souls in Purgatory—Advocates Fasting Communion—Bishop Samuel Wilberforce on Fasting Communion: "detestable materialism"—Opposes Evening Communion—Proofs that it is sanctioned by the Primitive Church—C. B. S. term it "spiritually and morally dangerous."—Eucharistic Adoration of C. B. S. Identical with that of Rome—Its Idolatrous character—The C. B. S. on the Real Presence—The "Eucharistic Sacrifice"— —Bishop Beveridge on Sacrifice—Transubstantiation advocated by name—Bishop Wilberforce Censures the Confraternity of the Blessed Sacrament.

CONTENTS.

CHAPTER VIII.—SOME OTHER RITUALISTIC SOCIETIES   -   227

A Purgatorial Society in the Church of England—The Guild of All Souls—Extracts from its Publications—Masses for the Dead in the Church of England—Festival on "All Souls' Day"—The Fire of Purgatory the same as that of Hell—Bishop of London (Dr. Temple) gives its President a Living—The Secret Order of the Holy Redeemer—An Inner Circle; The Brotherhood of the Holy Cross; its secret rules quoted—The "Declaration" of the Order of the Holy Redeemer—The Pope the "Pastor and Teacher of the Church"—Why its members stay within the Church of England—Extraordinary and Jesuitical letter of "John O. H. R." —Its mysterious Superior said to be a "Bishop," though not in the *Clergy List*. Who ordained and consecrated him?—The secret Order of St. John the Divine—Extract from its secret rules —Society of St. Osmund—Its rules and objects—Prays for the Pope—Its silly superstitions—Driving the Devil out of Incense and Flowers—The Adoration of the Cross—A degrading spectacle —Its Mary worship—Holy Relics—Advocates Paying for Masses for the Dead—The Society merged in the Alcuin Club—The Club joined by several Bishops—Laymen's Ritual Institute of Norwich —Its Secret Oath—Secret Guild Books of St. Alphege, Southwark —Guild of St. John the Evangelist, at St. Alban's, Holborn— Confraternity of All Saints', Margaret Street—The Railway Guild of the Holy Cross.

CHAPTER IX.—THE ROMEWARD MOVEMENT -   -   -   260

Corporate Reunion with Rome desired—Not individual Secession—The reason for this policy—How to "Catholicise" the Church of England—Protestantism a hindrance to Reunion— Reunion with Rome the ultimate object of the Ritualistic Movement—Newman and Froude visit Wiseman at Rome—They inquire for terms of admission to the Church of Rome—Secret Receptions into the Church of Rome—Growth of Newman's love for Rome—Newman wants "more Vestments and decorations in worship"—William George Ward: "The Jesuits were his favourite reading"—Publication of Tract XC.—Mr. Dalgairn's letter to the *Univers*—Secret negotiations with Dr. Wiseman— "Only through the English Church can you (Rome) act on the English nation"—Keble hopes that yearning after Rome "will be allowed to gain strength"—Mr. Gladstone on the Romeward Movement—He hopes those "excellent persons" who love all Roman doctrine will "abide in the Church"—"The Ideal of a Christian Church"—Dr. Pusey's eulogy of the Jesuits censured by Dr. Hook—Mr. Gladstone's article in the *Quarterly Review*— Pusey hopes "Rome and England will be united in one"—Pusey asks for "more love for Rome"—He praises the "superiority" of Roman teaching—Pusey believes in Purgatory and Invocation of Saints—He yet "forbids" his penitents to invoke the Saints—

Manning's remarkable letter to Pusey—Manning's visit to Rome in 1848—Kneels in the street before the Pope—His double dealing in the Church of England—The Roman Catholic *Rambler* on the Oxford Movement.

CHAPTER X.—THE ROMEWARD MOVEMENT - - - 307

The Association for the Promotion of the Unity of Christendom —*Sermons* and *Essays on Reunion*—Denunciation of Protestantism —Treasonable letter in the *Union Review*—The A. P. U. C. denounced by the Inquisition—Degrading Reply of 198 Church of England Dignitaries and Clergy—Archbishop Manning's opinion of the Romeward Movement—The Society of the Holy Cross Petition for Reunion with Rome—Signed by 1212 clergymen—The English Church Union—Its work for Union with Rome—Approves Dr. Pusey's *Eirenicon*—Pusey writes that there is nothing in the Pope's "Supremacy" in itself to which he would object—The Catholic Union for Prayer—A Colonial Priest on Reunion with Rome—The "levelling up" process—The real Objects of the English Church Union—The *Lord's Day and the Holy Eucharist*—Lord Halifax wants Benediction of the Blessed Sacrament—E. C. U. members find fault with the Book of Common Prayer—E. C. U. Petitions the Lambeth Conference for Reunion—Reunion asked for under "The Bishop of Old Rome" —Lord Halifax prefers Leo XIII. to the Privy Council—Dean Hook in favour of the Privy Council—Mr. Mackonochie's Evidence before the Ecclesiastical Courts' Commission—Asserts there has been no "Ecclesiastical Court" since the Reformation—A Ritualistic Curate supplies the "Kernel" to Roman Ritual—He preaches the Immaculate Conception of the Virgin Mary—Lord Halifax and "Explanations" of the Pope's Infallibility—The *Homilies* on the Church of Rome—Rome has already reaped an harvest from Ritualistic labours—Secession as well as union a Scriptural duty—Objections to Reunion with Rome.

APPENDIX.—WHAT THE RITUALISTS TEACH - - - 373

The Bible—The Book of Common Prayer—The Thirty-nine Articles—Reunion with Rome—The Pope's Infallibility, Primacy and Supremacy—The Reformers and the Reformation—Some Ritualistic "Ornaments of the Church"—The Real Presence—The Power and Dignity of Sacrificing Priests—The Sacrifice of the Mass—The Ceremonies of Low Mass—Some Cautions for Mass Priests—Purgatory—Auricular Confession and Priestly Absolution—Invocation of Saints—The Virtues of Holy Salt, Holy Water, and Holy Oil—Monastic Institutions—Protestantism —The Importance of Ritual—Dissent.

INDEX - - - - - - - 411

THE SECRET HISTORY

OF

THE OXFORD MOVEMENT.

CHAPTER I.

THE SECRET HISTORY OF THE OXFORD MOVEMENT.

Birth of the Movement—Its Secret Teaching—Promoters dislike their names being known to the Public—Tract "On Reserve"—Newman writes against Popery—"Eats his dirty words"—Ward on Equivocation—Newman Establishes a Monastery—Pusey gives his approval—Newman's double dealing about it—Lockhart's experience in this Monastery—Mark Pattison's experience—"Stealing to Mass at the Catholic Church"—Faber's visit to Rome—Faber kisses the Pope's foot—Desanctis on Jesuits in Disguise—Midnight secret Meetings at Elton—Dr. Pusey privately orders a "Discipline with five knots"—Dr. Pusey secretly wears hair shirts—Ritualistic Sisters of Mercy to take the "Discipline"—A Ritualistic Sister whipped most cruelly—Romanists sell articles of "Discipline" to Ritualists—Maskell's Testimony as to Tractarian evasions and trickery.

THE late Cardinal Newman, the first leader of the Tractarians, has stated in his *Apologia* that he ever considered and kept July 14th, 1833, as the start of the Tractarian Movement. Within three months from that date he published his work on the *Arians of the Fourth Century*, in which the " Disciplina Arcani," or the "secret teaching," which found such favour with a few of the early Fathers, was held up to the admiration of English churchmen of the nineteenth century. It was most appropriate that a religious movement in which secrecy has played so important a part should be inaugurated by the publication of such a work. It has served as a seed from which many a noxious weed has grown. Closely connected with the "Disciplina Arcani" is what is termed the "Economical" mode of teaching and arguing. The difference between the two is thus defined by Newman himself. "If," he writes, "it is necessary to contrast the two with each other, the one may be considered as withholding the truth, and the other as setting it out to advantage."[1] As an illustration of this "Economy" he quotes with approval the very objectionable advice of Clement of Alexandria:—

"The Alexandrian Father," he affirms, "who has already been quoted, *accurately* describes the rules which should guide the Christian in speaking and writing economically. 'Being fully persuaded of the omnipresence of God,' says Clement, 'and ashamed to come short of the truth, he is satisfied with the approval of God, and of his own conscience. Whatever is in his mind, is also on his tongue; towards those who are fit recipients, both in speaking and living, he harmonizes his profession with his thoughts. He both thinks and speaks the truth; *except when careful treatment is necessary*, and then, as a physician for the good of his patients, *he will* LIE, or rather utter a LIE, as the Sophists say. . . . Nothing, however, but his neighbour's good will lead him to do this. *He gives himself up for the Church.*'"[2]

As to the "Disciplina Arcani," Newman justifies it on several grounds, and affirms that in the Church of Alexandria the Catechumens were not taught all the doctrines of the Christian Faith. Many of these were treated by their teachers as secret doctrines to be held in reserve. "Even to the last," he asserts, "they were granted nothing beyond a formal and general account of the articles of the Christian Faith; the exact and fully developed doctrines of the Trinity and the Incarnation, and still more, the doctrine of the Atonement, as once made upon the Cross, and commemorated and appropriated in the Eucharist, being the exclusive possession of the serious and practised Christian."[3] It is worthy of note that Newman affirmed that these secret doctrines were not learnt from the Scriptures. "Now first," he writes, "it may be asked, How was any secrecy practicable, seeing that the Scriptures were open to everyone who chose to consult them? It may startle those who are but acquainted with the

[1] Newman's *Arians*, p. 65. Seventh edition. [2] *Ibid.*, pp. 73, 74. [3] *Ibid.*, p. 45.

popular writings of this day, yet, I believe, the most accurate consideration of the subject will lead us to acquiesce in the statement, as a general truth, that *the doctrines in question* [*i.e.*, the *secret* doctrines of the early Church] *have never been learnt merely from Scripture.*" And then he adds:—"Surely the Sacred Volume was never intended, and is not adapted, to teach us our Creed."[4] Thus early in the Tractarian Movement were its disciples taught not to look to the Bible only for what they should believe. The traditions of men were set up as of equal value with the Written Word. No wonder that such a Movement led to many and grievous departures from Christian truth. Teaching like this was eagerly imbibed by the disciples of Newman, who very naturally, though without sufficient reason, inferred that, if the Alexandrian Fathers were justified in hiding certain doctrines of Christianity from the popular gaze, as secrets to be made known only to the initiated whom they could trust, the Tractarians of the nineteenth century might lawfully imitate their example. Accordingly, they, at first, from their pulpits preached the ordinary doctrines of the Church of England, as they had been taught for nearly three hundred years; while secretly, and to those only who could be trusted, they taught those Romish doctrines and practices which they dared not then expose to the light of publicity.

There was a measure of secrecy observed even in the formation of the Tractarian Movement. As early as September 3rd, 1833, one of the party—the late Professor Mozley—writing to his sister, after announcing that with his letter she would "receive a considerable number of Tracts, the first production of the Society established for the dissemination of High Church principles," proceeds to give particulars of the plans of the party; but finds it necessary, before closing his letter, to add this caution for her guidance:—"But for the present you must remember all

[4] *Ibid.*, p. 50.

these details I have been going through *are secret.*"[5] Here, it will be observed, the real object of the Movement is frankly revealed. It is to be a Society for "the dissemination of High Church principles." But when the prospectus of the Society was made public, there was not one word in it which might lead the public to suppose that "The Association of the Friends of the Church"—as it was termed—had the slightest desire to promote High Church views. *That,* the *real* object, was kept back in reserve, to be imparted only to the elect of the party. In a letter to a friend one of the members of the new Association actually went so far as to assert :—"We want to unite all the Church, orthodox *and Evangelical,* clergy, nobility, and people, in maintenance of our doctrine and polity."[6]

"There was, indeed," writes one of the leaders of the Tractarians, the Rev. William Palmer, "much misapprehension abroad as to our motives, and we had no means of explaining those motives, *without the danger of giving publicity to our proceedings, which,* in the then state of the public mind on Church matters, *might have led to dangerous results.*"[7]

This dread of the light of day was fully shared by Newman, who, writing from Oriel College, Oxford, to his friend Mr. J. W. Bowden, on August 31st, 1833, remarks :— "We are just setting up here Societies for the Defence of the Church. *We do not like our names known,* but we hope the plan will succeed."[8] The very same day Newman wrote to another intimate friend, Mr. F. Rogers—subsequently known as Lord Blachford—as follows :—

"*Entre nous,* we have set up Societies over the kingdom in defence of the Church. Certainly this is, you will say, a singular confidential communication, being shared by so many; but the *entre nous* relates to *we*. *We do not like our names known.*"[9]

This dread of having their names "known" to the public

[5] Mozley's *Letters,* p. 33.
[6] Palmer's *Narrative of Events Connected with Tracts for the Times,* p. 212. Edition, 1883. [7] *Ibid.,* p. 108.
[8] Newman's *Letters and Correspondence,* Vol. I., p. 448. [9] *Ibid.,* p. 450.

is still felt by the members of several Ritualistic societies of the present generation. It is a noteworthy fact that for fifteen years—from 1880 to 1896—no list of the Brethren of the secret Society of the Holy Cross—though a fresh list is printed and circulated every year—came into Protestant hands. When the "Suggestions" for the formation of "The Association of the Friends of the Church" were printed and circulated, care was even taken that no outsider, into whose hands a stray copy might chance to fall, should be able to discover from it whence it came, or who were responsible for it. This was a matter for astonishment on the part of Mr. J. W. Bowden, who, writing from London to Newman, on November 4th, 1833, mentions that:—

"Those to whom I have shown the 'Suggestions' say, 'But where are the names? Who are they? Where are they?' For even the word Oxford does not appear thereon. For aught the 'Suggestions' say, the founders of the scheme might belong to the *operative* classes of Society, and their head-quarters might be in some alley in London. The year, too, should be put; a reader might, if he found a dirty copy, suppose the whole scheme ten years old."[10]

Amongst the prominent laymen who supported the Tractarian Movement was Mr. Joshua Watson. He drew up the first Lay Declaration organized by the Tractarians at the close of 1833. His brother wanted to know too much about the objects of the Declaration and was refused the information by Mr. Joshua Watson in the following terms:—

"As to the query, whence it comes and whither it goes, the only answer is, what does that signify? Never mind, if it dropped from the clouds. If you like it, sign it; if you do not, let it alone. As to its *ulterior destination*, I reply that, without the gift of second sight, I pretend not to answer."[11]

Dr. Pusey, at this time, had not publicly joined what Newman termed "the grand scheme."[12] But on November 7th, 1833, the latter was able to announce to the Rev. Hurrell Froude, then the most advanced Romanizer of the new

[10] *Ibid.*, p. 472.
[11] *Memoir of Joshua Watson*, by Archdeacon Churton, p. 209. Second edition.
[12] Newman's *Letters*, Vol. I., p. 478.

party, that Pusey was circulating the recently issued *Tracts for the Times*.[13] Six days later Newman privately informed Mr. Bowden that Pusey had joined the new party, but he adds the caution that his name "must not be mentioned as of our party."[14] It is interesting to note that Newman, at the same time, mentioned that Mr. Gladstone "has joined us." At this period Newman was writing a series of anonymous articles in the Evangelical *Record*, over the signature of "Churchman."[15] It is certain that if he had made known his High Church views to the then editor of that paper, his articles would have been refused.

Already Newman was himself practising his doctrine of Reserve. He had departed, in his own mind, from several of the Protestant doctrines of his forefathers, but the world knew nothing at all about the change in his views. What he kept secret from the public, he made known to his trusted friends. Thus, for example, he wrote, on November 22nd, 1833, to the Rev. S. Rickards:—

"I must just touch upon the notice of the Lord's Supper. *In confidence to a friend*, I can only admit it was imprudent, for I do think that we have most of us dreadfully low notions of the Blessed Sacrament. *I expect to be called a Papist when my opinions are known.* But (please God) I shall lead persons on a little way, while they fancy they are only taking the mean, and denounce me as the extreme."[16]

Here a truly Jesuitical spirit manifests itself. Hurrell Froude acted in a similarly underhanded manner. In one of his letters to a friend, written only one month after the commencement of the Movement, he remarked:—"Since I have been at home, I have been doing what I can to *proselytise in an underhand way*."[17] Is there not reason to fear that many of the clergy, who do not *call* themselves Ritualists, are in our own day imitating the bad examples shown by Newman and Froude, more than sixty years ago? The danger

[13] Newman's *Letters*, Vol. I., p. 476.
[14] *Ibid.*, p. 482.
[15] *Ibid.*, p. 483.
[16] *Ibid.*, p. 490.
[17] Froude's *Remains*, Vol. I., p. 322.

is to be looked for in nominally Evangelical parishes, as well as in those under avowedly High Church management. In looking through the privately printed Annual Report of the Merton College (Oxford) Church Society, for 1892, which supports several Ritualistic causes, and advocates reunion with the corrupt Eastern Church, I was surprised to read, in the list of members, the names of several clergymen who at the present time hold Evangelical incumbencies or curacies. These gentlemen would, no doubt, be considerably annoyed, were their connection with this private Society made known to their present congregations. It may, however, be fairly asked, why should they in *secret* be members of a High Church Society, while in *public* they profess to be Evangelicals? Let them be consistent, and if they do not hold High Church views, withdraw from such an organization. I do not assert that these gentlemen are insincere, for we cannot read the secret thoughts of others, but, until they cease to be members, I cannot help wondering whether they are acting on the Ritualistic principle of "Reserve in Communicating Religious Knowledge?"

Newman's views on Reserve and Economy when first published in 1833, created a great deal of interest; but this was as nothing when compared with the effect produced, in 1838, by the publication of Isaac Williams's pamphlet "On Reserve in Communicating Religious Knowledge." It formed No. 80 of *Tracts for the Times*, and this he subsequently supplemented by another and larger pamphlet on the same subject, being No. 87 of *Tracts for the Times*. The doctrine taught by Williams set the whole of the Church of England in an uproar. His Tracts were condemned by almost every Bishop on the Bench. In Bricknell's *Judgment of the Bishops upon Tractarian Theology*, pp. 424-472, there are printed extensive extracts from Episcopal Charges in which the doctrine of Reserve is condemned in the strongest terms. Tract 80 commences with a clear exposition of its purport.

"The object of the present inquiry," writes Isaac Williams, " is to ascertain, whether there is not in God's dealings with mankind, a very remarkable *holding back* of sacred and important truths, as if the knowledge of them were injurious to persons unworthy of them " (p. 3)

Amongst the doctrines which Williams mentions as those which are to be held back in Reserve from the uninitiated, as great secrets of Christianity, are those of the Atonement, Faith and Works, the free Grace of God, the Sacraments, and Priestly Absolution.

"Not only," he writes, " is the exclusive and naked exposure of so very sacred a truth [as the ' Doctrine of the Atonement'] unscriptural and dangerous, but, as Bishop Wilson says, the comforts of Religion ought to be applied with great caution. And moreover to require, as is sometimes done, from both grown persons and children, an explicit declaration of a belief in the Atonement, and the full assurance of its power, appears equally untenable." (*Tract* 80, p. 78.)

"These riches" [*i.e.*, certain 'sacred truths'] are all *secret*, given to certain dispositions—not cast loosely on the world. . . The great doctrines which of late years have divided Christians, are again of this ['secret'] kind very peculiarly, *such as the subjects of Faith and Works*, of the free *Grace of God*, and obedience on the part of man. . . They appear to be *great secrets*, notwithstanding whatever may be said of them, *only revealed to the faithful*." (*Ibid.*, pp. 48, 49.)

"With respect to the *Holy Sacraments*," Williams remarks, in his second pamphlet on *Reserve*, "it is in these, and by these *chiefly*, that the Church of all ages has held the Doctrine of the Atonement after a certain manner of Reserve. . . . Now here it is very evident at once that the great difference between these two systems [*i.e.*, what Williams terms the true Catholic, and the modern Protestant system] consists in this, that one holds the doctrine *secretly* as it were, and in Reserve; the other in a public and popular manner." (*Tract* 87, pp. 88, 89.)

"The same may be shown with respect to the powers of *Priestly Absolution*, and the gifts conferred thereby. It is not required for our purpose to show the reality of that power, and the magnitude of those gifts which are thus dispensed. But a little consideration will show that if the Church of all ages is right in exercising these privileges, *the subject is one entirely of this reserved* and mystical *character*. Its blessings are received in secret, according to faith: they are such as the world cannot behold, and cannot receive. The subject is one so profound and mysterious, that it hardly admits of being put forward in a popular way, and doubtless more injury than benefit would be done to religion by doing so inconsiderately." (*Ibid.*, p. 90.)

No wonder that the Bishops condemned such doctrines as these. "Far from us," wrote Dr. Musgrave, Bishop of Hereford, "therefore, be it to withhold from our Christian people any doctrine revealed in God's Word as needful for salvation, or to impose upon them for such, anything not there revealed."[18] Dr. Blomfield, Bishop of London, indignantly rejected the secret teaching of Isaac Williams. "Anything," he declared, "of the nature of a 'Disciplina Arcani,' I as promptly reject."[19] It is worthy of note here that in his *Autobiography*—which was not published until 1892—Williams admits that the Evangelical party, when his Tract on Reserve was published, took a right view as to its real meaning. "With regard to the great obloquy," he writes, "it [Tract on Reserve] occasioned from the Low Church Party, this was to be expected—it was against their hollow mode of proceeding; *it was understood as it was meant*, and of this I do not complain."[20] It is certain that Evangelical Churchmen understood it as meaning that the Tractarian clergy felt themselves justified in imparting to those only whom they could trust their real and Romish doctrines concerning the Atonement, Faith and Works, Grace, the Sacraments, Priestly Absolution, and other doctrines; and to Protestants this naturally looked like double-dealing and Jesuitism. No wonder they were indignant.

It is admitted by one who for many years held a prominent position amongst the advanced Ritualistic clergy (the Rev. Orby Shipley) that this "Doctrine of Reserve" was "both taught and acted upon" to "a *wide* extent" by the Tractarians.[21] And the Master of the secret Society of the

---

[18] Bricknell's *Judgment of the Bishops*, p. 434.   [19] *Ibid.*, p. 436.
[20] *Autobiography of Isaac Williams*, p. 91.
[21] Orby Shipley's *Invocation of Saints and Angels*, p. xi. London, 1869.

Holy Cross, addressing the May, 1873, Synod of that Society, said :—

"We look back to a time when Catholic truth and worship were in a condition almost resembling that of the Church of the Catacombs, *when the utmost reserve was thought necessary*, even in speaking of simple facts of the Creed. The Gorham case, and the intrusion of the Schismatical Hierarchy of Rome, with the anti-Catholic *animus* to which they gave force, were still hanging over us, and what was done for the truth *was mostly done in a corner.*"[22]

The subtlety of a Jesuit could not have invented a more ingenious scheme.

Early in 1836, both the *Standard* and the *Edinburgh Review* censured the Tractarian Party in strong terms. These attacks greatly annoyed Newman, who, writing to Keble on January 16th of that year, remarks :—" Now, since many of these notices are made under the impression that we are *Crypto*-Papists, here is an additional reason for tracts on the Popish question."[23] Dr. Pusey readily fell in with this subtle scheme for writing against Popery. He evidently thought it a clever dodge for throwing dust in the eyes of the public, and leading many Protestants, thus blinded, to adopt High Church principles, before they were aware of it. On this subject Pusey wrote to a friend :—

"I know not that the Popish controversy may not just be the very best way of handling Ultra-Protestantism, *i.e.*, neglecting it, not advancing against, but setting Catholic views against Roman Catholicism and *so disposing of Ultra-Protestantism by a side wind, and teaching people Catholicism, without their suspecting*, while they are only bent on demolishing Romanism. I suspect we might thus have people with us, instead of against us, and that *they might find themselves Catholics before they were aware.*"[24]

The impression that the leaders of the Tractarians were secretly Papists was a very natural one. Those who doubted could not produce legal evidence in proof of what they

---

[22] *S.S.C. Master's Address*, May Synod, 1873, p. 3.
[23] Newman's *Letters*, Vol. II., p. 153.
[24] *Life of Dr. Pusey*, Vol. I., p. 332.

feared: but the knowledge of the suspicions which existed led Newman to adopt a course to ward off suspicion, which, had it been understood by his opponents, would have greatly increased their impressions as to Crypto-Papists being at that time in the Church of England. He determined, as we have seen, to write against Popery. How could anyone, then, suppose that the man who said such strong things against the Church of Rome was in any sense a disguised Romanist? It was not the first time he had written against portions of the Roman system. No Protestant could have said fiercer things than he had said in the past, and continued to say, so long as it answered his purpose. Here are a few extracts from his utterances, beginning with the year 1833, and ending with 1839. I take the extracts as cited by Newman himself, in his famous letter to the *Oxford Conservative Journal*, January, 1843. In the *Lyra Apostolica*, published in 1833, he declared that the Church of Rome was a "lost Church." At page 421 of the first edition of his work on the *Arians of the Fourth Century*, he wrote of "the Papal Apostacy." In No. 15 of *Tracts for the Times*, in 1833, he wrote :—

"True, Rome is heretical now... If she has apostatized, it was at the time of the Council of Trent. Then, indeed, it is to be feared the whole Roman Communion bound itself, by a perpetual bond and covenant to the cause of Anti-christ."

Again, in the same year he wrote, in *Tract* 20. "Their [Papists'] communion is infected with heresy; we are bound to flee it as a pestilence. They have established a lie in the place of God's truth, and by their claim of immutability in doctrine, cannot undo the sin they have committed."

In 1834 Newman affirmed that :—

"In the corrupt Papal system we have the very cruelty, the craft, and the ambition of the republic; its cruelty in its unsparing sacrifice of the happiness and virtue of individuals to a phantom of public expediency, in its forced celibacy within, and its persecutions without; its craft in its falsehoods, its deceitful deeds and lying wonders; and its grasping ambition in the very structure of its policy, in an assumption of universal dominion; old Rome is still alive; nowhere have its eagles lighted, but it still claims the sovereignty under another pretence. The Roman Church I will not blame, but pity—she is, as I have said, spell-bound, as if by an evil spirit; she is in thraldom."

In the same year, in No. 38 of *Tracts for the Times*, Newman termed the Church of Rome "unscriptural," "profane," "impious," "blasphemous," "gross," and "monstrous." In the year 1838, in his lectures on *Romanism and Popular Protestantism*, he said of the Church of Rome:—

"In truth she is a Church beside herself, abounding in noble gifts and rightful titles, but unable to use them religiously; crafty, obstinate, wilful, malicious, cruel, unnatural, as madmen are. Or, rather, she may be said to resemble a demoniac, possessed with principles, thoughts, and tendencies not her own. . . Thus she is her real self only in name, and till God vouchsafe to restore her, we must treat her as if she were that evil one which governs her."

What Protestant could utter abuse of Popery more fierce than is contained in the above extracts from Newman's own words? But there is this marked difference between the two. The Protestant means what he says when he denounces Rome; while Newman did nothing of the kind. He meant his denunciation of Popery to be dust with which to blind the eyes of his opponents, and prevent them discovering his real aims; and there can be no doubt it, for a time, in a large measure served its purpose. When the denunciations had done their work, however, they were unreservedly withdrawn, and that by the author himself. In the letter to the *Oxford Conservative Journal* mentioned already, Newman cited all the extracts given above from his writings, together with other similar statements, and then he adds this remarkable confession of his guilt:—

"If you ask me how an individual could venture, not simply to hold, but to publish such views of a Communion [*i.e.*, the Church of Rome] so ancient, so wide-spreading, so fruitful in saints, I answer, that I said to myself, 'I AM NOT SPEAKING MY OWN WORDS, I am but following almost a *consensus* of the divines of my

Church. They have ever used the strongest language against Rome, even the most learned and able of them. I wish to throw myself into their system. While I say what they say I am safe. SUCH VIEWS, TOO, ARE NECESSARY FOR OUR POSITION.' Yet I have reason to fear still, that such language is to be ascribed, in no small measure, to an impetuous temper, *a hope of approving myself to person's respect,* AND A WISH TO REPEL THE CHARGE OF ROMANISM."

Accordingly he withdrew all the charges made against the Church of Rome in the above quotations from his writings. In those writings his denunciations of Rome are put forth, not as those of a "*consensus* of divines" of the Church of England, but as *his own*. And yet, all the while, he tells us, he was "*not* speaking his own words!" It was "necessary for our position" to write thus. There was no other effectual way to gain " person's respect" for his consistency, and to "repel the charge of Romanism." In short his conduct was a practical illustration of the doctrine of the "Economy" advocated in his book on the Arians, in which, as we have seen, he cites with approval the doctrine of Clement of Alexandria, that a Christian "Both thinks and speaks the truth; *except* when careful treatment is necessary; and then, as a physician for the good of his patients, he will lie, or rather utter a lie, as the Sophists say." Can we wonder that the men and women of that generation doubted the word of Newman? He did not tell the world at that time—so far as I can ascertain—that he had ever believed in his own denunciations of Romanism when he wrote them. It was nearly a quarter of a century after, that, in his *Apologia,* he let the public know that he " fully believed " all his accusations against Rome at the time he made them; but in the same book he admitted that his letter to the *Oxford Conservative Journal* was, after all, but "a lame apology."[25] There can be no question as to its lameness, and not all the subtlety displayed in the *Apologia* is able to deprive it of its crippled character. A few days before the retractation

Apologia Pro Vita Sua, pp. 201, 204. Edition, 1889.

was published at Oxford, Newman wrote to his friend, James R. Hope-Scott, to announce the coming event. "My conscience," he told his correspondent, "goaded me some two months since to an act which comes into effect, I believe, in the *Conservative Journal* next Saturday, viz., to eat a few dirty words of mine."[26] A few days later Mr. Hope-Scott acquainted Newman with the effect his retractation had produced on his acquaintances. "People whom I have heard speak of it," he wrote, "(few, perhaps, but fair samples) are rather *puzzled* than anything else."[27] Newman's conduct for several years before this date had fairly "puzzled" everybody, both friends and foes. They could not make him out; he was a mystery they could not penetrate. The suspicion that he was acting in an underhand way was not confined to Protestants, as the rejoinder he wrote to the last quoted letter of Mr. J. R. Hope-Scott, clearly shows. Writing to him, on February 3rd, 1843, Newman gives the following additional explanation of his retractation:—

"My reason for the *thing* was my long-continued feeling of the great inconsistency I was in of letting things stand in print against me *which I did not hold*, and which I could not but be contradicting by my acting every day of my life. And more especially (*i.e.*, it came home to me most vividly in that particular way) I felt that I was *taking people in;* that they thought me what I was not, and were trusting me when they should not, and this has been at times a very painful feeling indeed. I don't want to be trusted (perhaps you may think my fear, even before this affair, somewhat amusing); but so it was and is; people *won't* believe I go as far as I do—they will cling to their hopes. And then, again, *intimate friends have almost reproached me with 'paltering with them in a double sense, keeping the word of promise to their ear, to break it to their hope.'* They have said that my words against Rome often, when narrowly examined, were only what I meant, but that the effect of them was what *others* meant. I am not aware that I have any great motive for this paper beyond this—setting myself right, and wishing to be seen in my proper colours,

---

[26] *Memoirs of J. R. Hope-Scott*, Vol. II., p. 19.   [27] *Ibid.*, p. 20.

and not unwilling to do such penance for wrong words as lies in the necessary criticism which such a retractation will involve on the part of friends and enemies."[28]

Turning back to August 9th, 1836, we note that, on this date, one of Newman's friends, the Rev. R. F. Wilson, wrote to complain of his "unnecessary" Economy, and mentioned a case in which he had so acted. "By-the-bye," he asked Newman, "why will you economise so unnecessarily at times? as if to keep your hand in. You sent Major B. away with a conviction that you looked on D. as a very fine, noble character. As he had this information fresh from you, I did not venture to say anything subversive of your judgment; so now he will probably publish the high admiration and respect with which D. is looked up to by his late comrades—more especially by Mr. Newman."[29] There is something truly Jesuitical in the way Newman acted towards "Major B." on this occasion. Unfortunately there is reason to fear that it was by no means an exceptional case either with himself or his disciples. There is an absence of English straightforwardness and plain dealing in the whole business which is far from satisfactory.

The conduct, I may here remark, of Newman's successor as leader of the advanced Tractarians, viz., the Rev. William George Ward (author of the *Ideal of a Christian Church*) was even more Jesuitical. Writing of the period when Mr. Ward was still a clergyman in the Church of England, his son informs us that—

"He had long held that the Roman Church was the one true Church. He had gradually come to believe that the English Church was not strictly a part of the Church at all. He had felt bound to retain his external communion with her members, *because he believed that he was bringing many of them towards Rome;* and to unite himself to the Church which he loved and trusted, to enjoy the blessings

[28] *Ibid.*, pp. 20, 21. This remarkable letter is not reprinted in Newman's *Letters and Correspondence.* Why was it suppressed?
[29] Newman's *Letters*, Vol. II., p. 207.

of external communion for himself, if by so doing he thwarted this larger and fuller victory of truth, had seemed a course both indefensible and selfish."[30]

No man could have acted like this, unless his views of truthfulness had been strangely perverted. And this was markedly the case with Mr. Ward in his Tractarian days. His son relates of his father, that—

"In discussing the doctrine of equivocation, as to how far it is lawful on occasion, he maintained, as against those who admit the lawfulness of words literally true but misleading, that the more straightforward principle is that occasionally when duties conflict, *another duty may be more imperative than the duty of truthfulness*. But he expressed it thus: 'Make yourself clear that you are *justified in deception*, and THEN LIE LIKE A TROOPER.'"[31]

The establishment by Newman of a Monastery at Littlemore, near Oxford, affords another specimen of the secrecy and crookedness which characterized the Tractarian Movement. His plans for such a Monastery, which was first started in Oxford, and subsequently removed to Littlemore, appear to have been in a partly developed condition early in 1838; but at that time were shrouded in secrecy. On January 17th of that year he wrote to his friend Mr. J. W. Bowden:—

"Your offering towards the *young monks* was just like yourself, and I cannot pay you a better compliment. It will be most welcome. As you may suppose, we have nothing settled, but are feeling our way. We should begin next term; but since, *however secret one may wish to keep it*, things get out, we do not yet wish to commit young men to anything which may hurt their chance of success at any college in standing for a Fellowship."[32]

The scheme for a Monastery was, for some unknown reason, postponed for a time, but not abandoned. It was evidently in Newman's thoughts very much during the following year. "You see," he wrote to Mr. F. Rogers,

---

[30] *William George Ward and the Oxford Movement*, p. 356. First edition.
[31] *Ibid.*, p. 30.   [32] Newman's *Letters*, Vol. II., p. 249.

September 15th, 1839, "if things came to the worst, I should turn Brother of Charity in London—an object which, quite independent of any such perplexities, is growing on me, and, peradventure, will some day be accomplished, if other things do not impede me."[33] The secrecy so much desired by Newman, as mentioned in his letter cited above, seems to have been successful, at least in one instance. One of the body of young men who were Newman's disciples, succeeded, in 1840, in gaining a Fellowship at Lincoln College, Oxford, which certainly would not have been the case had the authorities been aware that he was at the time a "monk." The success of his policy of secrecy, in this instance, appears to have given Newman intense satisfaction. He wrote, on January 10th, 1840, in great glee to his friend Bowden, announcing the joyful news:—

"To return to Lincoln; after rejecting James Mozley for a Fellowship two years since for his opinions, they have been taken by Pattison, this last term, *an inmate of the Coenobitium.* He happened to stand very suddenly, *and they had no time to inquire.* They now stare in amazement at their feat."[34]

This letter implies that the "Coenobitium," or Monastic Establishment, was already in existence. It was possibly the same Institution as that mentioned in the late Professor Mozley's *Letters* as a "Hall" (p. 79). Professor Mozley was one of the first inmates of this "Hall." He was, as is well known, one of the most enthusiastic supporters of Tractarianism in its early days; but he failed to keep up with the pace at which its leaders were marching Romeward, and drew back. His subsequent work on the *Baptismal Controversy*, in which he justified the Gorham Judgment, gave great offence to his former friends. But at this period he enjoyed the fullest confidence of Newman. There are several allusions in Mozley's *Letters* to the mysterious "Coenobitium," though it is not mentioned by that name.

[33] *Ibid.*, p. 285.   [34] *Ibid.*, p. 297.

Writing on April 6th, 1838, to his brother, the Rev. Thomas Mozley, the future Regius Professor of Divinity, announces that "Newman intends putting some plan or other of a Society into execution next term, and I am to be a leading member—though whether principal or vice-principal I cannot tell you. But if there are only two of us, which seems likely at present, I must either be one or the other. Johnson, of Magdalen Hall, will join; he is the only one we are certain of. But after the Oriel contest is over, others may be willing."[35] Three weeks later Newman's plans were in a more developed condition, for Mozley writes to his sister:—"I must inform you that Newman has taken a house, to be formed into a reading and collating establishment, to help in editing the Fathers. We have no prospect of any number joining us at present. Men are willing, but they have Fellowships in prospect, as R. And P., who stood at Oriel, and passed a very good examination—the best, as some have thought—has a Fellowship at University in prospect, which would be interfered with by joining us, for we shall of course be marked men."[36] Though the house was taken in April, it was late in Autumn before it was occupied. To Mozley was entrusted the task of furnishing it, and getting it ready as a place of residence for the embryo "Monks." It was to be a comfortable place after all, and it is somewhat amusing to read Mozley's description of his preparatory labours, as sent by him to his sister on October 18th:—

"I have been busily engaged ever since coming up with making arrangements for the Hall—bustling about, calling at the upholsterers, giving orders for coal. The place is at present airing and warming. It will look decent enough when everything is in it. There are quite gay carpets in both sitting-rooms; as is natural in fitting up, one forgets the commonest things at first, till they come upon one one by one. I shall expect to find numerous deficiencies after all, when I come to the actual habitation of the place, and just at this moment, the

[35] Mozley's *Letters*, p. 75.   [36] *Ibid.*, p. 78.

thought of coal-scuttles has flitted by me, and I have booked it in my memoranda." [37]

In March, 1840, Newman seems to have been considering the advisability of moving his Monastic Establishment to Littlemore, about three miles from Oxford, and making it a Hall attached to, and recognized by, the University of Oxford. On the 21st of that month he wrote to his friend Rogers, asking for his advice on this subject :—

"Supposing I took theological pupils at Littlemore, might not my house be looked upon as a sort of Hall depending on Oriel, as St. Mary's Hall was? And if this were commonly done, would it not strengthen the Colleges instead of weakening them? Are these not precedents? And, further, supposing a feeling arose *in favour of Monastic Establishments*, and my house at Littlemore was obliged to follow the fashion, and conform to a rule of discipline, would it not be desirable that such institutions should flow from the Colleges of our two Universities, and be under their influence? I do not wish this mentioned by Hope to anyone else. I may ask one or two persons besides." [38]

Four days before this letter was written Newman wrote, from Littlemore (March 17th), to his more intimate friend, Dr. Pusey, putting his plans before him in a more unreserved fashion. "Since I have been up here," he wrote, "an idea has revived in my mind, of which we have before now talked, viz., of building a Monastic House in the place, and coming up to live in it myself." [39] Dr. Pusey appears to have heartily approved of his friend's monastic scheme. Pusey's biographer informs us that "the plan of life contemplated [by Newman] was substantially his [Pusey's] own." [40] On March 19th, Pusey replied to Newman's letter : "Certainly it would be a great relief to have a $\mu o\nu\eta$ in our Church, many ways, and you seem just the person to form one. . . . I hardly look to be able to avail myself of the $\mu o\nu\eta$, since I must be so busy when here on account of my necessary

---

[37] *Ibid.*, p. 83.   [38] Newman's *Letters*, Vol. II., p. 303.
[39] *Life of Dr. Pusey*, Vol. II., p. 135.   [40] *Ibid.*, p. 136.

absences to see my children, unless indeed I should live long enough to be ejected from my Canonry, as, of course, one must contemplate as likely if one does live, and then it would be a happy retreat." [41]

The subtle scheme of attaching his Monastery to a Protestant University under the guise of "a sort of Hall," fortunately did not succeed. But the scheme for erecting a Monastery at Littlemore was at once acted on. On May 28th, 1840, Newman informed Mrs. J. Mozley:—"We have bought nine or ten acres of ground at Littlemore, the field between the Chapel and Barnes's, and, so be it, *in due time shall erect a Monastic House upon it.*" [42] It was not, however, until February, 1842, that Newman actually removed to Littlemore, and started there his new Monastery. We gain some idea of the kind of building it was from a passage in the Rev. Thomas Mozley's *Reminiscences of the Oxford Movement* :—

"The building," writes Mr. Mozley, "in which Newman had now made up his mind to resume the broken thread of these noble [Monastic] traditions was a disused range of stabling at the corner of two village roads. Nothing could be more unpromising, not to say depressing. But Newman had ascertained what he really wanted, and he would have no more. He sent me a list of his requirements, and the only one of a sentimental or superfluous character was that he wished to be able to see from his window the ruins of the Mynchery [an ancient Convent] and the village of Garsington. There must be a library, some 'cells,' that is, studies, and a cloister, in which one or two might turn out and walk up and down—of course, all upon the ground floor. The Oratory or chapel was to be a matter altogether for future consideration." [43]

The Rev. Frederick Oakeley, one of Newman's early friends, and subsequently a pervert to the Church of Rome, tells us that this new building was known as the "Littlemore

---

[41] *Life of Dr. Pusey*, Vol. II., p. 137.
[42] Newman's *Letters*, Vol. II., p. 305.
[43] Mozley's *Reminiscences*, Vol. II., p 213.

Monastery";[44] and that "the fact is generally known, that the life at Littlemore was founded upon the rule of the strictest Religious Orders"[45]—that is, in the Church of Rome.

Of course Newman's removal from Oxford to Littlemore, and the erection in the latter place of a new Monastic-looking building, excited the greatest curiosity in the University. Visitors came to Littlemore in abundance, anxious to fathom the mystery, and to discover Newman's great secret; very much to his annoyance, since for many reasons he did not wish his privacy to be disturbed. In his *Apologia* he reveals to the world what his indignant feelings were like at the prying curiosity of his visitors:—"I cannot walk into or out of my house," he exclaimed, "but curious eyes are upon me. Why will you not let me die in peace? Wounded brutes creep into some hole to die in, and no one grudges it them. Let me alone, I shall not trouble you long."[46]

It was not the common members of the University only who took a natural interest in his new Monastery. "Heads of Houses," he tells us, "as mounted patrols, walked their horses round those poor cottages. Doctors of Divinity dived into the hidden recesses of that private tenement uninvited, and drew domestic conclusions from what they saw there. I had thought that an Englishman's house was his castle; but the newspapers thought otherwise, and at last the matter came before my good Bishop."[47]

The interference of the Bishop of Oxford annoyed Newman more than anything else. The Bishop wanted to know the whole of the facts of the case, and this was exactly what Newman did not wish to let him know. His lordship, in a gentlemanly and straightforward manner, sent him a letter, asking for full information; and Newman replied in accordance with his "Economical" policy, in which by

---

[44] Oakeley's *Historical Notes on the Tractarian Movement*, p. 93. [45] *Ibid.*, p. 94.
[46] Newman's *Apologia*, p. 172. Edition, 1889. [47] *Ibid.*, p. 172.

this time he had become quite an adept. The reader is already in possession of proofs, which cannot be refuted, that Newman *had* set up a Monastery at Littlemore, and that its rules were of the strictest kind. Bearing this in mind, the future Cardinal's Jesuitical dealing with his Diocesan can best be shown by reprinting here in full the Bishop's letter of inquiry, and Newman's evasive answer, as published by the latter himself, in his *Apologia*. The Bishop wrote on April 12th, 1842 :—

"So many charges against yourself and your friends which I have seen in the public journals have been, within my own knowledge, false and calumnious, that I am not apt to pay much attention to what is asserted with respect to you in the newspapers.

"In (a newspaper), however, of April 9th, there appears a paragraph in which it is asserted, as a matter of notoriety, that a so-called Anglo-Catholic Monastery is in process of erection at Littlemore, and that the cells of dormitories, the chapel, the refectory, the cloisters of all may be seen advancing to perfection, under the eye of a parish priest of the Diocese of Oxford.

"Now, as I have understood that you really are possessed of some tenements at Littlemore, as it is generally believed that they are destined for the purposes of study and devotion, and as much suspicion and jealousy are felt about the matter, I am anxious to afford you an opportunity of making me an explanation on the subject. I know you too well not to be aware that you are the last man living to attempt in my Diocese a revival of the Monastic Orders (in anything approaching to the Romanist sense of the term) without previous communication with me, or indeed that you should take upon yourself to originate any measure of importance without authority from the heads of the Church, and therefore I at once exonerate you from the accusation brought against you by the newspaper I have quoted; but I feel it, nevertheless, a duty to my Diocese and myself, as well as to you, to ask you to put it in my power to contradict what, if uncontradicted, would appear to imply a glaring invasion of all ecclesiastical discipline on *your* part, or of inexcusable neglect and indifference to my duties on *mine*."

On April 14th, Newman sent his reply to the Bishop of Oxford (Dr. Bagot). It was as follows :—

"I am very much obliged by your lordship's kindness in allowing me to write to you on the subject of my house at Littlemore; at the same time, I feel it hard both on your lordship and myself that the restlessness of the public mind should oblige you to require an explanation of me.

"It is now a whole year that I have been the subject of incessant misrepresentation. A year since I submitted entirely to your lordship's authority; and, with the intention of following out the particular act enjoined upon me, I not only stopped the series of Tracts on which I was engaged, but withdrew from all public discussion of Church matters of the day, or what may be called ecclesiastical politics. I turned myself at once to the preparation for the press of the translation of St. Athanasius, to which I had long wished to devote myself, and I intended, and intend, to employ myself in the like theological studies, and in the concerns of my own parish and in practical works.

"With the same view of personal improvement, I was led more seriously to a design which had been long on my mind. For many years, at least thirteen, I have wished to give myself to a life of greater religious regularity than I have hitherto led; but it is very unpleasant to confess such a wish even to my Bishop, because it seems arrogant, and because it is committing me to a profession which may come to nothing. For what have I done that I am to be called to account by the world for my private actions, in a way in which no one else is called? Why may I not have that liberty which all others are allowed? I am often accused of being underhand and uncandid in respect to the intentions to which I have been alluding; but no one likes his own good resolutions noised about, both from mere common delicacy, and from fear lest he should not be able to fulfil them. I feel it very cruel, though the parties in fault do not know what they are doing, that very sacred matters between me and my conscience are made a matter of public talk. May I take a case parallel, though different? suppose a person in prospect of marriage: would he like the subject discussed in newspapers, and parties, circumstances, &c., &c., publicly demanded of him at the penalty of being accused of craft and duplicity?

"The resolution I speak of has been taken with reference to myself alone, and has been contemplated quite independent of the co-operation of any other human being, and without reference to success or failure other than personal, and without regard to the blame or approbation of man. And being a resolution of years, and one to which I feel God has called me, and in which I am violating no rule of the Church any more than if I married, I should have to answer for it, if I did not pursue it, as a good Providence made openings for it. In pursuing it, then, I am thinking of myself alone, not aiming at any ecclesiastical or external effects. At the same time, of course, it would be a great comfort for me to know that God had put it into the hearts of others to pursue their personal edification in the same way, and unnatural not to wish to have the benefit of their presence and encouragement, or not to think it a great infringement on the rights of conscience if such personal and private resolutions were interfered with. Your lordship will allow me to add my firm conviction that such religious resolutions are most necessary for keeping a certain class of minds firm in their allegiance to our Church; but still I can as truly say that my own reason for anything I have done has been a personal one, without which I should not have entered upon it, and which I hope to pursue whether with or without the sympathies of others pursuing a similar course.

"As to my intentions, I purpose to live there myself a good deal, as I have a resident Curate in Oxford. In doing this I believe I am consulting for the good of my parish, as my population in Littlemore is at least equal to that of St. Mary's in Oxford, and the whole of Littlemore is double of it. It has been very much neglected; and *in providing a parsonage-house at Littlemore, as this will be*, and will be called, I conceive I am doing a very great benefit to my people. At the same time it has appeared to me that a partial or temporary retirement from St. Mary's Church might be expedient during the prevailing excitement.

"As to your quotation from the (newspaper) which I have not seen, your lordship will perceive from what I have said that *no 'Monastery is in process of erection,'* there is no 'chapel,' no 'refectory,' hardly a dining-room or parlour. The 'cloisters' are my shed connecting the cottages. I do not understand what 'cells of dormitories' means. *Of course I can repeat your lordship's words, that 'I am not attempting a revival of the Monastic Orders, in anything approaching to the Romanist sense of the term,'* or 'taking on myself to originate any measure of importance without authority from the Heads of the Church.' I am attempting nothing ecclesiastical, but something personal and private, and which can only be made public, not private, by newspapers and letter writers, in which sense the most sacred and conscientious resolves and acts may certainly be made the objects of an unmannerly and unfeeling curiosity."[48]

[48] Newman's *Apologia*, pp 172-176.

So it was only a "Parsonage House," and not a Monastery at all that Newman was setting up at Littlemore! Twenty-two years later, in his *Apologia*, he wrote that:—"There is some kind or other of verbal misleading, which is not sin."[49] This was no doubt a case of the kind. His previous statements, however, and the after history of the building, flatly contradict his assertions made in his truly "Economical" letter to his Bishop. As we have seen above, when Newman bought the land on which to build, he wrote to Mrs. Mozley that "in due time" he would "erect a Monastic House upon it"; and there is nothing to show that he ever altered his mind. His brother-in-law, the Rev. Thomas Mozley, refers to the building also, in his *Reminiscences*, as a Monastic establishment; and Newman's friend Oakeley, as we have seen, admits that it was known as the "Littlemore Monastery." Only three months before his reply to the Bishop, Newman wrote (January 3rd, 1842) to his friend, Mr. James Hope-Scott, in a way which clearly shows what were his real objects at the time:—"I am," he declared, "almost in despair of keeping men together. *The only possible way is a Monastery.* Men want an outlet for their devotional and penitential feelings, and if we do not grant it, to a dead certainty they will go where they can find it."[50] I do not assert that in thus wilfully deceiving his Diocesan, Newman thought he was doing anything wrong. There is such a thing as a "conscience seared with a hot iron" (1 Tim. iv. 2); and his certainly appears to have been at this period in that condition. Men may come to that lamentable state that they think it a duty to deceive others. And what sort of place was this "Parsonage House," which Newman falsely declared to his Bishop was not a Monastery? Let Father Lockhart answer. He and Mr. Dalgairns were the first inmates, and were actually in the Monastery at the very moment when the Bishop of Oxford wrote his anxious

---

[49] *Ibid.*, p. 348.   [50] *Memoirs of J. Hope-Scott*, Vol. II., p. 6.

letter of inquiry. The following is Lockhart's own description of the life they were then leading:—

"We had now arrived at the year 1842, when we took up residence with Newman at Littlemore. Father Dalgairns and myself were the first inmates. *It was a kind of Monastic life* of retirement, prayer and study. We had a sincere desire to remain in the Church of England, if we could be satisfied that in doing so we were members of the world-wide visible communion of Christianity which was of Apostolic origin. We spent our time at Littlemore in study, prayer, and fasting. We rose at midnight to recite the Breviary Office, consoling ourselves with the thought that we were united in prayer with united Christendom, and were using the very words used by the Saints of all ages. We fasted according to the practice recommended in Holy Scripture, and practised in the most austere Religious Orders of Eastern and Western Christendom. We never broke our fast, except on Sundays and the Great Festivals, before 12 o'clock, and not until 5 o'clock in the Advent and Lenten seasons." [51]

One day when the Evangelical Warden of Wadham College, Oxford, knocked at the door of the Littlemore "Monastery," *alias* "Parsonage House," Newman himself opened it. "May I see the Monastery?" asked the visitor. "*We have no Monasteries here*," replied Newman, who, thereupon, angrily and uncivilly slammed the door in the Warden's face![51] The Roman Catholic author to whom I am indebted for this story gives us further evidence tending to prove that it was a "Monastery" notwithstanding Newman's denial.

"The story of the life at Littlemore," he writes, "has never yet been told; and it would be impossible to glean from Newman's scanty allusions in the *Apologia*, or even from his letter to the Bishop, any idea of its primitive austerities and observances. I tell these as nearly as possible as they are told by Littlemore men to me. Lent was a season of real penance for the inmates. They had nothing to eat each day till 5, and then the solitary meal was of salt-fish. No wonder Dr. Wootten, the Tractarian doctor, told them they must all die in a few years if things went on so; and no wonder Dalgairns had a serious illness, at which some relaxations were

[51] *Biography of Father Lockhart*, p. 35. Leicester: Ratcliffe College.

[52] *Cardinal Newman: A Monograph*, by John Oldcastle, p. 23. The author of this work is editor of the *Weekly Register*.

made—a breakfast, of bread and butter and tea, at noon; taken standing up at a board—a real board, erected in the improvised refectory, and called in undertones by some naturally fastidious ones a 'trough.' The 'chapel' was hardly more pretentious than the dining-room. At one end stood a large Crucifix, bought at Lima by Mr. Crawley, a Spanish merchant living in Littlemore. It was what was called 'very pronounced'—with the all but barbaric realism of Spanish religious art. A table supported the base; and on the table were two candles (always lit at prayer-time by Newman), the light of which was requisite; for Newman had veiled the window and walls with his favourite red hangings. Of an altar there was no pretence; the village church at Littlemore being Newman's own during the first years of his residence there. A board ran up the centre of the chapel, and in a row on either side stood the disciples for the recitation of Divine Office, the 'Vicar' standing by himself a little apart. The days and hours of the Catholic Church were duly kept; and the only alteration made in the Office was that Saints were invoked with a modification of Newman's making—the '*Ora* pro nobis' being changed in recitation to '*Oret*.'"[53]

Amongst the inmates of Littlemore Monastery were Frederick S. Bowles, subsequently a Roman Catholic priest; and, as I have already stated, John B. Dalgairns, afterwards a priest at Brompton Oratory; Ambrose St. John, who became a priest at the Birmingham Oratory; Richard Stanton, subsequently an Oratorian priest; Lockhart (from whom I have quoted), who died, in 1892, as a Roman priest; and Albany Christie, who joined the Jesuit Order. Mark Pattison, afterwards the well-known Rector of Lincoln College, Oxford, paid a fortnight's visit to the Monastery, commencing at the close of September, 1843. He kept a diary while he was there, from which I take the following extract as exhibiting the kind of life which was led in the establishment:—

"Sunday, October 1st.—St. John called me at 5.30, and at 6 went to Matins, which with Lauds and Prime take about an hour and a half; afterwards returned to my room and prayed, with some effect, I think. Tierce at 9, and at 11 to Church-Communion.

[53] *Ibid.*, p. 25.

More attentive and devout than I have been for some time; hope I am coming into a better frame; thirty-seven communicants. Returned and had breakfast. Had some discomfort at waiting for food so long, which I have not done since I have been unwell this summer, but struggled against it, and in some degree threw it off. Walked up and down with St. John in the garden; Newman afterwards joined us. . . At 3 to Church; then Nones . . . Vespers at 8, Compline at 9; the clocks here very backward. Very sleepy, and went to bed at 10."[54]

When Newman seceded to the Church of Rome in 1845, the Littlemore Monastery was broken up, and most of its members followed their leader to Rome, and thus closed a noteworthy chapter in the secret history of the Tractarian Movement.

This may, perhaps, be an appropriate place to mention that some sort of a "religious community" was established at about this period, by the Rev. Frederick W. Faber (subsequently known as Father Faber of the Brompton Oratory), in the Parish of Elton, of which he became Rector in 1842, though he did not enter into residence until the following year. Meanwhile, between his acceptance of the living, and commencing work as Rector, Faber travelled abroad, and became desperately enamoured of the Roman Catholic system and religion. "He saw then," writes his biographer, "that he must within three years either be a Catholic, or lose his mind."[55] Faber went abroad with letters of introduction from Dr. Wiseman, subsequently Cardinal Wiseman, addressed to Cardinal Acton, and to the Rev. Dr. Grant, a Roman Catholic priest, both then resident at Rome. It was by no means uncommon at that time for young Tractarians to visit the continent, where, unknown and unobserved by prying eyes at home, they could indulge their taste for Popery to their hearts' content. "The disciples of the Oxford School," writes

[54] Mark Pattison's *Memoirs*, pp. 190, 191.
[55] Bowden's *Life of Father Faber*, p. 168. Second edition.

Father Oakeley, from personal experience, "had a general sympathy with all foreign churches."

"We endeavoured," Father Oakeley relates, "especially the younger and less occupied members of our Society, to improve our relations with foreign Catholics by occasional visits to the continent. For this purpose Belgium was preferred to France, because of the greater external manifestation of religion in that country. Whatever our Tractarian friends may have been on this side of the channel, there could be no doubt of their perfect Catholicity on the other. It was, in fact, of so enthusiastic and demonstrative a character as to astonish the natives themselves, and sometimes, even, perhaps, to shame them. Our friends used to distinguish themselves by making extraordinarily low bows to priests, and genuflecting, even in public places, to everyone who looked the least like a Bishop. In the churches they were always in a state of prostration, or of ecstasy. Everything, and everybody, was charming; and such a contrast to England! Catholics might have their faults like other people, but even their faults were better than Protestant virtues. There was always a redeeming point even in their greatest misdemeanours; their acts of insobriety were far less offensive than those of Englishmen, and evidences of their Catholicity might be traced in their very oaths."[56]

Of course, when these young gentlemen came back to England from their continental trips, they were careful not to let the English public know where they had been, what they had said, and what they had done, when abroad. At home they passed as faithful sons of the Reformed Church of England; on the continent they were seen in their true colours. Yet, even when at home, in Oxford, some of the young Tractarians indulged their passion for real Popery, in a daring though secret manner. The Rev. E. G. K. Browne, who, before his secession to Rome, was for some years a Tractarian clergyman in the Church of England, writing of events which transpired in the early period of the Movement, informs us that then men of the Tractarian party might "be found studying S. Thomas Aquinas, Bellarmine, and Perrone, and using the *Garden of the Soul* and the

---

[56] Oakeley's *Historical Notes*, pp. 73, 74.

Paradisus Animæ as books of private devotion, *but secretly, for fear of their fellow men*—*some might be seen stealing to Mass at the Catholic chapel*—humble and mean as it was—*but disguised*, and pouring out their hearts to their God, concealed from the view of man by some pillar, beseeching Him to guide them into the truth, for none dared trust another, or confer with the friend of his bosom, or the companion of his earlier days, on so sacred, so awfully sacred a subject as the salvation of the soul."[57] When Faber arrived at Rome, in 1843, he was "not scandalized" even by the "relic worship" he beheld there.[58] He wrote home, under date May 20th, 1843, to state that Dr. Wiseman's letters had engaged for him "the cheerful kindness of several of the Roman clergy, and a portion of almost every day is spent with them, either visiting the *holier* Churches, and Convents famous for miracles and the residence of Saints, or in amicable discussion of our position in England."[59] Paradoxical it must seem to my readers to know that in the same letter Faber declares :—"I find my attachment to the Church of England growing in Rome, the more I bewail our position." He rejoiced that "Protestantism is perishing," and that "what is good in it is by God's mercy being gathered"— not into the Church of England, but—"into the garners of Rome"; and he assured his correspondent that his whole life, "God willing, shall be one crusade against the detestable and *diabolical* heresy of Protestantism." On Holy Thursday he went to the Church of St. John Lateran. The Pope was present, and Faber was in an ecstasy. "I got," he says, "close to the altar, inside the Swiss Guards, and when Pope Gregory descended from his throne, and knelt at the foot of the altar, and we all knelt with him, it was a scene more touching than I had ever seen before. . . In the midst that old man in white,

---

[57] Browne's *Annals of the Tractarian Movement*, p. 41. Third edition.
[58] Dowden's *Life of Faber*, p. 156.   [59] *Ibid.*, p. 156.

prostrate before the uplifted Body of the Lord, and the dead, dead silence—Oh what a sight it was! . . . I bared my head and knelt with the people, and received with joy the Holy Father's blessing, till he fell back on his throne and was borne away."[60] On June 17th Faber had a private audience with the Pope. He appeared in "full dress" at the Vatican, and was told that "as Protestants did not like kissing the Pope's foot," he would "not be expected to do it." But this clergyman of the Reformed Church of England—Rome's greatest enemy—scorned to avail himself of the proffered dispensation! On entering the audience chamber—to quote Faber's own report of the interview—"I knelt down, and again, when a few yards from him, and lastly, before him; *he held out his hand, but I kissed his foot;* there seemed to me a mean puerility in refusing the customary homage. . . I left him almost in tears, affected as much by the earnest, affectionate demeanour of the old man, as by his blessing and his prayer. I shall remember St. Alban's Day, in 1843, to my life's end." Faber prayed at the shrine of "St." Aloysius, the Jesuit, on the feast of that "Saint;" and his biographer, Father Bowden, says that "he left the Church as if speechless, and not knowing where he was going." Twice he took up his hat to go to the English College at Rome, for the purpose of abjuring the Church of England; but on each occasion some unrecorded event prevented him from carrying out his impulse. The longer he stayed in Rome the more he loved both it and its Church. On July 5th, he declared:—"The nearest approach I can make to an imagination of heaven is that it is like Rome." He went to a Pontifical Mass, and the sight filled him with rapturous joy. "When the Pontiff, his eyes streaming with tears, slowly elevated the Lord's Body, suddenly from the roof some ten or twelve trumpets, as from heaven, pealed out with a long, wailing, timorous jubilee,

---

[60] *F.L.*, p. 162.

and I fell forward completely overcome."[61] From Rome Faber went to Florence, and while there he had gone so far away from the sound judgment of an English Churchman, that he was actually "persuaded to wear a miraculous medal"; and "on his return home he brought with him two rosaries blessed by the Pope."[62] After all this he actually began once more to act as a Church of England clergyman, by taking up his residence at Elton as its new Rector. How he could do so with an easy conscience is a mystery to any truth-loving Englishman. It certainly was not honest on his part; and the whole transaction has a very ugly look about it. I do not say that Faber was at this time a Papist in disguise, for I cannot prove it. But if anyone came forward now and proved it I should not feel the least surprise.

I am not one of those who suffer from "Jesuitism on the brain," and I do not, so to speak, see a Jesuit round every street corner. But I certainly am inclined to attach a good deal of importance to the revelations made by the late Rev. Dr. Desanctis, formerly parish priest of the Madallena, Rome, Professor of Theology, Official Theological Censor of the Inquisition, and subsequently Minister of the Reformed Italian Church at Geneva. Desanctis was a man of high personal character, and from the offices he held while at Rome was enabled to obtain an intimate acquaintance with the inner working of Romanism and Jesuitism. In his work on *Popery and Jesuitism in Rome in the Nineteenth Century*, a translation of which was published in London, in 1852, he gives a great deal of valuable information concerning the secret and inner working of Tractarianism, which, at that period, was popularly known in England and abroad as Puseyism.

"My Jesuit Confessor," says Dr. Desanctis, "was Secretary to the French Father Assistant [of the Jesuit Order], and as he esteemed me

[61] Bowden's *Life of Faber*, p. 170.   [62] *Ibid.*, pp. 175, 177.

much, and accounted me an affiliated member of the Society, he made many disclosures to me."

Amongst these disclosures were the following:—

"Despite all the persecution they [the Jesuits] have met with, they have not abandoned England, where there are a greater number of Jesuits than in Italy; that there are Jesuits in all classes of society; in Parliament; *among the English clergy;* among the Protestant laity, even in the higher stations. I could not comprehend how a Jesuit could be a Protestant priest, or how a Protestant priest could be a Jesuit; but my Confessor silenced my scruples by telling me, *omnia munda mundis*, and that St. Paul became as a Jew that he might save the Jews; it was no wonder, therefore, if a Jesuit should feign himself a Protestant, for the conversion of Protestants. But pay attention, I entreat you, to my discoveries concerning the nature of the religious movement in England termed Puseyism.

"The English clergy were formerly too much attached to their Articles of Faith to be shaken from them. You might have employed in vain all the machines set in motion by Bossuet and the Jansenists of France to reunite them to the Romish Church; and so the Jesuits of England tried another plan. This was to demonstrate from history and ecclesiastical antiquity the legitimacy of the usages of the English Church, whence, through the exertions of the Jesuits concealed among its clergy, might arise a studious attention to Christian antiquity. This was designed to occupy the clergy in long, laborious, and abstruse investigation, and to alienate them from their Bibles."[63]

On another occasion a Roman priest was asked by Desanctis:—"But do you not think it would be for the greater glory of God, that all the Puseyites should become Catholics?" The reply to this question was:—

"No, my son, the Puseyite movement must be let alone that it may bring forth fruit. If all the Puseyites were to declare themselves Catholics, the Movement would be at an end. Protestants would be alarmed, and the whole gain of the Catholic Church would be reduced to some million of individuals and no more. From time to time it is as well that one of the Puseyite leaders should become a Catholic, in order that, under our instructions, the Movement may be better conducted; but it would not be desirable for many of them to come over to Catholicism. Puseyism is a living testimony to the necessity

[63] Desanctis, *Popery and Jesuitism in Rome*, pp. 128, 134.

of Catholicism in the midst of our enemies; it is a worm at the root which, skilfully nourished by our exertions, will waste Protestantism till it is destroyed." [64]

I know very well that Ritualists will pooh pooh and laugh at these statements of Desanctis. But, for my part, I cannot see that I should reject his testimony merely because he was a convert from Rome. Why should I not trust the word of a Protestant, against whose character—so far as I can ascertain—nothing can be said, and who had exceptional opportunities of getting at the real facts of the case? If we reject the evidence of reliable persons, how can history be properly written? In dealing with the Secret History of the Oxford Movement it would be highly improper not to quote what Dr. Desanctis has written on this important subject. And those who have most closely studied the Secret History of Tractarianism, Puseyism, and Ritualism, will be more disposed than others to give credence to his statements.

To return to Faber. When he commenced his work at Elton, as Rector, he determined, says his biographer, "to model his pastoral operations on the system pursued by the [Roman] Catholic Church, and to work his parish, as he expressed it, 'in the spirit of St. Philip and St. Alphonso.'" [65] No doubt these two "Saints" were "St." Philip Neri, founder of the Oratorian Order, of which Faber subsequently became a member; and "St." Alphonsus Liguori, author of the *Glories of Mary*. Faber circulated amongst his parishioners a *History of the Sacred Heart*,[66] in which he advocated the adoration of the material heart of our Lord—a modern custom invented by the Jesuits. His biographer has to admit of this practice that it cannot "be said that it belongs to the genuine spirit of the Established Church." After he had been at Elton about six months, Faber found that it was not so easy as he expected to pervert his parishioners to his Romanizing views. On March 24th,

---

[64] Desanctis, *Popery and Jesuitism in Rome*, p. 17.
[65] Bowden's *Life of Faber*, p. 179.   [66] *Ibid.* p. 180.

1844, he wrote to a friend :—" I feel impatient, *thinking I could do all things in my parish as if I were a Roman.*" After a time, a measure of success attended his efforts, and he was able to start in his parish the Religious Community to which I have already alluded. The mystery and secrecy with which Faber shrouded this Community cannot be better described than in the words of Father Bowden :—

" A number of persons, chiefly young men, began," writes Faber's biographer, " to go to confession to him, and to receive Communion. Out of the most promising of these penitents he formed a sort of Community. *They were accustomed to meet in the Rectory every night at twelve o'clock*, and to spend about an hour in prayer, chiefly in reciting portions of the Psalter. On the eves of great feasts, the devotions were prolonged for three or four hours. *The use of the* DISCIPLINE *was also introduced on Fridays, eves of festivals, and every night in Lent, each taking his turn to receive it from the others.*" [67]

It may be well to explain here, for the benefit of the Protestant reader, who may be pardoned for want of information on the subject, that the " Discipline " secretly used by the fanatics at Elton, is a kind of cat-o'-nine tails, knotted, and made with either cord or steel, with which each penitent is whipped on the bare back, either by himself or another, as a penance for his sins. Very early in his career the late Dr. Pusey seems to have fallen in love with this form of Romish superstition; but his early regard for it remained concealed from the public gaze, until the publication of the *Memoirs of James Robert Hope-Scott*, in 1884, when a letter from Dr. Pusey to Mr. Hope-Scott, dated September 9th, 1844, first saw the light of day. The latter was travelling abroad at the time he received this letter, which contained two or three commissions for him to execute while on the continent. One of these was to purchase a number of Roman Catholic books, for Dr. Pusey's use; the second, to collect information concerning " the system as to Retreats " amongst Roman Catholics; and the third was, to

[67] *Ibid.*, p. 183.

purchase a specimen "Discipline." The latter commission was put into the postscript of his letter, and was as follows:—

"There is yet a subject on which I should like to know more, if you fall in with persons who have the guidance of consciences,—what penances they employ for persons whose temptations are almost entirely spiritual, of delicate frames often, and who wish to be led on to perfection. I see in a spiritual writer that even for such, corporal severities are not to be neglected, but so many of them are unsafe. *I suspect the 'Discipline' to be one of the safest*, and with internal humiliation *the best*. Could you procure and send me one by B.? What was described to me was of a very sacred character; *5 cords, each with 5 knots*, in memory of the 5 wounds of our Lord. I should be glad also to know whether there were any cases in which it is unsafe, *e.g.*, in a nervous person." [68]

One cannot help wondering, if a cat-o'-nine tails, or rather of five, with five cords, was not thought too severe for persons of "delicate frames," what would be the penance inflicted on those who possessed strong constitutions?

About two years after his letter to Mr. James Hope-Scott, Dr. Pusey appears to have commenced the use of "Hair Cloth" and "Disciplines." On the "Feast of St. Simon and St. Jude," 1846, he wrote to the Rev. J. Keble, who at about that period became his Father Confessor,—"Will you give me some penitential rules for myself? I hardly know what I can do, just now, in a bodily way, for nourishment I am ordered; sleep I must take when it comes; cold is bad for me; and I know not whether *I am strong enough to resume the Hair Cloth*. However, I hope to try." [69] The word "resume" in this letter proves that Pusey had used "Hair Cloth" before the date of his letter; but for how long I cannot tell. Later on in the same year he wrote again to Keble:—

"I am a great coward about inflicting pain on myself, partly, I hope, from a derangement of my nervous system. Hair Cloth I know not how to make pain: it is only symbolical, except when worn to an extent which seemed to wear me out. *I have it on again, by God's*

---
[68] *Memoirs of J. Hope-Scott*, Vol. II., pp. 52, 53.
[69] *Life of Dr. Pusey*, Vol. III., p. 99.

mercy. I would try to get some sharper sort. Lying hard I like best, unless it is such as to take away sleep, and that seems to unfit me for duties. Real fasting, *i.e.*, going without food, was very little discomfort, except in the head, when the hour of the meal was over, and Dr. Wootten said and says, 'It was shortening my life.' Praying with my arms in the form of a cross, seemed to distract me, and act upon my head, from this same miserable nervousness. *I think I should like to be bid* [*i.e.*, by Keble as his Father Confessor] *to use the Discipline*. I cannot even smite upon my breast much because the pressure on my lungs seemed bad. In short, you see, I am a mass of infirmities." [70]

This is, indeed, a most pitiful letter, and one to be wondered at. Instead of saying that he was wearing Hair Cloth again, "by God's mercy," it would have been more accurate to have said that he was wearing it through his own folly and superstition. He certainly could not plead either Scriptural or Church of England authority for the practice. One might make some excuse for Dr. Pusey on the score of his then enfeebled state of health, were it not that when he regained his ordinary health there is no evidence to show that he gave up the use of either Hair Cloth, or the Discipline. On the contrary, in his *Manual for Confessors*, published in 1878, he recommends both as penances for sinners. His biographer informs us that "with Keble's sanction" Pusey made it a rule "to wear Hair Cloth always by day, unless ill"; and that "he was very anxious to *use 'the Discipline' every night* with Psalm li. Keble did not advise it. Pusey entreated. 'I still scruple,' wrote Keble, 'about the Discipline. I could but allow, not enjoin it to anyone.'" [71]

The use of the "Discipline," and of other penitential "articles of piety," as they are sometimes termed, is, almost of necessity, kept secret by those who adopt them. Some idea, however, of the extent to which these articles of torture are used at the present time within the Church of England may be gained from the following article, which appeared

---

[70] *Ibid.*, p. 100. [71] *Ibid.*, pp. 104, 108.

in the *Westminster Gazette*, of September 9th, 1896—a paper which cannot be accused of any undue partiality for Protestantism :—

"John Kensit, 'the Protestant Bookseller,' has given Paternoster Row a new sensation this week. For some days past a large part of his window has been used for the exhibition of a large sheet displaying half a dozen 'instruments of torture,' *said to be used and recommended by 'members of the Church of England.'*

"Whoever they are used by—and it is pretty certain they are not mere ornaments or playthings—these 'instruments of torture' by no means belie the name Mr. Kensit has bestowed upon them. Take that broad stomacher of horse-hair, for example, and place it next to the skin; imagine the discomfort of the first five minutes as each bristly hair presses against the body, and picture the torture of each succeeding five minutes it is worn. Then turn from this mild 'Discipline' to the severer penance of the Barbed Heart. This is a maze of wire, the size of the palm of one's hand, upon one side of which barbs project, finer than the ends of the barbed fences of our fields. How many of these are pressing to-day against lacerated breasts! Of similar construction, and equally fiendish in purpose, are the Wristlets and Anklets and the broad band of netted barbs which the penitent fastens around his or her leg. All of these may possibly be worn under conditions which will mitigate the severity of the torture; but there would seem to be no way of softening the lash when applied to the bare skin, so what can be said of the two Scourges exhibited by Mr. Kensit? One is of hard knotted ropes, half a dozen ends attached to a pliant handle; the other is of well-hardened and polished steel, each end of the five chains neatly finished with a steel rowel. Every blow from this, when the penitent swings it over his shoulder upon his bare back, must produce five wounds, bruises, or sores. No wonder the crowd gazes incredulously until ordered to 'move on.'

"Since this queer little exhibition opened, the bookseller has stood a running fire of question and expostulation. The instruments had not been on view an hour before a gentleman entered the shop and delivered himself after this fashion :—

"'Look here, sir, whoever you are, if you're the proprietor of this place take those things out of your window. It's a lie. It never could be done. I believe it's just one of your advertising dodges. I won't believe that those things were ever made to be used in this day.'

"Mr. Kensit is accustomed to that sort of salutation, so he waited till his visitor had ended a long tirade, and then quietly remarked:—

"'Will you take the trouble to go into the shop next door and ask the shopman to show you a selection of these things. Ask him [a Roman Catholic publisher] to name his price, and let him tell you who buys them. Then you can come back and apologise to me.'

"'The gentleman,' said Mr. Kensit, when he told a representative the story on Monday, 'went into the shop next door. In five minutes he was back again with a bundle under his arm.' 'Mr. Kensit,' he said, 'you're right. They sell them, and I've bought a few to take home and show to my family. They'll never believe it unless I do.'

"'Well,' said Mr. Kensit, 'did you ask who purchases them?'

"'I did,' said the gentleman, 'and if you'll believe me, *the shopman said that for every one he sold to a Catholic he sold three to Church of England people!*'

"'I not only believe it,' said Mr. Kensit, 'but I know it.'"

There is certainly, as I have already said, no Scriptural authority for the use of the "Discipline." We do read that "By His stripes we are healed" (Isa. liii. 5); but never that we are spiritually healed by the stripes and bruises inflicted by ourselves. How far the use of the "Discipline" has spread amongst Ritualists at the present day is one of those secrets which have not been fully revealed. Yet there is reason to fear that it is on the increase, and is much more widespread than is generally supposed. There is cause to believe that in some Ritualistic Convents the "Discipline" is not unknown. Dr. Pusey, as is well known, in conjunction with the late Miss Sellon, founded several Convents, and retained spiritual authority over them until his death. In his *Advice on Hearing Confession*, for the use of Ritualistic Father Confessors, directions are given as to the penances to be imposed by the Confessor on Ritualistic Sisters of Mercy. One of these, if "the Superior of the Convent approves," is as follows:—For mortifications; the Discipline for about a quarter of an hour a day."[72] It may here be asked, if a

[72] Pusey's *Manual for Confessors*, p. 243.

Sister refused to undergo this severe and cruel penance, would she be considered as having broken her Vow of Obedience? The answer to this question is given by Dr. Pusey himself. His advice to Sisters of Mercy is:—
" Study to be perfectly obedient to your *spiritual father*. . . . Now perfect obedience implies prompt, punctual, willing, *unquestioning* obedience, unless the thing commanded be evident sin." [73] There can be no doubt, therefore, that the Sister would feel it a bounden duty to take the " Discipline for about a quarter of an hour a day," if ordered to do so by her " Spiritual father," the Confessor. The subject is not a pleasant one to those who hate cruelty; but it is of so secret a character that it seems almost impossible to discover the priestly culprits who order English ladies to be thus whipped on their bare backs, as *they* may think right and proper. One of these cases has fortunately come to light, in which the Discipline was used most cruelly and shamefully in a Ritualistic Convent, inflicted on the Sister, not by command of her Confessor, but by a " Mother " of the Convent. The story is related by Miss Povey, who, as " Sister Mary Agnes, O.S.B.," was for seventeen years a Nun in Convents controlled by the notorious " Father Ignatius." She writes:—

"One day I was coming from Nones at 2.45 P.M. This 'Mother' ['Mary Wereburgh of the Blessed Sacrament'] commanded me to stay where I was, and not to return to work, and then said:—'You have got the Devil in you, and I am going to beat him out.' All left the sacristy but myself, the Mother Superior, and one Nun, who was ordered to be present at the casting out of the devil. I was commanded first to strip. I saw ' *the Discipline*,' with its seven lashes of knotted whipcord in her hand, and I knew that one lash given (or taken by oneself) was in reality seven. I should mention that at certain times *it was the rule to Discipline oneself.* . . Then I began to undress; but when I came to my vest, shame again overcame me. 'Take that thing off,' said the Mother Superior. I replied, 'I cannot, reverend

---

[73] Pusey's *Manual for Confessors*, p. 245.

Mother; it's too tight.' The Nun who was present was told to help me to get it off. A deep feeling of shame came over me at being half-nude. The Mother then ordered the Nun to say the '*Miserere*,' and while it was recited *she lashed me several times with all her strength*. I was determined not to utter a sound, but at last I could not restrain a smothered groan, whereat she gave me one last and cruel lash, and then ceased. Even three weeks after she had 'Disciplined' me, I had a very sore back, and it hurt me greatly to lie on it (our beds were straw put into sacks). There was a looking-glass in the room I now occupied (Nuns do not usually have them), and I looked to see if my back was marked, as it was so sore. Never shall I forget the shock it gave me. I turned quickly away, for *my back was black, blue, and green all over*."[74]

Many of my readers, on reading this horrible yet true story, will naturally ask themselves, are there any other Mothers Superior who act in a similar manner? If the secrets of Convents were revealed, how many more tales of "Discipline" cruelty should we hear? We need not make rash and wholesale assertions, but is there not cause for inquiry and anxiety?

Faber, to whom we once more return, not only used the "Discipline" himself; he also, as a penance, wore "a thick horse-hair cord tied in knots round his waist."[75] He still, however, continued to act as Rector of Elton. On August 12th, 1844, he informed Newman:—"I seem to grow more Roman daily, *and almost to write from out the bosom of the Roman Church*, instead of from where I am."[76] By December he made the discovery—which he ought to have made long before—that his position in the Church of England was a dishonest one. "I feel as if I was living a dishonest life,"[77] he wrote to Newman. And yet, strange as it may seem to some, with this conviction upon him he continued for nearly another year to officiate in the Church of England. At this time he published a *Life of St. Wilfrid*, of which Father

---

[74] *Nunnery Life in the Church of England*, by Sister Mary Agnes, O.S.B., pp. 97-99.
[75] *Life of Faber*, p. 187.   [76] *Ibid.*, p. 187.   [77] *Ibid.*, p. 189.

Bowden says:—"It is difficult to conceive how" certain passages in it "could have been written by a member of the Church of England"[78]—so thoroughly Roman were they. Bowden quotes several passages from this "Life," from which I take the following specimens:—

"He (Wilfrid) saw that the one thing to do was to go to Rome, and learn under the shadow of St. Peter's Chair the more perfect way. To look Romeward is a Catholic instinct, seemingly implanted in us for the safety of the faith" (p. 4).

"Certainly, it is true that he materially aided the blessed work of rivetting more tightly the happy chains which held England to St. Peter's Chair—chains never snapped, as sad experience tells us, without the loss of many precious Christian things" (p. 84).

At last the time came when Faber publicly renounced his connection with the Church of England. On Sunday, November 16th, 1845, he addressed his congregation in Elton Church for the last time. He told them that "the doctrines he had taught them, though true, were not those of the Church of England; that, as far as the Church of England had a voice, she had disavowed them, and that consequently he could not remain in her communion."[79] The next day he left the parish, accompanied by his two servants, and by seven members of his "Religious Community," all of whom were admitted the same evening at Northampton, by Bishop Wareing, into the Church of Rome.

It would have been well for the Church of England had the case of Faber been the last of its kind. But I think that anyone who, during the past twenty years, has carefully read the Ritualistic newspapers, must be of the opinion that Faber's example is more or less followed at the present time by many hundreds, not to say thousands, of Ritualistic clergy, who have no greater moral right to remain in the Church of England than Faber had during the last two years of his ministry as Rector of Elton. The gates which admit to the ministry, be it remembered, are kept by the

[78] *Life of Faber*, p. 190. [79] *Ibid.*, p. 201.

Bishops, who have admitted to the ranks of the clergy of the Church, by ordination, every one of these traitors and conspirators, and therefore on the Episcopal Bench the responsibility of the mischief caused by them primarily rests. It is certain, therefore, that greater care is needed now than ever before, on the part of the Bishops, to prevent the ordination of men who hold Roman doctrines. And the laity have a right to complain, and they do complain justly and bitterly, that in many instances these Romanizing conspirators are preferred by the Bishops to influential dignities and valuable livings in their gift, while hard-working and law-abiding clergymen are coldly passed by, as quite unworthy of Episcopal notice or favour. These things are alienating the hearts of multitudes of the laity from the Church of England; and it is the truest wisdom of our rulers in Church and State to reflect that widespread discontent is not a thing to trifle with. The results of Archbishop Laud's efforts to Romanize the Church in the seventeenth century ought to serve as a salutary warning to Statesmen and Bishops of the nineteenth century. The dangers arising from the labours of the Ritualists are far greater than from those of their predecessors two hundred and fifty years ago. Laud and his party would never have dared to make such strides Romewards as have been made by our modern Ritualists. May God grant that the civil wars which were largely the result of Laud's foolish and disloyal operations, may not be repeated in England ere the close of the forthcoming century! We make no rash prophecy: no one can tell what the future may bring forth. But are there not already clouds in the ecclesiastical and political sky, which may suddenly grow larger and larger, until they burst forth in civil and religious convulsions which every lover of his country must dread?

I do not think that I could more appropriately close this chapter than by citing a very accurate description of the secret policy of the early Tractarians, given by one of the party, the Rev. William Maskell, Vicar of St. Mary's Church, in a letter which he published, in 1850, shortly before his secession to Rome.

"As a fact," wrote Mr. Maskell, "the Evangelical party, plainly, openly, and fully, declare their opinions upon the doctrines which they contend the Church of England holds: they tell their people continually, what they ought, as a matter of duty towards God and towards themselves, both to believe and practise. Can it be pretended that we [Tractarians], as a party, anxious to teach the truth, are equally open, plain, and unreserved? If we are not so, is prudence, or economy, or the desire to lead people gently and without rashly disturbing them, or any other like reason, a sufficient ground for our withholding large portions of Catholic truth? Can any one chief doctrine be reserved by us, without blame or suspicion of dishonesty? And it is not to be alleged, that only the less important duties and doctrines are so reserved: as if it would be an easy thing to distinguish and draw a line of division between them. Besides, that which we are disputing about cannot be trivial and unimportant; if it were so, we rather ought, in Christian charity, to acknowledge our agreement in essentials, and consent to give up the rest.

"But we do reserve vital and essential truths; we often hesitate and fear to teach our people many duties, not all necessary in every case or to every person, but eminently practical, and sure to increase the growth of the inner spiritual life; we differ, in short, as widely from the Evangelical party in the manner and openness, as in the matter and details of our doctrine. Take, for example, the doctrine of Invocation of Saints; or, of Prayers for the Dead; or, of Justification by Faith only; or, of the merit of good works; or, of the necessity of regular and obedient Fasting; or, of the reverence due to the blessed Virgin Mary; or, of the Propitiatory Sacrifice of the Blessed Eucharist; or, of the almost necessity of Auricular Confession and Absolution, in order to the remission of mortal sin;—and more might be mentioned than these. Now, let me ask you; do we speak of these doctrines from our pulpits in the same manner, or to the same allowed extent, as we speak of them one to another, or think of them in our closets? *Far from it;* rather, when we do speak of them at all, in the way of public, ministerial, teaching, *we use certain symbols and a shibboleth of phrases, well enough understood by the initiated few, but dark and meaningless to the many.* All this seems to me to be, day by day and hour by hour, more and more hard to be reconciled with the real spirit, mind, and purpose of the English Reformation, and of the modern English Church, shewn by the experience of 300 years. It does seem to be, daily, more and more *opposed to that single-mindedness of purpose, that simplicity and truthfulness and openness of speech and action, which the Gospel of our Blessed Lord requires.* We are, indeed, to be 'wise as serpents'; but has our wisdom of the last few years been justly within the exceptions of that law? Let me not be understood as if supposing that any motive, except prudence and caution, has caused this reserve; but there are limits beyond which Christian caution *degenerates into deceit,* and an enemy might think that we could forget that there are more texts than one of Holy Scripture which speak of persecution to be undergone, for His sake, and for the Faith.

"And if reserve in teaching carried to such an extent be, as I conceive it to be, unjustifiable, it is equally wrong, and to be condemned, in the practice of those who listen to, and endeavour to obey such teaching. What can we think—when honestly we bring our minds to its consideration—what *can* we think, I say, of the moral evils which must attend upon and follow conduct and rule of religious life, *full of shifts and compromises and evasions?* a rule of life based upon the acceptance of half one doctrine, all the next, and none of the third; upon the belief entirely of another, *but not daring to say so;* upon the constant practice, if possible, of this or that particular duty, *but secretly, and fearful of being 'found out';* doing it as if under the pretence of not doing it; if questioned, explaining it away, or answering with some dubious answer; creeping out of difficulties; ANYTHING, IN A WORD, BUT SINCERE, STRAIGHTFORWARD, AND TRUE. It would really seem as if, instead of being Catholics—as we say we are—in a Christian land, we were living in the city of heathen Rome, and forced to worship in the Catacombs and dark places of the earth."[80]

---

[80] *A Second Letter on the Present Position of the High Church Party in the Church of England,* by the Rev. William Maskell, pp. 65-68. Third edition. London: Pickering, 1850.

CHAPTER II.

THE SOCIETY OF THE HOLY CROSS.

Its secret birth in 1855—Brethren forbidden to mention its existence—Its secret Statutes—Its secret signs—Its mysterious "Committee of Clergy"—The Roll of sworn Celibates—Their Oath—Its secret Synods and Chapters—Brethren must push the Confessional amongst young and old—Its Confessional Book for little children—Its secret Confessional Committee—Issues the *Priest in Absolution*—Secret birth of the Retreat Movement—First secret Retreat in Dr. Pusey's rooms—Starts the "St. George's Mission" at St. Peter's, London Docks—Dr. Pusey a member of the Mission—The Bishop of Lebombo a member of the Society of the Holy Cross—Sensational letter from him—Ritualistic Holy Water—Brethren alarmed at publicity—The Society establish an Oratory at Carlisle—Its secret history—Organises a Petition for Licensed Confessors—Reports of speeches at its secret Synods—Their dark plottings exposed.

AFTER Tractarianism had become known as Puseyism, and both had developed into what is now termed Ritualism, it was felt by many members of the party that the time had come when the secret workers in what Hurrell Froude had so truthfully termed, in 1834, "the Conspiracy,"[1] should combine together in secret societies, the more effectually to carry out their objects. One of the most dangerous of these organizations is the Society of the Holy Cross, which was founded on February 28th, 1855. It began in a very small way, and gradually extended its borders, until it became the most powerful of all the secret organizations connected with the Ritualistic Movement. It began with only six members, of whom three subsequently joined the Church of Rome;[2]

[1] Froude's *Remains*, Vol. I., p. 377.
[2] *S. S. C. Master's Address*, to May Synod, 1875, p. 3.

and its founder was the Rev. Joseph Newton Smith,[3] who still survives. The only other surviving member of the original six is the Rev. A. Poole, Rector of Laindon Hills, Essex. A few others joined the Society during the year 1855, of whom the following are still living: viz., the Rev. John Sidney Boucher, now Rector of Gedding, Bury St. Edmunds (who withdrew in 1877); the Rev. Canon Francis H. Murray, Rector of Chislehurst (who withdrew in 1877); and the Rev. G. Cosby White, now Vicar of Newland, Malvern Link. It so happens that several of the secret documents of the Society of the Holy Cross have come into my possession, in an honourable and straightforward manner, and on these my description of the Society is mainly built. I have no more hesitation in making use of these documents than Her Majesty's Government would have in using the secret documents connected with a conspiracy against the State, should they come into their possession. For the early history of its movements I am much indebted to the *Master's* [the late Rev. A. H. Mackonochie's] *Address Delivered to the Society in Synod, on the Festival of the Invention of the Holy Cross*, 1870, and privately printed for the use of the brethren only. For the first twelve years of its existence, that is, until 1867, "caution was," said the Master, "enjoined upon the brethren in the matter of mentioning it" (p. 3). This one official statement is alone sufficient to show its secrecy, and how much it dreaded publicity. It has not lost its secret character yet. It so happened that I was at Folkestone during Church Congress week, in October, 1892, and while there I met a clergyman whom I knew to be still a member of the Society. I ventured to ask him—he knew who I was at the time—whether the Society of the Holy Cross had increased in numbers during the past fifteen years? "Don't you know, sir," was his very emphatic reply, "that

---

[3] *Twenty-one Years in St. George's Mission*, p. 18.

the Society of the Holy Cross is a *secret* Society, and that its members are pledged to *secrecy?*" "Oh, yes," I rejoined, "I know it very well; but I never before heard it so candidly acknowledged by one of its own members"! He declined to give me the information asked for, though I should have thought that such a very harmless question might easily have been answered.

The information which I am now about to give my readers concerning the Constitution of the S. S. C.—as it is commonly called—is taken from its official book, entitled *Societatis Sanctæ Crucis Statuta*, which is printed in English, the title alone being in Latin. So fearful is this Society of the Holy Cross lest anyone outside its ranks should see these Statutes, that it is expressly provided (chapter ii., sec. 10, page 4) that when a brother resigns his membership of the Society, he "shall return to the Master his Cross, and the Books of Statutes and Offices." The Cross is one of a peculiar pattern, made expressly for the Society, and is usually worn suspended on the breast, or from the watchchain, so that, as they walk along the streets, the brethren of the S. S. C. may be able to recognise one another as belonging to this secret Society, even though they may not know each other personally. The Books of Statutes and Offices are three in number, viz., the *Statuta*, already mentioned; the *Preparation for and Thanksgiving after Mass*, printed in English; and the *Societatis Sanctæ Crucis Officia*, which is entirely in Latin, and contains the "Officium Proprium"; the "Ordo ad Synodum"; the "Formula ad Cruces Benedicendas"; the "Ordo ad Recipiendum Candidatum Electum in Societatem"; the "Ordo ad Fratrem Admittendum," the "Ordo ad Admittendum Fratrem in Regulam Rubram"; a somewhat similar office for admitting to the "White Rule"; and an order for admittance into the Roll of Celibates.

The Society consists (*Statuta*, chapter i., sec. 1) "of Bishops, Priests, Deacons, and candidates for Holy Orders." "The Objects of the Society" are, as stated (in chapter i., sec. 2) "to maintain and extend the Catholic Faith and Discipline, and to form a special Bond of Union between Catholic Priests: (1) By promoting Holiness of life among the Clergy; (2) By carrying on and aiding Mission work at Home and Abroad; (3) By issuing and circulating Tracts and other Publications; (4) By the exercise of Temporal and Spiritual Charity among the Brethren; (5) By holding Synods and Chapters for Prayer and Conference; (6) By common action in matters affecting the interests of the Church; (7) By correspondence between the Brethren; (8) By the affiliation of Guilds of Laymen."

A prominent official of the S. S. C., with whom I had an interview about two years since, informed me that no action whatever has been as yet taken with reference to the last of these objects. With reference to the third of these objects a "Tract Committee" has been formed in the Society, whose work is (chapter vii., sec. 4) "to prepare, procure, revise, adapt, and *publish* Books and Tracts useful for furthering the objects of the Society." Now it is one of the proofs of the Jesuitical tactics adopted by the S. S. C. that although this Tract Committee has published a considerable number of books and tracts they never make known to the public the fact that they really emanate from the S. S. C. The most advanced Ritualistic doctrines are taught in these publications, which—I am happy to inform my readers—may henceforth be known to them by the statement on the title-page of each—"Edited by a Committee of Clergy." Whenever this is read on the title-page of any book or tract, it may be safely translated into "Society of the Holy Cross Tract Committee."

The identity of the Society with the "Committee of Clergy" seems to have been kept a profound secret, for some of the brethren appear to have known nothing at all about it. At the September, 1877, Synod, the Rev. Charles Edward Hammond expressed "the surprise he felt on discovering that the Tract Committee [of S. S. C.] and the

Committee of Clergy were the same body."[4] At the same Synod the Rev. Robert James Wilson " said that until then he had no idea of the identity of the Tract Committee and the Committee of Clergy."[5] The Rev. A. H. Mackonochie informed the brethren that "the Tract Committee came into existence soon after he became Master. Its work was to bring out Tracts, and it adopted some already in existence. He stated that the Tract called *Pardon through the Precious Blood*, and the *Altar Manual*, had been considered clause by clause by the Society."[6]

There are two classes of members, viz., "Brethren" and "Probationers." Both are required to "wear openly the Society's Cross," when "practicable" (chapter ii., sec. 5). This, of course, may be done with safety, since the outside public are not able to identify it. When two brethren meet "the one shall salute the other with the words, '*Pax tibi*,' to which the reply shall be, '*Per Crucem;*'" but it is cautiously provided that these salutations shall not take place "in the company of strangers" (chapter ii., sec. 6). One brother writing to another must begin his letter thus: —" P. ✠ T. My Dear Brother"; and end with "'In D. N. J. C.,' or some corresponding form of subscription" (*Ibid.*, sec. 7). It is provided by chapter ii., sec. 9, that:— " Upon the death of a brother notice thereof shall be given to the Secretary, as soon as possible, by any brother cognizant of it, and the Secretary shall, forthwith, inform the brethren, *that they may say Mass for the soul of their brother*, either on the day of the funeral, or as soon after as practicable." In this Statute the reader will perceive one proof of the Romanizing character of the Society.

"Every brother," says chapter ii., sec. 3, "shall be required to attend all the Synods and chapters he can, and positively the two Synods on May 3rd and September 14th

---

[4] *S. S. C. Analysis of Proceedings*, September Synod, 1877, p. 23.
[5] *Ibid.*, p. 24. [6] *Ibid.*, p. 24.

(Feasts of the Holy Cross), unless unavoidably prevented, in which case he shall state the reason to the Master, and ask for a Dispensation." These "two Synods," I may here remark, are held in the Church of St. Peter's, London Docks, with locked doors; and this has been the case for many years past. Is it not time that the Bishop of London prevented a church in his diocese from being used for secret meetings, where plots are continually being hatched for the destruction of Protestantism? The brethren are required to maintain strict secrecy as to what takes place in these Synods and Chapters. By chapter vi., sec. 24, it is provided that:—" The Brethren shall be *strictly forbidden to divulge the proceedings of the Synods and Chapters*, except so far as the publication is authorized by the Society." It is further ordered (*Ibid.*, sec. 8), that:—" The Brethren and Probationers in Synod shall sit vested in Cassock, Surplice, and *Biretta*, and in Chapter in Cassock and *Biretta*." These "Chapters" are meetings of the members, held on the second Tuesday of every month, except May and September. They have been held in various places during the history of the Society, including the House of Charity (1855-56); the Clergy House, 10, Great Tichfield Street (1856-57); the Mission House, Wellclose Square (1857-58); and the Clergy House, Crown Street, Soho. Next it shared a room with the Guild of St. Alban's, in Langham Street, from which they moved together to 3, New Boswell Court, Clare Market; and, again, in 1863, to the Clergy House, St. Alban's, Holborn. It was also located for some years in a house in a back street near St. Alban's Church, viz., 5, Greville Street, Brook Street, Holborn, now the head-quarters of the "Guild of St. Martin" for postmen. Its present meeting place I have been unable to discover. In addition to these Synods and Chapters, special District Meetings of the brethren, living in various parts of the country, are held in the provinces from time to time.

It is ordered that "Before the holding of any Synod, Mass

shall be Celebrated solemnly, with a short Sermon from a Brother, and the *Officium Proprium* shall be said" (chapter vi., sec. 4). "When the Synod shall extend over two days, a Mass shall be said for Departed Brethren on the second day, in a Church selected by the Master" (sec. 5). Those of the Brethren unable to attend the Synod, are expected, "if practicable, to say Mass for the Intention of the Society" (sec. 6), whenever an opportunity may be given them. It is also directed that "An Analysis of the Proceedings at Synod and Chapter shall be sent by the Secretary to all Officers, and to such Brethren who may desire it" (sec. 21). The Analysis is headed "S. S. C." The greatest care is taken to prevent copies falling into the hands of outsiders.

"There are," says chapter x., sec. 1, "four progressive degrees of obligation in the Society, termed respectively, the Ordinary, the Green, the Red, and the White Rule." The Ordinary Rule is "binding upon all the Brethren and Probationers. The other three (are) entirely voluntary, but recommended for adoption; the White Rule being restricted to Celibates." These Celibates are, apparently, considered as the very cream of the Society of the Holy Cross. Their names are kept on a separate list, which is known as the "Celibate Roll." A full list of the Brethren and Probationers of the Society is privately printed every year, for confidential use; but the "Celibate Roll," so far as I can ascertain, has never been trusted to print. There is a "Vicar" of this Roll. At the May Synod, 1881, the Rev. H. D. Nihill, then Vicar of St. Michael's, Shoreditch, was nominated as "Vicar of the Celibate Roll." In 1895 the Vicar was the Rev. E. G. Wood, Vicar of St. Clement's, Cambridge. By chapter xviii., sec. 5, "It is recommended that some external Symbol, and by preference a ring, be worn by Brethren of the Celibate Roll." A gentleman with whom I am acquainted, some years since came into the possession of one of these "rings," made of iron—I understand that others are made of silver, and some of gold—and he could not for some time make out its use. On looking more closely into it he discovered a very tiny indentation; but 'that was all. Wondering very much what it meant, he secured the assistance of a powerful magnifying glass, and then discovered within the indentation, the magic words " S. S. C." It was the Celibate Ring of the Society of the Holy Cross! Each member of this " Roll " takes a vow, or, rather, an oath of celibacy, "for a limited period, or *for life* " (chapter xviii., sec. 1). It is made in Latin, of which the following is a translation :—

" I, N——, profess and promise to Almighty God, Father, Son, and Holy Ghost, *and to all the Saints*, that I will lead a life of Celibacy for [so many years, or the rest of his life]. So help me God ! " [1]

The regulations for the guidance of the daily life of those attached to the various " Rules " are very minute. Those attached to the "White Rule"—that is, the Celibates —must " say Mass *daily* " (chapter xvi., sec. 4); " frequent the *Sacrament of Penance* at least *monthly* " (sec. 7); " say daily an office for each of the Hours, Prime, Terce, Sext, None, or Vespers, and Compline" (sec. 8); and " make a Retreat each year " (sec. 14). Those attached to the " Red Rule" must " say Mass on all Sundays and other Holy Days " (chapter xiv., sec. 4); " frequent the Sacrament of Penance at least *three times a year* " (sec. 7); observe the " Hours " of Prime, Compline, Sext, and None (sec. 8); and " make a Retreat each year " (sec. 15). Those attached to the " Green Rule," must also " say Mass (if practicable) on all Sundays and other Holy Days " (chapter xii., sec. 4); " frequent the Sacrament of Penance at least *once a year* " (sec. 7); make a yearly Retreat (sec. 12); and daily say a Mid-Day Office and Compline or Family Prayer (sec. 8). Those attached to the " Ordinary Rule," have a lighter set of directions than their brethren. The following "Rules and Usages of the Church " (*sic !*) are said to be binding on all

---

[1] *S. S. C. Officia*, p. 31.

who belong to the Society of the Holy Cross, which professes to be unable to grant any " dispensation therefrom " :—

" 1. To Celebrate, or at least to hear Mass (if practicable), on all Sundays and other Holy-days.

" 2. To say Mass or Communicate fasting since the midnight preceding.

" 3. To use Sacramental Confession as the conscience requires it."[8]

It will thus be seen that this secret Society of the Holy Cross is officially pledged to maintain much which ordinary loyal Churchmen consider as nothing less than Popery. The Confessional has always been a strong point with the Society. The importance attached to it is further seen in the Chapter of its Statutes devoted to "The Spirit and Discipline of the Society." Section 5 of that Chapter orders that :—

" The Brethren shall devote themselves diligently to the Science of the Care of Souls, and shall labour in bringing young and old who are under their influence to value duly the Sacrament of Penance."

We here discover that wherever members of the S. S. C. are found they are expected to act as missionaries of the Confessional, and that not only for the old, but also for the young. It is now many years since the Society, under its Jesuitical disguise of " A Committee of Clergy," issued a series of little " Books for the Young." No. I. of this series (a copy of the fourth thousand of which lies before me) was written for very little children, " six and a half or seven years old."[9] The following extracts from this book will show to my readers the fearful character of the Confessional teaching, imparted by the Society of the Holy Cross to very young children :—

" It is to the priest, and to the priest only, that a child must acknowledge his sins, if he desires that God should forgive him. Do you know why? It is because God, when on earth, gave to His

---

[8] *S. S. C. Statuta*, p. 34.

[9] "Books for the Young." No. I., *Confession*. Edited by a Committee of Clergy. Fourth thousand, p. 15.

priests, and to them alone, the Divine power of forgiving men their sins."[10]

"Go to the priest, who is the doctor of your soul, and who cures it in the name of God."[11]

"I have known poor children who concealed their sins in Confession for years. They were very unhappy, were tormented with remorse, and if they had died in that state, they would certainly have gone to the everlasting fires of hell" ! ! ![12]

"This acknowledgement, made in secret, once for all, this acknowledgement which the Confessor himself forgets the next minute."[13]

"Whilst the priest is pronouncing the words of Absolution, Jesus Christ pours the torrents of His grace into the soul of the penitent Christian. . . During this time the happy penitent ought to keep himself very humble, very little, at the feet of Jesus, hidden in the priest."[14]

"A little sinner of six and a half or seven years old, if he has sinned seriously, and if he repents and confesses seriously, has as much right to absolution as if he was twenty."[15]

"However painful it is to acknowledge a fault of this kind, it must be bravely confessed, without lessening it; it is almost always sins of impurity that weak penitents dare not tell in Confession."[16]

To help on its Confessional work the Society of the Holy Cross possesses a "Penitentiary Committee," whose work is "to advise, when referred to, on Cases of Conscience, and other matters connected with the Sacrament of Penance."[17] This Committee forms a consultative body to which Father Confessors throughout the country may apply for advice and help in their work. The latest privately printed list of Members of this Committee which I have seen, is that of 1895-96, issued with the official "Roll of the Brethren and Probationers of the Society of the Holy Cross," in that year. The members of the Committee were then: the Rev. E. G. Wood, Vicar of St. Clement's, Cambridge; the Rev. S. G. Beal, Rector of Ronaldkirk, Darlington; the Rev. A. Poole, Rector of Laindon Hills, Romford; the Rev. A. J. Mickle-

---

[10] *Ibid.*, p. 3.   [11] *Ibid.*, p. 4.   [12] *Ibid.*, p. 4.
[13] *Ibid.*, p. 7.   [14] *Ibid.*, p. 13.   [15] *Ibid.*, p. 15.
[16] *Ibid.*, p. 24.   [17] *S. S. C. Statuta*, chapter viii., sec. 4, p. 22.

thwaite, Vicar of St. Luke's, Chesterton, Cambridge (Secretary); the Rev. R. A. J. Suckling, Vicar of St. Alban's, Holborn; and the Rev. T. A. Lacey, Vicar of Madingley, Cambridge.

It was the Society of the Holy Cross that made itself responsible for that abominable book, written for the guidance of Ritualistic Father Confessors, and known as the *Priest in Absolution*. This work was issued in two parts, the first of which was published; and the second issued for private circulation amongst those Father Confessors who could be trusted by the S. S. C. The price of Part II. was, to the brethren, 5s 4d, post free. I possess a copy of both parts, which I purchased a few years since, after the work had been exposed in the House of Lords, in 1877, by the late Lord Redesdale. My copy contains a cutting, pasted on the inside, from the catalogue of Henry Sotheran & Co., the well-known London second-hand booksellers. After mentioning that the price of this copy was no less than £6. 6s, it is added :—

"So zealously guarded from public observation (for obvious reasons) is the *Priest in Absolution* that it is most unlikely that another copy will ever be offered for sale."

The second part was issued without even the printer's name attached. On the title-page it is stated that the book is "Privately Printed for the Use of the Clergy"; and it is dedicated :—

"To the Masters, Vicars, and Brethren, of the Society of the Holy Cross. This volume, *begun at their request*, and continued amongst many labours and infirmities, with the hope that it may serve to increase piety and devotion, is humbly and affectionately dedicated by an Unworthy Brother Priest."

The "Unworthy Brother Priest" carefully abstained from putting his name to his book, which was a translation with adaptations, from a filthy French Roman Catholic book, being *A Manual for Confessors*, by the Abbé Gaume. It so happened that this priest was dead when his translation was exposed in the House of Lords, but it was then made known to the public, for the first time, that his name was the Rev. J. C. Chambers. We shall return to this important event in the Society's history later on.

The "Retreat Committee" of the S. S. C. has increased its operations very much during recent years. In fact, the Society claims to have been the first to introduce Retreats into the Church of England. The Master of the Society, addressing the Synod of 1870, boasted that "the Retreat Movement" was "begun and fostered by the Society."[18] The first Retreat for the Clergy was held during the month of July, 1856, in Dr. Pusey's house at Oxford. It was marked by the secrecy which has ever characterized the movements of the Society of the Holy Cross. The outside public knew nothing at all about it; and so anxious were its promoters to prevent Churchmen generally from obtaining information, that the late Rev. Charles Lowder, who was present, and who was then a member of the S. S. C., and in charge of its East London Mission, found it necessary, in writing about it confidentially to his mother, to add this caution:—"*This account that I have given you is meant to be private, so do not let it go out of the house.*"[19] About seventeen or eighteen clergymen were present at this secret Retreat, which lasted a whole week. "Dr. Pusey has entered," wrote Mr. Lowder to his mother, "very kindly into it, and given us the greatest assistance, besides lodging and boarding us all."[20] The Romish offices of Prime, Terce, and Sext, were used at this Retreat, and several conferences were held by the members, at which various subjects of interest were discussed, including the Confessional. By the Statutes of the S. S. C. it is provided that the Retreat Committee shall "Prepare *and publish*, as near as practicable to the Feast of Epiphany in each year, a list of Retreats, stating the

---

[18] *The Master's Address*, 1870, p. 7.
[19] *Charles Lowder: A Biography*, p. 96. First edition. [20] *Ibid.*, p. 96.

place where each will be held; the persons to whom communications may be addressed; the times at which each will begin and end; the expense of living during the Retreat, and the name of the conductor" (chapter vii., p. 21). Now, here it seems as though all secrecy were cast aside, and the utmost publicity required. The Committee shall not only "prepare," but also "*publish*" the List of Retreats. And yet, notwithstanding this rule, a measure of secrecy is thrown around this List. It is periodically advertised in the *Church Times*, but no intimation is given that the Retreats have been organized by the Society of the Holy Cross. It would never do to make such a public display of its work, moderate High Churchmen might be thus frightened from taking part in Retreats organized by such a very advanced Society! Accordingly, a much needed "Economy" and "Reserve" is practised by the authorities. The Confessional is a special feature of these Retreats. The ordinary printer for the S.S.C., Mr. Knott, Brooke Street, Holborn, has published a four-paged tract, entitled *Instruction for Retreats*, which in all probability is the production of one of the brethren. Those who enter the Retreat are here directed that, before it commences, they should "go to Confession," and "join in the offering of the Holy Sacrifice"; and they are told:— "If you have made a Confession in Retreat, go back to your own Director as soon as possible." At these gatherings, whether for the clergy or the laity, for men or for women, the full Romanizing doctrines held by the Ritualists may be—and, I understand, really are—taught with safety, and with a frankness which could not be practised from the pulpit. Loyal Churchmen would do well to avoid Retreats, if they wish to retain their allegiance to the principles of the Protestant Reformation.

The year following the formation of the Society of the Holy Cross witnessed the starting, by that Society, of "The St. George's Mission," in the East End of London. The

Rector of St. George's, at that time, was the late Rev. Bryan King, and he approved heartily, not only of the general principles on which it was proposed to carry on the Mission, but also of that necessary secrecy as to certain parts of the scheme which it was desirable to keep from the knowledge of the public. The first clergyman placed by the Society of the Holy Cross in charge of the Mission was the late Rev. Charles Lowder, and to him, on May 31st, 1856, the Rev. Bryan King wrote as follows:—" Upon the principles of your scheme for the Mission, of course, I quite agree; as to the time for carrying some of them out, and the Christian *Economy and Reserve to be observed (respecting some of them)*, of course that must be left to the members of the Mission."[21] This Reserve and Economy was particularly shown in the earliest Reports of the " St. George's Mission," in which its Ritualistic character was studiously kept out of sight, and thus, no doubt, many were induced to aid it who would otherwise have withheld their subscriptions and donations on conscientious grounds. It is only fair to add here that this Economy and Reserve is no longer observed in the annual Report of the Mission. It is no longer necessary. The Mission was largely indebted to the assistance and advice of the late Rev. Dr. Pusey. There are several allusions to his help in the *Life of Charles Lowder*, and it would appear from one of these that Dr. Pusey was at one time himself a member of the Mission. Writing to his father, with reference to the Mission, on May 6th, 1856, Mr. Lowder said:—" I pray that it may be a good work for the Church; my desire is to make it a thoroughly Catholic one, a life of poverty, and self-denial, and dedication to God's service, and, if it may be, the revival of a really Religious Order for missionary work—men trained in holy living for the work of winning souls. *Dr. Pusey and the other members of the Mission* wish me to go, and we have had

---

[21] *Charles Lowder: A Biography*, p. 93. First edition.

already sufficient promise of support to justify our commencement. . . Dr. Pusey has about £150 or £160 at his disposal, which he will give it."[22] On May 16th, 1856, the Rev. Bryan King wrote to Mr. Lowder:—

"As we are beginning a very eventful experiment in the Church of England, it is most important that we should begin it upon a sound and safe basis. Both you and I may be deceived or biassed: you may regard the Mission too exclusively from your point of view, as of course I may from mine. Send then your letter and this *to Dr. Pusey for his counsel;* he, in Oxford, has the advantage of consulting far better and wiser heads than yours or mine, learned Canonists and earnest and experienced parish priests. *Beg him to draw up an experimental scheme or Constitution for the Mission.*"[23] There was a difficulty in securing a licence from the Bishop of London for Mr. Lowder to work in the Mission, and Dr. Pusey was consulted about the difficulty.[24] The late Dean Stanley, and the Archbishop of Dublin (Dr. French) gave help to the Mission from time to time. Even the late Bishop of Oxford (Dr. S. Wilberforce), in less than a year after its foundation, became quite infatuated with the Mission. On May 10th, 1857, he wrote to the Rev. W. J. Butler concerning it:—"I quite long to go and cast myself into that Mission."[25] Those dignitaries of the Church would never have given their aid had they been made fully acquainted with the objects of those who controlled the work. How the S. S. C. must have "laughed in their sleeves" at the success of their Jesuitical manœuvres! But what will straightforward Englishmen think of them?

In 1877 Mr. Lowder wrote a volume entitled *Twenty-One Years in S. George's Mission*, in which he describes at length the work carried on there. He tells us, amongst other interesting information, that in the Mission work:—

[22] *Charles Lowder: A Biography*, p. 86. First edition.
[23] *Ibid.*, p. 90. [24] *Ibid.*, p. 99.
[25] *Life of Bishop Wilberforce*, Vol. II., p. 341.

"When the soul is touched with contrition, and anxious to make her peace with God, we recommend Sacramental Confession, and have reason to be most thankful that *this has been our practice from the beginning*." [26]

"It is very gratifying to witness the reverence of our worshippers, and to know how many devoutly appreciate the blessings they enjoy in the constant Celebrations of the Holy Eucharist. . . . Is it a time of sorrow, the anniversary of a death or funeral? They fly to the Altar, and ask the Priest who Celebrates, and some of their friends also, to remember before God the soul of their departed one." [27]

The work of the Mission grew more and more Romanizing as the years went on, until at the present time the services are as advanced, if not more advanced, in a Romeward direction, than in any other church in London. The "Thirty-seventh Annual Report," issued in 1893, mentions that during the year 1892 no fewer than 3500 Confessions were heard in the church; and it is recorded that one of the former clergy of the Mission, "Father W. Edmund Smythe," had been appointed Bishop of Lebombo. In the *St. Peter's* (London Docks) *Parish Magazine*,[28] there is published a letter from this gentleman, who is a member of the Society of the Holy Cross (then only Bishop-Designate), dated Isandhlwana, Zululand, November 4th, 1892, in which he describes the opening of a new chapel in South Africa (towards which the S. P. C. K. gave £25), which clearly shows the Romeward tendencies fostered in its past and present workers in East London by the Mission of the Society of the Holy Cross.

"We can't," writes the Bishop-Designate, "do very much in the way of ceremonial out here of course, but the College students are getting to understand how to do things properly, and so we do our best. We vested in the Chapel and then went round the outside of the building in procession, the Bishop in Cope and Mitre, with two boys to support him, Mr. Gallagher, as Subdeacon, carrying the Cross in front. *We had Incense, but not Holy Water!*" [29]

[26] *Twenty-one Years in St. George's Mission*, p. 48.   [27] *Ibid.*, p. 54.
[28] The "St. George's Mission" is now popularly known by the name of "St. Peter's, London Docks."
[29] *St. Peter's Parish Magazine*, January, 1893, p. 3.

It is evident from the whole tone of this letter that this S. S. C. Episcopal Brother very much regretted the absence of the " Holy Water " ; but he comforts himself by adding :—
" By degrees we shall get more things." At the opening of the chapel he tells us that " High Mass " was celebrated by the Bishop, and then he describes a number of Romish ornaments already in use in the chapel :—

"It will interest you," he writes, "to know that the Altar Cross is one of the *large Crucifixes* which Fr. Massiah (another S. S. C. Brother) sent out for me. I have just received an anonymous present from England of some Cruets, one pair of which will go there. We have one Altar Frontal, which the Bishop has given us, and have managed to spare a linen Altar Cloth and *some Purificators*, &c., from our store at Isandhlwana. There is also *a large picture of Our Lady* ; so the Chapel is not altogether unfurnished. By degrees we shall get more things." [30]

It may be useful to mention here that the use of Holy Water is spreading considerably amongst the Ritualists. As far back as 1870 it was recommended, in a popular Manual of Devotion, which has had a large circulation amongst members of that party. The title of the book is the *Golden Gate*, and its author is the Rev. S. Baring-Gould, the well-known writer of novels, and now Rector of Lew Trenchard, Devon. In the service termed the "Last Agony," for a dying person, the author gives the following superstitious directions as to what should be done in the room immediately after death :—

"The body is then decently laid out, and a light placed before it. A small Crucifix is put in the hands of the deceased upon his breast, *while the body is sprinkled with Holy Water*." [31]

The *Priest's Prayer Book*, a large volume which has passed through seven or eight editions, was edited by two members of the Society of the Holy Cross, viz., the late well-known Rev. Dr. Littledale, and the Rev. J. E. Vaux.

[30] *St. Peter's Parish Magazine,* January, 1893, p. 4.
[31] *The Golden Gate*, by the Rev. S. Baring-Gould, Part III., p. 128. Edition, 1875.

It provides for the use of the clergy in the Church of England a special form for blessing Holy Water, to which it actually attributes the power of curing bodily diseases, and driving the devil out of people! Here is the rubric and prayer for this purpose:—

"*He* [the priest] *shall then bless the water on this wise:*—

"O God, Who, in ordaining divers mysteries for the salvation of mankind, hast been pleased to employ the element of water in the chiefest of Thy Sacraments: give ear to our prayers, and pour upon *this water* the might of Thy blessing, that as it serves Thee in those holy mysteries, so by Thy Divine Grace *it may here avail for the casting out of devils, and the driving away of diseases;* that whatsoever in the houses or places of the faithful is sprinkled therewith, may be freed from all uncleanness, and delivered from hurt." [32]

In the *Master's Address* to the Society of the Holy Cross, in 1870, he said:—"The policy of the Society, up to the September Synod of 1867, was that of privacy. Caution was enjoined upon the Brethren in the matter of mentioning it. It was thought, and no doubt wisely, that the first thing to be done was to deepen the inner life of the Brethren before launching out into greater publicity. In view, however, of the Church Congress at Wolverhampton, in the above year, it was determined to reverse this policy, and to distribute broadcast a new paper of the Nature and Objects of the Society, specially drawn up for the occasion. Together with this, was issued a short *Address to Catholics* and both obtained great publicity." [33] Three years later, the then Master of the S.S.C. in his "Address," said that the Society had "developed from secrecy to the most open publicity, so far as its existence and objects are concerned." [34] It is well for his veracity that the Master

---

[32] *The Priest's Prayer Book*, p. 221, seventh edition, issued in 1890. The same form appears in all the subsequent editions, including that still on sale. A similar form for blessing Holy Water is printed in the *Day Office of the Church*, p. xiii., together with another form for driving the devil out of the water before it is blessed.

[33] *The Master's Address*, S.S.C., 1870, p. 3.

[34] *Ibid.*, 1873, p. 4.

added the saving clause, "so far as its *existence* and *objects* are concerned"; because its essential secrecy has continued ever since, and at the present time is even more marked than ever. The Society gives to the public occasionally—very rarely, it should rather be said—a certain amount of information concerning its work, but as recently as its May, 1881, Synod, Brother the Rev. William Crouch said that "he thought the *secrecy* of the Society's doings a mistake,"[35] and, as we have already seen, the Statutes of the Society continue to enjoin secrecy on the Brethren.

The Master of the S. S. C., addressing the May, 1876, Synod, said that the Society "started with *its secrecy*";[36] and that "during the first eight years of the Society's life, its Statutes and Rules existed only in Manuscript."[37] He also said that from the formation of the Society, "The bond of union between the Brethren was to be as strict as possible. *None but themselves were to know their names*, OR OF THE EXISTENCE OF THE SOCIETY, except those to whom it might be named to induce them to join: but this only with leave of the Society."[38] Care was also enjoined on the Brethren to keep secret even the old documents of the Society, and, if necessary, to destroy them, lest any outsiders should know what was going on in their dark apartments. The Master, addressing the May, 1875, Synod, expressed his feelings of alarm on this point, in the following terms:—"The question has again arisen of the use of Post Cards in writing on Society business. I earnestly hope that the Society will let me press upon each Brother most strongly the undesirability of this practice. In these days there is great strength in a Society like ours being able to keep its private character. At present outsiders know only of our existence; but each little liberty, such as the use of these Post Cards, opens one more aperture for the entrance of inquisitive eyes. This

---

[35] *S. S. C. Analysis of May Synod*, 1881, p. 24.
[36] *The Master's Address*, May, 1876, p. 6.
[37] *Ibid.*, p. 3.   [38] *Ibid.*, p. 3.

same principle applies to taking the greatest possible care, either to *destroy*, or to keep in some safe place, the old Rolls, and other printed matter, such as Acta, Agenda, and Notice Papers."[39] At the September, 1876, Synod, the Master found it necessary to refer again to the subject. "Let me," he said, "urge upon you care with regard to the Statutes, Roll, Acta, and other documents of the Society. A description of it from a 'London Correspondent' appeared a few weeks ago in an Aberdeen newspaper. It was accurate enough to be correct in the names of the Saints to whom two of the local branches are dedicated. If we are to maintain the privacy which has hitherto been our rule, it can only be done by caution."[40]

At the May Synod, 1870, of the Society, a paper on "The Establishment of an Oratory in London by the Society of the Holy Cross," was read by Brother the Rev. Orby Shipley, who some years later seceded to the Church of Rome. Mr. Shipley was well known as the writer of advanced Romanizing works on various theological subjects, and was a very active supporter of the S. S. C. His paper was during the summer of 1870 "Privately Printed for the Society," at its expense, and in the following year was published by him, as an appendix to a book entitled, *The Four Cardinal Virtues*. The Oratory which he proposed was to be a centre for all the advanced Ritualists of the country, at which they could meet from time to time, and in which the Ritual should be of the most extreme character.

"Thus we should desiderate," for the Oratory, said Mr. Shipley, "these elements at the least:—The Asperges; the 'Censing of persons and things' or the use of Incense in a Ritual manner; the correct Introits, Graduals, Offertories, Communions; Gospel Lights; Consecration Lights on the Altar and Consecration Candles in front of the Altar, in addition to the Six Altar Candles and

[39] *Ibid.*, May Synod, 1875, p. 10.
[40] *The Master's Address*, September Synod, 1876, p. 8.

two Sacramental Lights; the use of the Altar Bell; the Lavabo; and, of course, the Eucharistic Vestments, for Celebrant, Ministers, Servers, and Acolytes."[41]

In short, the founders of the Oratory, Mr. Shipley said, "would not feel satisfied until they had restored to the Church of England a rendering of the sacred Mass which was fully Mediæval in the richness, costliness, taste, and perfection of its details." The Synod decided, after hearing Brother Shipley's paper, that the establishment of such an Oratory was deserving of further consideration. The idea of having such an Oratory in London appears to have been abandoned for a time, but not forgotten. Two years later it was determined to erect such an Oratory, not, however, in the Metropolis, but in the far North, in the city of Carlisle. For this purpose funds were necessary, but it was decided not to make a public appeal, but to set all the Brethren to work privately collecting amongst their friends the necessary pecuniary assistance. Accordingly the late Rev. A. H. Mackonochie wrote letters on the subject to the Brethren, but very much to the annoyance of the secret wire-pullers a copy of one of these letters came into the hands of the editor of the *Rock*, who published it in his columns, and thus removed the mystery which served as a protection to a dangerous movement, and made known to the public its real objects. Mr. Mackonochie's letter was as follows:—

"S. S. C.
"St. Alban's Clergy House, Holborn.
"*May* 11*th*, 1872.

"P. ✠ T.
"My Dear Brother,—The Vicar of the Carlisle Branch has asked me to commend to your notice the following resolution passed at the Synod last week:—

---

[41] *On the Establishment of an Oratory by the S. S. C.* Privately printed edition, p. 17. Mr. Shipley stated that the Society as such "is in no way responsible for the opinions" which he expressed in his paper; but it was certainly read by request of the authorities of the S. S. C., who paid £5. 11s for printing it, and who did not censure Brother Shipley's opinions.

"'That the S. S. C. approves of the scheme for the proposed Oratory in Carlisle, and, subject to the necessary funds being raised by private subscription among the Brethren, undertakes to treat for the securing of a site for the purpose.'

"The Carlisle Oratory is a work which the Synod considered to deserve the utmost attention of the Society—1. *The Carlisle clergy are completely overridden by an Ultra-Protestant clique*, the strength of which lies in the Dean,[42] and a powerful tradition left by the two late Bishops. . . . 4. The Bishop is quite willing to encourage work (especially an increase of celebrations), and he has consented to license a Chaplain to the proposed Religious House. 5. There is an earnest demand for the privileges which such a House would afford. A site may be had in the parish of Holy Trinity (the poorest in Carlisle), of which the priest has given his consent to the scheme, but it is of the utmost importance the site should be secured at once. If you will kindly exert yourself among your friends, and send any money you can get at once to Brother the Rev. C. H. V. Pixell, Skirwith Vicarage, Penrith, he will account for it to the Society, in Chapter, and send you a receipt.

"Believe me, Dear Brother,

"Yours most truly in our Blessed Lord,

"A. H. MACKONOCHIE."[43]

At that time the Rev. T. S. Barrett (now Rector of Teversall, Mansfield), was Rector of St. George's, Barrow-in-Furness, and, being one of the Brethren of the S. S. C., and living in the district, he naturally took a deep interest in the Oratory scheme. In November, 1872, he also made an appeal for furniture for the Oratory, mentioning that, amongst other things, it would require an Altar Cross, Altar Lights, Vesper Lights, Cottas, Cassocks and Stoles, a Sacring Bell, Frontals and Super Frontals, Banners, Flower Vases, &c.[44] These Ornaments were not then as common as they are now, and that they should be required for the new Oratory was a clear proof that its promoters intended to work on advanced Romanizing lines. But, unfortunately, the public knew nothing about Mr. Mackonochie's letter or

---

[42] That is, Dr. Close, who was then Dean of Carlisle.
[43] *The Rock*, July 4th, 1873, p. 448.
[44] Ibid.

Brother Barrett's appeal, until a full six months after the Oratory was actually opened, and the mischief done.

About a month before Mr. Mackonochie's letter was written, anonymous letters were sent to the Protestant Dean of Carlisle (Dr. Close), and these contained intelligence of such an alarming character that he at once wrote to the Bishop of Carlisle on the subject. The Bishop replied that an application had been made to him to grant a licence for certain clergymen to work in a Carlisle parish, under the "Private Chapels Act." He had taken a legal opinion on the question of his powers to do this, and had been "informed that it would be within the law." "This being so," continued the Bishop, "I said that in the event of an Institution being established upon the scheme described I would give a licence on certain conditions. The chief of these was that I should require to be satisfied that there would be no Ritual developments, contrary to what had been decided to be lawful."[45] Meanwhile, the clergy of Carlisle and neighbourhood had taken alarm, and towards the end of April, 1872, they presented an Address on the subject to the Bishop of Carlisle, signed by no fewer than 120 of their number, earnestly asking his lordship to give no encouragement to those who asked his licence for Brethren of the Society of the Holy Cross to officiate in the proposed Oratory. "Should such a step be taken," they said, "the consequences would be most disastrous to the best interests of the Church in this diocese. Schism and division would be multiplied and aggravated, and a permanent feud established in the heart of the Cathedral city." The Bishop was rather in favour of the scheme of the S.S.C., than otherwise, yet he could not ignore the opinions of such a large number of his clergy. So in his reply to their Address he tried to allay their fears, but would make no definite promise either way. And thus the matter rested until the

---

[45] The correspondence is published in full in the *Church Association Monthly Intelligencer*, June, 1872, pp. 146-148.

new Oratory was actually opened in the January of the following year, when another storm of public indignation arose. On January 17th, the Dean once more wrote to the Bishop calling his attention to the reports of the opening ceremony which had appeared in the Carlisle papers, and at which "the high Ritual" was witnessed which "usually characterised" the proceedings of the Society of the Holy Cross; and he asked the Bishop, "whether the building in question, or the officiating clergyman were licensed" by him, "or whether they have obtruded themselves on the citizens of Carlisle without your Lordship's permission"? To these questions the Bishop replied:—"The services to which you refer have had no sanction from me—unless it be regarded as a sanction that I have taken no active steps in opposition to them."[46] Thus the Society of the Holy Cross triumphed in Carlisle, mainly through a want of firmness on the part of the Bishop, who could easily have inhibited all the brethren, but did not. And so it has been ever since on the part of only too many of the Episcopal Bench, who, rather than permit a "row," have been willing to allow the Romanizing party to have their own way. These Bishops have reversed the Apostolic order which declares that "the wisdom that is from above is *first pure*, then peaceable" (James iii. 17). The fault has not been confined to our prelates, it has been shared also by both clergy and laity. It would be well if all these timid ones, who love peace more than the purity of the Faith, were to lay to heart the words and act in accordance with the spirit which moved Martin Luther when, at the Diet of Worms, he said:—"It is for me a great joy to see that the Gospel is now, as in ancient days, a cause of trouble and discord. That is the character and destiny of the Word of God. Jesus Christ hath said, 'I came not to send peace on earth, but a sword.' God is wonderful and terrible in His counsels; let us dread lest, in thinking to

---

[46] *Carlisle Journal*, January 31st, 1873, from which this correspondence was reprinted in the *Church Association Monthly Intelligencer*, March, 1873, pp. 20, 21.

stop discords, we persecute God's Holy Word, and bring down on our heads a fearful deluge of insurmountable dangers, of present disasters and eternal desolations."[47]

Early in 1873 a petition was presented to Convocation, signed by 483 Ritualistic priests, asking for Licensed Confessors in the Church of England. This petition naturally created a great sensation at the time, and led to many large anti-confessional meetings being held in London and the Provinces; to an important declaration on the subject by a Committee of the Upper House of Convocation for the Province of Canterbury; and a discussion in the House of Lords, on July 14th, in the course of which the Marquis of Salisbury denounced habitual confession. "We know," said his lordship, "that besides its being unfavourable to what we believe to be Christian truth, in its result it has been injurious to the moral independence and virility of the nation to an extent to which probably it has been given to no other Institution to affect the character of mankind." Everybody was talking about this daring petition, but not one of the public knew who its real organizers were. The real wire-pullers preferred to remain in the dark, and they were the authorities of the Society of the Holy Cross. On March 14th, 1873, the Rev. A. H. Mackonochie, who was then Master of the Society of the Holy Cross, sent out to all the brethren a printed circular letter, enclosing copies of the petition for signature, in the course of which he informed them that "The memorial was presented to the Society in Chapter last month, and again, after a further revision by the Committee, on Tuesday last. It was then adopted, considered clause by clause, a few verbal alterations being left to the final decision of the Committee, and finally agreed to." In the confidence of its secret May, 1873, Synod, the

---

[47] D'Aubigne's *History of the Reformation*, Book VII., chapter ix., p. 206. Edition, Edinburgh, 1846.

Master of the Society talked freely on the subject. "You are aware," he said, "that it [the petition] was not presented in the name of the Society, and the public papers have shown you that the blame of it is principally laid on me personally. It seems to have done for the Truth much more than the most sanguine expectations of its promoters anticipated, and, if I were entitled to it, I should gladly accept that blame as praise. I am, however, bound to say that it belongs to brethren senior to me, and far more able."[48] It had been organized by a special Committee of the S.S.C., who had collected the signatures. There was certainly something Jesuitical in the way it was managed. The petition asked for many things besides Licensed Confessors, and clearly proves that the Society of the Holy Cross, and large numbers of other Ritualists, are far from satisfied with the existing formularies of the Church of England. The Book of Common Prayer, says this petition, is "manifestly incomplete, through the absence in many particulars of such Services and Rubrics as would give adequate expression to this claim of the Church of England to be Catholic in her doctrine, usage, and ceremonial." This "want of completeness" is considered by the petitioners as a "distinct grievance." They object to any scheme which would "alter the Book of Common Prayer" in what they term "an un-Catholic direction"; but they are most anxious for a revision of that Book on Romish lines, for they suggest that Convocation should "promote" the "addition" to the Prayer Book of the following matters:—

"The doctrines, that is to say, of—

"I. The Real Presence of our Lord and Saviour Jesus Christ in the Holy Communion, 'under the form of Bread and Wine.'

"II. The adoration due to Him there present.

"III. The Sacrifice which He there offers by the hands of His Priest to the Divine Majesty."

The petitioners further pray that any "alterations"

---

[48] *The Master's Address*, S. S. C., 1873, p. 10, *note*.

which may be made in the Book of Common Prayer shall include :—

"The full provision of the ancient and proper Introits and Graduals, together with the Secreta, Communions, and Post-Communions, for Festivals, Sundays, and Ferial Days."

"That provision may be made for the decent and reverent Reservation of the Blessed Eucharist, and that an Office be prepared for the Communion of the Sick therewith."

"That the use of Unction may be restored in Holy Baptism and Confirmation, as well as in the Visitation of the Sick, together with the proper Services for the Consecration by the Bishops of the Oils for the said purposes."

The clause which gave its name to this petition of dissatisfied Ritualists was as follows :—

"That in view of the wide-spread and increasing use of Sacramental Confession, your Venerable House may consider the advisability of providing for the education, selection, and Licensing of duly qualified Confessors, in accordance with the provisions of Canon Law." [49]

There is one other feature of this petition worthy of special note. It mentions certain usages which, "while they are extensively promoted by or used under Episcopal countenance and sanction, are nevertheless neither expressly nor by necessary implication enjoyned by the Book of Common Prayer"—such as, "The use of solemn and other processions as well in Cathedral and Parish Churches as elsewhere. The formal presentation to Archbishops and Bishops of Croziers and Pastoral Staves, and the ceremonial use thereof. The use of Processional Crosses and Banners, Credence Tables, Chalice Veils, coloured Altar Cloths, and the like." It is indeed noteworthy that the Society of the Holy Cross should thus frankly admit that none of these things have the sanction of the Book of Common Prayer. But, it may well be asked, if not by that authority, by what other authority are they introduced?

---

[49] The full text of the petition was published in the *Rock*, June 6th, 1873, p. 383.

Of course Convocation declined to grant the impudent request of the petitioners. It had neither the power nor the will to do anything of the kind. Whatever official statements on the subject of Confession may have been issued by the Convocations of the Church of England, from time to time, they have never been favourable to the claims of the Society of the Holy Cross. The wish expressed for additions, of a Romanizing character, of services for special occasions, was really an attempt to alter the Constitution of the Church of England, and in such a manner that, if granted, every true lover of the Reformation would have been compelled, by the dictates of his conscience, to leave at once a Church which sanctioned ceremonies of such a Popish and superstitious character. Nothing less than Revision of the Book of Common Prayer on Romanizing lines will ever satisfy the aspirations of the Ritualists. It is sometimes said that we " shall *soon* have to fight the battle of the Reformation over again." But those who carefully study what is now going on in the Church of England do not *look forward* to the commencement of such a warfare. They know that the great battle has *already commenced*. It is an encounter of life and death. Bishops and Statesmen may wilfully shut their eyes to the dangers that surround the Reformed Church, and cry "Peace, peace, when there is no peace," and vainly strive to reconcile the opposing sections. But the attempt is in vain. It is impossible to reconcile Protestantism and Priestcraft, or Sacerdotalism; nor is such a peace on Christian principles desirable. The end of the struggle must be that either Protestant Churchmen—old-fashioned High Churchmen were not ashamed to call themselves Protestants—must retain their position, and recover the lost property which honestly belongs to them; or else the Sacerdotalists will oust them out of their rights and out of the Church of England, which will then once more place on itself that fatal chain of Papal bondage which has been the curse of every country that has submitted to it.

It may now be serviceable to take, as it were, a glimpse into a few of the Synods and Chapters of the Society of the Holy Cross, with a view to finding out the kind of business usually transacted at these secret gatherings. For this purpose we shall consult some of the official reports privately printed for the use of the brethren only. We commence with the "Analysis of Proceedings of May Synod, 1874," which, as the document itself records, "was held in St. Peter's Church, London Docks." At 10 A.M. on the first day of the Synod, there was a "Solemn Mass" offered. The special subject for discussion was "The Sacrament of Penance, its present position, and future prospects in the Church of England." It was opened by a speech from Brother the Rev. H. D. Nihill, who "contended that the great need of the present day was, to set forth the power and dignity of the Sacrament of Penance itself, as apart from all questions of the benefit of Direction, or the comfort of consultation with a clergyman."

Brother Canon Carter, of Clewer, maintained that before Penance can be regarded "as established on its true grounds, two points must be enforced, neither of which are as yet countenanced by authority—(1) Its *Sacramental* character, as really conveying grace; and (2) Its *habitual* use, as a means of growth of the spiritual life."

Brother Macfarlane, Vicar of Dorchester, Oxon, spoke of his experience in an agricultural parish. He found that the poor "when in earnest gladly receive the means of reconciliation for sins after Baptism"; but they "do not come habitually to confession, except in few cases." It is "not so generally welcomed by the tradesmen or farmers." As to the future prospects of the Confessional, that "seems to depend upon the degree of toleration which the Catholic Movement obtains at the hands of our rulers in Church and

State. If the Catholicity of the Church of England is preserved, the Sacrament of Penance must daily gain ground." He recommended the establishment of a "Chair of Moral Theology."

Brother the Rev. Charles Lowder thought they "must be prepared to show that Confession is neither unmanly nor un-English"—which was, I should think, a somewhat formidable task to undertake.

Brother the Rev. Rhodes Bristow, now Canon Missioner of the Diocese of Rochester, and Rector of St. Olave, Southwark, said that he valued the freedom accorded by the Church of England. We must, he said, "strive to raise the Sacrament of Penance to its due position, but we must be careful to do so as English Churchmen."

Brother the Rev. James Dunn, now Vicar of St. John the Baptist, Bathwick, Bath, "spoke of the difficulty felt by old people in going to confession to young priests. He suggested that more experienced priests should visit country parishes from time to time for the purpose of hearing Confessions."

Brother the Rev. H. P. Denison, now Vicar of St. Michael and All Angels', Notting Hill, "distinguished between voluntary and compulsory Confession. He maintained that the Church of England puts a man upon his honour to confess his mortal sins before Communion."

Brother the Rev. C. Bodington, now Canon of Lichfield, and Diocesan Missioner, lamented that "Our people do not realize what the Sacramental system of the Church is. If we get them to understand this, they will quickly see that, without Confession, there is a link missing."

Brother the Rev. R. C. Kirkpatrick, Vicar of St. Augustine's, Kilburn, "expressed a wish that country brethren would make it known that they were ready to hear Confessions."

The Synod next proceeded to consider a pamphlet by

Brother the Rev. E. G. Wood, now Vicar of St. Clement's, Cambridge, on "Jurisdiction in the Confessional," in the course of which he maintained that every Rector, Vicar, or Perpetual Curate of a parish "can, without license of the Bishop, give to another priest jurisdiction to hear the Confessions of all who may come to him at the church or other place, within the parish, appointed for the hearing of Confessions."[50]

Brother F. W. Puller, now Head of the "Cowley Fathers," "maintained that we should be careful to find out when our Absolutions are valid;" but it does not appear that he told his brethren *how* this difficult question was to be solved.

A discussion next took place as to the alteration of the fourth of the Society's Statutes, in which Brother W. M. Richardson (now Bishop of Zanzibar); Brother T. Outram Marshall (now Organizing Secretary of the English Church Union); Brother Bagshawe; Brother F. H. Murray (Rector of Chislehurst); and Brother G. A. Jones (Vicar of St. Mary's, Cardiff), took part. This closed the first day's proceedings of the Synod, at which one hundred and thirty-six brethren were present.

On the second day of the Synod, a "Mortuary Mass" was offered for the dead brethren at 9 A.M. I need not summarize the discussions on this occasion, further than to state that the subjects considered included the revision of the Statutes of the Society, the results of the London Mission, the position of the Ritualistic clergy in view of ecclesiastical proceedings against them, and the Public Worship Regulation Bill, then before the country. It is important, however, to record that Brother N. Dawes (now Bishop of Rockhampton, Queensland), who had become a Probationer of the Society of the Holy Cross in 1872, was at this Synod promoted to the ranks of the Brethren.

[50] *Jurisdiction in the Confessional*, by the Rev. Edmund G. Wood, M.A., p. 15. Printed for the Society.

The September, 1874, Synod met as usual in St. Peter's, London Docks. On the first day, after the "Solemn Mass" and the preliminary business had been transacted, a number of letters from absent brethren were read. Brother Hutchings (now Archdeacon of Cleveland) wrote, "expressing a hope that in Ritual, S. S. C. would move in the direction of the Roman rather than the Sarum Use." Brother J. E. Stocks (now Vicar of St. Saviour's, Leicester) also wrote with reference to a motion by Brother Bodington. After this the Synod discussed the following subject:— "That the action of the Society in 1868-9, committing itself to the principle of the Roman Ritual, be reconsidered."

Brother Linklater (now Vicar of Holy Trinity, Stroud Green) urged that "the Society should leave the brethren free in the matter of Ritual." He personally preferred the Sarum Use.

Brother Bristow, Canon Missioner of St. Saviour, Southwark, "hoped that the Roman Use would still prevail."

Brother C. Parnell (Curate of St. Bartholomew, Brighton) declared that he "would follow the Roman Ritual at the services of the Society, while individual brethren might follow their own bent."

Brother E. M. Chaplin "advocated the use of the Roman Rite, both for accuracy and uniformity."

Brother J. B. Powell (now Curate of St. Paul's, Knightsbridge, London) "was strongly in favour of the Sarum Use, but hoped that liberty would be granted by the Society to use either form."

Brother N. Green-Armytage (now Perpetual Curate of the Chapel-of-Ease, Boston), Brother Grieve (now dead), and Brother C. E. Hammond (now Vicar of Menheniot, Cornwall), would all "leave the brethren free."

Eventually it was decided to appoint a special Committee to consider the question more fully. Brother Bishop Jenner, it should be added, moved the following amendment, which was lost:—" That in the regulations hitherto laid down, the Society does not intend to bind the brethren to the adoption of the principle of any particular Rite."

The next subject considered by the Synod was "The Present Constitution and Reform of Convocation."

Brother Rhodes Bristow "reminded the brethren that Convocation might step in to-morrow, and take away our *locus standi* altogether."

Brother Charles Lowder said that "while Convocation needs much reform, it is the Assembly which, by God's providence, is the representative of the Church. We should welcome the co-operation of the faithful laity, as in Diocesan Conferences, while refusing to give them equal power to that of the clergy."

Brother Orby Shipley gave as "his opinion that Convocation is not the sacred Synod of the Church."

Eventually it was decided that "The Master be requested to communicate to the President of the English Church Union the opinion of the Society," which was that the Union should issue special Tracts on the subject of Convocation.

On the second day of the Synod (September 16th) after the "Mortuary Mass" had been offered, it was proposed by Brother Bagshawe (now dead), seconded by Brother Rhodes Bristow, and carried unanimously:—"That the Roll of the Brethren be referred to the Master's Council before it is republished." This motion led to a speech by Brother Bagshawe, which shows in a very marked manner, how much the Society of the Holy Cross dreads the light of day. He said that "we should be *most careful* to preserve the *strictly private and confidential character of the Roll*, but in the event of a copy falling into *hostile hands* it is most important that all the Brethren, whose names are therein printed, should be staunch and true to S. S. C." At that time the names of the members were quite unknown to the public, and it was not until 1877 that a copy of the *Roll* fell into the hands of the Editor of the *Rock*, who at once published it in his paper. The publication caused the utmost consternation in the ranks of the S. S. C., and, coming as it did immediately after the exposure of its Confessional book, the *Priest in Absolution*, in the House of Lords by the late Lord Redesdale, it led to the secession of nearly one-half of its members, who suddenly left the Society in a fright as soon as their identity was discovered. The *Roll* of the S. S. C. for 1895-96 has printed on its outer cover, and again on its title-page, the following significant directions, which clearly show how anxious the Society still is that the names of its brethren shall be kept secret :—

"PRIVATE AND CONFIDENTIAL. *To be returned to the Secretary by any brother leaving the Society; or by the representatives of a deceased Brother.*"

The Society of the Holy Cross still continues to exist, and its energies are as great as ever. But its secrecy is greater than ever. Amongst its members are the Bishops of Zanzibar and Lebombo, and many of the most prominent of the Ritualistic clergy. So carefully are its papers— generally headed with the letters "S. S. C."—kept, that I have been unable to get any reports of its Synods and Chapters dated later than 1881, with the important exception of a recent *Roll of Brethren*. If any of my readers are in a position to supply me with any of the more recent papers of the Society I shall be thankful, in order that I may use them in any later edition of this book which may be called for. I have, however, some reason for believing that a few years since a serious schism took place in its ranks, and that the seceders have formed themselves into another Society, whose name I have been unable to discover. Nearly all the old members, whose names appeared in the *Roll* for 1880, have disappeared in the more recent *Roll* which I possess.

CHAPTER III.

THE SECRECY OF THE RITUALISTIC CONFESSIONAL.

The Confessional always a secret thing—Confessional Scandal at Leeds—Dr. Pusey on the Seal of the Confessional—Ritualistic Sisters teach girls how to confess to priests—Secret Confessional books for penitents—Dr. Pusey revives the Confessional—Four years later writes against it—He hears Confessions in private houses—His penitent's "burning sense of shame and deceitfulness"—Bishop Wilberforce's opinion of Dr. Pusey—A Ritualistic priest's extraordinary letter to a young lady—How Archdeacon Manning heard Confessions on the sly—"A hole and corner affair."

AURICULAR Confession is always a secret thing. Both penitent and Father Confessor are expected to respect the secrecy of the Confessional. Were it a public transaction it would lose its attraction to a certain class of minds, and the power of the priest would cease to exist. It gives to the priest a power over the penitent which nothing can destroy but the grace of God. "I could never bear to meet him in the street," was the exclamation of a poor woman who had gone to Confession to her Vicar for more than a dozen years, but who, when I knew her, had learnt to be content with confessing her sins to Jesus Christ, and receiving direct from Him His all-sufficient absolution. She told me that whenever she saw her Father Confessor coming down the street towards her, she always went down a side street to avoid meeting him. The obligation of silence on the part of the penitent is thus taught in a widely circulated little book, edited by the Tract Committee of the secret Society of the Holy Cross:—

"There is a mutual obligation between the Confessor and the person making Confession, to keep secret what is said. He is solemnly bound to secrecy, and you also are bound to observe a reverent and religious silence upon what has been said. Be very careful yourself on this point. If you talk about what has passed in Confession, the priest may get the blame of its being known." [1]

The Confessional frequently interferes with the confidence which should exist between husband and wife. The wife will tell her Father Confessor things which she would not dare to mention to her husband; nor would she be expected ever to repeat to him the secret conversations between herself and her Confessor. An illustration of this took place in a Puseyite Church at Leeds, as far back as 1850. The Bishop of Ripon (Dr. Charles T. Longley, afterwards Archbishop of Canterbury) held an official and public inquiry as to a Confessional scandal connected with the Church of St. Saviour's, Leeds. After the inquiry he wrote, and published, a letter to the Vicar, the Rev. H. F. Beckett, from which I take the following extract:—

"It appeared in evidence," wrote the Bishop, "which you did not contradict, and could not shake by any cross-examination, that Mr. Rooke, who was then a Deacon, having required a married woman who was a candidate for Confirmation to go for Confession to you as a priest, you received that female to Confession under these circumstances, and that you put to her questions which she says made her feel very much ashamed, and greatly distressed her, and which were of such an indelicate nature that she would never tell her husband of them." [2]

Instead of trying to place the matter before Dr. Longley in a more favourable light, Mr. Beckett's reply to the

---

[1] *Pardon Through the Precious Blood*, edited by a Committee of Clergy, p. 31. Fifty-fourth thousand, 1883.
[2] *A Letter to the Parishioners of St. Saviour's, Leeds*, by the Bishop of Ripon, p. 37. London, 1851.

Bishop seemed to make the case even darker against himself, for he declared:—

"Your lordship cannot but see that Mrs. ——'s not mentioning what had passed between her and myself to her husband is nothing at all to the purpose, since NO WOMAN WOULD, I SUPPOSE, EVER TELL HER HUSBAND WHAT PASSED IN HER CONFESSION." ³

On the part of the Ritualistic Father Confessor, secrecy must be observed, no matter what the consequences may be. Rather than divulge the secrets entrusted to him the Confessor is recommended by the Rev. Dr. Pusey to resort to that which common-sense people would call lying and perjury.

"No Confessor," writes Dr. Pusey, "should ever give the slightest suspicion that he is alluding to what he has heard in the tribunal; but he should remember the canonical warning: 'What I know through Confession, I know less than what I do not know.' Pope Eugenius says that what a Confessor knows in this way, he knows it 'ut Deus'; while out of Confession he is only speaking 'ut homo': so that, 'as man,' he can say that he does not know that which he has learned as God's representative. I go further still: 'As man he may swear with a clear conscience that he knows not, what he knows only as God.' " ⁴

This is fearful teaching. Imagine the Confessor in an English Court of Justice. He is sworn to "tell the truth, the *whole* truth, and nothing but the truth" concerning the charge against the prisoner at the bar. He is asked, "Did the prisoner ever tell you that he stole those boots?" The Confessor has heard from the prisoner, in the Confessional, a full acknowledgment of his guilt, yet when asked this question, he may, according to Dr. Pusey, "swear with a clear conscience that he knows not, what he knows only as God." There is another alternative which Dr. Pusey does *not* advise the Confessor to adopt. He might respectfully

---

³ *A Letter to the Parishioners of St. Saviour's, Leeds*, by the Bishop of Ripon, p. 38. London, 1851.

⁴ Pusey's *Manual for Confessors*, "Adapted to the Use of the English Church," p. 402.

but firmly decline to answer concerning what he had heard in the Confessional, and then take the consequence like a courageous and honest man. But, instead of this, he is recommended to "swear," calling God's holy name to witness to the truth of a statement which he knows is a lie, and an abominable perjury! Is this the kind of teaching which ought to be given to the clergy of the Reformed Church of England? The book which contains it is a standard authority with Ritualistic Father Confessors.

Every effort is made by Ritualistic Confessors to bring young children, as well as adults, to the Confessional, even at a very tender age. Dr. Pusey teaches that it is "the ordinary and right custom among the faithful to bring young children to Confession from the time they are *seven years* old; and it is a great negligence of parents to omit doing so."[5] Sisters of Mercy sometimes help to bring the children to Confession. The "Sisters of the Church," otherwise known as the "Kilburn Sisterhood," and sometimes as the "Church Extension Association," have published several little books to teach little ones how to Confess to Priests.[6] The Sisters of St. Margaret's, East Grinstead, are expected to urge the girls under their care to make a full and complete Confession of their sins. Here are their instructions on this point, being the advice to them of their Founder and Father Confessor, the late Rev. Dr. Neale, as contained in their privately printed book, entitled, the *Spirit of the Founder. Dicit Fundator.*

"And this I say not so much about you, as about the confirmed girls. Whoever of you prepare these for their Communions, this above all things teach them, the great danger of a sacrilegious Confession: the utter uselessness as well as wickedness of each succeeding one, while that first sin remains unwiped out. And this more especially, that if any one of them leaves us in that state, in all

---

[5] *Ibid.*, p. 159.
[6] Such as their *Manual for the Children of the Church*, which has passed through several editions, but was suppressed when publicly exposed. It is also taught in several of their "Catechisms."

human probability she will never come out of it. Because, even granted that she is pressed about Confession, after she has gone out into the world, the sin will grow more and more terrible to look at; and if she kept it back from her first priest, small chance is there that she will have courage to make it known to a second." [7]

It is not uncommon for Ritualistic Father Confessors to circulate privately printed Manuals of Confession, for the use of children as well as adults. I have come across several of these. One is entitled *A Manual of Confession for Children.* "Translated and Adapted from the French. By a priest of the English Church. Privately printed." Even the printer's name is not given. As a specimen of the awful teaching thus imparted to our little ones, I quote the following from this *Manual* :—

"A good Confession ought not only to be humble and sincere, but also *full*. You must tell your Confessor *all* the sins you can remember. For if you hide one sin on purpose, you lie to God; you would be guilty of a great crime; and you would not even receive the pardon of those sins which you have confessed." [8]

When the practice of Auricular Confession was revived, about five years after the birth of the Tractarian Movement, great care was taken in keeping secret the numerous little books of devotion and manuals for Confession circulated amongst the Tractarians. The author of *Five Years in a Protestant Sisterhood, and Ten Years in a Catholic Convent,* published in 1869, relates her own experience in this matter, some fifteen years after Auricular Confession had been re-introduced. After mentioning some particulars concerning one of her lady friends, she proceeds :—

"We drove out together frequently, and from her I learned much of the habits and customs of the High Church party. She had all the little books of doctrine, which at that time had been 'adapted' from 'foreign sources;' all the little wonderful compilations about 'How to Prepare for a First Confession,' 'Prayers for the Penitential

---

[7] *The Spirit of the Founder*, p. 24. Privately printed for the use of the Sisters of St. Margaret's, East Grinstead.

[8] *A Manual of Confession for Children*, p. 12. Privately printed.

Seasons,' 'Devotions for the Holy Eucharist,' 'Hours for the Use of Members of the English Church,' which were ' privately printed,' *and handed about with a thousand injunctions to secrecy, from one to another of the initiated."* [9]

To the late Dr. Pusey is due the blame of reviving Auricular Confession in the Church of England. He commenced hearing Confessions in 1838. In 1850 Dr. Pusey wrote:— "It is now some twelve years, I suppose, since I was first called upon to exercise this office"—of Father Confessor,[10] that is, in 1838. Again, in 1851 he wrote to the Bishop of Oxford:—"What I say of Confession, I say upon the experience of *thirteen* years."[11] In a letter which he wrote to the *Times*, November 29th, 1866, Pusey remarked:— " During the *twenty-eight years* in which I have received Confessions, I never had once to refuse Absolution." Twenty-eight years from 1866 brings us back again to 1838. It seems almost incredible that four years after that date Dr. Pusey wrote a learned and thoroughly Protestant treatise to prove that in the early Church not a single trace can be found of private Confession to priests, with a view to thus obtaining God's pardon for sins! This appeared in 1842, in the form of lengthy "Notes" to the works of Tertullian, in the *Library of the Fathers*, extending from page 376 to page 408. In these notes Dr. Pusey quotes with decided approval the opinions of St. Chrysostom on the subject of Confession:—

"There could," wrote Dr. Pusey, "if Romanists would fairly consider this, be no way in which Confession to God alone, *exclusive of man*, could be expressed, if not here. S. Chrysostom says, 'to God alone,' 'apart in private,' 'to Him Who knoweth beforehand,' 'no one knowing,' '*no one present save Him Who knoweth*,' 'God alone seeing,' 'unwitnessed,' '*not to man*,' 'not to a fellow-servant,' 'within,' 'in the conscience,' 'in the memory,' ' Judging thyself' (in lieu of the Priest being the Judge), 'proving ourselves, each himself,

---

[9] *Five Years in a Protestant Sisterhood, and Ten Years in a Catholic Convent,* p. 15. London: Longmans, 1869.
[10] *Life of Dr. Pusey,* Vol. III., p. 269.   [11] *Ibid.,* p. 335.

not the one to the other,' 'in Church, to God' (*i.e.*, in the General Confession). Accordingly, one Romanist writer boldly pronounces all these passages spurious; and (since they are unquestionable) another of great name, Petavius, condemns them as 'being uttered in a declamatory way to the ignorant multitude for the sake of impressiveness.' But certainly, poor as such an excuse would be for what, according to Romanists, is false teaching, the passages are too numerous and too uniform to admit of it; they manifestly contain S. Chrysostom's settled teaching,' and Petavius condemns them as 'devoid of sound meaning, if fitted to the rule of the exact truth.'"[12]

Dr. Pusey thus summarized the whole question from an historical point of view:—

"The instances, then, being in each case very numerous, the absence of any mention of Confession in the early Church under the following circumstances, does, when contrasted with the uniform mention of it in the later, put beyond question that at the earlier period it was not the received practice."[13]

Who would have thought that the man who thus held up to the admiration of English Churchmen the teaching of St. Chrysostom, of "Confession to God alone, exclusive of man," was at the very moment hearing Confessions himself, and had been hearing them for four years previously! The utmost caution was exercised by Dr. Pusey in his Confessional work, and his very great dread of publicity led to practices which were anything but straightforward. His underhand proceedings disgusted some of even his warmest friends. As early as 1850, the Rev. W. Maskell, one of his disciples who subsequently seceded to Rome, published a *Letter to Dr. Pusey*, in which he exposed his secret Confessional tactics:—

"What, then," wrote Mr. Maskell, "let me ask, do you conceive that the Bishop of Exeter would say, of persons *secretly received* [to Auricular Confession] *against the known wish of their parents*, of Confessions heard in the houses of common friends, or of *clandestine correspondence* to arrange meetings, under initials, or in envelopes

---

[12] "Library of the Fathers." *Tertullian*, p. 401. Oxford: J. H. Parker, 1842.
[13] *Ibid.*, p. 405.

addressed to other persons?—and more than this, when such Confessions are recommended and urged as a part of the spiritual life, and among religious duties; not in order to quiet the conscience before receiving the Communion. Think not that I write all this to give you unnecessary pain; think not that I write it without a feeling of deep pain and sorrow in my own heart. But there is something which tells me, that, on behalf of thousands, this matter should now be brought before the world plainly, honestly, and fully. I know how heavily the *enforced mystery and secret correspondence regarding Confessions*, in your Communion, has weighed down the minds of many to whom you and others have 'Ministered.' I know how bitterly it has eaten, even as a canker, into their very souls: I know how utterly the specious arguments which you have urged, have failed to remove *their burning sense of shame and* DECEITFULNESS " (p. 21).

We get a further peep into Dr. Pusey's cautious mode of hearing Confessions, in Miss Cusack's ("The Nun of Kenmare") *Story of My Life*. This lady, in her early life, before her secession to Rome, was an inmate for some years of one of Dr. Pusey's sisterhoods.

"It was," writes Miss Cusack, "notable that no matter what the Doctor [Pusey] thought or said about the necessity of availing oneself of the 'Sacrament', he was very careful to whom he administered it. Further, it was well known that he administered the Sacrament of Confession, for the most part, in open defiance of the Bishop of the Diocese, where *he met his penitents, literally,* ' *on the sly.*' I believe that *the secrecy, and concealment,* and devices which had to be used to get an audience with the Doctor, for the purpose of Confessing, had a little, if it had not a good deal, to do with his success. The lady (few men went to Confession) who availed herself of the privilege, or who could obtain it, was looked upon with more or less holy envy, and felt correspondingly elated."[14]

It was at about this time that Dr. Pusey compiled, and secretly circulated, his *Hints for a First Confession.* Since his death they have been given to the world in the ordinary way, but for a period of upwards of thirty years after these *Hints* were first printed, I cannot find the slightest reference

---

[14] *The Story of My Life*, by M. F. Cusack, "The Nun of Kenmare," p. 63. London, 1891.

to them in any newspaper, biography, or any published book whatever. The world for that long period knew absolutely nothing about this little book, which all the while was working untold spiritual mischief in the Church of England. The teaching contained in these *Hints* was of a thoroughly Romanizing character. Here is an extract from the book, in proof of what I have said:—

"A Confession [*i.e.*, to a priest] avails which contains all you can recall. If other sins come back to your mind afterwards, which you would have confessed had you remembered them, they should be confessed afterwards, because *the forgiveness is conditional upon the completeness of the Confession*. Completeness implies that there should be care and faithfulness in discovering sins, and that *nothing so discovered should be kept back*."[15]

The High Church Bishop of Oxford (Dr. Samuel Wilberforce) was justly indignant with Dr. Pusey, when he fully realized the thoroughly Romanizing character of his Confessional work. For this, and for issuing "adapted" editions of Roman Catholic books, Bishop Wilberforce inhibited him, in November, 1850, from officiating in the diocese of Oxford, and did not remove the inhibition until nearly two years had passed by. On November 30th, 1850, the Bishop wrote to Dr. Pusey:—

"You seem to me to be habitually assuming the place and doing the work of a Roman Confessor, and not that of an English clergyman. Now, I so firmly believe that of all the curses of Popery this is the crowning curse, that I cannot allow voluntarily within my charge the continuance of any ministry which is infected by it."[16]

If the Bishops of the present day would only act as Bishop Wilberforce did, they would, unfortunately, find their hands full of this kind of work. The Confessional is now taught (in quite as Romish a form as that which was condemned by him) by thousands of nominally Church of England clergymen, who glory in what Dr. S. Wilberforce so truly termed

---

[15] *Hints for a First Confession*, by Dr. Pusey, p. 14. Edition, 1884.
[16] *Life of Bishop S. Wilberforce*, Vol. II., p. 99.

"the crowning curse" of Popery. Had the Bishops done their duty this "curse" would have been stamped out long ago.

A few other typical illustrations of the secrecy of the Confessional may here be added, out of many more which could easily be brought forward; the first from the year 1847; the second from the year 1853; and the third from 1872. The author of that well-known book, *From Oxford to Rome*, published in 1847, and written by one who was in full sympathy with the Tractarian Movement, informs us:—

"Confession the young Anglican has been accustomed to regard as one of his *secret privileges. Scarcely ever spoken of, even in the most confidential intercourse*, it is yet practised very extensively, and, as we believe, most beneficially, in the English Church." [17]

This is an important testimony, as coming from one who believed in the Confessional, and was not ashamed to acknowledge the mystery which surrounded its practice in his time.

The second instance is connected with the experience of the Rev. Lord Charles Thynne, who was for several years a clergyman in the Church of England, but seceded to Rome in 1853. After taking this decisive step his lordship addressed a lengthy letter to his late parishioners, giving his reasons for leaving the Church of England. The secrecy practised by the Tractarians with regard to Auricular Confession was one of those reasons.

"I believe," wrote Lord Charles Thynne, "that in order to obtain the remission of our sins by Absolution, it was necessary to confess them to some one possessed of authority to receive Confessions, and to give Absolution. I believe this to be necessary for all who have fallen into sin after Baptism. But when I had recourse to the only means within my reach, when I was a member of the Church of England, *I was pained by the very secret stealthy way in which alone my necessities could be met*, showing that so far as the Church of England was concerned there was something unreal and unauthorized in the act." [18]

[17] *From Oxford to Rome: and how it fared with some who lately took the Journey*, p. 205. London: Longmans, 1847.
[18] Browne's *Annals of the Tractarian Movement*, p. 296. Third edition.

The next illustration contains the unwilling testimony of a Ritualistic Father Confessor himself. At a meeting for the election of Proctors to Convocation, held at Durham, February 19th, 1874, the late Rev. G. T. Fox, a clergyman of high personal character, read to the audience a letter written by the Rev. Charles Jupp, a Ritualistic Father Confessor, to a young lady, making an appointment with her to receive her confession. The following was the letter read :—

"HOUGHTON-LE-SPRING. *May 26th,* 1872.

"MY DEAR MISS ———,—As usual, important letters are always delayed, and I fear my reply to yours of last week's date will not reach London till after you have left. I will, therefore, only say that I was very glad indeed to hear from you, and particularly on the subject you mentioned. I shall be quite ready and willing (in virtue of my office) to see you as you desire. Mrs. ——— *has left, and we have the house to ourselves.* Parishioners are so constantly coming on business of one kind or another, that your visits would not be noticed. *Please do not hint anything to Mrs. Jupp,* as I think all parochial affairs, of whatever kind, ought to be known to the priest only, and his lips sealed to every enquirer. We should be so glad to see you back after your long absence.

"In great haste,
"Yours faithfully in Christ,
"CHARLES JUPP." [19]

The late Cardinal Manning, in his Anglican days, while Archdeacon of Chichester, heard Confessions in the same stealthy manner. Mr. Purcell, his Roman Catholic biographer, relates that :—

"In his Diary, 1844-47, and in his letters to Laprimaudaye and Robert Wilberforce, Manning constantly makes use of the somewhat mysterious terms—*Under the Seal,* and *In Sacro.* To the initiated amongst High Church Anglicans these symbolic terms signified the Sacrament of Penance or Confession, and the Eucharistic Sacrifice; outside the Anglican community commonly called the Mass. These holy and wholesome Catholic doctrines Manning, as an Anglican, held and *taught,* if not in public, *in private.* In his sermons and

---

[19] *Church Association Monthly Intelligencer,* March, 1874, p 98.

Charges he practised οἰκονομία; or *spoke under reserve*, or in mere outline, of Confession and the Eucharistic Sacrifice. But in his *private* exhortations he inculcated these Catholic doctrines *in all their fulness*. The Archdeacon of Chichester practised what he preached. He offered up, as I have shown, the Eucharistic Sacrifice for the quick and the dead. He received penitents in Confession ; and exercising the power of the Keys, he loosed them from their sins; pronouncing in due form, whilst making over them the sign of the Cross, the words of Absolution.

" Protestant prejudice, popular ignorance, and the hostility of the authorities of their own Church, compelled the unhappy High Church Anglicans *to cast a veil of mystery or secrecy over the practice of Confession*. Instead of being an ordinary and common-place act of duty practised *coram ecclesia*, Confession amongst the Anglicans was, if I may so speak, *a hole-and-corner affair, spoken of with bated breath, and carried on under lock and key*." [20]

There were other difficulties which Father Confessors had to contend with. The Rev. William J. Butler, Vicar of Wantage, and subsequently Dean of Lincoln, writing to Archdeacon Manning, August 29th, 1840, remarked:—" The difficulty with which, as Vicar of Wantage, I am confronted in the practice of hearing Confessions *is the opposition to be feared on the part of the husband* to the wife's ' opening her grief' to another man." [21] It is hardly to be wondered at that husbands should object to their wives going to Confession, more especially to bachelor priests, since, according to the opinion of one of those Father Confessors quoted above (p. 82), " no woman would, I suppose, ever tell her husband what passed in her Confession." A married woman will tell her Father Confessor things which she would never dare to talk about to her own husband. Mr. Purcell throws some light on the secret way in which Archdeacon Manning heard the Confessions of his penitents:—

" It was a common practice for Manning, even in the days when in his Charges or sermons he was denouncing ' Romanism ' and the Popes, to hear Confessions at Lavington and Oxford, as well as at

[20] Purcell's *Life of Cardinal Manning*, Vol. I., p. 489.
[21] *Ibid.*, p. 490.

Wantage and elsewhere. It must be admitted that 'the halo of romance' thrown round the practice of Confession—of which the Vicar of Wantage so feelingly complained, was in no small measure due to the mystery or secrecy attached to the performance of the act, even by Manning himself. At Lavington, for instance, it was his practice to walk from the Rectory to the Church at a time when no service was going on, and no congregation present; in a few minutes, by appointment, his penitent would follow. On one occasion, when a near relative of the Archdeacon's was staying with her family at the Rectory, the children, playing of an afternoon in the grounds, were surprised to see 'Uncle Henry' walking towards the church. No bell had rung for service; the church was closed. Presently *their mother* passed along the gravel walk in the same direction. In their eager curiosity to discover the meaning of this novel proceeding, the children scampered across the lawn to the church door, when their wondering eyes discovered 'Uncle Henry' seated on a big arm-chair with his back to the altar, and their mother kneeling on the altar step." [22]

The facts I have already mentioned tend to show that our Ritualistic Confessors resemble the Roman Catholic Confessors, as described by one of themselves:—

"The most responsible office of the priest of God," writes Father Augustine Wirth, O.S.B., "is the hearing of Confessions . . . in the pulpit he can touch certain sins only with kid gloves, in the Confessional he probes the sores to the very bottom. In the pulpit he must be a lion, *in the Confessional a fox.*"[23]

---

[22] Purcell's *Life of Cardinal Manning*, Vol. I., pp. 492, 493.

[23] *The Confessional*, adapted by the Rev. Augustus Wirth, O.S.B., p. v, Fourth edition. Published at Elizabeth, New Jersey, 1882.

CHAPTER IV.

THE SECRET HISTORY OF "THE PRIEST IN ABSOLUTION."

Part I. of the *Priest in Absolution*—Praised by the Ritualistic Press—Part II. secretly circulated amongst "Catholic" priests only—Lord Redesdale's exposure of the book in the House of Lords—Archbishop Tait says it is "a disgrace to the community"—Secret letter from the Master of the Society of the Holy Cross—Statement of the S. S. C.—Special secret Chapter of the Society to consider the *Priest in Absolution*—Full report of its proceedings, with speeches of the Brethren—Refuses to condemn the book—Discussion in Canterbury Convocation—Severe Episcopal Censures—Immoral Ritualistic Confessors ruin women; Testimony of Archdeacon Allen—Dr. Pusey's acknowledgments of the dangers of the Confessional; "It is the road by which a number of Christians go down to hell"—Another secret meeting of the Society of the Holy Cross—Reports of the speeches and resolutions—Some Bishops secretly friendly to the Society—Canon Knox-Little's connection with the Society of the Holy Cross—Strange and Jesuitical Proceedings at the Society's Synod.

FOR many years the Ritualistic Father Confessors possessed no book of their own to guide them in their work, and were therefore entirely dependent upon Roman Catholic books written in Latin, or French, and as many of these Confessors were by no means Latin scholars, and numbers of them knew nothing of French, it was at length found necessary to make an effort towards supplying this long-felt want. The work was undertaken by the Rev. J. C. Chambers, a well-known clergyman, who, in 1863, was Master of the secret Society of the Holy Cross. Instead, however, of writing an independent treatise on the Confessional, he contented himself with translating and adapting a Roman Catholic work, written by the Abbé Gaume, which he issued under the now well-known title of the *Priest in Absolution*. It was divided into two parts. Part I. was published in 1866, and sold to the public; and a second edition was issued in 1869, but this was soon after withdrawn from *public* sale. When the first edition appeared it received a warm welcome from the Ritualistic press. The *Union Review* declared that it was "a golden treatise," "full of wisdom, sound teaching, and very valuable suggestions with regard to the Sacrament of Penance." But the reviewer evidently perceived a danger which was not realized by Mr. Chambers, for he wisely added that "It would have been far better to have issued the book in Latin."[1] No doubt it would have been "far better" for the Ritualistic Father Confessors had this warning been issued in time. It was clearly not wise to reveal to the English public in all its hideous deformity the moral filth of the Confessional. Had it been printed in Latin very few would have discovered its indecent character. The *Church Review* affirmed that the book could "be spoken of with the highest praise. It is a book which demands prayerful study, and our clerical readers will find it the greatest boon."[2]

The publication of the first half of the *Priest in Absolution* did not create any public excitement. It's unhappy birth appears to have been unnoticed by Protestant Churchmen. The second part was issued in 1872. It is dedicated "To the Masters, Vicars, and Brethren, of the Society of the Holy Cross," and the dedication states that it was "begun at their request." A note to the "Advertisement to the Reader" states that:—

"To prevent scandal arising from the curious or prurient misuse of a book which treats of spiritual diseases, it has been thought best that the sale should be confined to the clergy who desire to have at

---

[1] *Union Review*, Volume for 1867, p. 215.
[2] *Church Review*, March 23rd, 1867, p. 278.

hand a sort of vade-mecum for easy reference in the discharge of their duties as Confessors."

In this way the laity of the Church of England were kept in the dark as to what was going on. But not only was every effort made to keep the book out of their hands; but even ordinary Church of England clergymen were not allowed to purchase it, unless they were Father Confessors, or could give a reference to some well-known Ritualistic priest. One Church of England clergyman ventured to send Mr. Chambers himself stamps for a copy, and was not a little surprised on receiving the following reply:—

"18, SOHO SQUARE.

"DEAR SIR,—The book is only delivered to such priests of the English Church as are in the habit of hearing Confessions, or are known to me personally, or through friends. As your name is entirely unknown to me, I must require a reference to some well-known High Church priest, or I must return the stamps.

"J. C. CHAMBERS." [3]

When Mr. Chambers died there was a great danger lest the unsold copies of the *Priest in Absolution*—which was his private property—should be sold to some second-hand or other bookseller, and thus one of the great secrets of the Society of the Holy Cross should become widely known to the Protestants of England. There was no time to be lost. At the Monthly Chapter of the Society, held June 9th, 1874, a letter was read from the Rev. Joseph James Elkington, then Curate of St. Mary's, Soho, asking the Society to buy the copyright from the executors of Mr. Chambers. After some discussion, it was moved by the Treasurer, the Rev. John Andrews Foote, seconded by the Rev. E. M. Chaplain, and carried unanimously:—"That the copyright of the *Priest in Absolution* having been offered to the Society, the brethren be requested to subscribe towards the purchase, such subscriptions to be returned out of the proceeds of sale."[4] In the official report of the Chapter at which this resolution was passed, a special notice was issued, stating

[3] *The Rock*, June 6th, 1873, p. 391.   [4] *S. S. C. June Chapter*, 1874, p. 2.

that "the probable value of the copyright, together with the copies of the book on hand, is £100," and asking the brethren to lend £5 each towards the cost, the book when paid for to "remain the property of S. S. C." The subject was mentioned again at the next Monthly Chapter, but, as only one £5 had been promised, nothing definite was done, though a letter was read from Mr. Elkington, asking for a higher price. Matters, however, made rapid progress during the next month, for, at the August Chapter, the Master of the Society of the Holy Cross announced to the brethren that the "Copyright was now the property of the Society; the difficulties relating to the purchase having been satisfactorily settled."[5] However that may have been, on the following month the money had not all been paid, for the Treasurer of the Society had to issue, in that month, a special circular, announcing that £25 was still due to the executors of Mr. Chambers. From the "Balance Sheet" of the Society, presented to its September Synod, 1874, it appears that the copyright and stock of the *Priest in Absolution* had been bought for £75, or £25 less than was first asked for it. By a resolution passed at the May, 1875, Synod of the Society, it was decided that the money "lent by brethren for the purchase of the *Priest in Absolution*, be repaid out of the balance in hand of the general fund of the Society."[6] Part I. of the *Priest in Absolution* was sold to the public for 2s 6d; Part II. was sold to the brethren at 5s 4d, post free. How many copies were sold before the Society acquired the copyright I have no means of ascertaining; but after that date there must have been a considerable sale, to judge by the balance sheets of the Society of the Holy Cross. That for May, 1875, reported the sale of copies to the value of £20. 7s 6d; for May, 1876, £38. 17s 4d; September, 1876, £4. 11s 4d; and in September, 1877, £9. 16s 11d—making a total of £73. 13s 1d.

[5] *S. S. C. August Chapter*, 1874, p. 1.
[6] *S. S. C. Analysis of Proceedings of May Synod*, 1875, p. 6.

On June 14th, 1877, the late Lord Redesdale exposed the *Priest in Absolution* in the House of Lords. His lordship was not a fanatic, nor could anyone fairly describe him as an Evangelical Churchman. On the contrary he was, says Dr. Davidson, the present Bishop of Winchester, "a sober and trusted High Churchman, of the earlier sort."[7] Lord Redesdale quoted from the book itself, which he held in his hand. After this exposure it was commonly reported by the Ritualists that his lordship's copy had been stolen for his use from the library of a Ritualistic priest. No one, however, ventured to name the clergyman who had lost his copy, and as a matter of fact there was not a word of truth in the rumour. The copy was obtained in a perfectly honourable and straightforward manner by the late Mr. Robert Fleming. This false rumour was repeated again at Brighton, during the summer of 1890, by the Rev. C. Hardy Little, Vicar of St. Martin's, Brighton; but at a great public meeting held in the Dome, Brighton, on June 20th of that year, Mr. Fleming himself appeared on the platform, and told to the vast audience, which included a considerable number of Ritualists, the true story of how he came into possession of the *Priest in Absolution*, and his version of the case has never since been challenged by the Ritualists. Mr. Fleming, who held the original copy of the book in his hand, from which Lord Redesdale had quoted in the House of Lords, said that a gentleman occupying a prominent position in the Church of England had given it to him, at his request, for some little service which he had been enabled to render to him. As he presented him with the book that gentleman said smilingly to him, "you won't make a bad use of it?" To which he replied, "All right." The statement that the book was stolen, he emphatically declared, was an absolute falsehood.[8]

---

[7] *Life of Archbishop Tait*, Vol. II., p. 171. First edition.
[8] *English Churchman*, June 26th, 1890, p. 415.

Lord Redesdale, in the course of his speech in the House of Lords, quoted largely from the *Priest in Absolution*, to prove that it was a grossly indecent and abominable book. Some of the portions read were so vile that, as the Right Rev. Biographer of Archbishop Tait informs us, " many of the quotations were necessarily withheld from publication either in the newspapers or in *Hansard*."[9] Lord Redesdale concluded his speech by saying:—

"I must say, my Lords, that I think it high time the laity should move in this matter. Hitherto it has been treated too much as one exclusively for the clergy. In calling your lordship's attention to the subject, I am actuated simply by a sense of duty, for I feel that the time has arrived when there should be a decided condemnation of such practices."[10]

The Archbishop of Canterbury (Dr. Tait) addressed the House, after Lord Redesdale sat down. He said:—

"The fact that such a book should be printed and circulated is to my mind a matter of very great concern. The Noble Earl spared us from many details; but, at the same time, he read quite enough to show that *no modest person could read the book without regret,* and that IT IS A DISGRACE TO THE COMMUNITY that such a book should be circulated under the authority of clergymen of the Established Church. . . . I cannot imagine that any right-minded man could wish to have such questions [as those suggested in the *Priest in Absolution*] addressed to any member of his family; and if he had any reason to suppose that any member of his family had been exposed to such an examination, I am sure it would be the duty of any father of a family to remonstrate with the clergyman who had put the questions, and warn him never to approach his house again."[11]

As a result of this exposure great excitement was created in the minds of all loyal Churchmen, who were righteously indignant at learning the filthy character of the Ritualistic Confessional, as revealed in the *Priest in Absolution*. That indignation was greatly strengthened when, a few weeks

---

[9] *Life of Archbishop Tait*, Vol. II., p. 172.
[10] *Ibid.*, p. 172.
[11] *Church Association Monthly Intelligencer*, August, 1877, pp. 314-316.

later, the late Rev. A. H. Mackonochie, of St. Alban's, Holborn (who was for many years Master of the Society of the Holy Cross) published a correspondence which he had with another clergyman, in which he declared concerning the *Priest in Absolution*, that " Its principles are those which govern, I believe, all Confessors among ourselves."[12] The daily papers of the United Kingdom, almost without exception, gave expression to the feelings of the country, in leading articles condemning the Society of the Holy Cross, and its Confessional book, in the severest terms. About two months after the exposure Lord Abergavenny forwarded to the Archbishop of Canterbury an address on the subject signed by peers and noblemen of England, Ireland, and Scotland, in which they expressed their "sorrow and deep indignation at the extreme indelicacy and impropriety of the questions therein [in the *Priest in Absolution*] put to married and unmarried women and children." This address was signed by the Duke of Westminster, the Duke of Wellington, the Duke of St. Albans, the Duke of Manchester, the Duke of Grafton, the Duke of Leinster, the Marquises of Abergavenny, Bristol, Ailesbury, Conyngham, and Hertford; the Earls of Redesdale, Jersey, Harrowby, Fortescue, Cork, Morley, Fitzwilliam, Clancarty, Sydney, Bessborough, Seafield, Cadogan, Ilchester, Mansfield, Normanton, Harewood, Spencer, Bantry, Desart, Camperdown, Manvers, Lucan, Arran, Bradford, Shaftesbury, Roden, Haddington, Cowper, Darnley, Donoughmore, Chichester, Dunmore, Elphinstone, and Longford; by Viscounts Hardinge, Midleton, Hawarden, Lifford, Strathallen, Powerscourt, Sidmouth, and Torrington; and also by Lords Sondes, Henniker, Leconsfield, Wynford, Hampton, Ebury, Rivers, Sandys, Churchill, Bolton, Cottesloe, Oranmore, Talbot de Malahide, Clonbrock, Dynevor, Forester, Walsingham, Digby, Dorchester, Foley, Denman,

---

[12] *The Priest in Absolution and the Society of the Holy Cross*: a Correspondence between a London Priest and A. H. Mackonochie, p. 17.

Abinger, Crofton, Zouche, Ruthven, Penrhyn, Chelmsford, Huntingfield, Inchiquin, Colchester, Enfield, Eversley, Waveney, Airey, Ellenborough, Delamere, Ventry, Bateman, and Dudley.

I now proceed to relate the attitude adopted by the Society of the Holy Cross towards the exposure of the *Priest in Absolution*. My authorities for what I shall record are mainly the secret documents of the Society in my possession. Two days before Lord Redesdale's exposure, viz., on June 12th, at the Monthly Chapter of the Society, the Rev. Robert James Wilson, who subsequently became Warden of Keble College, Oxford, called the attention of the brethren to the notice which Lord Redesdale had given of his intention to bring the *Priest in Absolution* to the attention of the House of Lords. "After some conversation," says the official report of the proceedings, "it was decided that the Master should be left to use his own discretion in dealing with the matter."[13] The "Master" at that time was the Rev. F. Ll. Bagshawe, Vicar of St. Barnabas', Pimlico. On June 25th this gentleman sent out to the brethren the following printed letter:—

"ST. BARNABAS, PIMLICO.
"*June* 25*th*, 1877.

"P. ✠ T.

"DEAR BROTHER,—I think it will be satisfactory to you to know that I have not remained inactive during the present attack upon our Society in connection with the *Priest in Absolution*. The Bishops have referred the book to a Committee, consisting of the Archbishop of Canterbury, and the Bishops of London, Winchester, Gloucester and Bristol, and Ely. This Committee has asked us to meet them on Thursday, the 28th. I have reason to think that the Bishops are disposed to be friendly. The whole question was discussed at a Meeting of the Council, including the Assessors, on Saturday. You shall have immediate information when anything further is done.

[13] *S. S. C. June Chapter*, 1877, p. 6.

I have decided also not to accept the resignation of any brethren for the present, not to print the Roll of members, nor to permit the distribution of the *Priest in Absolution* until after the September Synod.

"You would perhaps like to know the true relation of S. S. C. to the *Priest in Absolution*. Some years ago, the Society requested Br. Chambers to prepare a book on the subject; when he had done so, he published the first part of the *Priest in Absolution*, but retained the second part for private circulation. It was entirely his own work, and executed on his own responsibility: its sheets were never submitted to the Society. When he died, the whole remaining stock would have been sold by his executors, and have been exposed for public sale.

"In order to prevent an action so contrary to the compiler's wish, and hurtful to the Society, to whom it was dedicated, we bought the book, and have been responsible for a limited and cautious supply to priests of known character.

"Believe me,
"Yours Faithfully,
"In D. N. J. C.,
"Francis Ll. Bagshawe."

There was need for Mr. Bagshawe's action in refusing to accept the resignations of the brethren for the time being. The more timid of the brethren were thoroughly frightened by the exposure which had taken place, more especially after the *Rock* had published a complete list of their names and addresses, which made them most anxious to leave an organization that had brought them into trouble with their parishioners. The Master acknowledges that the Society was "responsible for a limited and *cautious* supply to priests of *known character*" of the now notorious Confessional book; and it is quite evident from the whole of his letter how greatly the Society dreaded the light of publicity being thrown on its dark underground proceedings. There is reason to believe that most of the brethren who at this period left the Society did so, not because they disapproved of the Society or the *Priest in Absolution*, but simply through fear. The fact that scarcely any of them publicly repudiated either the one or the other is a proof of this. There were, however, a few exceptions, of which the most remarkable was that of the Rev. Frank N. Oxenham—he joined the S. S. C. in 1872—who, as early as June 19th, wrote to the Archbishop of Canterbury :—

"When, in consequence of your Grace's observations, I looked into the book, I felt that no words could be too strong to condemn the principles advocated, and the advice given in that book as to the questioning of persons who came to Confession. If the practice of Confession involved, which it certainly does not, any such questioning, I should regard it with abhorrence. I am sure, my Lord, that a very large number of the members of the Society of the Holy Cross are as ignorant as I was of the contents of this unhappy book, and would repudiate its principles in the matter to which I have alluded as sincerely and utterly as I do. In justice to those persons, as well as to myself, I am venturing to trouble your Grace with this communication. I very deeply regret that the Society of the Holy Cross ever came into possession of this book, and I shall take the earliest opportunity open to a private member, to move that all remaining copies of the second part of the *Priest in Absolution* be forthwith destroyed."[14]

This condemnation of the *Priest in Absolution*, I may here remark, came from one who was for many years an advanced Ritualist, and is therefore all the more valuable on that account, as showing its mischievous and dangerous character. Unfortunately for Mr. Oxenham's opinion, a "very large number of the members" of the Society of the Holy Cross did *not* "repudiate its principles." The proposal that the Society should burn the remaining copies in its possession was brought forward, though not by Mr. Oxenham, at the May Synod, 1878, when the following resolution was carried by thirty-four to eight :—" That this Synod is not in favour of the destruction of the remaining copies of the *Priest in Absolution* at the present time."[15] The Society would not even allow that there was any possibility of the advice on

---

[14] *Life of Archbishop Tait*, Vol. II., p. 174.
[15] *S. S. C. Analysis of the May Synod*, 1878, p. 16.

questioning, contained in the book, being misused, for when Mr. Oxenham, at the Special Chapter, held July 5th, 1877, moved that "the advice given in this book as to questioning penitents is at least liable to injurious misuse," his motion was lost. The report of the proceedings does not state how many voted for or against it.[16]

On the day before Lord Redesdale's speech the Master of the Society of the Holy Cross wrote to the Bishop of London on the subject, and informed him that the *Priest in Absolution* could "only be obtained by those who are known clergymen of the Church of England," and that "very few copies" had in consequence been distributed; and stating that "the Society bought the work up at considerable pecuniary loss." These statements can scarcely be described as accurate. The official statements of receipts for the sales before the Master wrote this letter, quoted above, clearly prove that there had been what may be fairly termed a *considerable* sale for such a work. As we have seen, £75 was paid for the copyright, and £73. 13s 1d had already been received from the sales. Where, then, was the "considerable pecuniary loss"? In addition to these sales, it is well to remember that Mr. Chambers himself must have sold a considerable number of copies before the Society purchased the book. Was it, therefore, truthful for Mr. Bagshawe to inform the Bishop that only a "very few copies" had been distributed? I think not. And was there not something like equivocation in the Master's further statement to the Bishop :—" I venture to assert that the great body of these clergy are not acquainted with the contents of this book, and some scarcely know of its existence"? The Master, in this letter, also informed the Bishop that the Rev. J. C. Chambers had compiled the book. This was startling news for the Bishop, who, in his reply to the Master's letter, wrote :—

"Few things have ever given me more pain than the very unex-

[16] *Minutes of the Special Chapter*, p. 11.

pected information that the late Mr. Chambers was the compiler of that volume which I have seen, and that you were Master of the Society which owns and circulates it. I am, of course, aware of the line of defence indicated by the term professional character; but I must say that, in my judgment, a system of Confession which makes such a book necessary or even useful to the Confessor, carries with it its own condemnation."

The Bishop's letter shows how carefully the leading authorities of the S.S.C. had kept their proceedings from the knowledge of their own Diocesan. Mr. Bagshawe's next letter to the Bishop was written on the day after the exposure in the House of Lords, and contained the following paragraph:—

"As you have written to me in such a kind way, I am quite entitled to tell you, as my Bishop, that I have never thought the book a useful one, or recommended it to others. It is a matter of sorrow that some of us differ with our Bishops at all, but I cannot help feeling, after listening to a debate such as that on Thursday night, that our practice with regard to Confession is very widely misapprehended. One of my objections to the *Priest in Absolution* is that its language is not calculated to remove that misapprehension."

It would be interesting to know what other objections the Master had to the book, which he in no way condemns as bad in itself. Yet the unsold copies of the book were, as he subsequently acknowledged, kept in his own care, and therefore no copies could have been circulated without his knowledge and sanction. In his Address to the May Synod, 1878, he said :—" Hitherto the book has been in my care—now it will cease to be so." [17] It is evident, therefore, that his letters to the Bishop of London were written for a purpose, viz., that of making his lordship think more highly of the Master than he really deserved. Actions speak more strongly than words, and Mr. Bagshawe's words seem to contradict his actions.

The interview of the representatives of the Society of the Holy Cross with the Bishops took place at Lambeth Palace,

---

[17] *S.S.C. Master's Address*, delivered at the May Synod, 1878, p. 6.

on Thursday, June 28th. The representatives were the Master of the Society, together with the following members of his secret Council:—The Rev. C. F. Lowder, Vicar of St. Peter's, London Docks; the Rev. Joseph Newton Smith, founder of the Society of the Holy Cross; the Rev. F. H. Murray, Rector of Chislehurst; the Rev. H. D. Nihill the Rev. R. J. Wilson, subsequently Warden of Keble College; the Rev. John William Kempe; and the Rev. G. Noel Freeling, the latter of whom, however, was not on the "Council." To the surprise of these gentlemen, instead of meeting the Bishops they expected, they found waiting for them the Archbishops of Canterbury and York, and the Bishop of London only. The Master had brought with him a carefully-prepared *Statement to the Bishops;* but he was only allowed to read about one-half of it, the remainder was sent to the Bishops on the following Saturday. This *Statement*, which, with the correspondence already alluded to, was subsequently printed for private circulation amongst the brethren, commenced with an account of the nature and objects of the Society of the Holy Cross, and then proceeded to give the history of its connection with the *Priest in Absolution*, which has, I think, already been sufficiently related above. But I may quote the following extract from the *Statement*, as having an important bearing on the revival of Auricular Confession in the Church of England:—

"All, or nearly so," said Mr. Bagshawe, "of our members had, as a matter of fact, found the blessing of Confession; and very many of them were constantly applied to by those who desired to share in that blessing. Perpetually, at our meetings, questions of difficulty were asked, as our members began to learn the existence of sin and its power in their parishes. They felt the need of guidance in the ministry to which they believed themselves to be called. Under these circumstances, the Rev. J. C. Chambers was asked, I believe informally, and before I joined the Society in 1868, to undertake a work for their assistance, adapted to the needs of the Church of England and the state of modern society. It was felt that they could not have made a better choice. He possessed, more than any of their number, the confidence of the Bishops for prudence, learning, moral integrity, and purity of purpose. His experience was vast. Members of both Houses of Parliament, Clergy, Barristers, Merchants, Tradesmen, and Costermongers were amongst his penitents. In 1869 the first part of the work was published. It was entirely on Mr. Chambers's own responsibility. The Society was responsible for the request, but not for the manner of execution. In 1872 or 1873, the second part was brought out."

Mr. Bagshawe made a singular error in stating that the first part was published in 1869. It was, as I have already mentioned, published in 1866, and the second edition was published in 1869. The Bishops referred to as having "confidence" in Mr. Chambers could hardly have been aware of his advanced Romanizing views, or that he was Father Confessor to so many influential people. The second half of that gentleman's official *Statement* to the Bishops consisted of an apology for the *Priest in Absolution*, concerning which he had, as we have seen, written but a few days before, that "he had never thought the book a useful one"; but of which he *now* affirmed that it was "a work upon an important subject from which good might be gained by those who read it with a right motive." "I consider," he continued, "very many propositions in the *Priest in Absolution* doubtful, and from some I completely disagree. Yet I should be very far from saying that the discussion of such questions is not productive of good." The Master next proceeded to call attention to the "various cautions with which the book abounds"; but goes on very candidly to acknowledge that :—

"We believe that in certain cases *questions must be asked of the penitent*, partly to clear what has been ambiguous in his statement, and partly to help him to confess what he really wishes to say, but is hindered in saying from shyness. In no case should any new matter be imported, unless there is very strong reason to believe that something has been suppressed, and then it should be approached with the utmost care."

It was evidently the desire of the Master to move as much

of the blame as possible from the Society of the Holy Cross, but he utterly failed in impressing the Bishops with his view of the case. Instead of repudiating the book altogether, he asserted that "no harm has been done by the kind of circulation which the Society has permitted." One result of this interview, as recorded in the official and privately circulated report of the proceedings, was "the surrender of a copy of the *Priest in Absolution* to the Archbishop, and the promise of a surrender of the Statutes. The Master took the Statutes and the Office Book to the Archbishop on the following day." On June 30th, the Archbishop of Canterbury wrote to Mr. Bagshawe :—" I understand from you that a meeting of your Society will be held on Thursday of next week. Let me, through you, urge upon the Society the duty of at once repudiating the book which has caused so much alarm. This is due both to yourselves and to the Church. It is absolutely necessary that I should be in possession, not later than Thursday evening, of any resolutions you pass." The reason for the Archbishop's haste was that on the following day, July 6th, the subject was to be discussed by the Bishops in the Upper House of Canterbury Convocation, and they had postponed the consideration of the subject for a day, to suit the convenience of the Society.

On Thursday, July 5th, a "Special Chapter" of the Society of the Holy Cross, to consider the action of the Society, was held at 5, Greville Street, Brooke Street, Holborn. Seventy-five brethren were present. Fortunately, I have come into possession of the official and secret report of this very secret meeting, held in a private house. From this I learn that the Master informed his brethren that it was "his opinion that unless the Society yielded to some extent to the wishes of the Bishops, we were in danger of a synodical statement by the Upper House against the Sacraments of the Catholic Church. To avert this, which would cause the gravest anxiety to many of the clergy and the laity, he advised the Chapter to pass a resolution to stop the further circulation of the *Priest in Absolution*." Canon T. T. Carter, of Clewer, who was the next speaker, moved a resolution, thanking the Master for the statement laid before the Bishops, and expressing " general approval of the same." This was seconded by the Rev. George Davenport Nicholas, Vicar of St. Stephen's, Clewer, and carried unanimously. Before it was passed, however, there was some grumbling on the part of a few of the brethren. The Rev. C. D. Goldie "thought that the Society had been betrayed into too hasty action "; while the Rev. A. H. Stanton, Curate of St. Alban's, Holborn, revealed the fact that " the Council was not unanimous " in its action, and that he and the Rev. Henry Aston Walker, now Vicar of Chattisham, Ipswich, " had strongly opposed the idea of a deputation." The well-known Rev. A. H. Mackonochie said that he " was one of the Master's Council who had been averse to any deputation to the Bishops at all." He believed that the Bishops " had got up this attack " upon the Society, and desired to fix upon it the stigma of " indecent publications." " He warned the brethren that if they gave up the book, they would not escape the stigma."

The Chapter next proceeded to read letters from absent brethren, including one from the Rev. Dr. Littledale, and also a resolution passed by the Edinburgh Local Chapter of the Society, to the effect that "the Society's further connection with the book was undesirable." On the other hand, the Cheltenham Local Chapter had sent up a resolution to the effect that it " was opposed to any repudiation of the book." The Rev. C. F. Lowder next addressed the meeting, and for politic reasons recommended "the Chapter to withdraw the book from circulation." He concluded by reading a further Statement which had been drawn up, he said, with the assistance of the Rev. T. W. Perry and Dr. Walter Phillimore (now Sir Walter Phillimore, Bart., Q.C.). This statement was discussed by the

Chapter, and after several amendments had been adopted, was carried unanimously. Thereupon Canon T. T. Carter moved that,—

"The Society presents this Statement to the Right Reverend the Bishops and the Reverend the Clergy in Convocation assembled, in deference to the expressed desire of the Archbishops of Canterbury and York, and the Bishop of London, whom the delegates of the Society met at Lambeth. In deference to the expression of the desire on their part, the Society has determined that no further copies of the book shall be supplied."

In moving this resolution Canon Carter said that he, "while revising the proof sheets of the work, had recommended the author to publish it in Latin." He was in favour of withdrawing the book "because we cannot heartily endorse it as a whole"; and "because the Bishops ask us to give the book up." The Rev. Charles Bodington (now Diocesan Missioner for Lichfield) supported the motion. He said that he did so "*because it kept clear of any condemnation of the book.* While he should consider it *injudicious* to endorse the book as it stands, he thought that withdrawing it in deference to the Bishops' wishes need not make the slightest difference in our teaching and practice with regard to Confession." The Rev. William Crouch, now Vicar of Gamlingay, however, "believed our position would be weakened by giving up the book. No doubt the book was imperfect, but as much might be said of all books, save one." The Rev. F. N. Oxenham "considered that the charges had been fairly brought against the book, though parts of it are exceedingly valuable, yet the general tone of the work, though guarded, he held to be deeply injurious if generally used. He felt that the Society ought to condemn the book." This courageous statement of Brother Oxenham appears to have received no encouragement from the brethren present, for, when he proposed an amendment embodying his views, it was lost. After a good deal of further discussion, with the consent of Canon Carter, the following resolution was passed, by twenty-eight against twenty, instead of that proposed by Brother Oxenham :—

"That, under these considerations, the Society of the Holy Cross, while distinctly repudiating the unfair criticisms which have been passed on the book called the *Priest in Absolution, and without intending to imply* ANY *condemnation of it,* yet, in deference to the desire expressed by the Archbishop of Canterbury to the representatives of the Society, resolves that no further copies of it be supplied."

This was a most important resolution. By it the Society declined to censure the book either in whole or in part. Mr. Oxenham proposed to insert the words "as a whole" after "condemnation of it"; but his proposal was rejected by twenty-one to eighteen. The promise to withdraw the *Priest in Absolution* from circulation served its purpose very well with the Bishops in Convocation the next day; but it was a promise which was valueless, for it was subsequently repudiated by the Society as a whole, very much to the annoyance of the Master of the Society, who considered, as we shall see presently, that by repudiating the resolution of the Special Chapter the Society had broken faith with the Bishops, and in such a way as to compel him, as an honourable man, to resign his position as Master of the Society of the Holy Cross. Before this Special Chapter closed the Rev. James Benjamin Parker said "he was prepared to move that a copy of the Society's Roll" of the Brethren should be given to the Bishops. But the Master very soon put a stop to Brother Parker's injudicious proposals. He informed the Chapter that he had already refused to give a copy to the Archbishop. Mr. Bagshawe was evidently too wide awake to do anything of the kind. There is nothing, I am certain, that the Society of the Holy Cross dreads more than that the names of its members shall be known to the general public. They could not even trust the secret to one Archbishop!

On Friday, July 6th, the Upper House of Canterbury met to consider the *Priest in Absolution.* There were present, in addition to the Archbishop of Canterbury, who, of course, presided, the Bishops of London, Llandaff, Gloucester and Bristol, Norwich, Hereford, St. Albans, Lichfield, Bath and Wells, Chichester, Salisbury, Oxford, and St. Asaph. Not one of these Prelates, whether High Churchmen or Evangelicals, had one word to say in favour of either the *Priest in Absolution,* or the Society of the Holy Cross, which they held responsible for the book. They unanimously condemned both the one and the other, though some of them bore testimony to the personal character of some of the members of the Society. My readers may find a *verbatim* report of the speeches of these Prelates, on this remarkable occasion, in the *Chronicle of Convocation,* Sessions July 3-6, 1877, pages 310-336. My quotations from the speeches are taken from this official report.

The Archbishop of Canterbury, who, in the course of his speech, presented to the Bishops the resolutions of the Special Chapter of the S. S. C. passed the previous day, said:—"The persons with whom we have now to deal, it appears to me, have adopted a system altogether alien from the system of the Church of England, which yet might not find its natural home, under existing circumstances, in the exaggerated Ultramontane form of the present Roman Catholic Church. This system must seek a home somewhere else than in the Reformed Protestant Church of England. . . I am sure your lordships will agree with me that it will be most dangerous to allow them in this Church powers to propagate doctrines, to introduce and carry into effect practices which are entirely alien from the spirit and teaching of the whole body of the Divines of the Church of England from first to last." The Archbishop then called attention to a little confessional book for children, "Edited by a Committee of Clergy," and entitled "Books for the Young," No. I., *Confession.* It must have had, he said, a very wide circulation, for the copy from which he quoted was one of the "Eighth Thousand." He said that he did not know who the "Committee" were who were responsible for that book. He trusted that they were few in number, and not more than two or three. What would he have said, if he had known that this little book, which he so sternly condemned, was, in reality, issued by the Society of the Holy Cross, but without its name being attached to it? Of course the Society was too wise to enlighten Dr. Tait on this important subject. The little book taught that little children from six and a-half years old should go to Confession; and these little ones were instructed that, "It is to the priest, and to the priest only, that the child must acknowledge his sins, if he desires that God should forgive him." In conclusion his Grace said, "I have now given your lordships all the information that I have on this subject; I do it with the greatest pain. I do it with a full appreciation of the goodness of the men with whom we have to deal: but no admiration of any points in their character ought, I think, to make us hesitate as to whatever may appear to be our duty in the endeavour to counteract *what I feel obliged to call a* CONSPIRACY *within our own body* against the doctrine, the discipline, and the practice of our Reformed Church."

The Bishop of London said that in the First Part of the *Priest in Absolution* there are some pages which contain things as bad as are to be found in the Second Part. He noticed that, by the resolution of the Society of the Holy Cross which had been sent to them, the remaining copies of the *Priest in Absolution* were not to be destroyed, but none others are to be supplied. "There, consequently," said the Bishop, who evidently suspected trickery, "they are to remain, and at some future opportunity, when the opinion of the Society undergoes a change, I presume they will again be available as they have hitherto been." "I shall," he continued, "ask your lordships to permit me to move, in the first place, that this House holds the Society of the Holy Cross responsible for the preparation and dissemination of the book called the *Priest in Absolution*. The question is, how far they have by their resolutions withdrawn that responsibility; and I am afraid I must say that they have not withdrawn it at all. They have not repudiated the book, nor expressed their regret that it has been published. They have given no opinion in condemnation of it; on the contrary, they say they do not intend to imply any condemnation of it, though, in deference to the desire expressed by the Archbishop, no further copies of it will be supplied. I shall, therefore, ask your lordships to agree to a resolution to this effect :—

"'That this House, having considered the first resolution appended to the "Statement of the Society of the Holy Cross, presented to this House on Friday, July 6th, 1877," is of opinion that the Society has neither repudiated nor effectually withdrawn from circulation the aforesaid work.'"

The Bishop of London then proceeded with his speech, and termed the little book on Confession, quoted by the Archbishop, "a wretched little book," after which he moved this further resolution :—

"That this House hereby expresses its strong condemnation of any doctrine or practice of Confession which can be thought to render such a book necessary or expedient."

The Bishop of Llandaff seconded the resolutions. He said :—"It appears to me, after reading a good deal of this book, that it and its papers are books and papers which ought to appear within the pale of the Roman Catholic Church, and not within the pale of the Church of England." In conclusion, the Bishop expressed his belief that dispensed Jesuits had in the past worked mischief within the Protestant Churches. "I am very unwilling," he said, "to suppose that anything of the kind is done at the present day, but this is an important fact in history which at any rate may well be borne in mind."

The Bishop of St. Albans, who was a High Churchman, said :—"I think it is high time that some restraint should be placed on the doctrine and practice of Confession that has become prevalent among us lately. I was, of course, well aware that this practice was beginning to prevail to a great extent; but I do not think it ever impressed itself on my mind so fully as it did when, on Good Friday last, I took part in the service, for the first time in many years, in a church which has acquired a very unenviable notoriety— I mean the Church of St. James's, Hatcham. In looking over that church after the service had concluded I saw in a transept or side chapel—I saw with my own eyes—a Confessional of the Church of Rome, with its seat for the Confessor, a place for the penitent to kneel upon, curtains, and the usual paraphernalia of such places. Now, I do not wish to say one unkind word concerning the Incumbent of that church, although I must say his conduct has cost me the most miserable weeks of the whole of my Episcopate. I repeat that I do not wish to say anything unkind of him; but I cannot forget on the present occasion that he is an office-bearer in this Society of the Holy Cross." The Bishop concluded by supporting the resolution. I may here note that Confessional Boxes, which so astonished the late Bishop of St. Albans, have now become very common in Ritualistic churches. The Bishops have the power to remove them, but, with a very few exceptions, they refuse to use their powers. Many of them can *talk* against Popery in the Church of England, but the laity are asking, Why do they not *act*? We need *deeds* more than *words* in these dangerous days.

The next speaker was the High Church Bishop of Lichfield (Dr. Selwyn). He said:—"I must say, from the observation which I have made of the documents placed before us, that they do contain the very gravest elements of suspicion, and that they would make me—although I do not pledge myself as to my future course either as regards an Incumbent or a Curate—entertain doubts as to whether I could appoint one of these clergymen to one of those offices or the other. . . We, as Bishops of the Church of England, cannot sanction their doctrines or practices, and therefore we call upon them in terms of earnest but affectionate expostulation to retreat from a position which we feel to be so utterly wrong."

The High Church Bishop of Oxford (Dr. Mackarness) declared that he cordially concurred in the resolution, but he added :—" I feel bound to say with respect to some of the persons who are said to be members of this Society, that I do not believe they have the slightest idea of any conspiracy against the doctrine and discipline of our Reformed Church." At the same time his lordship declared that he "disapproved" of the *Priest in Absolution*.

The Bishop of St. Asaph said :—" The system of Confession which we have been discussing, followed by priestly absolution, has no sanction from Scripture or from the formularies of the Church of England. I believe that it is most injurious to those who come to confess, and most detrimental to the Minister who receives Confession. . . . What was the result of the system in Ireland, when assassination was frequent in that country? Did not the assassin go to Confession the previous day and obtain relief to his conscience? And what was the effect on the priest's own mind? Was it likely that he could come in contact with so much sin and contract no defilement? Alas! let the moral aspect of many countries on the continent supply the answer."

The Right Rev. Dr. Moberly, Bishop of Salisbury, who next addressed the House, avowed that he believed Confession to be right, and yet even he condemned in very severe language the *Priest in Absolution*, and the teaching of the Society of the Holy Cross, as contained in its "Books for the Young," No. I., *Confession*. He said :—" I entirely agree with the resolution ; but I think that this matter is a much more difficult one than on the surface it appears. I cannot doubt that Confession and Absolution were enjoined by our Lord Himself, and that they form a real part of the system of the Church, and under certain circumstances are capable of being blessed in the highest possible degree for good to those who partake of them. At the same time, by carrying them to the excess taught and practised by the persons whose conduct is before us to-day they cannot but be productive of great and serious evil. . . . I believe the practice of habitual Confession to be mischievous in the highest degree, and I have a particular object in referring to it, for the greater part of my life, as that of others of your lordships, has been spent as a schoolmaster, and I confess that there is not one thing in all the world which is deeper in my heart and conscience than the corrupting mischief of any such system as this getting into our schools."

The Bishop of Bath and Wells said :—" We have seen how the authors of this book, by the doctrine and practice they have set forth, have scandalized the public mind, and I am sure that if we, the Bishops of the Church of England, were to aid and abet such doctrine and practice, we should lose the respect and confidence of the country. For these reasons, I think it most important that we should unanimously agree to the resolutions before us."

The last speech from which I shall quote was that of the High Church Bishop of Chichester. "I think," he said, "this is a very serious matter, and that it is the duty of this House to protest in the strongest manner against the teaching of these Romanizing doctrines, and the adoption of these Romanizing practices. There is not a single syllable in the Statutes [of the Society of the Holy Cross] about Confession to Almighty God, and seeking forgiveness through Jesus Christ. There is no intimation that the means of forgiveness are open to all who come to God through Christ. Nothing of the sort is said, and this is a case in which omission appears to me to be fatal. It leads the people to lean on the priest. You cannot find that in the Scriptures, and no one would say that it is inculcated in the formularies of our Church."

The resolutions were then put, and carried unanimously.

I have devoted a considerable amount of space to the speeches of the Bishops on this occasion, partly because of their intrinsic value, and also because the book in which alone they are recorded *verbatim* is exceedingly scarce, and is, therefore, quite out of the reach of ordinary Churchmen, who may be glad to have the chief points of the speeches within reach in these pages. It will be observed that the *Priest in Absolution* was thus unanimously condemned by all the Bishops of Canterbury Convocation present on this occasion, and since then not one Bishop of the Church of England has ever publicly said, or written, one word in its favour. Perhaps one of the most damaging exposures of the evil results of the *Ritualistic* Confessional ever made in public, was that made in the Lower House of Canterbury Convocation, on July 4th, 1877, two days only before the debate in the Upper House. The subject of Confession had been sent down to the Lower House, by the Bishops, for discussion, in consequence of the exposure of the *Priest in Absolution* in the House of Lords. In the course of the debate in the Lower House, Archdeacon Allen rose and said :—

"I find it printed that it is a shame to suspect any of these Clergymen of misusing this mode of treatment of spiritual disease. A shame to suspect them! If that is said, I must say something on the other side. I was talking to an elderly clergyman—a Rural Dean, older than myself—a man who has daily prayer in his church, and whom all his friends and neighbours respect—a venerable and wise High Churchman, and he told me that in his own experience *he had known three clergymen* who had practised this teaching of habitual Confession as a duty, *who had fallen into habits of immorality with women who had come to them for guidance.* That was the testimony of an old-fashioned High Churchman; and I will give his name to any one who asks me for it. You know it is said a discreet Confessor will make a proper use of this book [the *Priest in Absolution*]. A discreet Confessor! Is it possible that discretion can be a quality of every young clergyman who is a member of this Society, which is said to have a property in this book?" [19]

[19] *Chronicle of Convocation.* Sessions, July 3-6, 1877, p. 231.

The truth of Archdeacon Allen's charge against these three Ritualistic clergymen does not appear to have been ever challenged, much less refuted. It raises the very serious question, How far is the Ritualistic Confessional used for immoral purposes by wicked and evil-disposed clergymen? No one wishes to make sweeping and general charges on such a subject. But is there not just cause for anxiety? Is not human nature the same in all ages? That the Confessional has been grossly used for immoral purposes, by evil-disposed priests, and that to a gigantic extent in the Church of Rome, is amply proved, beyond the possibility of refutation, by the Bulls of the Popes themselves against solicitant priests. Anyone who wishes for clear and ample evidence on this point, based exclusively upon Roman Catholic authorities, should certainly read *An Historical Sketch of Sacerdotal Celibacy*, by Mr. Henry C. Lea, of Philadelphia. Mr. Lea's book is not sufficiently known in Europe, and I only wonder that an edition of such a learned work has never yet been published in England. He proves conclusively that the Confessional has been used, by wicked priests, for the vilest purposes in the past, and that the offence is not unknown to the nineteenth century. It appears that the Abbé Helsen, who for twenty-five years had been and still was a Roman Catholic preacher in Brussels, addressed an indignant remonstrance to the Archbishop of Mechlin, in 1832, in which he exposed to the light of day the awful immorality existing at that time amongst the Romish priesthood.

"Helsen," writes Mr. Lea, "alludes to the scandals of the Confessional as a cause of its avoidance by the faithful and as contributing powerfully to the growth of religious indifference, and that these scandals exist is not a mere matter of conjecture or inference. If it were so, there would be no need for reiterating the prohibitions against the absolution by Confessors of their fair partners in guilt, which is still occasionally found to be necessary by modern Councils; nor would Pius IX., in 1866, have felt himself obliged to declare that the power granted to Bishops to absolve in cases reserved to the Pope shall not in future extend to offences reserved for Papal absolution by Benedict XIV.'s Bull '*Sacramentum Pœnitentiœ.*' In fact, the crime of 'solicitation' must have *become notoriously frequent* before the Congregation of the Inquisition at Rome could have felt impelled, in 1867, to put forth an Instruction addressed to all Archbishops, Bishops, and Ordinaries, complaining that the Constitutions on the subject did not receive proper attention, and that in some places abuses had crept in, both as to requiring penitents to denounce guilty Confessors, and as to the punishing of Confessors guilty of solicitation [*i.e.*, soliciting women, while in the Confessional, to immorality]. It therefore urged the officials everywhere to greater vigour in investigating such offences, and gave a summary of the practice of the Inquisition in regard to these matters." [19]

Bearing these and other similar facts in mind, I am not at all surprised to learn, on the reliable authority of Archdeacon Allen, that within the experience of even *one* clergyman "*three*" instances were made known in which the Ritualistic Confessional has been used by Father Confessors for the vilest purposes. Are we to suppose that those three were the only guilty persons in England? If the experience of others could only be made public, is there not reason to fear that the instances would be considerably multiplied? Has not, at least, one clergyman, since 1877, been deprived of his living for the crime of seducing a young lady through the Confessional? Clerical celibacy is rapidly spreading amongst the Ritualists, and it is not at all a pleasant thought that our wives, daughters, and sisters may be going to Confession to some young bachelor priest, and talking with him on subjects which should never be alluded to. This sort of thing is bad enough when the Confessor happens to be a married man, but when he is a celibate the dangers are greatly increased. Let it not be said that I am bringing reckless and wholesale charges against the Ritualistic clergy. I am doing nothing of the kind. I am simply dealing with facts, and with possibilities, which we

---

[19] Lea's *History of Sacerdotal Celibacy*, p. 633. Second edition. Boston: Houghton, Miffen & Co., 1884.

cannot afford to ignore. That the Confessional may be used for the vilest purposes is acknowledged even by the author of the *Priest in Absolution*, who, as a Ritualistic Confessor of many years' experience, speaks with some authority on this point. While writing on the care which the Confessor should exercise in hearing the Confessions of females, he remarks:—

"Nothing more shows the fearfulness of Satanic devices than that it is possible that a Sacrament which was instituted to drive forth from souls sin and the devil, and make them living temples of the Holy Ghost, may be profaned by abusers of its ministrations to the grossest iniquity."[20]

This testimony of the Editor of the *Priest in Absolution* is corroborated by that of Dr. Pusey, given after he had himself been hearing Confessions for forty years. He tells us of one way in which the Confessional is still abused by Confessors:—

"It is a sad sight," writes Dr. Pusey, "to see Confessors giving their whole morning to young women devotees, while they dismiss men or married women, who have, perhaps, left their household affairs with difficulty to find themselves rejected with, 'I am busy, go to someone else!' so that, perhaps, such people will go on for months or years without the Sacraments. This is not hearing Confessions for God's sake, but for one's own."[21]

Again, Dr. Pusey warns the Confessor, when in the Confessional,—

"You may pervert this Sacrament [of Penance] from its legitimate end, which is to kindle an exceeding horror of sin in the minds of others, into a subtle means of feeding evil passions and sin in your own mind."[22]

He also warns the Confessor, who hears Confessions while "in a state of mortal sin," which does not necessarily imply what the world would term a *wickedness*:—

"If the ministry of a Confessor is beset with dangers, even for a

---

[20] *The Priest in Absolution*, Part II., p. 77.
[21] Pusey's *Manual for Confessors*, p. 108.   [22] *Ibid.*, p. 102.

good man, how can one in your condition hope to escape? There is but too great danger, that you will add fresh crimes to your account by an undue indulgence to faults in others which you have not overcome in yourself; or, worst of all, being the cause of temptation to others, thereby proving yourself no spiritual father, but rather a ravening wolf; no Minister of God, but of the devil; no physician, but the murderer of souls."[23]

And yet one more quotation from Dr. Pusey which, with all my heart and soul, I believe to be the solemn truth:—

"Be assured," he writes, "that this is one of the gravest faults *of our day* in the administration of the Sacrament of Penance, that it is the road by which a number of Christians go down to hell."[24]

When the Editor of the *Priest in Absolution*, and the Rev. Dr. Pusey, both experienced Father Confessors themselves, make such startling acknowledgments as those I have just quoted, is it surprising or unreasonable that Protestant Churchmen also should raise a loud note of warning, and urge people on no account to enter on that road, by which "a number of Christians go down to hell"? It cannot be Christ's road, for he who walks on *that* road, cannot possibly go astray. Such dire possibilities as those so frankly acknowledged by these two noted Ritualistic leaders, can never result from that Confession to the Great High Priest, the Lord Jesus Christ, practised by all devout Protestant Christians. The Father Confessor, as Dr. Pusey admits, is often, while in the Confessional, the "murderer of souls."

And now let us return once more to the Society of the Holy Cross and its proceedings, in relation to the *Priest in Absolution*. The ordinary Monthly Chapter of the Society was held on July 10th, 1877, when an address of sympathy with the Society was read from the so-called "Church of England Working Men's Society." The Rev. G. D. Nicholas rose and complained that the caution given to the brethren by the Master at the Special Chapter, as to the

[23] *Ibid.*, p. 99.   [24] *Ibid.*, p. 315.

"strictly confidential" nature of its proceedings, had been ignored. A lady had actually "told him, on the following morning, that she knew that the vote of the Society was not unanimous." Next a letter was read from Brother Oxenham, who was evidently anxious to keep his promise to the Archbishop of Canterbury. That gentleman enclosed a motion which he wished to bring before the September Synod, if approved by the Chapter. The motion was as follows:—

"That inasmuch as certain parts of the *Priest in Absolution*, relating to the questioning of penitents, are, in the opinion of this Synod, at least very liable to injurious misuse, this Synod resolves that all copies of the said book now in the possession of the Society shall be destroyed." [25]

To tolerate the discussion of such a very proper motion as this was what the brethren could never assent to. The very thought was treason. So, in pious horror, the Rev. Robert James Wilson exclaimed that "he hoped that the Chapter would not allow Brother Oxenham's motion to be placed on the Agenda" of the September Synod. So to make quite sure that the hated and dreaded discussion should not take place, Brother Wilson proposed, and the Rev. Edgar Hoskins (now Rector of St. Martin's, Ludgate, London) seconded the following resolution:—" That the Society thinks it undesirable to enter at the Synod into a reconsideration of its relations to the *Priest in Absolution*."[26] There was no difference of opinion in the Chapter as to the desirability of stifling discussion on Brother Oxenham's motion, and accordingly Brother Wilson's resolution was "carried unanimously." And yet, notwithstanding this decision of the July Chapter, when the September Synod was held the relations of the Society to the *Priest in Absolution were* very fully considered, as the official report of the proceedings fully shows, though, of course, Brother Oxenham's motion was rigorously boycotted.

[25] *S.S.C. July Chapter*, 1877, p. 2.   [26] *Ibid.*, p. 10.

One of the special subjects discussed at the July Chapter was " Our Action Towards the Bishops." It was introduced by the Rev. C. F. Lowder, who, after mentioning that the Upper House of Convocation had appointed a Committee to consider the Statutes of the Society of the Holy Cross and the *Priest in Absolution*, proceeded to congratulate the Society on having so far escaped Episcopal censure. That, it seems, was largely due to the Bishop of Oxford, who, while denouncing the Society and its Confessional Book in public, was at the same time secretly plotting for the purpose of shielding them from the expected censure of the Episcopal Bench. In the course of his speech Brother Lowder said that " Putting aside the rhodomontade and *ad captandum* words of the Archbishop about a ' conspiracy,' he saw grounds for hope in the line taken by the Bishop of Oxford, who, he believed, was friendly to us, *and had moved for a Committee in order to save the censure which was hanging over us*. That censure would be most serious to the Society at large, and especially to the younger brethren, and those holding positions under Government. He advised that a deputation of the Society should go before the Committee [of Bishops] with the object of explaining and defending the Statutes." Brother Lowder concluded his speech by moving a resolution to the effect that the Master in Council take such steps as might seem best to explain the work of the Society to the Committee of the Upper House of Convocation. This resolution was severely criticised by several of the brethren. In particular, Brother A. H. Mackonochie declared that he differed entirely from the course proposed. " The leading mind among the Bishops was," he said, " simply hatred to the Society as far as they knew it. . . At the meeting at Lambeth the Archbishop had surreptitiously got the Statutes out of the Master, and having obtained them the Archbishop of York announced that he should not feel himself bound to respect the confidence of the Society. The Bishops' object was to put down the

Society, which they hate and fear. They have already a great idea of its power."

Canon T. T. Carter said he "must agree with Brother Mackonochie as to the evident animus of the Bishops. They would destroy us if they could, and the principles we uphold. . . There were Bishops, he knew, who hated the way in which they were kept under by the Archbishop, and only wanted to be backed up; and our power against the Archbishop lay in those men being able to show our position. . . Now that we have gone so far, we must not withdraw from the course we have taken."

The Rev. T. Outram Marshall (Organizing Secretary o the English Church Union) said he could support Brothei Lowder's motion, if the powers of the deputation were limited. "He looked upon it as an opportunity to teach the Gospel to those who seldom hear us." This will no doubt be news to many. It was certainly impertinent on Mr. Marshall's part thus to imply that the Bishops seldom heard the Gospel, and that it was the duty of a secret Society of Father Confessors to "teach" it to them!

The Rev. Robert Eyton (now Canon of Westminster) declared that "He was glad of unburdening his mind, and stating what might have to be his course of action. There was a great tide of feeling in the country setting in towards Catholicism as the only safe ground. He hoped the Society would not by its policy at this great crisis check that tide. If it ever came to his having to choose between remaining in the Society, and ceasing to minister in the Church of England, he felt no doubt what he should do, deeply as he should regret his severance from S. S. C." It may help towards explaining Mr. Eyton's position if I mention that he at that time held a curate's license under the Bishop of London, and therefore what he meant was that rather than lose that license he would, though with deep "regret," leave the Society of the Holy Cross. As a matter of fact, he has since withdrawn from the Society, though whether his heart is still with it or not, now that he is a Residentiary Canon of Westminster, is more than I can say. Certainly, so far as I can ascertain, Canon Eyton has never *publicly* denounced the Society of the Holy Cross, and he must at one time have been anxious that his connection with it during seven years should be unknown to the general public.

The Rev. Nathaniel Dawes (now Bishop of Rockhampton, Australia) supported the motion. He said:—" Our weakness hitherto had been our 'secrecy.' He deprecated a spirit of uncourteous defiance towards the Bishops. . . . There is no need to go to the Bishops as penitents, but we must not forget our obligations to them." From this I gather that, in the opinion of Brother Dawes the Society of the Holy Cross had done nothing for which they needed to express sorrow.

One of the speakers, the Rev. Edmund Gough de Wood, Vicar of St. Clement's, Cambridge, is evidently of a subtle turn of mind. After declaring that if the Society went to the Bishops, without being first invited, it would be like "rushing into the lion's mouth," he recommended the Society to revise its Statutes. " Our Statutes," he said, " were not drawn up for the public. The Society used to be a secret Society. If now it becomes a public one it might be wise to alter them; perhaps to have certain Constitutions *for outsiders to see*, and an '*Interior* Rule' *for ourselves*." Some persons would term a proposition, such as this, thoroughly Jesuitical. Eventually the Chapter passed Brother Lowder's motion, but with the proviso that the Master should not go before the Committee of the Upper House, unless "summoned by them."

A short discussion followed on the "Resignations of Brethren." The Rev. Joseph Newton Smith (Founder of the Society of the Holy Cross) made a speech, in the course of which he displayed considerable hatred of publicity. He "thought we ought to cultivate 'the wisdom of the serpent.' He did not share the admiration some brothers had expressed for English honesty and straightforwardness. He thought our secrecy had been a protection to us, and he therefore was opposed to surrendering the Roll to the Bishops."

Before the Chapter closed protests were made by two of the brethren. The Rev. E. G. de Salis Wood said that he "wished to protest against the statement in the Address [of the Society of the Holy Cross] to Convocation, that 'the Church of England teaches that Confession is not a matter of compulsory obligation.'" The Rev. A. H. Mackonochie declared that "he agreed with Brother Wood in this sense, that for those who are in mortal sin there is no way generally of obtaining pardon, save in the Sacrament of Penance."

Two days before this Chapter was held the Rev. W. J. Knox-Little (now Canon Knox-Little) preached (on July 8th) a sermon on the subject of the *Priest in Absolution* to his own congregation at St. Alban's Church, Manchester, and subsequently he published it in pamphlet form. I refer to it here as illustrating the tactics of some leading Ritualists. The preacher had not the courage to tell his people plainly that he was himself a member of the Society of the Holy Cross, yet to save his conscience he thus referred to the matter:—

"My connection, indeed, with the Society of the Holy Cross is of the *slightest*, but my knowledge of the good and holy men who are leading members of it is intimate, and I believe, from all I *have heard* of it, that the Society of the Holy Cross is *a noble Society*, no matter what calumny may be heaped upon it."[27]

Was this a strictly accurate way for Canon Knox-Little to describe his connection with the Society of the Holy Cross? Was it right to say that his "connection" with it was "of the slightest," when he was a full member at the

---

[27] *The Priest in Absolution*, by Rev. W. J. Knox-Little, M.A., p. 26. London: Rivingtons.

very moment he was speaking? And notice the expression, "from all that I have *heard* of it"; as though he had no *personal* knowledge of its dark history and Popish Statutes! It may reasonably be asked here, If the S. S. C. "is a *noble* Society," why did Canon Knox-Little sever his connection with it the next year?

At the August, 1877, Chapter of the Society of the Holy Cross, a letter was read from the Master of the Society "to the effect that, as some of the brethren had expressed their disapproval of his action in surrendering the Statutes to the Archbishop, he thought it would be well to give an opportunity at the [September] Synod for an expression of opinion on the part of the Society as to his conduct." On the motion of the Rev. Anthony Bathe, now Vicar of Fridaythorpe, York, a resolution assuring the Master that he possessed "the full confidence of the Society" was carried unanimously. The Rev. Charles Stebbing Wallace (now Vicar of the Church of the Ascension, Lavender Hill, S.W.) brought before the Chapter the difficult circumstances in which he was placed. He said, "that the Archbishop of Canterbury had refused to license him to the Curacy of St. Barnabas', Beckenham, because he would not leave S. S. C." On the motion of the Rev. H. D. Nihill, seconded by the Rev. Anthony Bathe, a resolution was passed by the Chapter unanimously thanking Brother Wallace for his courageous conduct. At this Chapter, it may interest some to know, the late Archdeacon Denison was admitted into the Order of Probationers. The Archdeacon made no secret of his connection with the Society of the Holy Cross. In his *Notes of My Life*, he glories in the fact that he joined it because of the attack on it in 1877.

The September, 1877, Synod of the Society of the Holy Cross was looked forward to by the brethren with more than ordinary interest and anxiety. It was the first Synod of the whole Society held since Lord Redesdale's exposure of the *Priest in Absolution*. I am sorry to state that the

Sermon to the brethren, and the Master's Address to the Synod on this important occasion have not come into my possession. But I do possess the official and secret report of the Synod itself, which was held in St. Peter's Church, London Docks, on September 13th and 14th. The proceedings began each day at the early hour of 9 A.M. and lasted until 7 P.M.[28] At this Synod an effort was made by several of the brethren to nominally break up the Society, but to continue it under another name, so as to avoid the official censure of Convocation. The truly Jesuitical scheme seems to have been suddenly sprung on the Society, for Brother Mackonochie denied that the Synod had the power to discuss the question "after twenty-four hours' notice." It was said that "very many" of the brethren had received no notice of what was coming on. A series of resolutions bearing on the subject had been prepared. It was, however, soon evident that there would be a strong opposition to the proposals for disbanding the Society, and a protest was entered against the discussion of the question at that Synod. After an excited debate, it was decided that the Resolutions should be brought forward as an amendment to the first motion on the agenda paper. That motion was the result of the recent discussion in public of the *Priest in Absolution*. A desire was expressed at the Synod that the Statutes might be revised, with a view to toning down some of the expressions in the Statutes of the Society, not that anyone objected to the *doctrine* contained in those Statutes, but to the use of *terms*, such as "The Mass," and "Sacrament of Penance," &c., which had given offence to the Bishops. Accordingly, the Rev. William Henry Hutchings (now Archdeacon of Cleveland) proposed, and the Rev. Edgar Hoskins seconded, the following motion:—

"That in the opinion of this Synod it is advisable that a Committee be appointed to consider the form of the Society's Statutes, with a view to modification or otherwise."

[28] *Charles Lowder: a Biography*, p. 311. First edition.

In proposing this motion, Brother Hutchings said that:—
"It was the opinion of a well-known Oxford Professor[29] that to dissolve would be to create confusion in certain minds, and would involve some loss of self-respect; if we dissolved we acknowledged ourselves to be in the wrong, and destroyed the great instrument we had for promoting the Catholic Revival in this country. . . . To appoint a Committee to consider the form of the Statutes would be to withdraw the Statutes as they now stand, and so prevent the Bishops from considering them." This was a clever scheme, and proves to my mind that the motion of Brother Hutchings was mainly intended to "draw a red herring" across the trail of the Bishops.

The Rev. Edgar Hoskins, now Rector of St. Martin's, Ludgate Hill, London, in seconding the motion, "thought it would be very disastrous for the Society to disband. What we have to stand up for is Eucharistic Truth, and freedom of Confession in the Church of England."

The Rev. William Purton declared that, in his opinion, S. S. C. "was one of the outposts which we were bound to defend; he thought it would be cowardly to disband."

The Rev. W. J. Knox-Little (now Canon Knox-Little) "maintained that we must do what was right, and leave the result to God. Losing self-respect! A dread of what would be said! Fear of the laity! All this must be put out of the question. He was opposed to the mere withdrawal of terms;[30] that, he believed, would be inadequate to meet the difficulty. Did the Synod (he asked) believe in the certainty of a Synodical condemnation? Did we realize the force of such condemnation? It would be impossible to remain in the Society after such a condemnation. What was S. S. C. that Catholic work should be given up for it? To revise

---

[29] Who was this "well-known Oxford Professor"? I am inclined to think he was Dr. Pusey, who had evidently been consulted by the Society, for at this Synod a letter was read from him on the question of revising the Statutes.

[30] That is, to such "terms" as the "Mass," &c., in the Statutes.

the Statutes by the withdrawal of terms would not be to avert a Synodical condemnation. He would support the resolutions in favour of disbanding."

These were brave words, coming from one who soon after withdrew from the Society, without waiting for any "Synodical condemnation." I have altered the wording of his speech, in accordance with his own corrections, as given in the *October Chapter*, p. 1.

At this point, Brother E. G. de Salis Wood obtained permission to bring forward his resolutions, as an amendment to the motion of Brother Hutchings. They are somewhat lengthy, but I think it may be useful to quote them here in full, omitting only the last two clauses, as not of any importance. They reveal a plan for disbanding the Society, so far as the public knowledge of their proceedings went, while at the same time providing for its continuance under another name, by which scheme the general public would be led to suppose that it had ceased to exist altogether. The following were the resolutions (the italics are mine):—

"I. That on and after the 15th day of September, 1877, the Society of the Holy Cross be disbanded, and that all its members be and they are hereby freed from all obligations imposed by the Society in respect to its Statutes, Laws, or Rules of Life (*save and except the obligation of confidence as regards past proceedings of Synods and Chapters and of this Synod*), as well as from any formal bond of union or mutual obligations at present subsisting in virtue of Membership in the Society."

"II. (*a.*) That the Master, the Secretaries, the Treasurer, and two other Brethren chosen by them, shall be and are hereby constituted Trustees of the funds, papers, and other property of the Society, without power of disposition except as hereinafter provided.

"(*b.*) That it be and is suggested to the said Trustees, that from time to time, at their discretion, *they should invite to informal conference all whose names shall have been upon the Roll of the Society* on the 14th September, 1877, *as well as such other priests as they may choose*.[31]

---

[31] This was a plan for continuing the S. S. C. in existence under another name, together with power to add to their number. There was a great deal of subtlety in such a plan, which is more clearly developed in the next section.

"(c.) That the Trustees shall have power to transfer the property of the Society *to any other Society with similar objects and like constitution, which at any future time may be formed,* if they shall receive the sanction expressed by a vote of the majority of those present and voting at such a Conference as is provided for in the foregoing section; at least one month's notice having been given to all whose names were on the said 14th day of September on the Roll of the Society of the Holy Cross."

In moving this resolution as an amendment the Rev. E. G. Wood said that "the Society had been rushed down hill into the midst of its foes, and was now surrounded, and in danger of being cut to pieces. There was nothing for it but to 'take open order,' to skirmish as it were for a time, to pass through our enemies *and re-form in a stronger position.* In other words, he counselled disbanding the Society, *with the view of thereby escaping an Episcopal censure,* and of reconstructing the Society under the same or a similar title, at as early a date as possible. This it was well known was the opinion of at least one Bishop who was friendly towards us.[33] . . . . The course he (Mr. Wood) advocated derived great support from consideration of the policy of the Apostolic See, when the Jesuit Order was suppressed by Clement XIV.—not because it had done wrong, but simply, as the Pope emphatically asserted, for the sake of the peace of the Church. And that was the ground on which he (the speaker) urged the disbanding of the S. S. C. . . . The Society, as appeared from the list of resignations the Master had read out, was rapidly bleeding to death."

In thus comparing the Jesuits with the Society of the Holy Cross, Mr. Wood certainly used a most appropriate illustration. It is, however, a great pity that the authorities of the Church of England did not suppress the S. S. C., as Pope Clement XIV. did the Jesuit Order. Mr. Wood's amendment did not find favour with a section of the

---

[33] It would be interesting to know who the Bishop was, who thus played a double part, censuring the Society in public, and helping it on with a friendly lift in secret!

brethren in Synod, for no sooner had he concluded his speech than several of them raised the question, was the amendment in order? The Master of the Society definitely ruled that it was; but that did not satisfy the discontented brethren, who actually had the daring to challenge the Master's ruling. The Rev. H. D. Nihill moved, and the Rev. T. Outram Marshall seconded the following motion:— "That the ruling given by the Master was not correct." Of course, this was equivalent to a vote of censure, and an excited debate followed, in which Bishop Jenner took part. Eventually the Master triumphed, for only thirty-six voted for the resolution, while fifty-three voted against it. Mr. Wood's amendment was thereupon once more declared in order, and the general debate was continued.

Canon George Body (now Canon Missioner of Durham) "spoke strongly in favour of disbanding. He gave his reasons for having remained in S. S. C. under its altered circumstances. The Rule was a help to him. He desired to fight shoulder to shoulder with those who were fighting the same battle; but now he thought that the work of the Society could not be continued without great injury to the Church."

The Rev. C. D. Goldie moved another amendment to the effect that the Society should assure the Bishops that the Council would "be anxious" to "consider any recommendation which may be made by their lordships, and to coincide with any amendments which are in accordance with the teaching of the early Church, and the Formularies of our Church."

The Rev. Frederick William Puller (now head of the Cowley Fathers) supported Brother Goldie's amendment. He said that he was against disbanding, but "he admitted that it was possible that the wording of the Statutes might be improved, and he allowed the force of the arguments that they had been drafted under the idea that they would be seen only by those who would understand them."

The Rev. William H. Colbeck Luke affirmed that he "would shelve the question of disbanding for the present."

The Rev. A. H. Mackonochie declared that "for his own part (and many had expressed their agreement with him) he did not mean to be disbanded, but would hold on, with any who chose to join him, as the S. S. C., in spite of any vote for disbanding."

The Rev. T. Outram Marshall, spoke against disbanding, and then went on to make a very startling announcement. He declared that, " There were *five or six Bishops who wished us well, and who would be glad to do all in their power to prevent the Upper House of Convocation from condemning the Society.*" [33] Mr. Marshall proceeded, with an astuteness which would have done credit to the General of the Jesuits, to point out that, " They would be able to lay great stress on the fact that the *Statutes* were *under consideration ;* they [the ' five or six Bishops '] *wanted to stand by us,* and we should thus enable them to do so. f the Archbishop of Canterbury found that the Bishops were *divided,* he would probably shrink from pressing the matter ; and so this storm, like many others, would pass away."

In this Mr. Marshall was a true prophet. The Statutes *were* revised ; but rejected by the Society afterwards ; the Archbishop did not press the matter ; the storm passed away, and the Society went on its way rejoicing, mainly, I have no doubt, through the treachery of these five or six Bishops.

The Rev. Arthur Hawkins Ward, Vicar of St. Raphael, Bristol, informed the Synod that "he had come most reluctantly to the conclusion that we must, *for a time,* disband. Unless we did so the censure of the entire Episcopate would come upon us."

Archdeacon Denison spoke next. He asked, " What

---

[33] What hypocrites these " five or six Bishops " must have been! They succeeded in their underhand proceedings, for the dreaded censure of the Upper House did not take place.

advantage could there be in disbanding? We should part with some of the most precious things we possessed, and should gain nothing. He had turned towards that Society, believing that the brethren, at any rate, would stand firm. As to a Synodical condemnation, he laughed at it! On the vote of this Synod, he believed, hung the hope of the Catholic Church of England. We had heard very much about Episcopal condemnation, but such a condemnation would be based upon Protestant principles. Our attitude should be, 'You shall kill me, if you choose, but you shall not stop me.'"

After some further discussion, Brother Goldie withdrew his amendment. Brother Wood's amendment for disbanding was then put, and was lost by a great majority, only nine voting for it, and sixty-seven against it. At last Brother Hutchings's original motion, in favour of a Committee to revise the Statutes, was put to the Synod, and was carried, forty-one voting for it, and twenty against it.

On the second day of the Synod an important debate took place on the *Priest in Absolution.* The Rev. Orby Shipley (who is now a Roman Catholic) opened the discussion by moving the following very startling resolution:—

"That, in consequence of the evil effects which have ensued from the private circulation of the *Priest in Absolution*, the bad use made of its contents, and the false charges founded upon garbled quotations, it is due both to the memory of its compiler, and to the character of its owners, that the work be published in the ordinary course of trade, and this Synod hereby authorises the same."

Of course this resolution was equivalent to flinging defiance at the Bishops, and at all the opponents of that filthy book. Brother Shipley "declared, emphatically, that the book was *pure and holy.* Publicity, he held, was now the only safeguard for our personal character against the evil which had been done by its private circulation. . . He protested against the action of those brethren who had publicly condemned the book, which they admitted they had never read."

The Rev. H. D. Nihill seconded the resolution, and said that "the most miserable circumstance about the question was the condemnation of the book by those who had not read it."

The Rev. W. C. Macfarlane moved and Brother Goldie seconded as an amendment—"That all the words after 'That' be omitted, in order to insert the following 'inasmuch as the book called the *Priest in Absolution* has been withdrawn from circulation, the copies in possession of the Society be at the disposal of the Master.'"

The Rev. Joseph Newton Smith "opposed the publication of the book; he could not see how we should mend matters by increasing the opportunities of unprincipled people to sin by sowing the book broadcast."

What an acknowledgment this was, to be made by no less a person than the Founder of the Society of the Holy Cross! A more severe, though, apparently, unintentional, condemnation of the *Priest in Absolution*, could not have been passed by any Protestant Churchman. To circulate the book publicly would, in his estimation, "increase the opportunities" of committing sin in the world, and thus do the work of Satan more effectually. Those whose painful duty it has been to read its dirty pages, as I have, will quite agree with Brother Newton Smith, who does not, however, appear to have condemned the book itself. If the book would have had such an evil effect on the general public, is there not reason to fear that it may have already had an evil effect on some of the young bachelor Father Confessors who have already studied it, and who are made of the same flesh and blood as other mortals?

The Rev. W. J. Knox-Little delivered a speech on the subject, which I report as corrected by himself later on in the report of the October, 1877, Chapter of the Society. He said that "circumstances had compelled him to speak of the book in public. He had not seen the book, and therefore he acted upon the descriptions of it which he had seen and heard, by those able to speak accurately on the subject. He defended the general principle of the book, but deprecated the extracts, of which an unwarrantable use had been made. At the same time he acknowledged his disapproval of it as a work on moral theology, and he by no means repented of what he had said. With regard to the motion he argued that it would be hardly honourable to publish the book in the face of Convocation."

The Rev. A. H. Mackonochie "thought the book a most useful one for young priests, and expressed a hope that it might be circulated again at some future time." He supported the motion.

The Rev. Charles Parnell, Curate of St. Bartholomew, Brighton, "opposed the publication of the book"; and the Rev. Charles Stebbing Wallace "urged that, as men of honour, we had no right to publish the book."

The Master, in reply to a question, explained that "the amendment meant that the book should be destroyed *privately*, without casting any stigma upon the author. He maintained that, as honourable men, we could never put the book out again."

The Rev. T. Outram Marshall "opposed both the destruction and the publication of the book."

The Rev. R. Rhodes Bristow supported the amendment. "*If the book were published, it would be prosecuted,* he said, *as an obscene book.* We did not want the book. Dr. Pusey was bringing out a work on Moral Theology. He would therefore instruct the Master to deal with the book as with waste paper."

The book of Dr. Pusey, referred to by Mr. Bristow, was in reality only another adapted translation of the same book from which the *Priest in Absolution* was translated, namely, the Abbé Gaume's *Manual for Confessors.* Dr. Pusey's translation was published early in 1878.

At last the debate ended. The question was then put, "That the words proposed to be left out stand part of the question." This was carried by thirty-four to eight. The amendment was therefore lost. The original motion was then put. Twelve voted for it, and thirty-one against; and therefore it was lost.

The Society would neither publish nor destroy the book. I learn from the official report of this Synod that the Society received several messages of sympathy with the brethren for what they had suffered under the attack upon them for their connection with the *Priest in Absolution*. One message was from the "Church of England Working Men's Society"; another from the Bristol Branch of the English Church Union; and a similar one from the Penrith Branch of the Union; and two other resolutions of sympathy were received from the London Province of the Guild of St. Alban's and the Wolverhampton Branch of the same Guild. Several other branches of the English Church Union sent, later on, similar resolutions. At the October Chapter, a letter was read from the Rev. Richard Whitehead Hoare, Vicar of St. Michael's, Croydon, "enclosing a letter expressing the sympathy and goodwill which the Bishop of Grahamstown felt towards S. S. C."[31]

The action of this Synod led, eventually, to the resignation of the Master of the Society (the Rev. F. L. Bagshawe). At the October Chapter a long letter was read from him, in which he complained bitterly of the way in which he had been treated by the Society. His first thought had been, he said, to resign at once, immediately after the Synod, on the ground that his policy had been "distinctly negatived" by the Synod. "I asked leave," he wrote, "to destroy privately the copies of the *Priest in Absolution*, on the ground that we were bound in honour never to circulate that book again"; but the Synod refused to grant his request. He would not, however, resign at that time, lest it should hinder the success of the efforts being made to revise the Statutes "Negotiations of a private kind," he added, "have been already opened with several Bishops; but if these fail, either on

[31] *S.S.C. October Chapter*, 1877, p. 2.

your part or on theirs, and the work of the Committee is rendered fruitless, I have but one course open to me "—that is to ask them " to elect another Master who can carry out the policy of resistance " to the Bishops.

A letter such as this must indeed have been a bombshell in the Society, and have added greatly to the difficulties of its position. Before the Chapter concluded its sittings it passed unanimously a resolution expressing their "continued and complete confidence" in the Master, and a hope that he would not resign.

Several months passed by without anything being definitely done by the Society of the Holy Cross with regard to their Confessional book. But meanwhile the Committee appointed to revise the Statutes of the Society were hard at work. The Committee consisted of the following seventeen members, all of whom signed its report, presented to the May, 1878, Synod:—The Revs. F. Ll. Bagshawe (the Master), C. F. Lowder, John Andrews Foote, Edgar Hoskins, T. T. Carter (of Clewer), G. R. Prynne (Vicar of St. Peter's, Plymouth), Henry Edward Willington, William Henry Hutchings, L. Alison, R. Rhodes Bristow, J. W. Chadwick, Charles Bodington (now Canon of Lichfield), R. J. Wilson, Charles D. Goldie, Frederick William Puller, R. H. Parry, and George Body. At the April, 1878, Chapter of the Society, it was announced that the Committee of Revision had " communicated the Report (*without any signature of Members attached*)[35] to the following Bishops— London, Winchester, Oxford, Ely, Lichfield, Peterborough, Exeter, and Chichester, *but that no copies of the Report have been supplied to the two Archbishops.*" [36] This significant omission of the Archbishops, shows that the Committee were either afraid of their knowing too much of their proceedings, or was an intentional insult to their Graces. Perhaps it was both.

[35] This shows how afraid they were to be known to the Bishops. Their Report, as presented to the May, 1878, Synod, does contain all the names of the Members of the Committee mentioned above.

[36] *S. S. C. April Chapter*, 1878, p. 3. For a complete list of the Members of this secret Society up to the year 1897, *see Church Association Tract*, No. 244, price one penny.

And why, it may be asked, was not the Report sent to *all* the Bishops of the southern and northern provinces? Those in the north were left out altogether, while only eight Bishops in the southern province, out of twenty-two, received a copy of the document. I can only account for the omission by the dread of publicity and the light of day, which has ever characterised the owl-like proceedings of the Society of the Holy Cross.

When the May, 1878, Synod of the S.S.C. met, the Master's address was entirely taken up with the recent attack on the Society, and the revision of its Statutes. He mentioned that in 1877, the Society numbered exactly three hundred members, but that during the past year their had been no fewer than 122 resignations. He found, however, one consolation in the fact that the Society had "been honoured by the addition to its ranks of one of the most distinguished members of the Church of England, the Ven. Archdeacon Denison."[37] It is evident that the Master had a higher personal sense of honourable conduct than the Society as a whole possessed. He said, in the course of his address:—

"I pass on to another question that will be brought before you, simply because it involves what is personal to me. At a Special Chapter of the Society last year a printed letter was drawn up and sent to the Bishops, in which it was promised that the *Priest in Absolution* should not be circulated. The language was somewhat ambiguous. I thought I understood it, and assured the Archbishop and others that the book was absolutely and for ever withdrawn. Last September Synod I discovered that some brethren looked forward to its *re-circulation* at some future time. Hitherto the book has been in my care—now it will cease to be so. If the Society resolves to preserve the book it must be with a motive, and how that motive can be reconciled with my personal representation to the Bishops will be a difficult question for my own after-consideration."[38]

The sermon to the brethren at this Synod was preached

[37] *S.S.C. Master's Address*, May Synod, 1878, p. 7.
[38] *Ibid.*, pp. 5, 6.

by the Rev. Canon Carter, of Clewer, but as I do not possess a copy I am unable to quote it here. The *Report of Committee appointed to consider the form of the Society's Statutes*, I fortunately possess. The suggested alterations were twenty-six in number, and mainly consisted of the omission of the words " Mass," " Sacrament of Penance," and " Sacramental Confession" from the Statutes and Office Books of the Society. The report shows that four members of the Committee, not included in the list given above, refused to sign the report. The Rev. John Comber, Rector of St. Margaret's, Aberdeen, it is stated, was " opposed to such suggested alterations as would involve the removal of the terms ' Mass ' and ' Sacrament of Penance ' from the Statutes and Rules of the Society.' The Revs. A. H. Mackonochie, H. D. Nihill, and J. W. Biscoe, were " opposed to *all* the alterations suggested."[39]

Now, although this Committee were quite willing to delete the *terms* " Mass " and " Sacrament of Penance " from the documents of the Society, it is quite clear from their report that they saw no harm in them, and therefore they retained the *things* represented by these *terms*, while rejecting the *names* for politic reasons. As to the term " Mass," they declared that it "can be most legitimately used by English Churchmen at the present day, so only that scandal to the ignorant be avoided."[40] They also justified the use of the term " Sacramental Confession ";[41] and, as to the other expression they affirm that " the members of S. S. C. were in no way going beyond what the Church of England permits, when they spoke in their Statutes of the ' Sacrament of Penance,' that sacred rite which seals and completes the work of penitence for post-baptismal deadly sin."[42] It is, therefore, quite certain that this precious Report in reality withdrew nothing but empty names, and was primarily intended for the purpose of throwing more dust in the eyes

[39] *Report of Committee,* p. 16. [40] *Ibid.,* p. 5.
[41] *Ibid.,* p. 11. [42] *Ibid.,* p. 11.

of the Bishops. It was worthy of a conclave of Jesuits rather than of a committee of clergymen within the Reformed Church of England.

At the commencement of the Synod letters were read from Archdeacon Denison, and the Revs. Robert Herbert Godwin (of St. Cyprian's Theological College, Bloemfontein), G. P. Grantham, and William Webster (subsequently Dean of Aberdeen) "deprecating the suggested changes in the Statutes," and from the Revs. George Croke Robinson and Arthur Gordon Stallard ("suggesting amendments to certain of the proposed changes"); and from Charles John Corfe (now Bishop of Corea), who "advocated the suggested changes."

The Master rose to propose the following motion:— "That the Report of the Committee appointed to consider the Society's Statutes be received and adopted"; and was about to speak to it, when the Rev. T. Outram Marshall rose and declared that, in *his* opinion the motion was out of order. Of course this raised a discussion at once. The Master ruled that his own motion was "strictly in order"; but this did not satisfy the rebellious Organizing Secretary of the English Church Union (Mr. Marshall), who at once moved "That the ruling given by the Master is not correct." He found a seconder in the Rev. Lyndhurst Burton Towne, but the Master refused to put the rebel motion to the Synod, whereupon the discontented brethren had to "eat humble pie," and sit down.

The Master then delivered the speech he had prepared in support of his own motion.

The Rev. R. Rhodes Bristow seconded the Master's motion, and announced that "The Committee, while convinced that the Statutes contained nothing but sound doctrine, had sought the peace and unity of the Society by suggesting the changes in our terminology. . . Some might say that we were drawing back, but it was in order that we might strike a harder blow."

The Rev. A. H. Mackonochie complained of one of the

brethren, whose name does not appear to have been mentioned. "He asserted that the Society had been betrayed by one brother, who left the Society as soon as he got it into difficulties."

The Rev. John Edwards (now the Rev. J. Baghot De La Bere, Vicar of St. Mary, Buxted) "advocated the use of the terminology in the Statutes. The term 'Sacrament of Penance,' he maintained, was not only theologically correct, but expressed the intercourse which existed between a priest and a penitent."

The Rev. John William Kempe said that "to speak only of the one word 'Mass,' eternity alone will tell how grievously sacramental and supernatural life in England has suffered from the disuse of this venerable term." He moved as an amendment that the Synod, while thanking the Committee for their labours, "declines to admit any of their recommendations."

The Rev. Charles Bodington pointed out that "neither our teaching nor our practice would be altered by the adoption of the suggested changes of terminology."

Bishop Jenner, "as the only Episcopal brother present, appealed to the Synod for conciliation."

When the voting took place, fifty-one voted for the Master's motion, and fifty-eight against it. The motion was therefore declared lost. The Society refused to adopt the revised Statutes, and consequently reverted to the old Statutes. The amendment of Brother J. W. Kempe was then put, and was carried, fifty-seven voting for it, and fifty-one against. It is evident from the voting that the Society of the Holy Cross was very closely divided on the subject of revision.

On the second day of the Synod a very important protest was read by Brother Mackonochie. It was as follows:—

"We, the undersigned Brethren and Probationers of the Society of the Holy Cross, being, as members of that Society, part proprietors of a certain property consisting of a number of copies of the *Priest in Absolution,* do hereby refuse and withhold our consent to the destruction of that property; and we do hereby protest against any discussion upon the question of destroying that property in this Synod, on the ground that such destruction, without the consent of us as part proprietors, would be an illegal act."

This protest was signed by Archdeacon Denison, the Revs. John Edwards (now Baghot De La Bere), A. H. Mackonochie, Arthur Henry Stanton, H. D. Nihill, Charles Parnell, John Comper, Thomas Isaac Ball, William Moore Richardson (now Bishop of Zanzibar), John Barnes Johnson (Vicar of St. Mary, Edmonton), James Hipwell, Edward Heath, George Musgrave Custance (Rector of Colwall, Malvern), — Collins, Cecil Wray, and William Crouch (Vicar of Gamlingay).

The friends of the *Priest in Absolution* were determined, if possible, to stop discussion. They objected to the following motion being put to the Synod, but which had appeared on the Agenda paper:—

"That, inasmuch as the book called the *Priest in Absolution* had been withdrawn from circulation, the copies remaining in the Master's hands be destroyed."

So, before this resolution was brought forward, Brother Mackonochie moved "That the resolution on the Agenda paper is not in order."

This last motion was immediately put to the vote, and lost, sixteen voting for it, and twenty-three against.

Brother Macfarlane then moved the motion which had been placed on the Agenda paper; but he was careful to explain that "the book itself needed no commendation; the motion was quite irrespective of the merits of the book. A pledge had been given to the Bishops, and we were bound to redeem it."

The Rev. William Crouch, however, was of a different mind. He boldly declared that "to redeem the pledge to the Bishops would be to break the Eighth Commandment."

The Rev. Frederick William Puller "thought that this

was hardly the occasion for destroying it, but he thought at some future time we might destroy it as lumber."

The Rev. C. D. Goldie said that "we needed such a book as the *Priest in Absolution*.

The Rev. William John Frere (Principal of Hockering Training College, Bishops Stortford) "quoted Brother Bodington's opinion as to the value of the book. He thought that we might put forth another book on Confession, and remarked that Dr. Pusey's work does not touch upon the Seventh Commandment."

The Rev. Robert Eyton (now Canon of Westminster) "said that we were not called upon to give up our private copies of the book." He would support the motion.

The Rev. H. D. Nihill informed the Synod that "he burnt all *bad* literature; he was not ashamed of the *Priest in Absolution*."

Brother Macfarlane's motion was put to the Synod, and lost by a very large majority, forty-nine voting against it, and only eleven for it. After a great deal of discussion the following amendment was passed as a substantive motion, by thirty-four to eight:—

"That this Synod is not in favour of the destruction of the remaining copies of the *Priest in Absolution* at the present time."

What the Society of the Holy Cross has done, in its corporate capacity, with reference to the *Priest in Absolution*, since the Synod whose secret proceedings I have just described, is more than I can say, but I have reason to believe that it still retains possession of the book. So careful have the members of the S. S. C. been to keep their underground proceedings from the knowledge of the general public, that it was not until eighteen years had passed by, after the celebrated exposure of 1877, that any Protestant Churchman was able to see a single secret document of the Society connected with that important event in its history. I have reported the Society's secret proceedings, and the speeches delivered at its meetings, at considerable length, for what I believe to be sufficient reasons. There is no other way in which the general public can be made acquainted with what is going on underneath the surface. Secrecy cannot be defeated except by publicity. And it is important that the public shall know that many of the men whose secret utterances I have here reported, have since been promoted to high positions in the Church, possibly because their real sentiments were unknown to those in whose hands the higher patronage of the Church has been placed. I have no doubt they will be very much annoyed at being thus shown in their true colours, nor is there any doubt that they will bitterly denounce me for dragging their secret speeches out into the light of day. But it cannot be helped. Certainly the Society of the Holy Cross, as a Society—whatever may be said in favour of individuals—does not come out with much credit to itself. Its underhand dodgery and Jesuitical tactics deserve the contempt of all men who love straightforward dealing. Its filthy Confessional book has never been condemned by the Society as a whole, though a few of its members have written and spoken against it. On the contrary, the Society seems to glory in what many will consider its shame. Individual members of the Society found themselves, in the latter part of 1877, in many instances subject to a great deal of unpleasant criticism from their Protestant parishioners. Some of them put a bold face on the matter, while others published apologies for their conduct. As a rule, these were so worded as to commend the Society of the Holy Cross, instead of condemning it, and at the same time to represent themselves as the victims of unmerited censure. One of the most remarkable of these apologies was that issued by the Rev. John Erskine Binney, at that time Vicar of Summerstown, near Oxford. His parish was, immediately after Lord Redesdale's exposure, placarded with an address to the people, in which it was mentioned that the Vicar was a member of the Society of the Holy Cross. Mr. Binney did not, in his reply to the placard, deny the charge, nor did he in any way censure the *Priest in Absolution;* but he declared that he had "too much confidence" in the "good sense" of his people to suppose that the placard would "in any way affect" their "mutual relations as Pastor and Flock."

"The chief intent of the placard," he continued, "seems to be to reflect on a certain book called the *Priest in Absolution,* and it chooses to assume that this work is the text-book of the Clergy whose names are mentioned, in some of their most important ministerial relations with their parishioners. Now it may be well for me to say most distinctly that, though I glory in being a member of the Society of the Holy Cross, because I know that in its twenty-five [sic] years of existence it has done more, under God, to raise the personal tone of the parochial Clergy than any other institution, yet that I do not know the work in question, nor do I wish to know it."

This document was dated June 22nd, 1877, and although at that time Mr. Binney gloried in being a member of the Society of the Holy Cross, yet when the next secret list of its members appeared *his* name was withdrawn.

I believe that all loyal members of the Church of England will endorse the opinion of the late Dr. Harvey Goodwin, Bishop of Carlisle, who, writing to a member of the Society of the Holy Cross, on December 29th, 1877, emphatically declared that, "It [S. S. C.] has created a scandal in the Church of almost unparalled magnitude, and it seems to me that the only right course for wise and loyal Churchmen is to wash their hands of it."[43]

[43] *S. S. C. Copy of Correspondence,* p. 2.

CHAPTER V.

THE ORDER OF CORPORATE REUNION.

Origin of Order of Corporate Reunion shrouded in mystery—Its first "Pastoral"—It professes "loyalty" to the Pope—Prays for the Pope in its secret Synod—Its Bishops secretly consecrated by foreign Bishops—Who were they?—"Bishop" Lee and "Bishop" Mossman—"Bishop" Mossman professes belief in the Pope's Infallibility—Birth of the Order rejoices the Romanists—Its proceedings discussed by the Society of the Holy Cross—Some secret documents—Eight hundred Church of England clergy secretly ordained by a Bishop of the Order.

THE Order of Corporate Reunion is even more secret and mysterious than the Society of the Holy Cross, and what is more serious, it is more unblushingly Popish, going to the length of acknowledging the Pope as the lawful Head of the whole visible Church on earth. It does not, however, advocate individual secession to Rome, but acts on the lines which the late Rev. Dr. Littledale laid down for the Ritualists many years since. That gentleman, in a lecture on "Secession to Rome," which he delivered at Ipswich and Norwich, referring to those who had already seceded to Rome, remarked:—

"They go (over to Rome) to get something which they cannot get, do not get, or what often comes to the same thing, think they cannot get, in the English Church. When once they have got this notion fairly into their heads, all the No-Popery tracts and lectures in England will not keep them back. *The real cure is to give them here what they are going to look for;* and if they get *all* they want from us, you may be very sure few of them will take the trouble to go further. *Now, this is what the Tractarians,* as they are called, *are trying to do,* and it is for this that they are so heartily abused every day of their lives by persons who do not understand what they want."[1]

Dr. Littledale contented himself with supplying the rank and file of the Ritualists, in the Church of England, with the Romish doctrines and ritual for which they craved. It is true that he wrote a well-known book, entitled *Plain Reasons Against Joining the Church of Rome*, but in that work he did not bring forward what he evidently considered the strongest argument to prevent people going over to Rome. He supplied *that* argument in the lecture just cited, and acted upon it in his *Priest's Prayer Book*, of which he was joint editor with the Rev. J. E. Vaux. In that book will be found a large collection of the most superstitious of Romish practices, together with most of the peculiar doctrines of the Church of Rome. But the Order of Corporate Reunion goes further than Dr. Littledale. It professes to supply not only Popish doctrines, but also Orders and Sacraments such as even the Church of Rome must admit to be valid, though she refuses to acknowledge those of the Church of England. It has Bishops secretly consecrated, and these are prepared to give conditional re-ordination to such of the clergy of the Church of England as may choose to submit to the process. It admits the laity of both sexes to its ranks, and these are, as a general rule—with possibly a few exceptions—conditionally re-baptized when they join the Order. These laymen and women being in the secret, no doubt know where to go to in order to receive valid Sacraments. It is stated that no one is admitted to the Order but *bonâ-fide* members of the Church of England. As a matter of fact several of its officials have seceded to Rome.

The actual origin of the Order of Corporate Reunion is shrouded in mystery. Its rulers made known to the public the existence of the Order during the summer of 1877, but it appears to have been organized, more or less

[1] *Defence of Church Principles*, "Secessions to Rome," by the Rev. Dr. R. F. Littledale, p. 4.

imperfectly, about a year before that date, and even at that early period to have been known to a trusted few on the Continent, as well as at home.[2] It held a secret Synod, in London, on July 2nd, 1877, at which a "Pastoral" of the Rulers was approved, which had been previously drawn up. A copy of this document was subsequently written out, and taken abroad, where it was attested by a foreign Roman Catholic Notary, named "Adrian De Helte," to be a true copy, and as such signed by him on August 15th. The Pastoral was formally promulgated by being read on September 8th, in the presence of witnesses whose names have not been made public, on the steps at the west end of St. Paul's Cathedral, and in other places throughout the land.[3] This Pastoral was also printed in the *Reunion Magazine*, an official periodical issued by the Order, but which was withdrawn from circulation about a year after its commencement. It is too lengthy a document to reprint here in full, and therefore I must confine myself to a few extracts. It commences thus:—

"In the Sacred Name of the Most Holy Undivided and Adorable Trinity, Father, Son, and Holy Ghost. Amen.

"*Thomas*, by the favour of God, Rector of the Order of Corporate Reunion, and Pro-Provincial of Canterbury; *Joseph*, by the favour of God, Provincial of York, in the Kingdom of England; and *Laurence*, by the favour of God, Provincial of Caerleon, in the Principality of Wales, with the Provosts and Members of the Synod of the Order, to the Faithful in Christ Jesus, whom these Presents may concern; Health and Benediction in the Lord God everlasting."

The Pastoral proceeds to deplore "the evil state into which the National Church of England has been brought by departure from ancient principles and by recent events"; and it positively asserts, as "certain" that "all semblance of independent existence and corporate action has departed from the Established Church." A brief history of the Church of England to the present day is then given, in the

[2] *Reunion Magazine*, p. 11.   [3] *Ibid.*, p. 11.

course of which it is affirmed that the Act of Submission of the Clergy, in the reign of Henry VIII., "is the root of all our existing evils and miseries." The reign of Edward VI., the Protestant King, is described as "a period of wild confusion," while that of the Romanist, Queen Mary, is referred to as one "of Catholic reaction." The glorious Revolution of 1688 comes in for a measure of abuse, and it is declared that after "the riot, blasphemy, and general wickedness of the Great Rebellion, the Revolution of 1688 was the beginning of yet more serious trouble for the Established Church." Coming down to our own day, it affirmed that "every vestige of distinct corporate entity has utterly disappeared from the Church." Against these and a host of other real or imaginary evils the Order of Corporate Reunion raises its protesting voice. It protests, in particular, "against the disuse of Chrism in Confirmation, and the inadequate form for the administration of that Sacrament now in use within the Church of England; as well as against the total abolition of the Apostolic practice of Anointing the Sick with Oil—by which every baptized person is curtailed in his spiritual privileges, and robbed at the hour of death of an important part of his rightful heritage. Many persons," continues the Pastoral, "have lamented the loss of this last-named Sacrament: We, by the favour of God, are now enabled to restore it."

Next, the Pastoral grumbles at the School Boards, and the existing relations of Church and State; and at last announces the remedy which the Order has provided for all the "evils" which trouble their minds. "We affirm," they triumphantly declare, "that in the Providence of God, the evil itself has opened the door to a remedy. For the Bishops of the Church of England, having yielded up all canonical authority and jurisdiction in the spiritual order, can neither interfere with, nor restrain, Us in Our work of *recovering from elsewhere* that which has been forfeited or lost—*securing three distinct and independent lines of a new Episcopal Succession,* so as to labour corporately, and on no sandy foundation, for the healing of the breach which has been made."

Here is their grand remedy for everything. The Orders and Sacraments conferred in the Church of England are, in their opinion, open to grave and serious doubt; but now, "three distinct lines of a new Episcopal succession," have been secured by the Bishops of the Order of Corporate Reunion—though they carefully abstain from mentioning their source, or by whom they were conferred—who are thus able to remedy all defects in the Church of England, in the hope of eventually securing that Corporate Reunion with the rest of Christendom, which it is their "chief aim" to secure. Of course they think it necessary to make known the doctrinal basis on which the new Order is built.

"In thus associating ourselves together," says the Pastoral, "we solemnly take as the basis of this Our Order the Catholic Faith as defined by the Seven General Councils, acknowledged as such by the whole Church of the East and the West before the great and deplorable schism, and as commonly received in the Apostles' Creed, and the Creed of Nicaea, and the Creed of St. Athanasius. To all the sublime doctrines so laid down, We declare our unreserved adhesion, as well as to the principles of Church constitution and discipline, set forth and approved by the said Seven General Councils. Furthermore, until the whole Church shall speak on the subject, *We accept all those dogmatic statements set forth in common by the Council of Trent* and the Synod of Bethlehem respectively, with regard to the doctrine of the Sacraments...

"Thanking Almighty God most humbly for the restoration of Brotherhoods, Sisterhoods, and Guilds, We solemnly affirm that the Monastic Life, duly regulated according to the laws of the Catholic Church, is a most salutary institution, in perfect harmony with the spirit of the Gospel; and is full of profit to those who, being carefully tried and examined, make full proof of their calling thereto. Our services will always be at the disposal of such—upon whom We invoke the Divine blessing."[4]

The thought which naturally suggests itself to a loyal Churchman on reading this Pastoral for the first time, is

[4] *Reunion Magazine*, pp. 88-98.

one of astonishment, that men who thus doubt the validity of the Orders and Sacraments of the Church of England, should, notwithstanding, continue to act as her Ministers, or in any way remain within her communion as members of such a Church. How they reconcile their conduct with their Ordination vows is a puzzle hard, indeed, to unravel, except on a theory very little to their credit. When it becomes lawful to do evil that good may come, then, and not till then, can their conduct be justified. The real object of such a policy is, of course, to bring not only themselves, but the whole Church of England with them, back to the Pope—and this is what they mean by "*Corporate* Reunion," as distinguished from *individual* secession. The same policy was set forth as far back as 1867, in the columns of the *Union Review*, by a Ritualist, in the form of a letter to a foreign Roman Catholic.

"With such a position," wrote the Ritualist, "it is surely, I say, much better for us to remain working where we are—for what would become of England if we were to leave her Church? She would be simply lost to Catholicism, and won to Rationalism. . . . Depend upon it, it is only through the English Church itself that England can be Catholicised; . . . and so long as the Church of England remains what she is, to join you [Rome] in any but a corporate capacity would be, in our view, to sin against the truth." [5]

The utter disloyalty of this secret Order of Corporate Reunion to the Church of England, and its real loyalty to the Pope of Rome, is more clearly revealed to us by a glimpse at its first Synod, afforded to us by no less a person than a high official in the Order itself, viz., " Laurentius, O.C.R., Provincial of Caerleon." This official states that :—

" It is quite true that we [O. C. R.] do not assume an attitude of independence towards the Holy See. We frankly acknowledge that, in the Providence of God, *the Roman Pontiff is the first Bishop in the Church*, and, therefore, ITS VISIBLE HEAD ON EARTH. We do not

---

[5] *Union Review*, Volume for 1867, p. 410.

believe that either the Emperor of Russia or the Queen of England is the head of the Church. As the Church must have some executive head, and as there is no other competitor, *we believe the Pope to be that head.* But he is more to us than this, for he is our Patriarch as well. *So that we admit his claim to the veneration and* LOYALTY *of all baptized men,* and in a special degree of all Western Christians, and in these capacities we prayed for him in our Constituent Synod."[6]

Probably the authorities of the Order of Corporate Reunion think they can best show their "loyalty" to the Pope by acting a double part. Ordinary people, however, will think that they are traitors in the camp, and that the sooner they are drummed out of it the better.

There has been a good deal of conjecture as to the identity of the men whose names appear at the head of the Pastoral. Who are "Thomas," Pro-Provincial of Canterbury; "Joseph," Provincial of York; and "Laurence," Provincial of Caerleon? We can only answer this question from indirect sources of information. The first guess at their identity appears to have been made by the Rev. W. Allen Whitworth, a Ritualistic clergyman opposed to the Order, who, in a long letter to the *Church Review,* December 28th, 1878, affirmed that the Rev. F. G. Lee, Vicar of All Saints', Lambeth, was one of the three Bishops of the Order of Corporate Reunion; and he distinctly terms him "Bishop F. G. Lee"; and he refers to "the Roman, Greek, and Armenian Bishops who joined together, secretly to consecrate Dr. F. G. Lee and his colleagues."[7] A lay official of the Order of Corporate Reunion, a Mr. William Grant, who is referred to in the *Reunion Magazine* as "Registrar" of the Order, published in pamphlet form a reply to Mr. Whitworth's attack.[8] Mr. Grant denies many of Mr. Whitworth's assertions, but he does *not* deny that Dr. Lee was a Bishop

---

[6] *Reunion Magazine,* p. 242.
[7] *Church Review,* December 28th, 1878, p. 623.
[8] *Is the Order of Corporate Reunion Schismatical?* by William Grant. London: D. Nutt.

of the O. C. R., or that he and his colleagues were secretly consecrated Bishops by three "Roman, Greek, and Armenian Bishops." There can be no doubt that he would have denied these statements also had they been false, and as "Registrar" of the Order he must have been fully acquainted with the facts of the case. The next attempt to identify the three mysterious Bishops of the O. C. R. was made by the *Whitehall Review*, early in 1879. That paper published the following paragraph:—

"The three Anglican clerics who have obtained Episcopal consecration from the Dutch Jansenists, for the purpose of 'revalidating' the Orders of clergymen having doubts about their priesthood, are singularly modest in their signatures. The 'Rector Provincial, Canterbury' is '✠ Thomas,' the 'Provincial of Caerleon' is '✠ Laurence,' the 'Provincial of York' is '✠ Joseph.' Might I suggest that 'Thomas' sign for the future, '✠ Frederick George Lee'; Bishop 'Laurence,' '✠ Joseph Leycester Lyne'; and Bishop 'Joseph,' '✠ Thomas W. Mossman'! Perhaps Bishop 'Laurence' might prefer to call himself '✠ Ignatius'; if so, one would not object, as it would give a better idea of his real name." [9]

It is not a little remarkable that the *Whitehall Review* was certainly correct in at least two out of the three names which it identified, and, for anything I know to the contrary, may have been right as to the whole three of them. Dr. Lee, and the Rev. Thomas W. Mossman (now dead), for many years Rector of West Torrington, Lincolnshire, were certainly Bishops of the O. C. R., and I have never heard that the Rev. Joseph L. Lyne, *alias* "Father Ignatius," has denied the accusation of the *Whitehall Review*, though I have serious doubts as to his identity.

Seven years after the foundation of the Order, the *Birmingham Daily Gazette*, in a leading article, remarked:— "Strange as it may seem, Dr. Lee and certain other clergy of the 'Establishment' are said to have been consecrated as Bishops by some mysterious triumvirate of an Eastern, a

[9] Quoted in *Church Times*, March 14th, 1879. p. 163.

Latin, and an Anglican prelate, no one knows when, where, or by whom. It is certain that Dr. Lee has been challenged over and over again to say explicitly what is the fact, and has never done so. It is said that there is no doubt that he does exercise Episcopal functions, and has been seen in Episcopal vestures, of course of a more mediæval pattern than the 'Magpie' attire familiar to the House of Lords. It is said also to be beyond doubt that individuals have been re-baptized, re-confirmed, if not ordained by him or his supposed colleagues."[10]

The Rev. A. Jerome Matthews, a Roman Catholic priest, wrote to the *Trowbridge Chronicle*, of October 16th, 1886, a letter, in which he asserted that Dr. Lee was reputed to be " one of three Anglican clergymen who went in a vessel for a sea voyage in company with three foreign schismatical but real Bishops. That when in mid-ocean, the three clergymen were conditionally baptized, ordained Deacons and Priests, and then consecrated Bishops. That they went to mid-ocean to be in nobody's diocese, and that Dr. Lee does not deny the allegation."[11] In the same paper, in its issue for November 29th, 1886, another Roman Catholic priest, the Rev. W. F. Trailies, wrote that " the Order of Corporate Reunion is under Dr. Lee, who is undoubtedly a Bishop, which is more than can be said by anybody of his neighbour at Lambeth Palace."[12]

So much for Dr. Lee. As to the Rev. Thomas W. Mossman, that gentleman publicly acknowledged that he possessed Episcopal Orders, in a letter to the *English Churchman* :—

" I believe," he wrote, " that the Bishops of England ought to be elected by the Christian people of England, and that the election ought to be approved and confirmed by the Pope, as the *visible head of God's Catholic Church here on earth*. . . . *All I have ever claimed*

---

[10] Quoted in the *English Churchman*, January 1st, 1885, p. 10.
[11] Quoted in Brinckman's *Controversial Methods of Romanism*, p. xvi.
[12] *Ibid.*, p. xvi.

for myself is to be in what are termed Episcopal Orders, and even that not publicly." [13]

The advanced views held by these two "Bishops" concerning the Pope and Papal Infallibility, will no doubt surprise many of my readers. Dr. Lee has published a little volume of sermons, entitled *Order Out of Chaos,* from which I quote the following passage:—

"The government of the Catholic Church by Bishops, Primates, Metropolitans, and Patriarchs, *with One Visible Head,* is so exactly of that practical nature, that no wholly independent and isolated religious body can possibly partake either in its government or in the blessing of being rightly governed, so long as it remains independent.... The Visible Head of that One Christian Family, as Christendom has universally allowed, is the Bishop of the See of St. Peter. Unlike all other Bishops, he has no superior either in rank or jurisdiction. Now, when any part of a family, by misunderstanding and perverseness, becomes disobedient to, or out of harmony with, its Visible Head, weakness and confusion, as regards its oneness, are certain to supervene." [14]

In this book "Bishop" Lee reprints a letter, which he had addressed to the *Guardian,* in which he declares:—

"As I am personally challenged on this point, I hold, *and have always held* (mere rough contradictions have no effect on me) that *the Pope is the Archbishop's* [of Canterbury] *direct spiritual superior both in rank and authority.*" [15]

He even expresses approval of the modern doctrine of the Immaculate Conception of the Virgin, which was not made an article of faith in the Church of Rome until December 8th, 1854. "It seems to many," Dr. Lee writes, "that the doctrine of the Immaculate Conception of our Blessed Lady is but the due and reasonable complement of the *Theotokos* of Ephesus.[16]

Since he wrote these last words, Dr. Lee has written a

---

[13] *English Churchman,* March 5th, 1885, p. 110.
[14] *Order Out of Chaos,* by Frederick George Lee, D.D., pp. 60-62. London, 1881.
[15] *Ibid.,* p. 50.   [16] *Ibid.,* p. 6.

large volume to prove that the Immaculate Conception, as defined by Pius IX., ought to be believed by all Christians.

"Bishop" Mossman professed faith in the Pope's personal Infallibility, as defined by the Vatican Council of 1870, and yet remained nominally in communion with the Church of England until his death, in 1885, when he was received into the Church of Rome by Cardinal Manning. Writing to the *Church Review*, in 1881, Mr. Mossman remarked :—

"I used to be as opposed to the doctrine of Papal Infallibility as it was possible for anyone to be. Deeper reflection has, however, convinced me that there is really nothing in it to which exception need be taken. Granting an administrative Head of the whole Catholic Church, granting a Primate of Christendom, by the same right even that the Archbishops of Canterbury profess to be Primates of the English Church—namely, 'by Divine Providence,' it is surely only reasonable to believe that, if this Head of the Universal Church were to teach *ex-cathedrâ*, or authoritatively, anything pertaining to faith or morals, to the whole flock of God, of which he is the Chief Shepherd upon earth, he would most surely be guided by the Holy Ghost in such a way as not to teach Satan's lie instead of the truth of God. This is the way in which I should feel disposed to understand the Vatican Decree. And so far from seeing anything inconsistent with reason, or history, or Holy Scripture, or the Catholic Faith, in that Decree, thus understood, it appears to me that natural piety itself, and a belief in God's providential guidance of His Church, would lead us to accept it."[17]

The birth of the Order of Corporate Reunion was hailed with delight by the Romanists of England and the continent. This, of course, was quite natural. They knew very well who would get the benefit of the labours of the O. C. R., and they were quite willing to encourage its growth, and to wait patiently for the harvest time to come. About two years after its birth a correspondent of the *Church Times* declared that Roman Catholics at home and abroad only ridiculed the Order of Corporate Reunion. Thereupon Mr. William Grant, who signed himself as "Registrar, O. C. R.," wrote to that paper :—

[17] *Church Review*, November 3rd, 1882, p. 531.

"In reply to one paragraph in the letter printed in your last issue from ' H. A. B.,' will you permit me to say that my own experience is diametrically opposed to that of your correspondent. In the place of 'ridicule' I have found respectful interest and good wishes. Personally, I have received, at the very least, over fifty letters of inquiry and 'Godspeed' from eminent Roman Catholic priests and members of Religious Orders, and well-known Roman Catholic laymen. I was lately shown a letter addressed by his Eminence Cardinal Manning to an Anglican layman, who had requested the Cardinal's opinion of the O. C. R., in which his Eminence, whilst insisting on the fact that individual secession was the rule of his Church in England, utterly refused to condemn the aims and objects of the O. C. R., stating that every organization which tended to a restoration of unity was to be respected." [18]

The *Civilita Cattolica*, the organ of the Jesuits, and published at Rome, in its issue for April 20th, 1878, printed a letter from its English correspondent on the O. C. R.

"The Order of Corporate Reunion," he writes, "actively pursues its labours, and its officers have sent forth a Pastoral Letter containing an exposition of its views and ends. It is known that several Anglican ministers in connection with this Society have induced a Greek Bishop—whose name, however, it has not as yet been possible to ascertain—to ordain them under certain conditions, in order that the doubt to which Anglican Orders are subject may not be alleged as a reason for taking exception to the validity of their operations. The three leading officers of the Order have received Episcopal consecration from the same quarter—a quarter which, according to what is said, is of such a character as to completely exclude any question as to the validity of the Orders so conferred, when once the time shall come for submitting the matter for examination to the Holy See. So soon as a sufficient number of the Anglican clergy shall have in this way removed the difficulty which arises from their ordination, the Order hopes to be able to present its petition for Corporate Reunion with the Catholic Church, signed by a number of members so imposing as to render it impossible for the Holy See not to recognise the gravity and importance of the movement." [19]

The schemes of the Order of Corporate Reunion did not

---

[18] *Church Times*, August 22nd, 1879, p. 528.
[19] Quoted in *Church Association Monthly Intelligencer*, Volume for 1878, p. 238.

receive the approval of the great majority of the Ritualistic party. It is ever the fate of the pioneers of ecclesiastical movements to receive a good deal of censure from the rank and file far away behind them. Yet it is generally found that where the pioneers of a religious movement stand at any particular year, the rank and file will be found standing a quarter of a century later on. Such has been the rule with the Ritualistic Movement since its birth in 1833. The Order of Corporate Reunion is at present the pioneer of the Ritualistic Movement, being much nearer to Rome than any of its predecessors. It has consequently come in for a great deal of criticism from the rank and file of the Ritualistic party. Even the secret Society of the Holy Cross has taken up arms against the Order of Corporate Reunion. At the monthly Chapters of the former of these Societies during the close of 1878, and in the early portion of 1879, and also at its September Synod, 1878, the action of the O. C. R. was again and again discussed by the brethren in their secret gatherings. The S. S. C. even appointed a Special Committee to examine the whole question, "Bishop" Thomas W. Mossman was at that time a member of the S. S. C., and in its secret conclaves fought valiantly for the Order of which he was a "Bishop." The "Bishop" even presented a "Report" of his own on the subject to the Society of the Holy Cross, some time during the year 1878, the most remarkable passage in which is the following :—

"The O. C. R. admits none but those who accept the whole Catholic Faith; and its work is to gather them together, and form them into one great spiritual Order : and then, when the time appointed comes, as most surely in God's Providence it will come, whoever lives to see it, we shall go with our thousands of faithful clergy and laity, and we shall say to the Patriarchs of the East and West, ' We all hold the Catholic Faith in its fulness and integrity, can you refuse to admit us to intercommunion?' *I have the best possible ground for believing that*, whatever might be the action of the other Patriarchs, *the Patriarch of the West* [the Pope] *would not look coldly on our plea,* and would not only grant it, but would give besides every concession that could in reason be demanded."²⁰

At the November, 1878, Chapter of the Society of the Holy Cross the " Report " of Brother Mossman was read to the brethren, but did not receive any approbation from them, for they passed the following motion unanimously :—" That although Br. Mossman's Report is printed and circulated amongst the brethren, the Society distinctly repudiates the opinions expressed in it."²¹ At this Chapter the preliminary Report on the O. C. R. of the special Committee of the S. S. C. was read. There was attached to it, as an Appendix, several extracts from letters which the Committee had received from " Bishop " Mossman. In one of these letters he wrote :—

"I can only speak profitably of what I am able to testify of my own personal knowledge. The most important part of this is that a Consecration has undoubtedly taken place. I have been frequently asked what is meant by 'three distinct and independent lines of Episcopal Succession' in the First Pastoral of the Order of Corporate Reunion. Let me distinguish carefully between what I have been told and what I know. What I have been told is, that three Anglican clergymen have been consecrated Bishops from three distinct sources. That may be true, or it may be the reverse. What I know is, that one Anglican clergyman²² has been consecrated a Bishop by a Catholic Bishop; and by a Catholic Bishop I mean one who is now at this present time, and who was when he performed the act of consecration, in full communion with either the See of Rome, the Patriarch of Constantinople, or the Archbishop of Canterbury. It will thus be seen that the Bishops of all so-called heretical or schismatical bodies are excluded *vi terminorum*. More than this I am pledged not to reveal at present. I know it will appear very strange to many that such a thing could have taken place. I am not sure that I should have been able to believe it myself, had not the documents which attest the consecration, signed and sealed by the consecrating Prelate himself, attested by witnesses, and other

[20] *Br. Mossman's Report on the Order of Corporate Reunion. Presented to S.S.C.*, p. 10.
[21] *S.S.C. November Chapter*, 1878. *Acta*, p. 4.
[22] There can be no doubt that " Bishop " Mossman here referred to himself

corroborative evidence, been placed in my hands for examination in the most frank and unreserved manner possible."[23]

It will thus be seen that the mystery which surrounds the identity of the Consecrating Bishops was not altogether removed by "Bishop" Mossman. He was evidently "pledged" not to make their names public. A great many guesses have, from time to time, been made as to who the Consecrating Bishops really were, but nothing certain has been made known to the public from that day to this. Since its foundation the Order of Corporate Reunion appears to have influenced for evil a considerable number of the Ritualistic clergy. In the November, 1881, issue of the *Nineteenth Century*, Dr. Lee wrote an article on "The Order of Corporate Reunion," in the course of which he asserted that "Already there are representatives of the O. C. R. in almost every English diocese" (p. 755). The Roman *Catholic Standard and Ransomer*, edited by a priest who was formerly an advanced Ritualistic clergyman, in its issue for November 22nd, 1894, p. 323, says:—"We have heard just lately that there are now *eight hundred* clergymen of the Church of England who have been *validly* ordained by Dr. Lee and his co-Bishops of the Order of Corporate Reunion. If so, Dr. Lee's dream of providing a body with which the Pope could deal seems likely to be realized."

[23] *S. S. C. Report of Committee on the Order of Corporate Reunion.* pp. 9, 10.

CHAPTER VI.

RITUALISTIC SISTERHOODS.

Ritualistic Sisterhoods formed on Roman models—Dr. Pusey visits Romish Convents in Ireland—Borrows Rules from English and Continental Nunneries—Hislop on the Pagan origin of Convents—Dr. Pusey's first Sister visits Foreign Convents—Miss Goodman's experience of Dr. Pusey's Sisterhood—Rule of Obedience—Shameful tyranny over the Sisters—The Sister must obey the Superior, "yielding herself as wax to be moulded unresistingly"—The mercenary Rule of Holy Poverty—Are Ritualistic Convents Jails?—The Vow of Poverty at St. Margaret's, East Grinstead—A secret Convent Book quoted—Life Vows—Is it easy to embezzle the Sister's money?—The secret Statutes of All Saints' Sisterhood, Margaret Street; and Clewer Sisterhood—Sisters and their Wills—Evidence before the Select Committee—Bishop Samuel Wilberforce on Conventual Vows—Archbishop Tait on Conventual Vows—Ritualistic Nuns Enclosed for Life—"Father Ignatius's" Nuns—Whipping Ritualistic Nuns—Miss Cusack's experience of Dr. Pusey's Sisterhood—"A Hell upon earth"—Cases of Cruelty in Dr. Pusey's Sisterhood—Hungry Sisters Tempted—Private Burial Grounds in Ritualistic Convents—Secret Popish Service in a Ritualistic Convent Chapel—A Mass "in Latin from the Roman Missal"—Superstitious Convent Services—Extracts from a secret book of Dr. Pusey's Sisterhood—Sisterhoods and Education: A Warning to Protestant Parents.

I HAVE nothing whatever to say against any good work which Ritualistic Sisterhoods may undertake, nor would I treat the Sisters themselves otherwise than with personal respect. But in writing about Ritualistic Sisterhoods I remember that I have to deal with a system which at the Reformation was entirely ejected, root and branch, out of the Reformed Church of England, and, as most loyal Churchmen believe, for very good reasons. The so-called "Religious Life" in Ritualistic Sisterhoods is an exact reproduction of that system which the Church of

England abolished in the sixteenth century. The spread of this Conventual system in the Church of England is witnessed with serious and reasonable alarm by many of the wisest of Churchmen and Churchwomen. There are at the present time, within the Church of England, a greater number of Sisters of Mercy than were in this country before the suppression of Monasteries and Convents by Henry VIII. The wealth possessed by Ritualistic Convents is, I have no doubt, far greater than that possessed by the Roman Catholic Convents of England in the early part of the sixteenth century. These institutions are not legally recognized by the Church of England, but efforts are constantly being put forth to obtain for them that legal sanction which they possessed in this country before the Reformation. In view of these efforts I have thought it desirable to devote a chapter of this book to Ritualistic Sisterhoods. It is most appropriate that this should be so, since every Ritualistic Sisterhood is as truly a *secret* Society as is the Society of the Holy Cross, or the Order of Corporate Reunion. What passes within Convent walls is a secret known only to the initiated, or to outsiders by means of revelations made by Sisters who have forsaken the so-called " Religious Life." The secret Statutes, regulating not only the lives of the inmates, but also the disposal of their property, are quite unknown to the general public.

The rules of the first of these Tractarian Sisterhoods were copied from Roman models. The thought of establishing such institutions came into the minds of the Tractarian leaders several years before the first was founded. As early as February 21st, 1840, Dr. Newman wrote to his friend Bowden:—" Pusey is at present eager about setting up Sisters of Mercy."[1]

At this period Dr. Hook, Vicar of Leeds, was anxious to establish a Sisterhood in that town, but on the sly.

[1] *Life of Dr. Pusey*, Vol. II., p. 155.

Writing to Dr. Pusey from the Vicarage, Leeds, June 9th, 1840, he remarked:—

"I perfectly agree with you in thinking it to be most important to have a class of persons acting under us, and answering to the Sisters of Charity in some foreign Churches. But there will be great difficulties in the way. Although we shall obtain the co-operation of the really pious of all classes ultimately, there will be much opposition from those 'Evangelical' ladies who at present control the visiting societies. . . . What I should like to have done is this: for you to train an elderly matron, full of zeal and discretion, and thoroughly imbued with right principles, and for her to come here and take lodgings with two or three other females. *Let their object be known to none but myself, and I would speak of them merely as well-disposed persons willing to assist my Curates and myself*, as other persons do, in visiting the sick."[2]

In the following year Dr. Pusey spent two months in Ireland for the special purpose of studying the Roman Catholic Sisterhoods.[3] The Irish Romanists very naturally gave him a hearty welcome. Writing to Newman, August 9th, 1841, Pusey remarked:—"The Roman Catholics have been so civil I have not known what to make of it. I have had to fight off being introduced to the one and the other, and they shake hands so cordially, and are so glad to see one! *e.g.*, a Roman Catholic Bishop of British Guiana."[4] He saw also the Roman Catholic Archbishop Murray, of Dublin. Some of Pusey's friends were greatly distressed at the rumours which were flying about as to the object of this mysterious journey to Ireland, and one of them, the Rev. E. Churton, wrote to him about it, in evident alarm. Three years after the commencement of the first Sisterhood, Dr. Pusey wrote to his friend Mr. A. J. Beresford Hope, describing the plan upon which it was founded. "We naturally," he wrote, "went by experience. Lord John Manners procured us the rules of the Sisters of Charity at Birmingham. I had

---

[2] *Life of Dr. Pusey*, Vol. III., p. 7. [3] *Ibid.*, Vol. II., p. 243.
[4] *Ibid.*, p. 246.

some rules by me, used by different bodies in England and on the Continent."[5]

The system which Dr. Pusey thus imported into the English Church was not only Popish, but also Pagan in its origin. Nuns and Monks existed long before Christianity, and they still exist to-day amongst those who do not worship the true God. Mr. Hislop, in his learned work entitled the *Two Babylons*, tells us that, in connection with the ancient Babylonish religion—

"There were Monks and Nuns in abundance. In Thibet and Japan, where the Chaldean system was early introduced, Monasteries are still to be found, and with the same disastrous results to morals as in Papal Europe. In Scandinavia, the priestesses of Freya .. who were bound to perpetual virginity, were just an order of Nuns. In Athens there were Virgins maintained at the public expense, who were strictly bound to single life. In Pagan Rome, the Vestal Virgins .. occupied a similar position. Even in Peru, during the reign of the Incas, the same system prevailed, and showed so remarkable an analogy, as to indicate that the Vestals of Rome, the Nuns of the Papacy, and the Holy Virgins of Peru, must have sprung from a common origin."[6]

It seems that as early as June 5th, 1841, a young lady, named Miss Marian Hughes, who subsequently became the Mother Superior of one of Dr. Pusey's Convents at Oxford, took "a vow of celibacy," under the guidance of Dr. Pusey himself.[7] Newman celebrated the Holy Communion on this occasion, in St. Mary's Church, Oxford. Shortly after this event Miss Hughes went abroad. The biographer of Dr. Pusey informs us that she went in company with the Rev. C. and Mrs. Seager—

"In order to study, as far as might be possible, the 'Religious' Life among women in France. At Bayeux they made the acquaintance of the Bishop, and of the Abbé Thomine, Canon of the Cathedral and Archdeacon of Caen. M. Thomine was the Director of fifteen Convents, and he allowed Miss Hughes to go as a visitor to the Hotel

---

[5] *Ibid.*, Vol. III., p. 22.
[6] Hislop's *Two Babylons*, p. 223. Seventh edition.
[7] *Life of Dr. Pusey*, Vol. III., p. 10.

Dieu in Bayeux, which was served by a community of White Augustines or Ursulines. She was received with great cordiality, and was allowed to ask as many questions as she liked. She found the Nuns as fervent and simple-hearted as could be wished: perfect harmony reigned between the different grades of Sisters, and the hospital and schools under their management were admirably conducted. The Rule of this House had not been published; but Miss Hughes was allowed by M. Thomine to learn much of it. She afterwards visited the Convent of the Visitation at Caen, which was, of course, under the published Rule of St. Francis de Sales. Pusey was much interested in these details, and in such information as Mr. Seager could collect about the conditions under which temporary vows were allowed in the French Church. In the regulations of the first English Community of Sisters, it is not difficult to trace the influence of the information thus conveyed. Indeed, the Rule first adopted was largely taken from that of St. Francis de Sales, though it was modified after a few years of practical experience."[8]

Of course, visits to Popish Convents such as that made by Miss Hughes and her Puseyite companions, were kept as secret as possible. It would never have done to have taken the public into the confidence of men and women about to revive that Conventual system which Englishmen everywhere hated and dreaded. Already, it will be observed, the taking of Conventual Vows was contemplated by the leaders of the new Movement, and Miss Hughes had actually taken one of those Vows, that of celibacy. From that day to this the authorities of the Convents founded by Dr. Pusey have never given to the public any idea of the actual terms of the Vows taken by their Sisters. They form a part of the secret work of the Ritualists, which sadly needs Government Inspection, as much in the interests of the Sisters themselves, as of that of their relatives and friends. Fortunately, however, a lady of high personal character, who was for several years one of Dr. Pusey's Sisters in a Convent, of which the late Miss Sellon was the Mother Superior, in the year 1863 gave the public the benefit of her painful experience, in a

[8] *Life of Dr. Pusey*, Vol. III., pp. 10, 11.

volume entitled *Sisterhoods in the Church of England*, and with it the rules which regulate two out of the three Vows taken by these Sisters. The following is an extract from the "Rule of Holy Obedience":—

"Ye shall ever address the Spiritual Mother with honour and respect; avoid speaking of her among yourselves; cherish and obey her with holy love, without any murmur or sign of hesitation or repugnance, but simply, cordially, and promptly obey with cheerfulness, *and banish from your mind any question as to the wisdom of the command given you.* If ye fail in this, ye have failed to resist a temptation of the Evil One." [9]

There is nothing in the "Blind Obedience" of a Jesuit worse than this "Rule of Holy Obedience." In the hands of a wicked Mother Superior it might at any time lead to the commission by a Sister of the foulest crimes. If the Mother Superior gives a command to commit a crime, the Sister must obey, banishing from her mind "any question as to the wisdom of the command given" her! In later years Dr. Pusey required a similar blind obedience to be given by the Sisters of Mercy to their Father Confessors. In his *Manual for Confessors*, published in 1878, he gives the following directions to Sisters of Mercy:—

"I would have great respect paid in Confession to your Confessor, for—(to say nothing of the honour due to the priesthood)—we ought to look upon them as Angels sent by God to reconcile us to His Divine goodness; and also as His lieutenants upon earth, and therefore we owe them all reverence, even though they may at times betray that they are human, and have human infirmities, and perhaps ask curious questions which are not part of the Confession, such as your name, what penances or virtues you practise, what are your temptations, &c. I would have you answer, although you are not obliged to do so." [10]

We may indeed pity the unfortunate Sister who has to

---

[9] *Sisterhoods in the Church of England*, by Margaret Goodman, pp. 79, 80. London: Smith Elder, 1863. It were much to be desired that a new edition of this valuable book should be published. It is now out of print.

[10] Pusey's *Manual for Confessors*, p. 190.

submit to priestly rule of this infamous kind. If that priest is a bad man, what terrible moral evils he may be guilty of! As we have learnt already (see page 117) three Ritualistic Confessors were mentioned by the late Archdeacon Allen who had fallen into acts of immorality with women who came to them in Confession. Who can wonder at it that reads Dr. Pusey's *Manual for Confessors*, or the *Priest in Absolution?* It will be observed that the Sister is forbidden to show any "hesitation or repugnance" in carrying out the orders of the Mother Superior. Here is an instance of an indignity offered to one of Dr. Pusey's Sisters, by Miss Sellon, the Mother Superior. It is recorded by the late Rev. W. G. Cookesley :—

"One of the Sisters was one day employed in the menial office of lacing Miss Sellon's boots. Whilst she was thus employed with one of the Lady Superior's feet, that dignitary thought fit to bestow her other foot *on the head* of the stooping Sister. Some little disposition to objection and resistance to this disgusting insult being manifested, was immediately checked by the Lady Superior, who remarked that such humiliation *was good* for the Sister." [11]

The orders of a Father Confessor are, it appears, sometimes equally disgusting. Of one of the inmates of Dr. Pusey's Sisterhood, Mr. Cookesley records that—

"A Sister who had been hasty with her tongue, and had thrown out some unguarded expression, was commanded by the Rev. Mr. Prynne, one of the Confessors to the Institution, *to lie down flat on the floor, and with her tongue to describe the figure of a Cross in the dirt.*" [12]

The Rev. R. M. Benson, who for many years was Superior of the "Cowley Fathers," and Chaplain of several Ritualistic Sisterhoods, wrote an introduction to a little book for the guidance of Sisters of Mercy, entitled :—*The Religious Life Portrayed for the Use of Sisters of Mercy*, and this is what he says to them about their Vow of Obedience :—

---

[11] *A Letter to the Archbishop of Dublin*, by the Rev. W. G. Cookesley, p. 76. London: Ridgway, 1853. [12] *Ibid.*, p. 11.

THE VOW OF POVERTY.

"A Religious [*i.e.*, a Sister] has made the sacrifice of her will in taking the Vow of Obedience: she is no more her own, but God's; and she must obey her Superiors for God's sake, *yielding herself as wax, to be moulded unresistingly*" (p. 13).

Anyone who submits to a Vow of Obedience like this, "yielding herself as wax to be moulded unresistingly," is more truly a slave to her Superiors than any negro slave is to his master, since slavery of the mind and soul is in her case added to that of the body. Moral slavery is the greatest of all tyrants. Is it right that any free born Englishwoman should be permitted to take a Vow of Obedience of this horrible character? The victims are truly objects of pity. Another lady, who was for a time one of Dr. Pusey's Sisters, commenting on the Rule of Obedience quoted above, very truly remarks:—

"Plainly, this whole Rule of Obedience is simply the *counterfeit* of that entire self-consecration which the Christian, whose soul has been redeemed, owes to his Redeemer. To Him, indeed, and to His holy will revealed in the Scriptures, the Christian owes an unhesitating, unquestioning obedience. If His providential dealings appear mysterious, child-like trust and entire confidence and submission are due from those who know that the Judge of all the earth 'must needs do right,' though His ways are past finding out. . . But this Rule of Holy Obedience is, in fact, a part of that corrupt and perverted Christianity which, since its first manifestation in the Church, has beguiled ignorantly devout souls—a system which, indeed, 'admits the whole canon of truth, and yet contrives that it should teach only error.' It is part of a carefully devised system for depriving the soul of obedience to God." [13]

We now come to the consideration of the "Rule of Holy Poverty" in Dr. Pusey's Sisterhood. It is as follows:—

"It is not permitted to any Sister to appropriate anything, however small, or under whatever pretext, to herself; since each shall, on the day of her entrance, renounce in favour of the Community, not only the possession, but the use and disposition of *everything* which is hers, or shall be given to her. All this being under the entire regulation of the Superior. Ye shall neither ask for, nor receive anything

---

[13] *The Anglican Sister of Mercy*, pp. 62, 63. London: Elliot Stock, 1895.

without permission; and when ye shall have received it, ye shall place it in the hands of the Mother Assistant for the use of the Society."[14]

There is certainly in this "Rule of Holy (?) Poverty" something which looks very much like what City men term "sharp practice." It is a grand scheme for relieving English ladies of their money. "A lady," writes the Rev. W. G. Cookesley, "who joined Dr. Pusey's establishment, as a Sister, carried into the common stock a capital producing, I believe, so large a sum as £1200 *per annum*; when she subsequently left the Society, which she did to join the Church of Rome, she did not possess a penny!"[15] Here we are face to face with another very serious evil, which sadly needs a remedy at the hands of Parliament. A Sisterhood which retains the property of a Sister who desires to leave its walls, ought to be compelled by law to return her fortune, after deducting a reasonable amount for her support while in the Convent. This "Rule of Holy Poverty" is manifestly unjust on the face of it. A provision should be made, in every case, which shall secure the pecuniary rights of each Sister, and not leave her dependent—should she decide upon leaving the Sisterhood—on the doubtful charity of the authorities. But even if such a provision were made, something more should be done to remove the difficulties which surround a Sister desirous of leaving a Sisterhood. Miss Goodman, writing from the standpoint of one who had practical experience, informs us that—

"The fact that these Conventual establishments are closed against all unwelcome visitation, and that any of the inmates may be secluded from all intercourse and communication with their family and friends, at the will of the Superior, is, if not a breach of the law of England, *at least an alarming and dangerous innovation, and in direct opposition to the spirit of civil and religious liberty in this country.* Since *it is*

---

[14] Goodman's *Sisterhoods in the Church of England*, pp 82, 83.
[15] Cookesley's *Letter to the Archbishop of Dublin*, p. 12. London: Ridgway, 1853.

possible for a young girl to be kept secretly, in strict seclusion, in a Convent professedly connected with the Church of England, *not only against her own inclinations, but against the wishes of her parents and friends*, and even in despite of their efforts to remove or communicate with her, it is superfluous to add that this fact is one of grave importance, *and demands the consideration of the Legislature.* The unfortunate inmates of lunatic asylums, private as well as public, are shielded by the law from ill usage and unjustifiable restraint; surely the inmates of Religious Houses, who devote themselves to the good offices of nursing and comforting the sick and afflicted, teaching ignorant adults and training children—or even if solely engaged in prayer and worship—ought not to be left entirely to the tender mercies of high-handed and uncontrolled power, exercised by irresponsible Superiors, whose authority is absolute." [16]

If what Miss Goodman here states be true—and I have discovered no reason for doubting it—it follows that Ritualistic Convents are, in some instances, nothing better than jails for innocent young ladies, and consequently that, like jails, they ought to be under Government Inspection. Nominally, in most if not all of these Convents, the Sisters may be free to leave when they please; but even here *moral* bolts and bars are used which more effectually prevent their escape than any material ones could.

"A Sister," writes Miss Goodman, "under some circumstances would find it very difficult to leave. Those who enter Sisterhoods abandon family ties; they acquire peculiar habits; are ignorant of the state of things without their Nunnery gates. . . . I have known several Sisters who have spent every penny of their capital; and Dr. Pusey also knows them much better than I do. Without money; without friends; without clothes (Sisters who persist in leaving Miss Sellon's are sent forth in Sisters' garb, and they are instructed to send everything back as soon as they can clothe themselves); without an idea which way to look for occupation; what is a Sister to do who leaves a Nunnery? . . . The foregoing is no overdrawn picture of the difficulties: I am speaking from certain facts which came under my own observation." [17]

The Vow or Rule as to Poverty varies in different Convents. The Sisterhood of St. Margaret's, East Grinstead, is

---

[16] Goodman's *Sisterhoods*, pp. vii., viii.   [17] *Ibid.*, p. 113.

a very large one, devoted mainly to nursing, but also paying a great deal of attention to the publication of books, and the production of ecclesiastical embroidery. It so happens that I possess a secret book written for the use of this Sisterhood, entitled *The Spirit of the Founder*. It consists of extracts from addresses privately delivered to the Sisters by the Founder of the Sisterhood, the late Rev. Dr. Neale. From this book I take the following extracts relating to the Vows taken by the Sisters:—

"Of the three Vows," said Dr. Neale, "that every Sister implicitly or explicitly takes—Poverty, Chastity, and Obedience—the two last are perfectly easy to understand. *They bind you to a Sister's life*, not certainly here, but certainly somewhere, *as long as you live*" (pp. 5, 6).

We thus learn that at East Grinstead the Vows are taken *for life*, making it morally impossible for a Sister to withdraw from her profession, so long as she retains a belief in Ritualistic principles as to the so-called "Religious Life." Dr. Neale seems to have insisted very much upon the alleged wickedness of a Sister ever withdrawing from a Sister's life. "Let me repeat to you," he said to them on one occasion, "once more, that, henceforth, ever to draw back from a Sister's life *is sacrilege: sacrilege in the highest degree:* inasmuch as the Doctors of the Church have always taught that sacrilege of person is worse than sacrilege of place" (*Ibid.*, p. 89). It seems that in this Sisterhood the Sisters are not required to part with the whole of their property to the Convent on joining it.

"A Sister coming to us," says Dr. Neale, "and not able to pay any, or all, of the dowry of this House, is then *bound* to mention in Confession why not, and *to tell the priest how she disposes of her income*" (*Ibid.*, p. 11).

I am afraid that there is in the Confessional a great deal too much interference with the disposal of the property of Sisters. It is open to grave objection that an excitable and enthusiastic young lady should be expected to tell her Father Confessor what she has done with her money. It is no business of his, and if he is a bad man he can easily use his opportunities to enrich the Convent at the expense of justice.

"Let us imagine," said Dr. Neale, on another occasion, to his Sisters, "a Sister wishing to join us with a certain income belonging unrestrictedly to herself; when she makes the Vow of Poverty, what does she promise, and what does she not promise ? She promises, in the first place, to give up what is called the usufruct of it; that is, neither directly nor indirectly to lay out a farthing of it on herself. She promises to keep nothing in hand, to have, as the usual expression goes, no pocket money, to buy nothing for herself with her own money, either necessary or unnecessary. She does not promise— God forbid—to devote all her income to this House. When I say God forbid, I mean what I say. There have been some griping, grasping Religious Houses which have been satisfied with nothing less, but they have always been regarded the plague spots of Religious Communities" (*Ibid.*, pp. 7, 8).

I wonder whether Dr. Neale had Dr. Pusey's Sisterhood in his mind, when he thus denounced those "griping, grasping Religious Houses" which—as was the case with Dr. Pusey's—requires the Sister to devote *all* her income to the Convent ? Dr. Neale understood what he was talking about, and when he terms such Convents "plague spots," it leads us to express a hope that such places may speedily be removed from the Church of England, and thus prevent the spreading of the "plague." At St. Margaret's, East Grinstead, the Sisters may not spend their own money. The Mother Superior kindly spends it for them! I wonder whether Convent authorities ever give a really satisfactory and business-like account to the Sisters of the way their money is spent? Immense sums of money flow into some Convent coffers. Is there ever any auditing of accounts by a *public* auditor ? There ought to be, and Parliament should insist upon it. History proves that there have been very wicked Mother Superiors, and very wicked Father Confessors of Convents. The present Ritualistic system makes it *very easy* for the authorities to embezzle the Sisters' money, with but little or no risk of discovery, should they feel tempted at any time to do so. To plead that all these people are pious and quite above acting dishonestly, is not sufficient to allay doubt and suspicion. It is a plea which is never used with regard to our public religious Societies, as a reason why their accounts should not be publicly audited; and therefore it ought not to be used to shield those secret Societies which exist within Convent walls. The Vow of Poverty is quite unnecessary. Why cannot a private Sister attain to holiness while retaining control over her fortune, and spend her own money as she likes? This Vow keeps her in cruel bondage. And then, after she has thus parted with her whole fortune —in some cases amounting to many thousands of pounds— she is, perhaps, coolly insulted by such advice as the following, given in "Father Benson's" *Religious Life Portrayed for the Use of Sisters of Mercy* :—

"Accept the food set before you, as though given out of mere charity; and however coarse and uninviting it may be, reflect that you do not deserve even that" (p. 33).

A considerable amount of useful information about Ritualistic Sisterhoods may be read in a Government Blue Book, published in 1870, and containing the *Report from the Select Committee on Conventual and Monastic Institutions*. As an appendix to this *Report*, there are printed the, till then, strictly secret Statutes of two Sisterhoods, viz., that of All Saints', Margaret Street, and the Clewer Sisterhood. This *Report* is, unfortunately, but very seldom seen, and, like many other Blue Books, is quite unknown to the general public. From it I learn that in the Clewer Sisterhood the Statutes declare that—

"The Sisterhood is formed *without* Vows, for the observance of the Rules of Poverty, Chastity, and Obedience, in which state of life the Sisters offer themselves *perpetually* to God, to live alone for His glory, in the love of Jesus, and to serve Him in the persons of His poor and suffering ones."[18]

[18] *Report*, p. 224.

But, surely, if they promise and offer themselves to God "perpetually" to observe the Rules of Poverty, Chastity, and Obedience, such an offer is, practically, the same thing as a Vow? It would be hard to define the difference. Canon T. T. Carter, who has been Warden of the Clewer Sisterhood from its commencement, has written a treatise to prove, amongst other things, that "the dedication" of a woman to a life of celibacy in a Sisterhood, "whether expressed or implied, or however expressed, was regarded as tantamount to a vow."[19] The Rev. Dr. Neale, Warden of the East Grinstead Sisterhood, said that "a Vow is tantamount to an Oath."[20] The Rules which regulate the property of the Clewer Sisters, though open to abuse, are not so bad as those which obtain in Dr. Pusey's Sisterhood. They are as follows:—

"15. Sisters who are able, are expected to contribute each £50 annually to the Community Fund, but this sum may be increased at the desire of any Sister.

"16. The sum to be contributed by each Sister, shall be settled between herself and the Warden and Superior; the arrangement being strictly confidential.

"17. In the event of any Sister desiring to give or bequeath any property to the Community, or any of its Houses, she shall satisfy the Visitor that she has informed the next-of-kin, or the next in degree, if more than one (*or give to the Visitor a sufficient reason for her not having done so*) of her intention, that any objections on their part may be duly considered, and that they may have the opportunity of laying such objections before the Visitor."[21]

According to these Rules the amount of a Sister's contribution to the Community Fund is kept a profound secret, known only to the priest who acts as Warden, the Mother Superior, and herself. Even the Council of the Sisterhood are to know nothing at all about it. Those two "old hands" working on a susceptible young lady, could

---

[19] *Vows and the Religious State*, by the Rev. T. T. Carter, p. 73. London: Masters, 1881.

[20] *Spirit of the Founder*, p. 71. [21] *Report*, p. 226.

easily, if they pleased—I do not say that they would so act—work the arrangement very much to the advantage of the Community Fund. And then, supposing the Sister subsequently desires to "give"; or, when dying, "bequeath" a part, or the whole, of her property to the Sisterhood, it can be very easily managed under Rule 17, even though that Rule seems at first sight so fair to the next-of-kin. It is very right that she should inform her nearest relations as to what she proposes to do with her property, but, it will be observed, there is an important exception made to this salutary provision. She may "give to the Visitor a sufficient reason for her *not having done so*," and then, calling in the aid of her Father Confessor, the Warden, and the Mother Superior, the result of their conference will, no doubt, be quite satisfactory to the Convent. But what will her next-of-kin think about it? Even if they are permitted, according to Rule 17, to lay their objections to losing the money (which they might reasonably expect from their relative) before the Visitor, it does not necessarily follow that their protests will be successful. In either case the Convent has an unfair advantage. We know from the history of Romish countries what the threats of a priest can accomplish at a dying bed.

An illustration, I do not say of undue influence, but of the way in which Ritualistic Convents benefit largely by the wills of dying Sisters, is thus given by Miss Goodman, in her *Sisterhoods in the Church of England*, p. 16 :—

"The father of H—— [one of Dr. Pusey's Sisterhood] was a Scotch baronet, and when he died, his property went to his eldest son; but Lady ——, the mother of H——, was an heiress, and a considerable part of her own *large property* was settled on herself for life, to be divided equally afterwards among her daughters and younger sons. When H—— was dying at Bradford [Convent], her mother and sister were sent for; but they were allowed to stay only two days, of which one was Sunday. On the Monday H—— made a will leaving her share of her mother's property absolutely to Miss Sellon [the Mother Superior], or to the Sisterhood, which is much the same thing. *The mother expressed a wish that her daughter should do otherwise, but in vain;* so Lady —— went away with the pleasant reflection that Miss Sellon, through whom she was sent away from her daughter's death bed, will inherit as a daughter from her."

In the Sisterhood of All Saints', Margaret Street, it is provided by the Statutes, that no Sister leaving the Sisterhood, even if "dismissed," shall have any right to any portion of the money or property which she has given to it, whether as a dowry or otherwise. The rule, which is very stringent, is as follows:—

"18. No Sister, *whether dismissed or not*, or whether remaining or not, or her heirs, executors, or administrators, shall have or be entitled, either in her lifetime or after her decease, to, or shall have power to claim, either at law or in equity, any estate, right, title, interest, property, or share whatsoever in or to the real estate or chattels real, houses, leasehold or copyhold estates, stocks, funds, and monies, or in or to the household furniture, books, linen, china, and other chattels personal, and effects belonging to or held in trust for or used for the purposes of the said Society, or any of them, or any part or parts thereof, anything herein contained to the contrary thereof in anywise notwithstanding."[22]

It is evidently quite possible that a Sister may, whether intentionally or otherwise, be "dismissed" contrary to strict justice, yet, according to this rule she is, even in such a case, barred from any claim for compensation on the property of the Sisterhood, which, of course, includes what she has given to it. Such a rule is open to grave abuse. By Rule 22 the first Mother Superior, Miss H. B. Byron, is excepted from the operations of Rule 18, to this extent, that, should the Sisterhood be dissolved in her lifetime "the houses and property of the said Society in Margaret Street, Cavendish Square, shall be reconveyed to and vested in the said Harriet Brownlow Byron, her executors, administrators, and assigns." It is evident that Miss Byron looked after her own interest very well. It would have been well had the authorities shown an equal regard for the interests of the

[22] *Report*, p. 215.

other Sisters. By this same Rule 22, it is provided that the "whole of the property and effects" of the Sisterhood shall, in the event of its being dissolved, "be disposed of to such charitable purposes in connection with the Church of England" as the trustees may select, the unfortunate Sisters being in no way provided for by the Statutes, though they have probably contributed the greater portion of the Sisterhood property out of their own private fortunes. On July 21st, 1870, Mr. W. Ford, the Honorary Solicitor of this Sisterhood, was examined before the Select Committee of the House of Commons on Conventual and Monastic Institutions. He was questioned by the Committee on this subject, as follows :—

"3768. They [the Sisters] have not precluded themselves by these Statutes or regulations from taking property by trustees ?—No ; they may receive property in their own names or in the names of trustees ; when the Sisters go away or die they or their representatives shall not be considered to have any right to a share of the property of the Community.

"3769. *Though they may contribute some, they are not to take any away ?*—It is not put so in express words, but that is the legitimate inference I think." [23]

In the course of his evidence Mr. Ford stated that at All Saints', Margaret Street, the Sisters take no Vow of Poverty, and may continue to hold any personal property of their own, which they may not have handed over to the Sisterhood. The Statutes are signed by all the Sisters, who promise to observe them "God being our helper." Mr. Ford was asked by the Committee, if this was not equivalent to an oath : but he denied that it was, though he admitted that "a great many persons of tender conscience might feel" that, in thus invoking the name of God as a witness to their promise, "they were entering into a solemn obligation, and that if they failed in it, they would feel it some sort of a burden on their conscience." [24] Mr. E. E.

[23] *Report*, p. 173.   [24] *Ibid.*, p. 17 .

Freeman, Solicitor of the Clewer Sisterhood, also gave evidence before the Select Committee, and stated that in that institution a similar, but verbal declaration of consent to the Statutes was made by each Sister, ending with the words, "God being our helper."[25] From this gentleman's evidence we further learn that the rules as to the possession of private property are more severe at Clewer than at All Saints', Margaret Street, as the following questions and answers show :—

"4097. Do I rightly understand that they [Clewer Sisters] give up nothing on entering the Community?—They give up nothing on entering; they make arrangements for the disposing of their property, *and they do not deal with their money after entering the Institution.*"

"4100. But is it the arrangement, or one of the rules, that they shall not hold any property for their own benefit?—Yes."

"4103. But it is understood that they shall not employ any moneys or properties that they may receive for their own purposes, after they have joined?—Yes."[26]

What the rules are as to the Vows of Poverty, Chastity, and Obedience, which obtain in the numerous other Sisterhoods within the Church of England I have been unable to ascertain.[27] They are kept as great secrets, known only to the initiated. Could not the Charity Commissioners make inquiries on this subject? The Rules of the Sisterhoods which I have come across, may, of course, have been altered since those were issued which I have quoted, but I have no reason to hope that, if altered, they have been altered for the better.

This subject of Conventual Vows demands the serious attention of loyal Churchmen everywhere, and especially of our Bishops, whose influence is, in some instances at least,

---

[25] *Ibid.*, p. 193. [26] *Ibid.*, p. 190.

[27] From a letter published in the *Life of Archbishop Tait*, Vol. I., p. 456, I learn that in the "Sisterhood of the Holy Cross," which works in connection with the St. George's Mission at St. Peter's, London Docks, "*Perpetual* Vows" are taken by the Sisters. By the way, is there any connection between this "Sisterhood of the Holy Cross," and the secret "Society of the Holy Cross," both of which work in the same parish?

considerable over the Sisterhoods in their dioceses. In the opinion of many of the most learned Divines of the Church of England these Vows are most dangerous, and wholly without Scriptural authority. A case is mentioned in the *Life of Archbishop Tait*, in which a clergyman of the Church of England administered a Vow of perpetual Celibacy to a young lady who was only *eighteen* years of age! No wonder that the Archbishop termed the taking of such a vow "a *sinful* act."[28] It is very common nowadays to see very young Sisters of Mercy walking in our streets. How many of them have taken Perpetual Vows? It would be easy to fill several pages with extracts from the writings of English Divines in proof of their opposition to Conventual Vows, and certainly it is quite reasonable to ask the question, Why cannot we have Sisterhoods without any Vows, direct or indirect? Is it not possible to be kind to the sick and poor, and to educate the young without them? The history of many Deaconesses' Homes, conducted on Protestant principles, is an ample answer to the question. No sensible person objects to Christian women banding themselves together for Christian work; on the contrary, they ought to be encouraged in their good resolutions to the utmost. But, surely, he is not to be considered an enemy of Christian charity who faithfully points out the dangers and evils which invariably follow the taking of Vows of Poverty, Chastity, and Obedience? The late Bishop Samuel Wilberforce was ever a great friend to women's work in the Church, yet he, old-fashioned High Churchman though he was, felt bound to raise a warning cry on this grave subject. Writing on April 14th, 1850, to a clergyman who had submitted to him the rules of a proposed Sisterhood, he remarked:—

"I object, then, absolutely, as un-Christian *and savouring of the worst evils of Rome*, to the *Vows* involved in such a context in the statement as, 'She is for ever consecrated to the service of her

---

[28] *Life of Archbishop Tait*, Vol. I., p. 466.

heavenly Spouse.' I object to the expression itself as *unwarranted by God's Word and savouring of one of the most carnal perversions of the Church of Rome*. . . . I add my solemn warning that such tampering with the language, acts, and temper of the Church of Rome in young women of our communion must tend to betray them into infidelity to their mother Church, and to perversion to the Papal schismatical and corrupt communion."[29]

At the Oxford Church Congress, in 1862, Bishop S. Wilberforce delivered a stirring speech on the subject of Vows, strongly condemning them, whether taken for life, or for a shorter period, and this although he was quite in favour of Sisterhoods, when free from this and other Romanizing peculiarities. He said:—

"I think so far we are agreed—but if it were to be imagined from the silence of any that those who were silent went on to approve, in the first place, of Vows of Celibacy being made *for life*; or, secondly, of the taking Vows of Celibacy *for a fixed time* by those who give themselves to that life, I believe it would be an entire mistake of the meeting. I am bound to say this, in order that there may be no mistake of one holding the office God has given me, that I should not have felt at liberty to take any part in the engagements of any Sisterhood of which such Vows formed a part[30]—because, firstly, *I see no warrant for them in the Word of God*—and it would seem to me that to encourage persons to make Vows, for which there is no distinct promise given that they should be able to keep them, would be *entangling them in a yoke of danger*; secondly, because it seems to me that our Church has certainly discouraged such Vows. . . . I feel, therefore, that I may venture to say that, instead of the Perpetual Vows representing the higher, it is the admission of a lower standard. . . I believe that the abuses of that life have come, first from the promises of *perpetuity*; and, secondly, from the abuse connected with the admission of persons having *property*, and being *led to give that property up, in a moment of excitement, to this purpose*. . . . One single word on the use of the term 'Religious.' I confess

---

[29] *Life of Bishop Wilberforce*, Vol. III., pp. 330, 331.
[30] In his diary for November 30th, 1860, the Bishop records that during a visit he had that day made to the Clewer Sisterhood, he "would not consent to altering rule about *no Vows*." (*Life of Bishop Wilberforce*, Vol. III., p. 332.) It is evident from this that the authorities wished to introduce Vows. Have they been introduced since then?

that I have the very deepest objection in any way whatever to applying the word 'Religious' to such a life. I think it was adopted at a time when the standard of lay piety was very low, and at all events, as no good seems to me to be got by the use of a word ambiguous at least in its meaning, and which seems to imply that God can be better served in the unmarried Sisterhood than in the blessed and holy state of matrimony, I think it is a pity that it should be used." [81]

Archbishop Tait, a Broad Churchman who, like Bishop Wilberforce, had no objection to Sisterhoods, if they could be kept free from Romish corruptions and abuses, was equally stern in his denunciation of Vows. Writing to a gentleman, on December 27th, 1865, who had asked for his opinion on the subject, Dr. Tait, who was then Bishop of London, replied:—

"There is no warrant for supposing that I in any way approve of Sisterhoods in which Perpetual Vows are administered. I have on more than one occasion stated publicly my belief that all Vows or oaths administered under the circumstances you describe, not being sanctioned by the Legislature, and being taken by persons not authorized to receive them, are of the nature of illegal oaths. It is a grave question whether a clergyman of the Church of England, administering such an oath, does not make himself amenable to prosecution before the magistrates." [32]

A London Sisterhood, whose name is not given, applied to Dr. Tait to licence a certain clergyman as their Chaplain. His lordship replied, expressing his willingness to do so, provided only "that habitual Confession shall not be urged upon the Sisters or any inmates of the House"; and, secondly, "that no Vows whatsoever shall be administered or sanctioned by the Chaplain." These very reasonable and moderate conditions were, however, rejected by the Chaplain. He would subject himself to no such conditions, and consequently the Bishop very properly refused to licence

---

[81] *Life of Bishop Wilberforce*, Vol. III., pp. 332, 333.
[32] *Life of Archbishop Tait*, Vol. I., p. 457.

him. The Bishop wrote to the Mother Superior of the Sisterhood, giving his reasons for his refusal to license the Chaplain:—

"It is felt," he wrote, "that such Vows are not warranted by anything in the teaching of our Church, and are rash, as binding the conscience not to follow the leadings of God's providence in case of a change of circumstances. If, notwithstanding this, any ladies choose to bind themselves by Vows, I do not see what can be done to prevent their acting in *a way unwarranted by the Church*, and rash, from a mistaken notion that real devotion of life to Christ's service is strengthened by this attempt to forecast the events of our changeful life which God retains in His own keeping. The Church of Rome, in sanctioning such Vows, sanctions also a power of dispensing with them; but the claim to such dispensing power is rightly repudiated by us—so that a Vow for life may be *an entanglement of the conscience*, when God plainly, in our changing relations, prescribes for us a change of duty. The only Vows which the Church of England sanctions are such as the Formularies recognize as based on the teaching of God's Word; and for these the law of the land provides by giving its additional sanction to the Formularies."[33]

The Bishop's exhortations were in vain. The Mother Superior wrote to him, in the name of all her Sisters, to say that they would rather go without a licensed Chaplain than have one on the condition laid down by his lordship.[34]

There is another subject connected with Ritualistic Sisterhoods, which needs to be mentioned here. There are now, scattered throughout the country, several Ritualistic Convents of *Enclosed* Nuns, who are supposed to never leave the Convent walls. Miss Goodman mentions that, in her time, there was an order of Enclosed Nuns in Dr. Pusey's Sisterhoods. "The Sisters at Plymouth," she states, "do not speak of themselves under the title of 'Nuns'; they are Sisters of Mercy; but those of the community belonging to the Order of the 'Sacred Heart' are termed 'Nuns' by the Sisters of Mercy, and the place of their habitation a 'Nunnery.' As I have before observed, the 'Order of the

---

[33] *Ibid.*, p. 461. [34] *See* the Mother Superior's Letter, *ibid.*, p. 462.

Sacred Heart,' or, as it is often termed, the 'Order of the Love of Jesus,' *is strictly* '*Enclosed*,' and their time is supposed to be spent in almost perpetual prayer, for the living or the dead, according as their prayers are solicited."[35]

Miss Goodman further mentions that the rules of this Enclosed Order of the Sacred Heart are modelled after those of the Poor Clares in the Church of Rome, but that in the former Order the discipline is, in some respects, more cruel than in the Church of Rome.

"The relatives of a Poor Clare," writes Miss Goodman, "can speak with her through a 'grille'; the relatives of an Anglican are to think of the Sister as in the grave, and it is esteemed a falling away from the rule for a recluse to desire even to see one so near and dear to her as a mother. An aged lady has for years been trying every means to obtain, as she says, 'only one word' from a beloved daughter at Miss Sellon's, but without success: she has written most imploringly to Miss Sellon, and has begged the interference of the Bishop of Exeter, who declares himself powerless in the matter; yet there is nothing to forbid the meeting except the rule of the Order to which the daughter has devoted herself."[36]

Another Order of Enclosed Nuns existed for several years at Feltham, Middlesex, from whence it was removed to Twickenham; and, later on, to West Malling, Kent. Its Home is known as the "Convent of S. Mary and S. Scholastica." I have no idea how many Nuns reside within its walls. Originally this Nunnery was under the control of the Rev. J. L. Lyne, who calls himself "Father Ignatius," after Ignatius Loyola, founder of the Jesuit Order. A schism took place in its ranks, and the Feltham Nuns seceded from the control of "Father Ignatius." That gentleman, however, keeps on another Nunnery of his own at Llanthony, where he has also a Monastery. In 1879 this Convent was in Slapton, Devonshire, where, in company with two others, I had an interview with " Ignatius " himself, who told me that his Nuns " never see the face of man "—his own face,

[35] Goodman's *Sisterhoods in the Church of England*, p. 125. [36] *Ibid.*, p. 213.

I presume, excepted. "Sister Mary Agnes, O.S.B.," who was for seventeen years one of the Nuns under "Father Ignatius," states that the "Discipline," or cat o' nine tails, was used by the Nuns in the Convent,[87] and this is confirmed by the *Monastic Times*, June 24th, 1884, a periodical issued by "Ignatius" himself. Sometimes this "Discipline" was inflicted by the "Mother Superior" against the will of the unfortunate Nun, an instance of which is given above (p. 40).

That horrible, but perfectly true story, the accuracy of which has not been publicly denied by "Ignatius," reads like a chapter of Convent life taken from the Dark Ages. I wish I could think it were an isolated case; but when I remember that one in the position of the late Dr. Pusey, as recently as 1878, recommended, as I have already stated, this self-same "Discipline," as a penance for Sisters of Mercy, I cannot help feeling anxious about the fate of the unhappy creatures subject to it. In his well-known *Manual for Confessors*, Dr. Pusey recommends Ritualistic Father Confessors to prescribe for Sisters of Mercy, as a penance, and "For mortifications, *the Discipline for about a quarter of an hour a day*" (p. 243). There is something truly horrible in such a penance. A "quarter of an hour a day" of whipping on the bare back, amounts to *ninety-one hours of whipping every year!* What an outcry there would be raised all over England if it were discovered that the humblest woman in East London were subject to such torture as this, even though it were inflicted by herself! Is it not evident that the inherent evils of Convent life are growing up rapidly in what used at one time to be termed the *Reformed* Church of England? This "Discipline"—which is sometimes made of spiked steel instead of whipcord—is in itself quite enough to make a Convent an abode of misery and woe, rather than a paradise on earth which some of the friends of the so-called "Religious Life" assert it to be. Would to

---

[87] *Nunnery Life in the Church of England*, by Sister Mary Agnes, O.S.B., p. 97.

God that the history of the inmates of Ritualistic Convents could be written for the benefit of the public! A cry of horror would, I have no doubt, then be heard throughout the length and breadth of the land. A few ladies only of those who have left Ritualistic Sisterhoods have published their bitter experiences for the good of the public. The principal of these are Miss Cusack, who, after leaving Dr. Pusey's Sisterhood, became a Roman Catholic, and was known as "The Nun of Kenmare," and who has now become a Protestant; Miss Margaret Goodman, who has written two books on the subject, viz., her *Experiences of an English Sister of Mercy*, and *Sisterhoods in the Church of England*; Miss Wale, who wrote the *Anglican Sister of Mercy*, giving her experience of Dr. Pusey's Sisterhoods; and "Sister Mary Agnes," who wrote *Nunnery Life in the Church of England*, being her experience of life in Father Ignatius's Nunnery. All these writers agree as to the misery of the so-called "Religious Life" in Anglican Convents.

Miss Cusack was one of the earliest of those who joined Dr. Pusey's Sisterhood, of which she remained a member for about five years. She joined the branch of the Sisterhood which then existed at Osnaburgh Street, London, and of which a Miss Langston was at that time Superior. One of the ladies in this Convent was known as Sister Jane. This lady, Miss Cusack states—

"Let drop many little hints as to the state of affairs [in the Sisterhood], with which she was far from being satisfied, but above all she warned me against Miss Sellon, and not without cause. Her description of the Plymouth Sisterhood was that it was '*a hell upon earth*,' and later, I knew, from personal experience, that she was not far astray." [38]

A very curious story is told by Miss Cusack as to the way in which Dr. Pusey heard the Confessions of the Sisters. It implies that he systematically broke the "Seal of Confession." Miss Sellon, she states—

[38] *Story of My Life*, by N. F. Cusack, p. 65.

"Made one strict rule for her own protection, which was never broken. No Sister was allowed to go to Confession unless she was in the house, and she always remained in the room next to the one which Dr. Pusey occupied when he heard the Sisters' Confessions. When he had heard one Sister he always went into her room before he heard the Confession of another Sister; hence I think we were not unreasonable in concluding that he told Miss Sellon—if not in words, at least by implication—what had passed. And this was religion!"[39]

It may be well to remark here, that Miss Cusack is not the only person who has brought such a charge as this against Dr. Pusey. The late well-known and highly esteemed Rev. Mark Pattison, Rector of Lincoln College, Oxford, wrote as follows:—

"I once, and only once, got so low by fostering a morbid state of conscience as to go to Confession to Dr. Pusey. Years after it came to my knowledge that Pusey had told a fact about myself, which he had got from me on that occasion, to a friend of his, who employed it to annoy me."[40]

The Confessional, when in the hand of a bad-tempered Confessor, must be often the means of making the life of the poor Sisters burthensome. Certainly what Miss Cusack relates about Dr. Pusey has a very suspicious appearance, indirectly corroborated as it is by Mr. Mark Pattison's revelation.

Miss Cusack mentions the case of a clergyman and his wife who were foolish enough "to give up their baby girl to Miss Sellon to train her for a Convent life."

"Alas," she writes, "for their utter ignorance of the person to whom they had given their treasure. I pitied the poor babe from my heart. It was treated shamefully; and I believe some years later the parents found out their mistake, and reclaimed their child. But the poor little thing was for years at the mercy of a woman who knew no mercy, and at the caprice of one who never considered the feelings or the welfare of anyone except herself."[41]

It is possibly to the case here mentioned that Miss Margaret Goodman refers, in her *Sisterhoods in the Church*

[39] *Ibid.*, p. 71.   [40] Mark Pattison's *Memoirs*, p. 189.
[41] Cusack's *Story of My Life*, p. 77.

of England. Miss Goodman wrote from a bitter experience of Miss Sellon's Sisterhood, of which for several years she was a member. This child, if she were the one referred to by Miss Cusack, was named Lucy, and it appears that there were several other "child novices" in the branch Convent at Bradford, Wilts:—

"One day," writes Miss Goodman, "the little novices, attended by the lady who had charge of them, were spending their hour of silence in the grounds at Bradford. During this time the children were not only required to refrain from speaking or crowing, but they were expected to remain perfectly still. Little Lucy had a great fear of wasps: indeed, she was altogether rather a timid little one; so, as one of these insects wheeled nearer and nearer, the child shrank back. 'Sit still, Lucy,' was the admonition she received. Poor Lucy obeyed, but watched the wasp in agony; at length it almost touched her face, and then she pleaded, 'Please, may I move just a very little bit; I am so frightened.'" [42]

No wonder that poor little Lucy's mother, when she was only eight years old, came and took her away from the Convent. "It was found," Miss Goodman informs us, "that her mind had been overwrought, and, at the direction of the medical attendant, who feared a disease of the brain, all tasks were suspended for more than a year" (p. 132). I think my readers will consider that, under such treatment as is described above, the wonder is that Convent training did not drive the poor sensitive little child mad. Miss Cusack's estimate of Miss Sellon is shared by Miss Goodman, though the latter, by way of apology, pleads that it was her office which spoiled the woman in Miss Sellon. Both these ladies were Sisters at the same time. Miss Goodman quotes a letter which she once received, which she states confirms her own opinion of the Mother Superior.

"Those under Miss Sellon suffered from want of the commonest care. Anything that affected her own comfort or that of —— was ordered immediately—other things were forgotten. It was a fault even to do anything for a sick person without the 'Mother's' orders;

---

[42] Goodman's *Sisterhoods in the Church of England*, p. 135.

and she, late at night, late in the morning, unpunctual at all times, would forget to give any. At the same time, it was always thought right to do anything for her, with or without orders; and so, sharing none of the hardships of others, she was unaware what they were."[43]

Miss Goodman boldly brings charges of "cruelty" against the authorities of this Sisterhood, and supports her charges by evidence which has never been refuted. She mentions, amongst other cases, that of a Sister, whose sufferings at the hands of Miss Sellon appear to have facilitated her death.

"The Sister of whom I am now writing took a cold which, being neglected, proved fatal, from being constantly obliged to remain many hours with damp feet. She had asked for new boots some *months* previously, but her request had been overlooked, I suppose; while, to add to her necessity, she was Portress at the House in Osnaburg Street, and in taking her messages to the Superior, she had to cross an exposed courtyard, during a wet and cold season. If the poor Sister's death had been occasioned by a cold caught while in the execution of some act of mercy, we might not so much have deplored it, but it seems extremely sad that *a valuable life* should *have been sacrificed to an absurd rule.* Her work as Portress must have taken her frequently into the presence of her Superiors, therefore it is strange that the need of shoes was not observed. . . I must distinctly affirm, that her death ought not to have been unexpected, and could only have been so to those who were wholly absorbed in other matters—that is, in administering to the slightest wish and whim of the Lady Superior. The contrast is more evident in this case, because the Sister was one of those who came and went to the several Houses in the train of the 'Mother'; and thus, while all was confusion in the anxiety and confusion of so great an arrival, SHE CRAWLED ABOUT UNNOTICED AND UNPITIED."[44]

A story like this is enough to make a Briton's blood boil with righteous indignation. Where was the womanly kindness of the women who ruled this Convent, to allow a poor creature thus to die "unnoticed and unpitied," and all for the want of a pair of shoes! And does not the thought that there may be scores of other tenderly-reared ladies at present in these Ritualistic Convents, suffering similar

[43] *Ibid.*, p 18.   [44] *Ibid.*, pp. 19, 20.

cruelties, and "crawling about unnoticed and unpitied," make us justly anxious that *these* Convents, as well as those of the Church of Rome, should be open to Government inspection? The objections commonly brought against such inspection are of the feeblest kind, and might just as reasonably be brought against the existing Government inspection of factories. The sensible way to argue is that, if factories need inspection, how much more do Ritualistic Convents? And if the Government inspection of factories in recent years has—as everybody admits—remedied many and grave abuses, why should not a similar reformation of abuses be expected as the natural result of Government inspection of Convents?

Honour and attention were paid to this young lady when too late to do her any good. "If a splendid funeral," remarks Miss Goodman, "could atone for any want of care in her lifetime, poor Sister Fridswida's would certainly have gone a long way. The coffin was very beautiful, and the pall was a gorgeous mass of white and gold" (p. 23).

While the comfort of poor Sister Fridswida was thus shamelessly neglected, that of Miss Sellon (the Lady Superior) and Dr. Pusey (the Father Confessor of the Convent), were very carefully attended to.

"Most elaborate was the care bestowed in preparing the suite of rooms [in the Convent] in which Miss Sellon and Dr. Pusey lived. I may mention that some *hundreds of pounds* were spent in making ready their apartments, which formed a suite of rooms in the tower of the Abbey. I do not mean in furniture only, but in carrying hot-water pipes into every room and passage, in addition to the open grates; in opening walls for extra doors, &c. A long spiral flight of stone steps was covered with wood, on which was nailed rich carpeting; and whenever the Lady Superior ascended or descended, these pieces of carpeted wood were fitted on to each step, and taken up again when she had ceased to walk upon them."[45]

Certain ladies held office in the Convent, who were known as "Eldresses." These, like Miss Sellon, appear to have

---

[45] Goodman's *Sisterhoods in the Church of England*, p. 37.

had their share of the good things of this life, not enjoyed by the ordinary Sisters :—

"Two young Novices having occasion to go into the kitchen late one evening, saw on the dresser a large dish of cold soup prepared for next day's dinner. One said, 'How good it looks'! and drawing near, they observed suet dumplings floating in it. They declared they must taste the dumplings; but they took a morsel more, and a morsel more, until they had made most alarming inroads, and went to bed trembling, lest a searching inquiry should be made the next morning. Will there be 'an hour' for stealing the dumpling? It was at the time, just before we went to bed, that *we were apt to feel most ravenously hungry;* and, in winter, *terribly cold also,* and *altogether woe-begone.*

"Though opposed to the rules, the Chapel was at one time often without a fire, and we left it for bed after two hours of almost incessant repeating aloud of Psalms and other prayers, nearly all of which were said standing. On leaving one night, myself and the Novices were met, as we passed down the corridor to our respective cells, by a droll girl, a kind of servant in the house, and who from having lived amongst the Irish, before being taken by the Sisters, had acquired many of their expressions. She invited us to 'Come and see true "Holy Poverty,"' as practised by the governing powers in the Abbey: Eldresses as they were termed. 'Sure,' said Martha, 'if its cold and hungry ye are, come here, and its Holy Poverty I'll show ye.' She tripped on before, and threw open the door of an Eldress's cell, saying, 'Sure, and arn't this Holy Poverty?' We stood peering over each other's shoulders round the open door, perfectly fascinated. After an interval of years, every object in that little cell is clearly before me; so strong was the impression which, *from contrast with our own state,* it made upon me. The cell of the Eldress contained a blazing fire, a heaped-up feather bed, instead of a healthy hard mattress, and on her table stood a bountiful plate of cold meat, and a small horn of wine." [46]

The existence of Nunneries in the Church of England, the inmates of which are supposed never to leave their walls, makes it all the more important that I should call public attention to the fact that *private* burial grounds now exist within some Ritualistic Convents. I have heard of several such places, the existence of which is, as far as possible,

---

[46] *Ibid.*, pp. 105-107.

kept a profound secret from the outside world. One such *private* burial ground certainly exists within Ascot Priory, one of Dr. Pusey's Sisterhoods, within the premises of which Dr. Pusey died. Miss Goodman says that Ascot Priory is the head-quarters of the " Order of the Sacred Heart," which I have already mentioned. Several of the Nuns are buried within those walls, though whether their deaths were properly registered or not is more than I can say. Certain it is that the existence of such places is naturally calculated to arouse suspicion. They ought not to be tolerated by the Government, and those already existing ought to be at once closed by authority. It would be well if some Member of Parliament were to question the Government on this subject, and make an effort to secure a return of all such *secret* burial places, whether connected with Ritualistic or Roman Catholic Sisterhoods.

The very existence of such burial grounds within Convent walls would, at any time, facilitate the commission of crime. In Roman Catholic Convents, it is well known, illegitimate infants, and even the Sisters themselves, have been murdered, and secretly buried. Human nature is the same all the world over, temptation and opportunity are all that are needed to rouse certain natures to deeds of evil, and though we have heard of no such foul deed as murder in Ritualistic Convents, it is just as well that nothing shall be tolerated which is calculated to arouse suspicion and help on iniquity. Depend upon it, once the people of England realize that such secret burial-places do exist, their just indignation will not be removed until they are closed for ever. It is better and wiser far to prevent evil and crime, than to cure them after they have been committed.

Ritualistic Sisterhoods mainly exist for the propagation of what ordinary and loyal churchmen term advanced Romanizing practices and doctrines. In the chapels attached to several of these institutions advanced Ritualism is secretly practised which the world at large knows nothing about. It is nothing uncommon now for the Reserved Sacrament to be kept in the chapels, and even "Benediction of the Blessed Sacrament" is not unknown. The Rev. Owen C. H. King, a Ritualistic clergyman was, before his ordination, frequently present at the services of the St. Margaret's, East Grinstead, Sisterhood, in the chapel attached to their Convent in Queen Square, London, and at which the Rev. Dr. Littledale officiated. When Mr. King became a Roman Catholic he published a pamphlet, entitled, *The Character of Dr. Littledale as a Controversialist*, in which he described the secret services at which he was present. The pamphlet was published during Dr. Littledale's lifetime, and I have never heard that he publicly, or otherwise, denied the facts mentioned by Mr. King in the following statement, nor yet have the Sisters themselves done so :—

"Not many years ago, while preparing for the ministry of the Church of England, I was engaged in voluntary lay work in connection with St. Alban's, Holborn. During this time . . . I was *on many occasions* present at certain services performed in the chapel connected with the branch of the East Grinstead Anglican Sisters, established in Queen Square, London. Dr. Littledale is the Chaplain of this institution, and Dr. Littledale (the author of '*Plain Reasons against Joining the Church of Rome*') several times was the officiant. Now as an 'Anti-Roman' controversialist, he has written against the following :—

"1. The doctrine of 'Concomitance,' *i.e.*, that Christ is present whole and entire under either species in the Blessed Sacrament—from which it follows that the Blessed Sacrament cannot be reserved in one kind only.

"2. The 'modern Roman Rite' of Benediction of the Blessed Sacrament.

"3. The use of the Latin tongue in Church Services.

"4. The use of images of the Blessed Virgin and the Saints.

"But as Chaplain to the East Grinstead Sisters, Dr. Littledale adopts all these customs. Everyone of these things is practised by him, *and I am prepared, if called upon, to prove my assertion* by the production of such evidence as it will be impossible to resist. Once I attended a '*Mass*' at Queen Square, which, to my utter astonishment, *was said in Latin from the Roman Missal*, and although Dr. Littledale was not the officiating minister on that occasion, still the demeanour of the assembled Sisters showed that they were witnessing a service to which they were quite accustomed. On the altar, at which this 'Mass' was said, is a Tabernacle, and in this Tabernacle is kept a vessel called a Ciborium, which contains consecrated altar breads—that is to say, the Anglican Sacrament is Reserved in one kind by Dr. Littledale for the purposes of Communion, and for another purpose also, which I will explain presently. People outside the circle no doubt will think this an extraordinary performance for a Church of England clergyman to go through who has penned his name to the Thirty-nine Articles. What, then, is to be thought of one who has been engaged by the S. P. C. K. to write against all these things? But more than this. On Sunday afternoon the 'modern Roman Rite of Benediction of the Blessed Sacrament' is performed at this singular Anglican altar, and Dr. Littledale exposes on the altar a 'consecrated' wafer, in a Monstrance, for the worship of the Sisters, *and the chosen few who are permitted to be present.* The hymns which are used on this occasion are sung in Latin, and in fact the whole performance is an exact imitation of the well-known service of the Roman Catholic Church. After this, one would scarcely be surprised to hear that the chapel is not without *a sacred image,* surrounded with *flowers and candles.* I challenge Dr. Littledale to deny these things; as I said before, I am prepared to prove them all." [47]

The services provided for the clothing of a Novice, and the Installation of a Mother Superior of a Ritualistic Sisterhood, as provided in the Ritualistic *Priest's Prayer Book,* have much of superstition connected with them. This book has had an immense circulation amongst the Romanizing clergy during the past thirty years, and I regret to state that it has been recommended to town curates by the Bishop of Truro (Dr. Gott) as one of those books which he has "found exceptionally valuable" to himself.[48] The service for "Clothing of a Novice in a Sisterhood" in this *Priest's Prayer Book,* assumes that a "Bishop, or some one in his stead, vested in Albe, Stole, and Cope," shall perform the

---

[47] *The Character of Dr. Littledale as a Controversialist,* by Owen C. H. King, pp. 5-7. London: Burns and Oates.

[48] *The Parish Priest of the Town,* by John Gott, D.D., pp. 214, 216. First edition. London: Society for Promoting Christian Knowledge, 1887.

ceremony. At one point in the service "the Benediction of the Candle" takes place; after which "the Officiant shall light the Candle, and place it in the hands of the Postulant." Later on it is ordered that "the Novice's Habit shall be blessed," and it is asserted that *this dress* will be to the Postulant "a sure protection, a token of her profession, *a beginning of holiness, and a strong defence against all the darts of the enemy.*" There is certainly no Scriptural or Church of England authority for supposing that the dress of a Sister of Mercy will protect her from the devil, or be to her in any way a "beginning of holiness." The marvel is how Church of England clergymen, in this enlightened nineteenth century, can believe in such superstitions. Yet, after all, it must be admitted that there is no limit to the superstitions and follies which men will believe, when once they have forsaken the Bible as their only Rule of Faith. And what are we to think of the following portion of this service, published in all seriousness?

"The Bishop shall then deliver the Habit to the Postulant, saying—
"Receive this Habit that thou mayest *wear it unspotted before the Judgment seat of our Lord Jesus Christ.*"[49]

Surely, this is an impossible task to give to the poor Postulant? The said "Habit" will, no doubt, be worn out long before she appears "before the Judgment seat." How, then, can she wear it, and in an "unspotted" condition too, on that great occasion? Besides, one may reasonably ask, what authority is there, in earth or heaven, for assuming that anybody will be dressed in the "Habit" of a Ritualistic Sister of Mercy on the great Day of Judgment?

When the time comes for the Postulant to become a fully professed Sister, another religious service is provided for the occasion, termed a "Form for the Profession of a Sister." In this it is directed that the Bishop shall bless the Habit

---

[49] *The Priest's Prayer Book*, pp. 302-306. Seventh edition. Eighteenth thousand. London, 1890.

if it be a new one, in the same words as in the case of a Postulant, and, in addition, he "shall bless the Veil and Ring" to be worn by the Sister on the occasion, and also a "garland of flowers." [50] The *Priest's Prayer Book* also contains a form of religious service for the "Installation of a Mother Superior." The Mother Superior, like a Lord Bishop, must needs have a "Pastoral Staff" of her own, and it is ordered at a certain point in the service—"Then shall the Bishop proceed to bless the Pastoral Staff;" and, accordingly he has the daring to pray to God thus:— "Almighty and Merciful God, Who of Thine unspeakable goodness hearkenest to our supplication, and of Thine abundant loving kindness givest to us the desire to pray, *plenteously pour the might of Thy bless ✢ ing upon this Staff.*" The Bishop must then "bless the Ring of office" to be worn by the Mother Superior, and say:—"Bl ✢ ess, O Lord, and hal ✢ low this Ring, *and send upon it Thy sevenfold Holy Spirit.*" [51] Is there not something very much like blasphemous irreverence in asking that God the Holy Ghost shall be poured out on a gold ring? Things like these are what have made men Infidels in France and elsewhere. Certainly if holiness consists in the possession of material objects blessed by a Bishop, Sisters of Mercy possess holiness to an extraordinary degree. They possess, as we have seen, Holy Candles, Holy Habits, Holy Veils, Holy Rings, Holy Flowers, and even a Holy Pastoral Staff for each Convent. Poor, deluded victims, of a superstitious system! Is there any valid reason why Christian women should not band themselves together—as is the case in many Deaconesses' Homes—without adopting the superstitious customs of Popery and Paganism?

It is not to be wondered at that superstition follows the Sisters within the Convent walls. In the secret *Manual of*

---

[50] *The Priest's Prayer Book*, pp. 306-311. Seventh edition. Eighteenth thousand. London, 1890.

[51] *Ibid.*, pp. 311-314.

Prayers According to the Use of Devonport, which is also known to the Sisters as the *Devonport Manual*, many superstitious services are provided for. I should explain that this secret book is for the use of Dr. Pusey's Sisterhood, and is printed at their own private press. In the "Office of the Choir of the Holy Sepulchre" is a hymn in honour of the winding sheet which wrapped our Lord's dead body. The first verse is as follows:—

> "The glories of that sacred Winding Sheet
>   Let every tongue record;
>   Which from the Cross received with honour meet
>   The Body of the Lord." [52]

In the "Office of the Choir of the Pierced Heart" is a hymn in praise of the spear which pierced our Lord's side, and of the nails which fastened Him to the Cross!

> "What tongue, illustrious Spear! can duly sound
>   Thy praise, in heaven or earth?
>   Thou who didst open that life-giving Wound,
>   From whence the Church had birth.
>
> "And equal thanks to you, blest Nails! whereby
>   Fast to the Sacred Rood,
>   Was clench'd the sentence dooming us to die,
>   All blotted out in Blood." [53]

On reading this one cannot but feel that it would be just as reasonable to have a hymn in praise of the man who thrust the spear in our Saviour's side; and another in honour of the man who drove the nails into His Body; for they were but instruments for carrying out their master's orders.

I possess also a copy of the first part of the secret *Devonport Manual*, "printed at the Printing Press of the Devonport Society, A.D. 1861." From it I learn that the Sisters wear useless and superstitious Scapulars.

"On putting on the *Scapula*:—

"Lord, protect me under the shadow of Thy Wings." [54]

---

[52] *Devonport Manual*, Part III., p. 338. There is no date to the edition of this book which I possess.
[53] *Ibid.*, p. 332.   [54] *Devonport Manual*, Part I., p. 4.

What, in the opinion of this Sisterhood, are the virtues of their Scapulars, we are not told, but we can hardly be thought uncharitable if we assume that, in their opinion, they are the same as those derived from the Scapulars worn by Roman Catholics. Scapulars were the product of the Dark Ages, and are, in the Church of Rome, generally supposed to be a protection against fire and drowning, and enable the wearer to pass into heaven soon after they have entered Purgatory. I cannot find in either of the two parts of the *Devonport Manual* in my possession, that the Sisters are ever required to specially pray for their own relatives and friends outside of the Convent. At page 4 of Part I. the Sister is directed to pray thus:—" Bless my dear Mother and my Community," but the Mother is the Mother Superior, and not the Superior Mother at home. It would appear that the Sisters are expected to act as though they had no mothers, relatives or friends outside the Convent; or, as if they were all dead and buried.

"Of what use," asks the *Devonport Manual* of the Sister, " will it be having left the world, if you still dwell on its news, or *to have given up your relations* if you are taken up or entangled with *the wish to receive letters or visits from them?* " [56]

In many of the Ritualistic Sisterhoods much of the time of the Sisters is devoted to the care of the sick, and not a few of them act as nurses for the sick and dying. Dr. Pusey said, at the Oxford Church Congress, that " the Sister is the Pioneer of the priest," which amounts to this: wherever the Sister goes, she prepares and makes ready the way, as a pioneer, for the priest to follow her. We may be quite sure that the priest whom the Sister may recommend is, whenever possible, one of the Father Confessor class. In only too many instances the Nursing Sisters act as zealous missionaries of the Ritualistic cause, and use their influence to persuade young ladies—more especially those with large fortunes—to enter Ritualistic Convents.

[56] *Devonport Manual*, Part I., p. 32.

In the secret book for the use of St. Margaret's, East Grinstead, Sisterhood, the *Spirit of the Founder*, Dr. Neale, their Warden, is reported as having said to them: " You stand, if not in the place of priests, yet in the place of God's ambassadors, to those to whom you are sent."[57] Nor is their influence in the matter of will-making to be despised. It would be interesting to know how many legacies to Convents, and bequests for the erection of new Romanizing Churches, are the result of the influence of Nursing Sisters of Mercy. Protestant families are never theologically safe with Ritualistic Nursing Sisters in their houses.

The influence of Ritualistic Sisterhoods in destroying a love for Protestantism, and planting a love for more or less of Roman Catholic doctrine in its place, is most of all seen in their educational work, whether it be carried on by means of schools or books. Convent Schools for the upper and middle classes are now very numerous, and constitute a serious danger to the Protestantism of the Church of England. The specially sad thing is that many parents who dislike Ritualism exceedingly, send their daughters to these schools to be educated, merely because they are cheap. The policy is a selfish one, and cannot be justified by those who believe that the welfare of the souls of their children should be, to Christian parents, a first consideration. In elementary schools for the poor also these Sisters are frequently seen as teachers. The " Sisters of the Church," who are known by various *aliases*, such as " The Kilburn Sisterhood," " Church Extension Association," &c., devote themselves largely to the work of education, and are publishers of many works, in which Auricular Confession for young and old is taught, as also the Real Presence, and the Eucharistic Sacrifice. The Sisterhood of St. Margaret's, East Grinstead, publishes the most extremely Romanizing books of any Sisterhood I am acquainted with. One of the worst of these is the *Night Hours of the Church*, in three

[57] *The Spirit of the Founder*, p. 94.

volumes. In the "Editor's Note" to the second volume it is stated that these *Night Hours* are translated from the "Roman Breviary," and that the work has "been carefully brought into accordance with the Latin original." In this work services are provided for "All Souls' Day," and for the festival of "Corpus Christi," two Roman Catholic holidays which are not found in the Kalendar of the Book of Common Prayer; the first of these being held in support of the doctrine of Purgatory, and the second in honour of Transubstantiation. Throughout these volumes the Intercession of Departed Saints is asked for, and they are invoked by name, especially the Virgin Mary. The following extracts prove the Invocation of the Virgin :—

"Blessed art thou, Virgin Mary, Mother of God, that believedst the Lord: for there hath been a performance of those things which were told thee: behold thou art exalted above the choirs of Angels. Intercede for us to the Lord our God." [58]

"Holy Mary, Virgin Mother of God, intercede for us." [59]

In a "privately printed" volume of *Offices from the Breviary*, dated 1885, for use in St. Saviour's Hospital, Osnaburgh Street, London, N.W., which is under the control of another Sisterhood, is contained a Hymn to the Virgin, the first verse of which is as follows :—

> "Those five wounds of Jesus smitten,
> Mother! in my heart be written,
> Deep as in thine own they be!
> Thou, my Saviour's Cross who bearest,
> Thou, thy Son's rebuke who sharest,
> Let me share them both with thee." [60]

On the question of the general work of Ritualistic Sisterhoods, and their objects, I cannot do better than quote here the following wise remarks from *Cautions for the Times*, edited by the late Archbishop Whately :—

"The principal method of decoy, at present, is not so much argument as other kinds of persuasion. Among these, none seem

---

[58] *Night Hours of the Church*, Vol. II., p. 175.   [59] *Ibid.*, p. 128.
[60] *Offices from the Breviary*, p. 95.

more popular just now than what are called 'Brotherhoods' and 'Sisterhoods of Mercy'; the real grand object of which appears to be, not so much almsgiving itself, as, under pretence of that, imbuing with Tractite" [now called Ritualistic] "principles those who receive, and those who administer 'the charity.' And it is part of the system not only to make a great parade of their works of charity, but also to represent themselves as the *only* persons who pay any regard to the wants of the poor in those localities where such associations have been at work. Bold and persevering assertions often gain credence with the thoughtless; and thus it has come to be believed by many, in some cases which have lately made much noise in the world, that in such and such districts the poor were left wholly unthought of till these Sisterhoods arose; the truth being the very reverse: *twenty times as much* was being done for the poor, and in a more judicious and efficient way, by persons who were content to go about their labour of love quietly, without blowing a trumpet before them, or wearing any fantastic uniform." [61]

[61] *Cautions for the Times*, p. 344.

CHAPTER VII.

THE CONFRATERNITY OF THE BLESSED SACRAMENT.

Protestant Martyrs and the Mass—Latimer's testimony—Restoration of the Mass by the Ritualists—Birth of the Confraternity of the Blessed Sacrament—Its objects and work—Its secret *Intercession Paper*—Ordered to be "destroyed" when done with—Its "medal" may be buried with deceased members—First exposure of an *Intercession Paper* at Plymouth—Great excitement—How the *Rock* found an *Intercession Paper*—Secret proceedings at New York—The secret " Roll of Priests-Associate "—Dread lest it should fall into Protestant hands—Curious letter from a Priest-Associate—Extracts from the papers of the C. B. S.—Requiem Masses for Souls in Purgatory—Advocates Fasting Communion—Bishop Samuel Wilberforce on Fasting Communion; "detestable materialism"—Opposes Evening Communion—Proofs that it is sanctioned by the Primitive Church—C. B. S. term it "spiritually and morally dangerous"—Eucharistic Adoration of C. B. S. Identical with that of Rome—Its Idolatrous character—The C. B. S. on the Real Presence—The "Eucharistic Sacrifice"—Bishop Beveridge on Sacrifice—Transubstantiation advocated by name—Bishop Wilberforce Censures the Confraternity of the Blessed Sacrament.

THOSE who have read the History of the Reformation are aware that in the estimation of the Church of Rome, the principal offence of the Protestant Martyrs of that period was their opposition to the Sacrifice of the Mass, and to the doctrine of Transubstantiation on which it is founded. Those holy Martyrs would rather die than express one word of approval of the Mass. In the course of a Disputation which Bishop Latimer held at Oxford, on April 18th, 1554, he said :—" These famous men, viz., Mr. Cranmer, Archbishop of Canterbury; Mr. Ridley, Bishop of London; that holy man, Mr. Bradford; and I, old Hugh Latimer, were imprisoned in the Tower of London for Christ's Gospel preaching, and for *because we would not go a Massing."*[1] No one who has read the writings of the Reformers can fail to see how much they hated and loathed the Sacrifice of the Mass. They always used the strongest possible language in denouncing it; and yet not stronger than the Church of England still uses in her Article XXXI.: "The Sacrifices of Masses, in the which it was commonly said that the priest did offer Christ for the quick and the dead, to have remission of pain and guilt, were blasphemous fables, and dangerous deceits." Probably there was not one of the men who were God's instruments for delivering England from Papal bondage, who would not have subscribed to Latimer's opinion of the Mass and Mass priests. "Another denying of Christ," he said, "is this Mass-monging. For all those that be Mass-mongers be deniers of Christ; which believe or trust in the Sacrifice of the Mass, and seek remission of their sins therein. For this opinion hath done very much harm, and brought innumerable souls to the pit of hell; for they believed the Mass to be a Sacrifice for the dead and living."[2]

That which the Protestant Martyrs protested against with their dying breath: those "blasphemous," "dangerous," and "deceitful" things—as the Church of England still terms them—have, unhappily, been restored by our modern Ritualists within the Church of England. The only difference between them is that the one is said in Latin, and the other in English. Even this difference has, in some instances, been removed. The Rev. Owen C. H. King, now a Roman priest, but formerly a Ritualist, states that he was present at a "Mass" offered up in the Chapel of the East Grinstead Sisters in Queen Square, London, which *"was said in Latin from the Roman Missal;"*[3] and Mr. King's statement, though made in a published pamphlet, has never, so far as

---

[1] Latimer's *Remains*, p. 258. Parker Society edition.
[2] Latimer's *Sermons*, p. 521. Parker Society edition.
[3] *The Character of Dr. Littledale as a Controversialist*, by Owen C. H. King, p. 6.

I am aware, been refuted. And that there may be no mistake as to the identity of the Roman Mass and the Ritualistic Mass we read in the St. Margaret's, Leytonstone, *Parish Magazine*, for April, 1894, the following statement:—
" *The Mass of the Church of England is identical with the Mass of the Church of Rome.*"

The early Tractarians, when they commenced their work, taught the doctrines of the Real Presence and the " Eucharistic Sacrifice," but they were very guarded in their language, and carefully abstained from extreme statements. In this direction they practised the doctrine of " Reserve in Communicating Religious Knowledge." It was soon realized that the propagation of these doctrines was essential for the success of the ultimate object of the Movement—Corporate Reunion with Rome. It was not, however, until 1862 that a society was founded for the special purpose of teaching the Real Presence and the " Eucharistic Sacrifice." The name which the new society assumed was that of the " Confraternity of the Blessed Sacrament." I look upon this Confraternity as *a semi-secret* Society, which shrinks as much as possible from the light of publicity. I am not aware that its members are under any vows of secrecy as to its proceedings, but there is a manifest dread lest its privately printed documents should fall into Protestant hands. As an instance of this I may mention that the Confraternity issues every month, to all its members, an "*Intercession Paper*," containing the subjects for which the members are to pray each day, and also subjects for their "thanksgiving." Every care is taken to prevent a copy of this *Paper* falling into Protestant hands. There are about 15,000 printed every month, yet, large as the number is, it is but rarely that anyone sees a copy who is not a member of the Confraternity. The reason of this is explained, I have no doubt, by the advice given to the members by the Superior General of the C. B. S. (Canon T. T. Carter, of Clewer), at its annual secret meeting, on June 20th, 1878.

"Let me add, however," said Canon Carter, "that it is a matter of importance to *be careful not to leave about the Intercession Papers*, to be misused by ill-disposed persons [as I am using them in this Chapter?], and that *they should be destroyed when no longer in use.* We are taught to be 'wise as serpents,' as well as 'harmless as doves'; and we shall do well not to encourage the modern tendency to attack all that savours of Catholic truth or Catholic use. I would add, that it is most desirable that Associates should not fail to notify changes of address, as far as may be possible, so as to *avoid the miscarriage of the Intercession Papers*. In consequence of the want of such care a considerable number of such papers wander about the country unclaimed, *liable to all kinds of misuse.*" [4]

At the annual meetings of the C. B. S., none are admitted unless they can produce the medal which proves that they are members, so that these gatherings are of a private character. The rulers of the Confraternity are naturally nervous lest anyone should gain an entrance into the annual meeting with a member's medal to which he, or she, may not be entitled. It was thought necessary, at the annual meeting on June 1st, 1893, to give the Associates a word of warning on this subject, and also to repeat the warning of 1878 concerning the Intercession Papers. In the course of his annual address, on the former date, the Superior General said:—

"I have also to remind Associates that care be always taken as to notices of changes of addresses, that our Papers may not wander broadcast through the Post Office: and also that notice be given in case of death. The Secretary tells me that he has only just been able to stop Papers that had been sent every month to an Associate who had been dead fourteen years. Moreover, for the medals special care is needed. *They might be buried with deceased persons*,[5] if so desired, *or they should be at once returned.* Otherwise, our medals run a great risk of being used by unfit persons, who may thus pass themselves off as members of the Confraternity." [6]

---

[4] *Address of the Superior General at the Conference*, June 20th, 1878, pp. 4, 5.

[5] What good would that do for the dead? The suggestion tends towards superstition.

[6] *C. B. S. Annual Report*, 1893, p. ix.

So far as I have been able to ascertain, no copy of the *Intercession Paper* of the C. B. S. came into the possession of an Editor of either of our daily papers until thirteen years after the founding of the Society.[7] On July 15th, 1875, the *Western Daily Mercury*, of Plymouth, published an analysis of the contents of the *Intercession Paper* for the July of that year, together with a list of the officers of its various Branches, and a leading article on the subject, in the course of which it remarked:—"Not a few people, we fancy, will be surprised at seeing [in the C. B. S. list] men, whom they believed to be honest, straightforward clergymen of the Established Church, allied with this dangerous Guild; and some clergymen, who have been one thing to members of the Confraternity, and another to the rest of the community, will hardly thank our correspondent for making apparent their double dealing. . . We name these gentlemen because they deserve notoriety, and it will be well if their friends and neighbours fittingly recognize their connection with the Confraternity. If they all, or any of them, have hitherto found it convenient to keep their connection with their Guild a secret, shared only by a few congenial spirits, they can do so no longer, for they now stand before the world in their true colours. They stand officially connected with an organization which is deliberately setting itself to undo the work of the Reformation, which desires to substitute for the Protestantism for which our fathers bled an Anglican counterpart of Romish sacerdotalism."

The exposure by the *Western Daily Mercury* was reprinted in several London papers, and produced a great deal of excitement and dismay in the Ritualistic camp. Indeed, a reward was offered, by advertisement, of Three Pounds to anyone who would give to a local solicitor, information as to who "stole" the *Intercession Paper* which had caused such a commotion. Although the *Western Daily Mercury* was, as I have said, the first daily paper to call attention to the

[7] *The Rock*, a Protestant Church paper, published an exposure in 1873.

C. B. S., the honour of being actually the first of all the papers to expose its *Intercession Paper* is claimed by the *Rock*, which, in its issue for May 23rd, 1873, tells its readers the very interesting story of how it came into possession of the secret document.

"Even Ritualists," said the *Rock*, "are not exempted from human frailties. One of the number seems to have let his copy [of the C. B. S. *Intercession Paper*] drop in the public street, where the word 'Confidential' placed at the top did not prevent its being picked up, and eagerly scanned by the first youngster who passed that way. In this case it luckily happened that the lad to whose lot the treasure fell, not knowing what to make of it, took it to his father, a worthy shoemaker in the district of St. Alphege, Southwark, who . . was as much puzzled as his boy had been, and left the *Paper* lying on the parlour table. Presently, in walks a Sister of Mercy (they swarm in those parts), whose quick eye instantly recognized the strayed *Paper*, which, with the remark (true enough we don't doubt) that 'it belonged to her master,' she immediately clutched. Mr. Crispin, however, not relishing this summary mode of doing business, insisted on having the *Paper* back; but, as the Sister positively refused to part with it, a tussle ensued, which ended in her discomfiture and the recovery of the prey. Our friend, who had now become quite alive to its importance, took an early opportunity of showing it to the Scripture Reader of his district, and he, we may readily imagine, saw at once what an important evidence of the stealthy manner in which the Ritualistic moles and bats are working had thus providentially been thrown in his way, for although the C. B. S. had been many years at work, it had hitherto contrived to keep its proceedings pretty secret."[8]

Probably it was the action taken by the *Rock* which led the Superior General of the C. B. S., at its next anniversary, to say to the members:—"We must endeavour to make our position accord with our constitution, *in keeping, as far as possible, out of public notice.*"[9] How forcibly this statement reminds us of the words of our Saviour:—"For every one that doeth evil hateth the light, neither cometh to the light, lest his deeds should be reproved" (*margin*, "discovered,"

---

[8] *The Rock*, May 23rd, 1873, p. 335.
[9] *Report of the Twelfth Anniversary of the C. B. S.*, p. 3.

John iii. 20). The *Rock's* exposure led to a considerable amount of local controversy in the provinces, where the Priests-Associate were very angry at having their names made known to their own congregations, as connected with such a Romanizing society. One of them wrote a long letter to the *Banbury Guardian* on the subject, in the course of which he asked two questions, to which, at the same time, he gave his own very candid answers. "But it may be said," wrote the Rev. James Hodgson, who described himself as "Superior of the Bloxham Ward C. B. S.," "why are they [*Intercession Papers*] marked 'confidential'? *Does not this imply* SECRECY? UNDOUBTEDLY. But anyone can see in a moment why it is. We are members of a Church that has two great sections in it, and we live among a people a large portion of whom 'care for none of these things.'" [10]

Later on in this same year the Confraternity of the Blessed Sacrament held its local anniversary in New York. Reports of its proceedings were kept from all the Church papers of that city, whether High Church or Evangelical. But what was undoubtedly an official report was sent to the Ritualistic *Church Times*, of England, where in due course it appeared. When the news of what had occurred came to the ears of the loyal members of the Protestant Episcopal Church of America, they were naturally very indignant. The *Church Journal* of New York, which was by no means unfriendly towards moderate High Churchmen, commenting on what had occurred, remarked :—

"By way of London comes to us an account, *carefully withheld from the American Church papers*, of a meeting in June last in this city, of what appears to be a *secret association* of American clergymen. If there is wrong done to anyone in the account given, we shall be ready and glad to give room for the righting of the wrong. But if a *secret and confidential Confraternity* exists among us, *whose purposes and meetings are carefully concealed from publicity* in the American Church,

---

[10] Mr. Hodgson's letter is reprinted in the Ritualistic *Church Review* July 5th, 1873, p. 400.

it is time we all knew it. The thing, like murder, 'will out,' and the mass of the clergy, bound by their ordination vows, and doing their work openly and honestly in the light, feel it unfair that there should be *an inner motive circle where the profane are not admitted; a Brotherhood of secret purposes and secret ties.*" [11]

The secrecy of the Confraternity of the Blessed Sacrament is also seen in another direction. It never prints, even for private circulation, a list of its lay Associates. But it does print yearly a *Roll of Priests-Associate.* Every possible care is taken to keep this *Roll* strictly secret. Scarcely any one outside of its ranks can procure a copy for love or money. Yet even this secretly circulated *Roll* does not contain the names of all the Priests-Associate. The Confraternity possesses in its ranks a body of priests who are so afraid that their connection with it shall be known, that they refuse permission to the authorities to print their names even in this secret and confidential *Roll*. So, every year, as the new *Roll* comes out, there are found printed therein the two following official notices:— [12]

"NOTICE—Priests who do not wish their names to appear in the printed list should give notice to the Secretary to that effect." [13]

"N. B. There are in addition [to those whose names *are* printed] certain Priests-Associate who do not wish their names to appear in print." [14]

Another notice proves how much afraid the rulers of the C. B. S. are lest some Protestant should get hold of a copy of the *Roll*:

"The Secretary General would be most grateful if Priests-Associate would kindly inform him of their changes of addresses from time to time. So many of the *Rolls* are returned through the G. P. O., and *very many copies fall into the hands of those who had better not have them.*" [15]

An amusing incident in the history of the C. B. S. took

---

[11] *The Rock*, October 24th, 1873, p. 717.
[12] I copy from the *Roll of Priests-Associate* for 1894, the last which I have seen.
[13] *Ibid.*, p. 88, *note.*   [14] *Ibid.*, p. 23.   [15] *Ibid.*, p. 77.

place in 1877. In that year the Editor of the *Rock* published a pamphlet entitled the *Ritualistic Conspiracy*, containing a list of clergymen who had supported the Ritualistic cause by joining Ritualistic societies, or signing Petitions in support of Ritualism. One of the clergymen whose name appeared in this pamphlet was the Rev. H. P. Denison, a nephew of the well-known Archdeacon Denison. This gentleman sent fourpence to the Editor of the *Rock* for a copy. On this, the Editor wrote to Mr. Denison, asking him, as a member of the C. B. S., to send him a copy of the last *Roll of Priests-Associate*. To this Mr. Denison sent the following reply:—

"Sir,—I am sorry to have forgotten to answer your letter sooner. Personally, I should be delighted to send you the C. B. S. *Roll*, for you to correct your list, *but I could not do so without the consent of the Superior-General*. If he gives his consent I shall be very happy to forward it.—Yours truly, "HENRY PHIPPS DENISON.
"East Brent, Highbridge, *November 8th*." [16]

I need hardly add that the Superior-General never gave his consent.

And now I come to the task of describing more fully what is the real work of the Confraternity of the Blessed Sacrament. It is a Society composed of bishops, priests, laymen, and women. It was founded in the year 1862; and in 1867 was united to the "Society of the Blessed Sacrament." In the year 1894, no less than 1682 clergymen in the Church of England, and 13,444 laymen and women, were members of this Confraternity.[17] The Rev. Orby Shipley informs us that the C. B. S.—as it is usually termed —is the "daughter"[18] of the notorious Society of the Holy Cross, which was responsible for that very indecent Confessional Book, the *Priest in Absolution*.

We learn from the official *Manual of the Confraternity of*

---

[16] *The Rock*, November 16th, 1877, p. 961.
[17] *Annual Report of C. B. S.* for 1894, p. iv.
[18] Shipley's *Four Cardinal Virtues*, p. 249. London, 1871.

the Blessed Sacrament—a book which is on public sale—that its "Objects" are:—

"1. The Honour due to the Person of our Lord Jesus Christ in the Blessed Sacrament of His Body and Blood.

"2. Mutual and special Intercession at the time of and in union with the Eucharistic Sacrifice.

"3. To promote the observance of the Catholic and primitive practice of receiving the Holy Communion fasting." [19]

We here discover what the work of the Confraternity of the Blessed Sacrament really is. It is nothing less than the propagation, in the Church of England, of the blasphemous Sacrifice of the Mass, under the name of "The Eucharistic Sacrifice!" As to "Fasting Communion," it is sufficient to say that the *first* and *best* Communion administered by our Saviour Himself, was received immediately after a meal. Even a Roman Catholic Sub-Dean of Maynooth College has admitted that—

"The Blessed Eucharist was instituted by our Lord after supper, and for a short time was celebrated and administered only after supper. Martene shows that for the first three centuries, and even much later, it was still in many places celebrated after supper." [20]

Among the "Recommendations" printed in the *Manual* is the following:—

"To make Offerings for the due and reverent celebration of the Holy Eucharist." [21]

This looks very much like a revival of that sacrilegious custom of the Church of Rome, *paying* for Masses! St. Peter forewarns us—"There shall be false teachers among you"; and of these teachers he says—"And through covetousness shall they with feigned words *make merchandise of you*" (2 Peter ii. 1, 3). The way in which the priests of the Church of Rome, at the Reformation, made "merchandise" of men's souls, by their Masses, was that which, as much as

---

[19] *Manual of C. B. S.*, p. 5. Ninth edition.
[20] *Notes on the Roman Ritual*, p. 261, by the Rev. James Kane. Dublin, 1867.
[21] *Manual*, p. 6.

anything, made Englishmen first detest and hate the Mass. The Confraternity of the Blessed Sacrament is now apparently trying hard to revive this scandalous custom in our Reformed Church of England, under the name of "*Offerings* for the due and reverent Celebration of the Holy Eucharist!"

Another of these " Recommendations " is, to offer up at the Holy Communion, " Prayers for the Visible Unity of Christendom." At page 70 we read the prayers for this object recommended by the Confraternity. The following is an extract from the first of these:—

"We earnestly pray Thee for the restoration of visible unity of worship and communion between the divided members of the Catholic Church, both East and West."

Here we find the Confraternity of the Blessed Sacrament praying that the Church of England, and the Eastern Churches, may again be in "visible unity," not only with the Eastern Church, but also with the Church of Rome. On this subject, and the many objections which may be brought against Corporate Reunion with Rome, I shall have a great deal to write in a later chapter.

In the " Laws of the Confraternity " it is provided that—

"Grants of Altar Vessels, Vestments, or Altar Linen shall be made by the Council-General, according to the means placed at their disposal, to such poor Parishes and Missions as may need assistance." [22]

The "Vestments" here referred to are, mainly, such as the Popish Chasuble, Alb, Tunicle, Stole, &c., all of which have been declared illegal by the Courts of Law.

Every member of the Confraternity is expected to offer prayers for the dead. A service used by the C. B. S. is entitled " Vespers of the Blessed Sacrament." It concludes with this prayer :—

"May the souls of the Faithful, through the mercy of God, rest in peace. Amen." [23]

[22] *Manual of C. B. S.*, p. 13. Ninth edition.   [23] *Ibid.*, p. 34.

The Church of England, on the contrary, exhorts her children, saying:—

"Neither let us dream any more, that the souls of the dead are anything at all holpen by our prayers."[24]

But the Confraternity rests by no means satisfied with Prayers for the Dead. She now holds an annual Mass for the Dead, under the name of a "Solemn Requiem." This service is announced every year in the October number of the *Intercession Paper*. The Confraternity believes, in common with the Church of Rome, that the faithful departed are benefited spiritually by the offering up by a sacrificing priest of consecrated bread and wine. It has held this view for many years. At its secret Annual Conference, May 27th, 1880, the Hon. C. L. Wood (now Lord Halifax) read a paper, which was afterwards privately printed by the Confraternity, in which he asserted that :—

"As the Cross sums up in one single act the atoning efficacy of the offering which Christ made throughout His whole life, and by his death upon the Cross, so *the Eucharist, which perpetuates and applies that offering*, enables us to offer up our whole souls and bodies in life and in death as an acceptable sacrifice to the Father of all. . . . Are we *troubled about those who in the shadow of death* are awaiting the Judgment? The blood of the Sacrifice reaches down to the *prisoners of hope*, and *the dead as they are made to possess their old sins in the darkness of the grave*, thank us as we offer for them *the Sacrifice which restores to light* and immortality."[25]

Here we have, in reality, though the *words* are not used, Masses for the Dead to get them out of Purgatory, taught by the Confraternity of the Blessed Sacrament.

In *Suggestions for the Due and Reverent Celebration of the Holy Eucharist*, privately printed for the Confraternity of the Blessed Sacrament, the priest is directed, at page 9, to offer the following prayer :—

"Receive, O Holy Father, Almighty, Everlasting God, this pure

---

[24] *Homily Concerning Prayer.* Part third.
[25] *Eighteenth Annual Report of C. B. S.*, p. xii.

Oblation, which I, Thy unworthy servant, offer unto Thee, the Living and true God, for my numberless sins, offences and negligences; for all who are here present, as also for all faithful Christians, living *and departed*, that it may avail to our salvation unto life eternal. Amen."

Who can doubt that here we have a Mass for the Dead? At the "Solemn Requiem" of the Society, on November 10th, 1890, the preacher, the Rev. E. de S. Wood, used the *word* Purgatory without a blush of shame. He said "The souls in Paradise are offering the homage of their spiritual sufferings in *the realms of Purgatory*, and are helped by our prayers and Eucharistic offerings on their behalf."[26] How different all this is from the teaching of the Church of England, which, in her Homily Concerning Prayer, instructs us that "These words [Luke xvi. 19-26], as they confound the opinion of helping the dead by prayer, *so do they clean confute and take away the vain error of Purgatory*."

We learn more about the work and objects of the Confraternity of the Blessed Sacrament from the secret *Intercession Papers* which it issues every month. To commence with the latest of these which has come to my hands, that for May, 1897, I find amongst the subjects for prayer: "That obstacles may be removed . . . to the celebration of the Holy Eucharist with the traditional and ancient ceremonial sanctioned by the Church."[27] Anyone who reads the *Suggestions for the Due and Reverent Celebration of the Holy Eucharist*, issued by the C. B. S., cannot doubt that by "the traditional and ancient ceremonial" is meant that of pre-Reformation times. The officiating clergyman is, in this pamphlet, required to have, for use at Holy Communion, amongst other things, "a clean Purificator," "Burse," "Corporals," "Cruets for wine *and water*," "a Perforated Spoon . . . for the removal of flies and other impurities from the Chalice." He is also required to say a number of secret and Popish prayers taken from Popish Missals, those

---

[26] *Church Times*, November 14th, 1890.
[27] *Intercession Paper*, May, 1897, p. 8.

provided by the Book of Common Prayer being evidently not adequate for his purpose.

The Associates of the Confraternity were required, on May 7th, 1897, to pray "That the Primitive and Catholic practice of Fasting Communion by priests and people may be generally recognized, and that obstacles to Fasting Communion may be removed."[28] The late Bishop Samuel Wilberforce, though an old-fashioned High Churchman, had very decided opinions on this subject of Fasting Communion.

"It is not," he said, "in a light sense that I say this new doctrine of Fasting Communion is dangerous. The practice is not advocated because a man comes in a clearer spirit and less disturbed body and mind, able to give himself entirely to prayer and communion with his God; *but on a miserable degraded notion* that the consecrated elements will meet with other food in the stomach. *It is a detestable materialism.* Philosophically it is a contradiction; because, when the celebration is over, you may hurry away to a meal, and the process about which you were so scrupulous immediately follows. *The whole notion is simply disgusting.* The Patristic quotations by which the custom is supported are mis-quotations."[29]

On May 27th, 1897, the Associates of the C. B. S. were required to pray "That Evening Communions may cease."[30] We have already learnt, on the authority of the Roman Catholic Professor Kane, that in the Primitive Church Evening Communion was the rule. Singularly enough this testimony is confirmed by that of the Rev. "Father" Puller, head of the "Cowley Fathers," who, in the course of a paper which he read at the annual conference of the C. B. S., on May 28th, 1891, said :—

"We have, I hope, got beyond the notion that the early Church objected to Afternoon and Evening Celebrations. The early Church in no sort of way objected to Evening Celebrations *per se*. She celebrated continually in the afternoon or evening. She had an Evening Celebration every day in Lent. In some Churches all through the year there were ordinarily three Celebrations in the week,

---

[28] *Ibid.*, p. 9.
[29] Dean Burgon's *Lives of Twelve Good Men*, Vol. II., p. 56. First edition.
[30] *Intercession Paper*, May, 1897, p. 24.

namely, on Sunday, Wednesday, and Friday; and two of these Celebrations were Afternoon Celebrations, and only one of them was early. It is a complete mistake to suppose that the early Church had any objection to Afternoon or Evening Celebrations." [31]

Ritualists are never tired of exhorting us to take the Primitive Church as our model. Why, then, should the C. B. S. every month in the year pray to God that the truly Primitive custom of Evening Communion "may cease"? Surely it cannot be wrong to follow a custom sanctioned by the practice of our Lord Himself at the first Lord's *Supper?* Possibly the authorities of the C. B. S. were not altogether satisfied with "Father" Puller's candid acknowledgment on this important subject, for at their annual conference on June 1st, 1893, a paper specially devoted to the question of "Evening Communion," was read by the Rev. T. I. Ball, Provost of Cumbrae College. This gentleman tried to get out of the Scriptural difficulty in a very daring, not to say wicked, manner. While he admitted that "our Lord Jesus Christ instituted the Eucharist on the Paschal *evening*," [32] he boldly declared that—

"As *Holy Scripture* does not help us [Ritualists] much in this matter, we may boldly say, that *it was not intended to help us in this;* but that we were meant to learn all that we need to learn from the practice and precept of the faithful companion of the Bible—the Catholic Church." [33]

Is not this a case of "Down with the Bible, and up with the Church"? Or, rather, does it not remind us of the conduct of those Pharisees—the Ritualists of their day—of whom our Saviour said:—"Full well ye reject the commandment of God, that ye may keep your own tradition"? (Mark vii. 9.) Mr. Ball proceeded to heap up insult and abuse on a custom which certainly had the Saviour's Holy sanction. "Evening Communion," he said, "is an act of schism, in the gravest sense of the term." [34] "They are spiritually and morally dangerous." [35] "It is

---

[31] *Twenty-Ninth Annual Report of C.B.S.*, p. xxiii.
[32] *Thirty-First Annual Report of C.B.S.*, p. xv.
[33] *Ibid.*, p. xv.   [34] *Ibid.*, p. xvii.   [35] *Ibid.*, p. xxi.

profane to invite men by Evening Communion to undertake a religious duty." [36]

The members of the C. B. S. are required to pray " That obstacles to the due and reverent Reservation of the Blessed Sacrament for the Sick may be removed, and that the use of the Sacrament of Holy Unction may be restored throughout the Anglican Church." [37]

As to the first of these I shall have some comments to make further on. It may, therefore, suffice if I here simply quote the words of Article XXVIII. :—" The Sacrament of the Lord's Supper was not by Christ's ordinance *reserved*, carried about, lifted up or worshipped." And there is certainly no trace in the New Testament of either of these customs being observed by the Apostles. As to the worshipping of the Sacrament, this is a practice which is much encouraged by the C. B. S. It would be easy to multiply proofs of this, but I will here content myself with quoting the *Altar Book for Young Persons*, issued by the Confraternity itself:—

> " I worship Thee, Lord Jesu,
> Who on Thine Altar laid,
> In this most awful service,
> Our Food and Drink art made.
>
> " I worship Thee, Lord Jesu,
> Who, in Thy love divine,
> Art hiding here Thy Godhead
> In forms of Bread and Wine." [39]

On this important point of adoration of the consecrated Sacrament the teaching of the Confraternity is identical with that of the Church of Rome. This was acknowledged by its Superior General at the annual conference on May 31st, 1877. I may here be permitted to mention that the anniversaries of the Confraternity are always held on

---

[36] *Ibid.*, p. xxii.

[37] *Intercession Paper*, May, 1897, p. 15.

[38] *Altar Book for Young Persons*, p. 69. Twenty-sixth thousand, 1884. The number printed shows how widely the spiritual poison has been spread.

"Corpus Christi Day," a Popish festival not to be found in the Kalendar in our Prayer Books. It was instituted by the Popes in the Dark Ages in honour of the doctrine of Transubstantiation. The Superior General said:—

"Whatever other differences, therefore, there may be between us and *the Church of Rome* (and I do not wish to question the fact that there are important differences) *yet no such difference as is commonly supposed exists between us on this great doctrine of Eucharistic Adoration.* We adore the same mysterious presence of our Blessed Lord, veiled from mortal eyes, through the grace of a like consecration." [39]

As to the "Sacrament of Extreme Unction" it may be sufficient to remark that the Church of England knows no such Sacrament. At the Reformation she ejected it from her system, for wise and sufficient reasons. I am not aware that the C. B. S. has published any form of service for the administration of Extreme Unction. Probably its Priests-Associate use that provided in the *Priest's Prayer Book*. In this form the priest is required to anoint the five senses of the sick person with oil "on his right thumb." When the time comes for anointing the sick person's nose, the following directions are given:—

"*Then upon the nostrils, saying,*

"Through this anointing, and His most loving mercy, the Lord pardon thee whatever thou hast sinned by smelling." [40]

Another subject for the intercessions of the Associates was "That there may be true repentance and due use of Sacramental Confession on the part of those needing it." [41] The Confraternity is very fond of Auricular Confession, even though the Church of England, in her Homily of Repentance, Part Second, teaches:—"It is most evident and plain, that this Auricular Confession hath not the warrant of God's Word." In its *Altar Book for Young*

---

[39] *Fifteenth Annual Report of C. B. S.*, p. x.
[40] *Priest's Prayer Book*, pp. 91, 92. Seventh edition, 1890.
[41] *Intercession Paper*, May, 1897, p. 16.

Persons the Confraternity prints a form of Confession in the presence of a priest (p. 29).

The Associates are also required to pray:—"That there may be a more widespread belief in the Catholic doctrine of the Real Presence and of the Eucharistic Sacrifice."[43] It would be easy to fill many pages with extracts from the documents of the Confraternity showing what its teaching is on these subjects. To commence with a sermon preached before the Confraternity by the Rev. A. H. Ward, in 1871. That gentleman then declared—

"That the Holy Eucharist is the Body and Blood of Christ under the forms of Bread and Wine, that therein is Christ Himself, His Body, Soul and Divinity, *as truly as at Bethlehem, or Nazareth, or Calvary*, or at the right hand of God, we take as certain."[43]

On the following year the annual sermon on behalf of the Confraternity was preached by the Rev. George Body, now Canon of Durham. We find that gentleman declaring that—

"The Eucharistic Sacrifice is a necessary consequence of the Real Presence. If the Bread and Wine become, by the action of the Holy Ghost in consecration, the Body and Blood of Christ, it follows that when we offer the Sacrament we offer the Body and Blood of Christ, *i.e.*, Christ Himself under the forms of Bread and Wine."[44]

A remarkable sermon was preached before the C. B. S. at its anniversary, June 20th, 1889, by one who has since made a name for himself in the world, viz., the Rev. Charles Gore, now Canon Residentiary of Westminster, and Examining Chaplain to the Bishop of Lincoln. Canon Gore said:—

"Christ is present in the Eucharist indeed externally to us, objectively and really; He is present as the Bread of Life, the Sacrifice for sins, the Object of worship. *He is present wherever the consecrated elements are.*"[45]

---

[42] *Ibid.*, p. 12.
[43] *The Holy Eucharist and Common Life*, by Rev. A. H. Ward, p. 8. London: Hodges.
[44] *Jewish Sacrifices and Christian Sacraments*, p. 27. London: Rivingtons, 1872.
[45] *The Eucharistic Sacrifice*, by Charles Gore, p. 13. Privately printed for the Confraternity.

This teaching is undoubtedly strong, and quite without warrant from the formularies of the Church of England. Many hundreds of volumes have been written on the Real Presence, and it is manifestly impossible for me to give space to an exhaustive treatise on the subject in this book. But I may point out that a localized presence of Christ "wherever the consecrated elements are" is contrary to the teaching of the great English Divine, Richard Hooker, who wrote: "The Real Presence of Christ's most blessed body and blood is not therefore to be sought for in the Sacrament, but in the worthy receiver of the Sacraments."[46] The Church of England teaches that there may—in her sense of the words—be a real eating and drinking of the Body and Blood of Christ, without the aid of a consecrating priest—a theory which is certainly inconsistent with the Ritualistic idea that the Presence is only the result of priestly consecration. In one of the Rubrics attached to "The Communion of the Sick" the Church orders that—

"If a man, either by reason of extremity of sickness, or for want of warning in due time to the Curate, or for lack of company to receive with him, *or by any other just impediment*, do *not* receive the Sacrament of Christ's Body and Blood, the Curate shall instruct him, that if he do truly repent him of his sins, and steadfastly believe that Jesus Christ hath suffered death upon the Cross for him, and shed His Blood for his redemption, earnestly remembering the benefits he hath thereby, and giving Him hearty thanks therefore, HE DOTH EAT AND DRINK THE BODY AND BLOOD OF OUR SAVIOUR CHRIST, profitably to his soul's health, ALTHOUGH HE DO NOT RECEIVE THE SACRAMENT WITH HIS MOUTH."

In this case the Body and Blood of Christ is certainly not eaten with the sick man's mouth. It is an act of faith, not of the body. And is not this the same way in which *ordinary* communicants are said by the Church of England to eat the

[46] *Hooker's Works*, Vol. II., Book V., lxvii., 6, p. 84. Oxford edition, 1865.

Body of Christ:—"Take and eat this," saith the Minister, "and feed on Him *in thy heart by faith* with thanksgiving." And again, in her Twenty-eighth Article she instructs us that "The mean whereby the Body of Christ is received and eaten in the Supper *is faith*"—not a man's mouth, as the Ritualists teach. Our Saviour has never had more than *one* Body. Of that Body, in its *glorified* condition as it now exists in heaven only, the Black Rubric at the end of the Communion Service says:—"The natural Body and Blood of our Saviour Christ are in heaven, and NOT HERE; it being against the truth of Christ's natural Body to be at one time in more places than one." If that Body, the *only one* our Saviour possesses, is "NOT HERE," how can it be in the consecrated bread and wine, as the C. B. S. and the Ritualists teach? I once went into a Ritualistic Church on an Easter Sunday morning, and saw behind the Communion Table, in large letters, the text of Scripture:—"He is risen; He is not here" (Mark xvi. 6). What an undesigned sermon *that* was against a localized Real Presence on the so-called "Altar"! Let us take heed to the warning words of our Saviour:—"Then if any man shall say unto you, Lo, here is Christ, or there; *believe it not*. For there shall arise *false Christs*, and false prophets, and shall show great signs and wonders; insomuch that, if it were possible, they shall deceive the very elect" (Matt. xxiv. 23, 24).

And as to the so-called "Eucharistic Sacrifice," which our modern Ritualists admire so much, and which they consider as a true, proper, and propitiatory sacrifice, and not a mere *commemoration* of the Sacrifice once for all offered upon the Cross by our Saviour, I cannot do better than quote the convincing argument of the High Church Bishop Beveridge, as contained in his book on the Thirty Nine Articles. These, then, are his words, while explaining Article XXXI. They ought to be sufficient to convince any earnest seeker after truth:—

"And as this doctrine is contrary to Scripture, so is it repugnant to reason too, there being so vast a difference betwixt a Sacrament and a Sacrifice: for in a Sacrament God offereth something to man, but in a Sacrifice man offers something to God. What is offered in a Sacrifice is wholly or in part destroyed, but what is offered in a Sacrament still remaineth. And there being so great a difference betwixt the one and the other, if it be a Sacrament it is not a Sacrifice, and if it be a Sacrifice it is not a Sacrament, it being impossible that it should be both a Sacrament and a Sacrifice too. To which we might also add, that, according to this opinion, Christ offered up Himself before He offered up Himself. I mean He offered up Himself in the Sacrament before He offered up Himself on the Cross; which offering up Himself in the Sacrament was either a perfect or an imperfect Sacrifice or oblation. To say that Christ should offer up an imperfect Sacrifice to God is the next door to blasphemy; but yet a perfect one that Sacrifice could not be, for then it need not have been repeated again upon the Cross. But I need not heap up more arguments to pluck down that fabric, the foundation whereof is already destroyed. It is Transubstantiation that is the ground of this fond opinion, therefore do they say the Body of Christ is really offered up to God, because the bread is first really turned into the Body of Christ; but now it being proved before that the bread is still bread after, as well as before consecration, and not the very Body of Christ; though the bread be consecrated by man, the very Body of Christ cannot be offered to God in the Sacrament; and therefore, if they will still call it a Sacrifice, they must acknowledge it is such a Sacrifice wherein there is nothing but bread and wine offered to God, and by consequence no propitiatory Sacrifice: for, as we have seen, 'without shedding of blood there is no remission,' and in the breaking and pouring forth of bread and wine there is no shedding of blood, and not, therefore, any remission of sins."

In many of the papers printed by the C. B. S. the term "Mass" is applied to the Lord's Supper. The Hon. C. L. Wood used it in his paper read at its eighteenth anniversary, in which he spoke of the custom of "getting up in the morning to go to "Mass."[47] In 1882, the Rev. J. B. Wilkinson said that "Children should be instructed, not only by oral teaching, but by bringing them to Celebrations

---

[47] *Eighteenth Annual Report of C. B. S.*, p. xv.

of the Blessed Sacrament for Children, or to put it more simply, *to Children's Masses.*" [48]

The teaching given in meetings of the C. B. S. sometimes amounts to the full modern Roman Catholic doctrine of Transubstantiation. At a meeting of the St. Mary's, Prestbury, Ward of the Confraternity, in 1871, the Rev. A. L. Lewington, now Chaplain of Ardingly College, Hayward's Heath, read a paper, which was subsequently published, in the course of which he said:—

"When we say that the Presence of Christ is objective, we understand that It is there without communion as with communion, abiding under the outward and Visible Form *in the consecrated Elements,* so long as the consecrated Elements are unconsumed. Again, we say that the Presence of Christ is *Whole. Whole* Christ comes to us, and is incorporated with us, in His Sacrament. His Body, His Blood, His Soul, His Divinity, are present. And not only that, but *He is wholly present in every particle, just as much as in all that is consecrated.*"

"When we separate from the notion of substance everything gross and material, *we may regard the term* TRANSUBSTANTIATION *as a convenient definition of the results of consecration* which the Articles do not exclude. . . . But those who *rightly* maintain the term Transubstantiation understand it to signify that what is in outward *accidents*—in sight, taste, and touch—Bread and Wine, by consecration becomes, not in *accidents* but in *substance,* the Body and Blood of Christ." [49]

Even more bold were the Romanizing utterances of the Rev. E. W. Urquhart, at a "Synod" of the C. B. S. held at Salisbury on April 30th, 1889. I attach more importance to what Mr. Urquhart said than to the paper of Mr. Lewington, because it was read at a much larger gathering of the Confraternity, and because it was subsequently published "by request of members present." Mr. Urquhart advocated, without reserve, the modern teaching of the Church of Rome, and frequently admitted that he believed in the

---

[48] *Twentieth Annual Report of C. B. S.*, p. ix.
[49] *The Doctrine of the Real Presence,* by Rev. A. L. Lewington, pp. 6, 9. Oxford: Mowbray, 1871.

doctrine of Transubstantiation, both name and thing. Here are some extracts from his address, which has never been repudiated by the authorities of the C. B. S. :—

"Those teachers who profess to accept a real Objective Presence, while repudiating Transubstantiation, are placed in a hopeless dilemma; as was plainly seen by Zuinglius, when he maintained that there was no alternative between Transubstantiation and the figurative view which he himself upheld. But the great Church of the West [that is, the Church of Rome] does not stand alone in its clear definite enunciation of the *Divine truth* in Eucharistic doctrine.[50]

"On this great subject, therefore [*i.e.*, the Real Presence], there is, happily, no room for difference between these two great Branches of the Church Catholic [*i.e.*, the Eastern Church and the Church of Rome]. *And if the unity of Christendom is ever to be restored, it can only be by the Church of England frankly accepting the full statement of Eucharistic truth as expressed in the authorized formularies of West and East alike.*[51]

"We are bold to maintain that the Eucharistic teaching of the Church of England *is essentially one* with that of the whole of the rest of Catholic Christendom, East as well as West. It is, indeed, that which, if she would make good her claim to be an integral part of the Catholic Church, she is bound to maintain.[52]

"But if it be asked why I lay such stress on a term which has given rise to so much odium and has been so misunderstood as *Transubstantiation*, I would answer, first, because I would remove all needless barriers between ourselves and the rest of Catholic Christendom, and, secondly, because experience shows that *no other expression defines what we mean so unmistakably*.[53]

"If ours be indeed, as we maintain it to be, the same Church of England which was planted by S. Augustine on the Mission of S. Gregory the Great, ours is the Church, and *ours the faith* of Wilfrid and Anselm, of Edmund Rich and *Thomas More*, quite as truly as it is of later worthies; *and we may look forward to a time*, though we all may be gathered to our rest, *when such open repudiation of Eucharistic Truth, even by our Ordained Ministry,* as we now deplore, *may be as impossible as it is now in the Priesthood of the Latin and Eastern Communions.* But the consciousness of our own grievous

---

[50] *The Doctrine of the Real Presence*, by Rev. E. W. Urquhart, p. 9. Oxford: Mowbray.
[51] *Ibid.*, p. 10.   [52] *Ibid.*, p. 11.   [53] *Ibid.*, p. 13.

shortcomings should prevent us from being high-minded, and check that bitter and spiteful attitude towards *our brethren of the Roman Communion*, which is so painful a feature in too much of the controversy of the day. Remember that, whatever be their shortcomings, they, throughout the ages, *have been faithful guardians* of the central verity of the Incarnation, and along with it, of the precious deposit of *Eucharistic truth*, which we have in years past insulted, neglected, and profaned. And in conclusion, to avoid misunderstanding, whilst *I hold that the time has come when we must ourselves recognize the identity of our own teaching with that which is expressed in the Tridentine canons by Transubstantiation*, and with the authorized formularies of the Eastern Church; it is only gradually, as they are able to learn, that we should expect to bring this conviction home to the minds of our weaker brethren, *whom we are striving to bring over to the faith*." [54]

With such a love for Popery as that which is exhibited by this Confraternity we need hardly wonder that during the year 1892, it requested all its members to pray "That the Ecclesiastical authorities in foreign countries, both East and West, may become willing to give Communion to English Catholics, on conditions which the latter may lawfully accept." [55]

It is a sad thing to see a Confraternity, engaged in teaching some of the worst doctrines of Popery, so widely supported by clergy of the Church of England. And even sadder is it to find that many of them have been promoted to high offices in the Church, and to livings in the gift of the Crown and the Bishops. In 1894 amongst its members were the Bishops of Zululand, Zanzibar, Nassau, Lebombo, and Corea, Bishops Hornby and Jenner, and the Deans of Rochester and Chichester.

One High Church Bishop, early in the history of the Confraternity of the Blessed Sacrament, had his eyes open to its dangerous and Popish character. Bishop Samuel Wilberforce wrote as follows to its Superior General, Canon T. T. Carter:—

"It is," wrote Bishop Wilberforce, "sure to stir up a vast amount

[54] *Ibid.*, pp. 14, 15.   [55] *Intercession Paper of C. B. S.*, June 1892, p. 18.

of prejudice from *its singularly un-English and Popish tone.* . . . I view with the utmost jealousy any tendency to ally that reviving earnestness to the unrealities and morbid development of modern Romanism. You may do much one way or the other. I entreat you to consider the matter for yourself, and *as Bishop I exhort you to use no attempts to spread this Confraternity* [of the Blessed Sacrament] amongst the clergy and religious people of my diocese."

In closing this chapter, let me once more quote Bishop Latimer. His words are as necessary now, within the Church of England, as when they were first spoken:—

"Wherefore stand from the altar, you sacrileging (I should have said, you sacrificing) priests; for you have no authority in God's Book to offer up our Redeemer: neither will He come any more into the hands of sacrificing priests. . . . *And I say, you lay people,* as you are called, *come away from forged sacrifices,* which the Papists [and now Ritualists] do feign only to be lords over you." [56]

[56] Latimer's *Remains*, p. 259.

CHAPTER VIII.

SOME OTHER RITUALISTIC SOCIETIES.

A Purgatorial Society in the Church of England—The Guild of All Souls—Extracts from its Publications—Masses for the Dead in the Church of England—Festival on "All Souls' Day"—The Fire of Purgatory the same as that of Hell—Bishop of London (Dr. Temple) gives its President a Living—The Secret Order of the Holy Redeemer—An Inner Circle; The Brotherhood of the Holy Cross; its secret rules quoted—The "Declaration" of the Order of the Holy Redeemer—The Pope the "Pastor and Teacher of the Church"—Why its members stay within the Church of England—Extraordinary and Jesuitical letter of "John O. H. R."—Its mysterious Superior said to be a "Bishop," though not in the *Clergy List?* Who ordained and consecrated him?—The secret Order of St. John the Divine—Extract from its secret rules—Society of St. Osmund—Its rules and objects—Prays for the Pope—Its silly superstitions—Driving the Devil out of Incense and Flowers—The Adoration of the Cross—A degrading spectacle—Its Mary worship—Holy Relics—Advocates Paying for Masses for the Dead—The Society merged in the Alcuin Club—The Club joined by several Bishops—Laymen's Ritual Institute of Norwich—Its Secret Oath—Secret Guild Books of St. Alphege, Southwark—Guild of St. John the Evangelist, at St. Alban's, Holborn—Confraternity of All Saints', Margaret Street—The Railway Guild of the Holy Cross.

PROBABLY the majority of my readers will be surprised to learn that there exists a Purgatorial Society nominally within the Church of England. Yet, strange and almost incredible as this may seem, it is a fact. This Society bears the title of "The Guild of All Souls," and was founded in the year 1873, for the special purpose of propagating within the Church of England a belief in Purgatory, and as a result of this, the offering of Prayers for the Dead, and of Masses to get them out of Purgatorial flames. It is a widespread organization, with branches all over England, and also in Scotland, the United States, Madras, Montreal, Prince Edward Island, Port

Elizabeth, Barbados, and New South Wales. According to the annual report for 1897—as recorded in the *Church Times*, May 28th, 1897—the Guild possesses seventy-one Branches. It includes amongst its members 646 clergymen, which is certainly a large number for such an extremely Romish society. The semi-secrecy of the Guild is shown in the fact that the public are never permitted to know who these clergymen are, with the exception of those who form its Council. The Guild issues a quarterly *Intercession Paper*, which is a strictly secret document. It always contains a list of churches in which Masses for the Dead are said every month, together with the names of deceased persons for whom prayer is asked. The latest copy of the *Annual Report* which I have been able to secure is that for 1895. It states that "During November, in addition to those on All Souls' Day, there were 991 Special Requiem Masses [offered] in connection with the Guild, and the regular Requiem Masses maintained throughout the year are now, at least, 480 each month."[1]

For the use of its members the Guild of All Souls has issued a book entitled the *Office of the Dead According to the Roman and Sarum Uses*—certainly not according to the use of the Book of Common Prayer, which is altogether too Protestant a compilation to suit the purposes of the Guild of All Souls. It has also published a book, entitled the "*Treatise of S. Catherine of Genoa on Purgatory*, edited with an Introductory Essay by a Priest-Associate of the Guild of All Souls." The title-page states that it is published by "John Hodges"; but it has on several occasions been officially advertised in the *Church Times* as one of the "Publications" of the Guild, and therefore I hold it responsible for its contents. In the portion which contains the translation of what Catherine of Genoa wrote, we read (in the chapter entitled "Of the Necessity of Purgatory:

---

[1] Guild of All Souls, *Report*, 1895, p. 3.

What a terrible Thing it is ") that the pains of Purgatory are "as sensible as the pains of hell."[2] The Priest-Associate of the Guild of All Souls who writes the Introductory Essay is evidently enraptured with what he actually terms "*the extreme moderation of the Roman Church upon the doctrine of Purgatory.*"[3] This gentleman's Popish sympathies are further manifested by his unblushing avowal that he believes in Transubstantiation!

"It is only," he writes, "within the last eight or nine years, since the publication of Mr. Cobb's *Kiss of Peace*, that *Anglicans* have begun to realize that there *is no essential difference between the doctrine of the Real Presence, as they hold it, and the doctrine of Transubstantiation, as defined by the Council of Trent.*"[4]

In the official *Manual of the Guild of All Souls* several "Litanies for the Faithful Departed" are printed. From these I take the following extracts:—

> "That it may please Thee to give rest to the souls of the faithful departed,
> That it may please Thee to cause light perpetual to shine upon them,
> That it may please Thee to wash them in Thy Precious Blood and to clothe them in white robes."[5]

> "From the shades of death, where they sit desiring the light of Thy Countenance,
> From Thine Anger, which they grieve to have provoked by their negligence and ingratitude,
> From the bonds of sin, wherein they have been entangled by the disorder of their affections,
> *From the pains*, which are the just penalty of their sins."[6]

> "Give Thy holy dead, O Lord,
> Portion in the Sacrifice,
> And prayers offered in Thy Church,
> Hear us, Holy Jesu.

"*We beseech Thee to hear us Sweet Jesu.*" "*Good Lord, Deliver them.*"

---
[2] *S. Catherine of Genoa on Purgatory*, p. 40.
[3] *Ibid.*, p. 11.
[4] *Ibid.*, p. 12.
[5] *Manual of G. A. S.*, pp. 16, 17.
[6] *Ibid.*, p. 20.

> "Make them share, O Jesu Blest,
> In the intercession
> Of the Saints before Thy Throne,
> Hear us, Holy Jesu.
>
> "Make all prayers and pious deeds,
> Holy rites and services,
> To increase their happiness,
> Hear us, Holy Jesu." [7]

In a sermon preached for the Guild of All Souls, on "All Souls' Day, 1883"—a Popish festival not found in the Prayer Book Kalendar—by the Rev. H. Lloyd Russell, Vicar of the Annunciation, Chislehurst, that gentleman affirmed that—

> "We believe that the mercy and justice of God in His dealings with their [faithful departed] souls, are reconciled by their being detained for a certain time in a middle place, *there to be punished*, and purified, and dealt with, according to His good pleasure, until He sees fit to admit them to the enjoyment of the Beatific Vision." [8]

Six years later, in 1889, the annual sermon before the Guild of All Souls was preached in St. Alban's, Holborn, by the Rev. John Barnes Johnson. The preacher told his deluded hearers that—

> "Blessed are they whom the Divine Fire thus changes now in the time of this mortal life. Blessed are they who know this Fire here on earth as the Fire of Love. But those who know it not, those who flee from it, yet cannot escape the Fire. If they remain in the world, St. Peter tells us the world is reserved for Fire. If they die, and go hence, *the Fire awaits them in Purgatory*; or, more terrible, in Hell. And everywhere the Fire that awaits them is the same Fire." [9]

> "God, even in the Fire, shall be known [by the faithful dead] to be their Father, burning out all the falsehood and revealing the truth. *Therefore let us join together now in offering the Sacrifice of the Mass for all departed souls.*" [10]

---

[7] *Manual of G. A. S.*, p. 26.

[8] *The Intermediate State*, by the Rev. H. L. Russell, p. 9. Published by the Guild of All Souls.

[9] *Things Present and Things to Come*, by J. B. Johnson, p. 17. London. Kegan Paul, 1890.

[10] *Ibid.*, p. 22.

For the year 1894 the annual sermon for the Guild of All Souls was preached by the Rev. E. G. de Salis Wood, Vicar of St. Clement's, Cambridge. Mr. Wood said that—

"Amongst all the consoling truths of our holy religion there was none more consoling than what Christian doctrine taught concerning Purgatory; and the consideration of the state of the holy souls detained there, though at all times most salutary, was especially salutary at the present. . . . The merits of Christ reigned everywhere, in Purgatory as well as on earth; the glorious, merciful work which was done for Christian souls in Purgatory was done by the merits of Christ alone. Never let the objection weigh with them for a single moment that the Christian doctrine of Purgatory evacuated the merits of Christ. It did nothing of the kind; on the contrary, it extended them to the other world as well as to this; *and so we did well to intercede for the souls in Purgatory.* Theirs was a blessed state, *though one of pain.*" [11]

Now, of course, for all this, as every well-informed and loyal Churchman knows, there is not to be found, either in Scripture or in the formularies of the Church of England, the slightest approach to an appearance of any authority whatsoever. You may search your Bible and Prayer Book from cover to cover, and you will not find one word in either of them which sanctions the teaching of the Guild of All Souls. The only proper place for such teaching is within the Church of Rome, and it would be a great blessing to the Church of England if every one of its members went there at once, without waiting for Corporate Reunion; though, of course, they would not be spiritually improved by their secession. But is it not an extraordinary thing that when the important living of St. Matthias', Earl's Court, London, fell vacant in 1892, the Bishop of London (now Archbishop of Canterbury), Dr. Temple, as patron, gave it to the Rev. Jonas Pascal Fitzwilliam Davidson, President of this very Guild of All Souls! This is the way in which many of our Bishops too frequently act. Not having the fear of loyal Churchmen before their eyes, they become indifferent

[11] *Church Times*, November 9th, 1894, p. 1195.

to their opinions, and not seldom treat an earnest remonstrance with contempt. But a day of reckoning will surely come, when the Bishops will be required to put their house in order. Just now, in connection with various Bills in Parliament, they are seeking to increase the powers they already possess. But how can we trust them with more power, so long as we behold them using that which they already possess in shielding—through the Episcopal Veto—law-breakers from the punishment of their misdeeds; and even in promoting these very law-breakers to positions of honour and trust? The powers the Bishops at present possess are too often used to the injury of the truth, and in the propagation of error.

I have, in the chapter on the Confraternity of the Blessed Sacrament, given quotations from the Homilies of the Church of England condemning both Prayers for the Dead and Purgatory. It is very well known that Purgatory is no part of Christianity; it is purely heathen in its origin. It is a doctrine well calculated to make the dying beds of Christians miserable. Who could have "a desire to depart" from this life with the prospect of Purgatorial pains before him? The religion of Purgatory, as it exists in the Church of Rome, is a very hard one for poor people, who cannot afford to pay their priests liberally for Masses for the Dead. And there are signs that the payment for Masses is about to be restored within the Church of England. Bishop Latimer spoke very truly of "Purgatory Pick Purse." Is there any limit to the toleration of the Church of England? Is the time coming when she will tolerate anything and everything —except decided Protestantism? At present she is torn with dissensions. The present state of things cannot go on very much longer. We have infallible authority for saying:—"If a house be divided against itself, that house *cannot* stand" (Mark iii. 25).

There is another mysterious and very secret Society nominally within the Church of England, whose special delight it is to work in and "level up" Protestant parishes. It is known as the "Order of the Holy Redeemer." From what I have been able to ascertain concerning its mischievous operations, I should not be surprised to hear that it is secretly affiliated to the "Order of Corporate Reunion." No owl ever loved the darkness more than does the "Order of the Holy Redeemer." It possesses an inner circle known as the "Brotherhood of the Holy Cross." I possess a copy of its secret "*Manual for Brethren of the B. H. C.*" It states that "this Brotherhood was started by a few friends who were studying for Holy Orders." The third of its Rules is as follows:—

"That, as the work of the B. H. C. can be best accomplished without opposition, *its very existence be kept in strict secrecy.*"

The fourth Rule is "That Brethren shall be *faithful* members of the Anglican Church"—though how *that* can be is hard indeed to understand. They may be nominally members of the Church of England, but that they are "faithful" members I will never admit. The Brethren are required "To endeavour to get others to join this Brotherhood"; but it is cautiously added that "Before speaking to anyone about it you should obtain advice and instruction how to proceed from your Superior." In a secret *Intercession Paper* of the Brotherhood of the Holy Cross for August, 1889, the members are requested to pray "For help for band of Catholics, working with success in Islington"— a thoroughly Protestant neighbourhood. A list of "Recommended books" is added, which includes the *Glories of Mary*, a most idolatrous book in honour of the Virgin Mary, written by "St." Alphonsus Liguori. It is so superstitious as well as idolatrous that even some Roman Catholics are found who are ashamed of its utterances.

As to the larger Order of the Holy Redeemer I learn from its secretly circulated *Monthly Leaflet* for April, 1891, edited by "the Secretary General," that those who join the Order as "Postulants," must make and sign a "Declaration" of their faith, which is printed in this same issue of the *Monthly Leaflet*. It is as follows:—

"THE DECLARATION REQUIRED OF POSTULANTS FOR ADMISSION TO THE ORDER OF THE HOLY REDEEMER.

"I................having signed the Nomination Form of the above Order, desire to profess my faith.

"I believe:—

"I. The Catholic Faith, as defined by the Seven General Councils accepted by the Undivided Church, and as commonly received in the Apostles' Creed, the Nicene Creed, and the Creed of St. Athanasius.

"II. The common Sacramental statements of the *Western Council of Trent* and the Oriental Synod of Bethlehem. The following is a digest of these propositions:—

"That there are Seven Sacraments instituted by our Lord, viz.:—
  i. Baptism which, necessary to all men for Salvation, remits original and actual sin, and is the instrumental cause of justification.
  ii. Confirmation.
  iii. The Holy Eucharist in which, after Consecration, our Lord Jesus Christ, true God and Man, is truly, really and substantially present under the species of Bread and Wine, and a whole and perfect Christ is contained in each kind, and in every part thereof. Furthermore, that in the Holy Eucharist a true and propitiatory Sacrifice is offered for the faithful, both living and dead.
  iv. Orders. v. Matrimony. vi. Penance. vii. Extreme Unction.

"III. The position of *the Bishop of Rome* is that of 'Archbishop of all the Churches,' *i.e.*, Chief Bishop (*and consequently* Pastor and *Teacher*) *of the Church*."

This is certainly a very sensational document, but the whole history of the Order of the Holy Redeemer, so far as I have been able to unravel it, is quite in accordance with its teaching. In the *Barnet Times* of May 6th, 1892, appeared a very noteworthy letter, in reply to a correspondent, from one who, as I happen to know from other sources, held high office in the Order of the Holy Redeemer. He signed himself as "John, O. H. R.," and gave some important information as to the real objects of the Order.

"In 1887," he wrote, "I joined the Order of the Holy Redeemer, a body working within the English Church *under Episcopal approval*. On behalf of the Order in particular, I have written when my multifarious duties have permitted me. I daily receive orders from the ecclesiastical Superior of the Order, and I hope faithfully execute them, but the reception of Holy Orders opens another question, which I leave him [his opponent in the correspondence] to propound, and to which I will happily give an equally candid answer. Finally, I do utterly and entirely love, with my whole heart and soul, all Christian bodies, *more especially the Church of Rome, which, I believe*, despite accidents and not inherent faults of discipline, *to be the purest and most apostolic body that has ever existed*, impeccable AND INFALLIBLE. Likewise, I believe that the Pope is not by honorary Primacy, but *by Divine appointment* and by the mercy of God, *Supreme Head of the whole Church of Christ* throughout the world, *and that those who refuse his rule forfeit all title to the name of Catholicity*. . . .

"Moreover, I believe that in discipline, doctrine, and in morality, *the Church of England has been utterly corrupt*, as the need of the Oxford Revival and the malignant opposition to it from the children of this world has fully attested, *and I believe that no man is justified in staying within that Church*, SAVE WHEN HE FEELS THE VOCATION OF GOD TO ASSIST IN RESTORING HER TO HER LOST PLACE, IN HUMBLE, IMPLICIT, AND UNQUESTIONING SUBMISSION TO THE SEE OF PETER, AND TO THE AUTHORITY OF OUR HOLY FATHER, THE POPE, WHICH IS THE OBJECT OF THE ORDER OF THE HOLY REDEEMER."

Here we have, indeed, the very essence of what is commonly termed Jesuitism, and in its most virulent form. Where was the *conscience* of the man who wrote like this? And yet it can scarcely be considered worse than the statement of the Rev. Dr. Ward's biographer, that he (Dr. Ward) stayed for years in the Church of England for the sole purpose of bringing over a greater number to Rome.[12]

A "Notice" which appears in the *Intercession Paper* of the Order of the Holy Redeemer, for February, 1890, shows how

---

[12] See above, p. 15.

terribly afraid the Order was lest its secret documents should be lost:—" It may be interesting to the Brethren to learn that the legal proceedings recently taken by the Order have been perfectly successful. The documents unlawfully detained were yielded, and further steps rendered unnecessary." In the following April the Order was in a most joyful condition, for it expected to receive the approval of the Bishop of London (Dr. Temple). In its *Intercession Paper*—or *Leaflet*, as it is sometimes called—for that month, appears the following announcement:—" It may interest the Brethren to hear that the approval of the work of the O. H. R. was asked of the Bishop of London. His decision is yet pending." Later on a High Church Vicar wrote to the Bishop on the subject, and received as an answer that he had never given any approbation to the Order. This gentleman, the Rev. V. H. Moyle, Vicar of Ashampstead, sent the Bishop's letter to the *English Churchman*, in which it appeared on June 2nd, 1892. Mr. Moyle, in sending this letter, added this further information concerning the O. H. R.:—" They have recently taken and opened a Convent at Stamford Hill, London. . . . Their object being the ultimate subjection of England and England's Church to Popery, I would warn all your readers against them." The March, 1890, *Intercession Paper* had a mysterious request for prayer " For several men, wishing to work for God, who are labouring at present under a false banner." Does that mean that they were labouring for Ritualism under the " false banner " of Protestantism? It looks very much like it. A pamphlet circulated by the Order affirms that its " Superior General " " was ordained priest "; [13] but it does not say by whom he was ordained. In a correspondence which has since appeared in the Roman Catholic *Tablet*, this gentleman asserted that he was also in Episcopal orders. I have since found out his real name, and it does not appear in the *Clergy List*, or *Crockford's Clerical Directory*. Was he ordained and

[13] *O. H. R. Tracts*, No. I., p. 12.

consecrated secretly by " Bishop " F. G. Lee, of the " Order of Corporate Reunion " ? This is another Jesuitical mystery which needs unravelling. I once had a letter from the " Brother John " who wrote the letter to the *Barnet Times*, quoted above, in which occurs the following paragraph :— " Shall I have the pleasure of seeing you personally at All Saints', Lambeth, next Wednesday night, or shall I send tickets ? I can get you a seat in the choir of Lady Chapel *with the Order*," that is, the Order of the Holy Redeemer. I did not accept the invitation, for I did not wish anyone to suppose that I had anything to do with such a society. But Brother John's letter was that which first led me to suspect that there was a connection of some sort between the O. H. R. and the O. C. R., for All Saints', Lambeth, is the Church of which " Bishop " F. G. Lee was and still is the Vicar. In 1891 the O. H. R. issued to its members a monthly paper entitled the *Catholic*, which described itself as " The Official Publication of the Order of the Holy Redeemer." In the October issue amongst the intercessions asked for was this :—" That devotion to Our Lady may spread in England ; " it also contained a Hymn to the Virgin of a most idolatrous character, and an article in favour of " Invocation of Saints and Angels." This was followed, in the January, 1892, number by the following interesting item of news :—

"On S. Thomas Day, 1891, the Chapter of S. Thomas, of Canterbury met at the Home of the Good Shepherd. The Superior presided, and after Evensong had been sung, proceeded to the admission of a Postulant. The chapel was well filled, and included among the congregation were many who are not members of the Order. The Rev. Fr. Square delivered a short address upon our work, and upon the conclusion of the office all adjourned to enjoy the unfailing hospitality of the Rev. Br. Philip, the Provincial of S. W. London."

It will be observed that mention is here made of two clergymen, the " Rev. Fr. Square," and the " Rev. Br. Philip," but who they are I cannot tell. In a leaflet issued by the Order, which I had lent to me in 1893, the names and addresses were printed of those to whom application might be made—by those wishing to join—for further particulars concerning the Order. Only one of these was a clergyman, and he was simply styled "Father George." By the aid of the address given I was able to find this person out, in the far East of London. What was my astonishment when I discovered that he was, and had been for the previous two years, acting as curate to the only Protestant incumbent in that part of London! I felt it my duty to see the incumbent, who, there and then, sent for this "Father George," and asked him, in my presence, if he was the person mentioned in the leaflet of the O. H. R., which I had brought with me? "Father George" was very much astounded at being found out, and very much frightened, too; but he was compelled to acknowledge that he *was* "Father George." The old Protestant Vicar sternly, and yet with a kindly voice, asked him if he thought it right or honourable to come to him—an Evangelical and Protestant clergyman—as curate, while he held office in an Order which was engaged in bringing the Church of England back to the Pope? The result of our interview was that the curate had to leave his curacy. He was "run to earth." On looking through the *Clergy List* for 1897, I was pleased to find that "Father George" had had no curacy since 1893, when he left East London. The old Vicar pleaded so hard with me to spare him the worry of publicity that I have, out of, it maybe, mistaken kindness to him, abstained from mentioning the case in print, with one exception, until now. I am prepared to give names and addresses to those who prove to me that they have a right to question me on the subject.

I am not going to say that the Order of the Holy Redeemer is a large body. I do not think it is. But it claims to have a great many Branches, and to have even extended its borders into several of our Colonies. There is evidently money at the disposal of the ostensible leaders, while the real leaders keep themselves within their native darkness. A few men of this class can do a great deal of mischief, probably where it is least expected. A young man who joined the Order told me that he was introduced to it by the teacher of his Bible-class in an Evangelical Sunday-school in Islington. The case I unearthed at East London shows further the wish of the Order to play a subtle part in Protestant parishes. Moral obligations sit loosely on a certain class of minds. Many persons are not particular as to the weapons they use, so that what they term "The Church" gains the benefit of their operations.

I wish that I could think the Order of the Holy Redeemer the only secret Ritualistic Society which, like the owl, loves most to work in the dark. I have heard—and on what I consider reliable authority—that there exist Ritualistic Societies, the members of which are required never to part with their rules to anyone outside their ranks. There lies before me, as I write, the Rules and Constitution of a Society which terms itself the "Order of St. John the Divine," and which is being pushed just now by Ritualists in East London. It contains the following "Notice":—

"The Objects, Rules, and Constitution of the Order are submitted for your perusal and consideration *in strict confidence*. In accepting this sheet for perusal *you pledge yourself that you will neither show it, nor impart its contents in any way, to any other person.*"

The Order, says the document, requires that "none shall be admitted who are not Communicants of the Church Catholic in England." The *real* objects of these secret organizations are never, I believe, fully committed to print or to writing, but are given verbally only.

There is a small section of the advanced Ritualistic party who have become so bold that they flaunt their Romeward leanings in the face of the public in the most unblushing manner. Some members of this section formed themselves into a society which termed itself the "Society of St. Osmund."

It was founded in 1889, and several men of note joined its ranks. In 1885 it printed, in its Annual Report, the names of the Bishop of Bloemfontein, the Bishop of Pretoria, the Bishop of Cairo, United States, the Dean of Argyll and the Isles, and the Dean of Bloemfontein in its list of Vice-Presidents. It was permitted to hold its annual meetings for 1891, 1892, 1893, 1894, and 1895 in the Church House, Westminster. In 1892 the chair was taken by Sir Theodore C. Hope, K.C.S.I., who is also a member of the Council of the English Church Union; and in 1893 by Mr. Athelstan Riley, also a member of the Council of the E. C. U., and one who has made himself very prominent as a member of the London School Board. In the handbill of the anniversary for 1892 it was announced:—"The Bishop-elect of Bloemfontein, South Africa (a Vice-President of the Society of St. Osmund) will be presented with a Set of Low Mass Vestments at this meeting." At its anniversary in 1894, as announced in the Annual Report printed beforehand, "The Holy Eucharist" was "offered up" in St. Margaret Pattens, Rood Lane, London, "by the Right Rev. the Lord Bishop of Cairo (Illinois)." During the London School Board Election, in 1894, the Society of St. Osmund was exposed in the *English Churchman*, and as the exposure was reprinted in a large number of daily papers it created a great deal of excitement. Down to that period the Society had been in the habit of printing with its Annual Report a list of those churches in London, the Provinces, and the Colonies in which Holy Communion would be celebrated "for the intention of the Society"; but after the exposure a fit of dread seems to have seized the Council, for in the Report for 1895 the list was suppressed, for obvious reasons. In an official paper of the Society it is stated that its "Objects" are:—

"1.—The Restoration and Use of English Ceremonial in the English Church, the rubrical directions of the Sarum Liturgical Books being taken as the basis.

"2.—The publication of such books, pamphlets, or leaflets as, in the judgment of the Council, are likely to promote the objects of the Society.

"3.—The encouragement of Liturgical study among the Members of the Society.

"4.—The assisting by advice, and in other ways, those who are desirous of following English customs in their Churches."

All this looks comparatively innocent. The Society was not going to promote the advance of "Roman" Ritual. It only wanted to restore "English Ceremonial." What could be more commendable from a loyal Churchman's point of view? But it also wished to restore—and here lay the real cause of its existence—the use of "the Rubrical directions of the Sarum Liturgical Books," and this meant a great deal; more, in fact, than the general public were aware of. It meant the restoration of the Ritual which was in use in England *before* the Reformation, a Ritual which had as great an authority and sanction from the Pope as that which is technically termed "Roman Ritual." The chief difference between the two is that Sarum Ritual is far more elaborate, superstitious, and puerile than that termed "Roman." Anyone who needs proof of the thoroughly Popish character of the Ritual advocated by the Society of St. Osmund cannot do better than consult a book which it published, entitled *Ceremonial of the Altar*, compiled by a clergyman on its Council, who subsequently seceded to the Church of Rome. This book has been frequently advertised amongst its "Publications," though the title-page states that it is published by a London firm. The work is remarkable also for its very advanced Romish doctrine, implied in its prayers and directions. It tells the Ritualistic priest how to use his eyes, how to use his hands, and when he is to turn his little finger in certain directions, and how to place his thumbs. With regard to his hands, there is a whole section devoted to telling the priest how to manage them; when they are to be "joined," when "extended," and when "laid on the altar." He is to bless the people with "fingers outstretched, little finger towards persons blessed." He is warned not to "fidget at the altar," told that he must "stand evenly on *both* feet"; and on no account must he forget to "keep the elbows to the sides when praying with hands extended." He is even told when to "kiss" the table and the Gospel book, and other things; and how "with the right thumb (to) make a small sign of the Cross." On no account must the priest omit "at the name of Mary to bow slightly," and also "at the name of the Saint of the day"; and he must not forget to say the words of consecration "with his elbows resting on the edge of the altar." The directions are so numerous and minute that it is no wonder if they give a fit of the "fidgets" to any nervous priest who has to observe them.

The *Ceremonial of the Altar*, in its "Ordinary of the Mass," directs the priest to say:—

"I confess to God, to Blessed Mary, to all the Saints, and to you, that I have sinned exceedingly in thought, word, and deed, by my fault: I beg Holy Mary, all the Saints of God, and you to pray for me." [14]

The most startling prayer of all is that which is printed on the portion entitled the "Canon of the Mass." The priest is directed to pray—

"That Thou [God] wouldst be pleased to keep it [the Church] in peace, to preserve, unite, and govern it throughout the world; and also for Thy servant OUR POPE N., our Bishop N., our Sovereign N." [15]

Some excuse might be made for praying for the Pope. We should pray for all men. But to pray for the Pope as "*our* Pope" is quite a different matter. He is not the Pope of English Churchmen, and a Society which recognizes him in that position cannot be said to be loyal

---

[14] *Ceremonial of the Altar: a Guide to Low Mass*, compiled by a Priest, p. 22. Second edition.   [15] *Ibid.*, p. 45.

to the Church of England. It has been said by friends of the Society of St. Osmund that this book was issued for the purposes of Liturgical study, and not for the actual use of the clergy of the present day. But this theory is refuted by the statement of the editor in his Preface, who declares that "The directions have been drawn up *for the use* of loyal [?] sons of the Church of England." [16] I ought to have mentioned above that one of the directions, which, I think, may reasonably be termed disgusting, is that which tells a clergyman, just after he has given the Communion to a sick person—

"Wash your fingers, and let *the sick man* drink the ablution." [17]

The Society of St. Osmund has shown itself a warm friend to Mariolatry. Mr. Athlestan Riley translated for it the *Hours of the Blessed Virgin Mary, According to the Sarum Breviary*, and also the *Mirror of Our Lady*. When we remember that there is not to be found in the Bible a single petition from a saint on earth to a saint in heaven, and that no such petition or invocation can be found within the Book of Common Prayer, it is easy to see that those who bring in such Popish practices are thoroughly dissatisfied with what they must consider the meagre provision for their devotional life placed at their disposal by either the Word of God or the Church of England. In this *Mirror of Our Lady* we read the following statements:—

"Our merciful Lady is that Star that succoureth mankind in the troublesome sea of this world, and bringeth her lovers to the haven of health, therefore it is worthy that she be served and praised at Mattins time." [18]

"*When all other succour faileth our Lady's grace helpeth.* Compline is the end of the day; and in the end of our life we have most need of our Lady's help, and therefore in all these hours *we ought to do her* WORSHIP, and praising." [19]

"It is reasonable that *seven times each day she* [Mary] *be* WORSHIPPED and praised." [20]

[16] *Ibid.*, p. iii.
[17] *Ibid*, p. 118.
[19] *Mirror of Our Lady*, p. 7.
[19] *Ibid.*, p. 8.
[20] *Ibid.*, p. 9.

"After ye have then called yourself and others to the praising of God and of His glorious mother, our Lady, *ye sing an hymn in* WORSHIP *and praising of her.*"[21]

"Here ye incline, both in token and in reverence of our Lord's meek coming down for to be man, and also *in worship of that most clean and holy Virgin's womb.*"[22]

There is nothing, I think, in the whole range of Roman Catholic literature more awfully idolatrous in the way of Mary worship, than this. So long as God's Word stands:— "Thou shalt worship the Lord thy God and Him only shalt thou serve," so long must this worship, whether it be termed *Latria, Doulia,* or *Hyperdoulia,* be condemned by all true friends of Christianity.

Idolatry and superstition are closely related. It is so in the Society of St. Osmund. It has published another book full of superstition as well as idolatry, entitled the *Services of the Holy Week.* The friends of the Society have pleaded that it, like the *Ceremonial of the Altar,* was issued for the purposes of Liturgical study, and not for actual use by English Churchmen of the nineteenth century. But in this case also the documents of the Society itself refute the plea put forward. In the annual report for 1895 the Council state that "a second edition of the *Services of Holy Week* has been published," and it adds that "a considerable demand for this publication points to the fact that there is an increasing desire to become acquainted with the *special offices* of this holy season, ruthlessly swept away at the Reformation, *but now being happily revived among us.*"[23] This proves that the book is designed or use, and not for study only. On turning to the services for "Good Friday," as provided in this work, we find that of the Adoration of the Cross set forth in full. This very idolatrous performance is now actually to be seen in several Ritualistic Churches each Good Friday. At St. Cuthbert's, Philbeach Gardens, London, for several years past, the Vicar has

[21] *Mirror of Our Lady,* p. 20. [22] *Ibid.,* p 34.
[23] *Annual Report of Society of St. Osmund,* for 1895, p 4.

issued a printed notice of services to be held in his Church in Passion Week. It has always included the announcement that the "Adoration of the Cross"—as it is therein termed—would take place at 9.30 A.M. on Good Friday. I have a copy of the notice for 1896 by me as I write. In that year I was present at the service, and beheld the clergy, choir, and about two hundred men, women, and children, adore the Cross—which lay at the foot of the steps on the floor—by throwing themselves flat on the floor, and kissing the foot of the Cross while in this literally "sprawling" attitude, the choir meanwhile singing, from *Hymns Ancient and Modern*, No. 97, the hymn addressed to the Cross:—

> "Faithful Cross, above all other
> One and only noble Tree,
> None in foliage, none in blossom,
> None in fruit thy peer may be;
> Sweetest wood and sweetest iron;
> Sweetest weight is hung on thee."

This was sung in accordance with the directions given in the *Services of Holy Week*. The following extract from the service for the Adoration of the Cross still further reveals its thoroughly idolatrous character:—

"*Then the Priests, uncovering the Cross by the right side of the Altar, shall sing this Antiphon:—*

"Behold the Holy Cross, on which the Saviour of the world did hang for us. O come and let us worship.

"*The choir, genuflecting, reply:—*

"*Antiphon.* We venerate Thy Cross, O Lord."

"*Then the clerks shall proceed* TO VENERATE THE CROSS, *with feet unshod, beginning with the Senior.*"

"When this is done, the Cross shall be solemnly carried through the midst of the choir by the two aforesaid priests, the Candle-bearers preceding them, and shall be set down before some Altar, *where it shall be* VENERATED *by the people.*" [24]

For "Easter Eve" a service is provided for "Blessing the Fire," in which it is stated that "*Holy Water* is sprinkled

---

[24] *Services of Holy Week*, pp. 30-32.

over the fire."[25] Incense is to be used, and a form is given for driving the devil out of it, as follows:—

"I exorcise thee, *most unclean spirit*, and every illusion of the enemy, in the Name of God the Father Almighty, and in the Name of Jesus Christ His Son, and in the might of the Holy Ghost, that *thou mayest go forth and depart from this creature of Frankincense* with all thy fraud and malice: that this creature may be sanc✠tified in the Name of our Lord Jesus Christ; that all who taste, or touch, *or smell* the same may receive the strength and aid of the Holy Ghost."[26]

A collect is then offered up, in which God is asked to send down His blessing "upon this incense," that "*by the smoke thereof* every illusion whereby the enemy doth assault soul or body may be put to flight."[27] Soon after follows "The Blessing of the Paschal Candle."[28] A Deacon is ordered to "put Incense into the candle in the form of a cross"; and God is asked to accept "this solemn oblation *of wax, the work of bees.*"[29] The officiating priest is ordered to put on a red Cope, and "stand before the Altar," while the Litany of the Saints is sung. The Litany is too long to print here entire. I therefore select from it the following items:—

> "Holy Mary, Pray for us.
> Holy Mother of God, Pray.
> Holy Michael, Pray.
> St. Peter, Pray.
> All ye holy Apostles and Evangelists, Pray.
> St. Gregory, Pray.
> St. Sixtus, Pray.
> St. Denys with his companions, Pray.
> St. Augustine, Pray.
> St. Agnes, Pray.
> All Saints, Pray."[30]

Later on in the service the priest is required to "drop wax from the candle into the font in the form of a cross"; and to "dip the candle into the font, making the sign of

---

[25] *Services of Holy Week*, p. 40. [26] *Ibid.*, p. 38. [27] *Ibid.*, p. 39.
[28] *Ibid.*, p. 40. [29] *Ibid.*, p. 42. [30] *Ibid.*, pp. 47, 48.

the cross with it."[31] All this to every loyal and soberminded Churchman must seem childish and puerile to a degree, and those persons may be pardoned who doubt whether anyone in a state of sanity could, with a solemn face, publicly perform such an outrageous farce. But it is no laughing matter. Unless this sort of thing is put down by authority it will increase as the years go on, and the evil will grow worse with time. Some, as they read this, will naturally ask, Have the Bishops gone asleep? They have taken an oath to "banish and drive away" all false doctrine contrary to God's Word, and the ritual which I have described is designed to teach false doctrine. Why, then, do not their lordships act? When an unfortunate Protestant Minister does anything extreme the Bishops become wide awake at once, and soon show that they possess power to put down what they dislike. Suppose they were to publicly declare that they would not license a curate to any Vicar who tolerates these idolatrous and superstitious practices in his Church? That would soon bring many of them to their senses, and compel these lawless rebels to submit to authority. We want a Bench of Bishops who will fearlessly do their duty. As Episcopal Sees fall vacant, pressure must be brought to bear on the Prime Minister to recommend for the vacant Sees men who will insist on the supremacy of law and order in their dioceses, and sternly put down these Ritualistic Anarchists, whose own will is their only supreme law, and who persist in doing that which is right only in their own eyes.

To return to the *Services of Holy Week*. It provides a service for "Palm Sunday," which commences with a "Sprinkling of Holy Water,"[32] and is followed by the priest driving the devil out of "the flowers and leaves" to be used in the service:—"I exorcise thee," he exclaims, "Creature of flowers or branches . . . and henceforth let all the strength of the adversary, all the host of the devil,

[31] *Ibid.*, p. 52.   [32] *Ibid.*, p. 3.

every power of the enemy, every assault of fiends, be expelled and utterly driven away from this creature of flowers or branches."[33] I did not know, until I had read this Service, that the devil ever resided within flowers. Ritualistic young ladies especially will now need to be careful. Would it not be wise for them, before going with a bouquet of flowers to the theatre, to take it to some priestly "Father," in order that he may, in this way, drive the devil out of the flowers? If he could drive the devil out of *the people* who carry the flowers, it would be much more profitable. The priest next sprinkles "the flowers and leaves" "with Holy Water";[34] and he is required to carefully observe the following Rubric:—

"When the Palms are being distributed, A SHRINE WITH RELICS [that is, with the holy bones of some supposed Saint] shall be made ready, in which shall hang in a Pyx the Host; and two clerks, not joining the procession to the first station, shall come to meet it at the place of the first station; a lantern shall precede it, with an unveiled cross and two banners."[35]

Where they are to get the "*Relics*" from I do not know. Can they purchase them at Rome for money? These "Relics" are mentioned in several other portions of the service. Another service is here provided, by the Society of St. Osmund, for "Maundy Thursday." It is ordered that the sub-deacon shall "prepare three Hosts to be consecrated," one of which, after consecration shall "be placed with the cross *in the sepulchre.*"[36] On this day, it appears, "the oilstock of the Holy Chrism is kissed in place of the Pax." After this the "altar" is to be washed by the priest with wine and water, who is to finish up the business by kissing it.[37] Before closing my remarks on this book I must mention that on Good Friday the Pope is ordered to be prayed for in terms which can only be used by those Ritualists who are thoroughly disloyal to the independence of

---

[33] *Services of Holy Week*, p. 3.   [34] *Ibid.*, p. 5.   [35] *Ibid.*, p. 6.
[36] *Ibid.*, p. 17.   [37] *Ibid.*, pp. 19, 20.

the Church of England of all Papal control. The following extracts prove this:—

"Let us pray also for *our* most *blessed Pontiff* N., that our God and Lord, who hath chosen him from the Order of the Episcopate, would preserve him in health and safety to His Holy Church, for *the governance* of God's holy people."

"Almighty and everlasting God . . . regard our prayers: and with Thy mercy preserve *our* chosen prelate; that *all* Christian people *governed by such authority, and obeying so great a Pontiff*, may ever increase in faith and works." [38]

The wonder is that the people who teach this sort of thing, do not consistently "obey so great a Pontiff," by at once going over *openly* to his communion. If the Pope is appointed by God, as is here asserted, "for the governance of God's holy people" without exception, then the conduct of those Ritualists who believe this is undoubtedly that which is usually termed "double dealing." We cannot afford to laugh at or despise this sort of thing. It has a tendency to grow and multiply, like weeds in a garden. The sooner these Popish weeds are pulled up out of the garden of the Church of England the better it will be for those healthy plants whose proper place is in her soil. It is nearly thirty years since the Ritualists first published a translation into English of the *Liturgy of the Church of Sarum*. Canon T. T. Carter, of Clewer, Superior General of the Confraternity of the Blessed Sacrament, wrote an Introduction to it in which he affirmed that the translation was "a boon of the greatest value"; and expressed his own personal "sense of its great value." [39] In the "Canon of the Mass" this translation also contains a prayer for "our Pope"; [40] and as a specimen of superstition I may mention that one of the rubrics in it directs:—"Let the Priest rinse his hands, lest any remnants of the Body or Blood should have remained *on*

---

[38] *Ibid.*, p. 26.
[39] *The Liturgy of the Church of Sarum*, with Introduction by Rev. T. T. Carter, pp. vi., vii. Second edition. London: Hayes.
[40] *Ibid.*, p. 63.

his fingers or in the chalice."⁴¹ The following prayer is very disloyal and Popish :—

"*For the Pope.*

"Let us pray also for the Blessed N. *our Pope;* that our God and Lord, who elected him to the Order of the Episcopate, may preserve him safe to His Holy Church that he may govern the holy people of God."⁴²

There is not one word of warning in the book which contains this prayer, reminding the reader that God never did appoint the Pope to "govern the holy people of God."

There is one other publication of the Society of St. Osmund which I must notice, because it proves how anxious some of the Ritualists are to revive the evil custom of paying for Masses for the Dead, and at the same time to restore many of the most degrading death-bed customs of the Papacy, which obtained in England during the Dark Ages. It is entitled *Ceremonial and Offices Connected with the Burial of the Dead.*

"It will be seen," writes the author, "that Chauntry priests were not overpaid: but as half a loaf is said to be better than none, surely it would be worth the while of some aged or infirm priest to accept a moderate stipend or voluntary offering of £60 or £70 a year to act in that capacity.⁴³ One of the most distressing things I know of in the Anglican Church is the difficulty of getting a priest to say Mass for some departed friend or relation, because when asked he will tell you *he does not like being paid for Sacraments,* &c.; but *surely this is a prudish line to take*—the 'labourer is worthy of his hire'—and as St. Paul said, 'They which wait at the altar are partakers with the altar.'

"Let priests then awaken to a greater sense of duty in this respect, and the great work of charity they have the power of bestowing, and remember that *in accepting an Honorarium for a Mass* they are not receiving a fee, but an offering."⁴⁴

All this means, of course, however covered over with

---

⁴¹ *The Liturgy of the Church of Sarum,* with Introduction by Rev. T. T. Carter, p. 78. Second edition. London: Hayes.

⁴² *Ibid.,* p. 114.

⁴³ That is, to act as a "Chauntry Priest," whose sole work would be that of offering Masses for the Dead to get them out of Purgatory.

⁴⁴ *Transactions of the Society of St. Osmund,* Part III., "Ceremonial and Offices Connected with the Burial of the Dead," pp. 73, 74.

words, a revival of what Bishop Latimer justly denounced as "Purgatory Pick Purse." The "honorarium for a Mass" is *not*, says the writer of this pamphlet, "a fee, but an offering." But when the priest refuses to say the Mass without his "honorarium," would not that refusal be equivalent to a demand for a "fee"? It would be the same as saying:—"I cannot sell the Lord's Body in this Mass, like Judas sold it of old for thirty pieces of silver. That would be very wicked; but for all that, if you cannot give me a money 'offering,' you cannot have the Mass." What is the essential difference, in a case like this, between the conduct of Judas and that of the Ritualistic priests? Judas might have said to the chief priests, "I cannot sell the Lord Jesus to you; but it is quite open to you to make me an 'honorarium,' or free-will 'offering' of thirty pieces of silver for my services in handing Him over to you."

The writer of this pamphlet, towards its close, tells us that he has in it sketched those "beautiful rites of our Holy Mother the Church with which, in the plenitude of her glory, peer and peasant alike were fortified and honoured, and through the wickedness of man alone were lost to long generations that followed. *It becomes nothing less than a solemn duty* devolving upon us, in this so-called enlightened age, *to restore and resuscitate* ALL *that our forefathers so dearly cherished.*"[45] Amongst the "*beautiful* rites" which, in the opinion of this Society of St. Osmund, it is our "solemn duty" to "restore," are the following, as described in the pamphlet which I am considering :—

"Richard Marsh, Bishop of Durham, in 1220 enjoins as follows :— 'When the Eucharist is taken to the Sick, let the priest have a clean and decent Pyx, so that one always remains in the Church, and in the other he carries the Lord's Body to the Sick, the Eucharist itself being enclosed in a very clean purse. The Pyx will be covered with a clean linen cloth, and a light will be carried before it, and a cross also, unless the cross has already been carried to another sick man. A

[45] *Ibid.*, p. 71.

little bell will also be rung before the priest to excite the devotion of the faithful. The priest will always have with him a stole when he carries the Eucharist to the Sick, and when the sick man is not very far off the priest will go to him in a surplice. He will have a vessel of silver or tin, kept especially for the purpose, that he may give to him [the sick man] the ablutions of his fingers after Communion.' " [46]

" Arriving at the sick man's house, the priest sprinkled it with Holy Water, saying, 'Peace be to this house,' and having heard his Confession, absolved him and given him the kiss of peace, he administered the Viaticum and Extreme Unction." [47]

"This service [for deceased Guildsmen in the Dark Ages] was followed . . by three solemn Masses, at each of which every brother present went up at offertory time to the altar and put his MASS PENNY for the good of the departed soul into the hands of the sacrificing priest." [48]

I have no doubt that the " sacrificing priest " thought that the custom of each brother paying a " *Mass Penny* " into his hands was a very " beautiful rite " indeed, as it appears the Society of St. Osmund also does at the present time; but I should imagine that the overwhelming majority of Englishmen are now of a very different opinion. We think the other " rites " described above to be far from " beautiful," especially that one in which the sick man is to drink the dirty water in which the priest has washed his hands!

On February 18th, 1897, the Hon. Secretary and Treasurer of the Society of St. Osmund sent out a circular-letter to the members announcing that a " general meeting " would be held on February 25th " for the purpose of dissolving the Society of St. Osmund." This would indeed have been good news for English Churchmen, had it been strictly in accordance with the facts. What was actually " dissolved " was, not the *Society*, but its *name*, as is clear from the Secretary's letter which appeared in full in the *English Churchman* of February 25th, 1897, page 126.

---

[46] *Transactions of the Society of St. Osmund*, Part III., " Ceremonial and Offices Connected with the Burial of the Dead," p. 55.
[47] *Ibid.*, p. 56.   [48] *Ibid.*, p. 62.

"Enclosed," wrote the Secretary to the members of the Society of St. Osmund, "are particulars of the *Alcuin Club*, whose work will cover more ground than our Society has been able to touch, and *I consequently presume that you will continue your support* of English Ceremonial *by joining the Club*, at least as an Associate, at the annual subscription of five shillings. *Unless I hear from you to the contrary*, on the dissolution of the Society of St. Osmund, *I shall* therefore assume that you wish to become an Associate of the Club, and will accordingly *propose you for election.*"

The Secretary of the new "Alcuin Club" is the gentleman who had hitherto acted as Secretary of the Society of St. Osmund; and several of the Committee of the "Club" are the same gentlemen who served on the Council of the Society of St. Osmund. There is, therefore, but little, if any, room for doubt that the "Club" and "Society" are to all intents and purposes the same. An article on the new "Club" appeared in the *Church Times* of March 19th, 1897, from which I learn that it will be a larger and more influential organization than the Society was. "Both members and associates," it states, "must be in communion with the Church of England"; and it announces that "The Club has already been joined by the Bishops of Oxford, Salisbury, and Edinburgh," and by Professor W. E. Collins, of King's College, London; Canon J. N. Dalton, of Windsor; Canon A. J. Mason, of Canterbury; the Rev. Hugh P. Currie, Principal of Wells Theological College; and Canon W. E. Newbolt, of St. Paul's Cathedral. The names of the Committee are given by the *Church Times*. The clergy are all extreme Ritualists.

"The work of the Alcuin Club," says the *Church Times*, "will be chiefly in books and tracts, illustrated by exact reproductions of miniatures and photographs of Church furniture, ornaments, vestments ... the ornaments of the altar and the liturgical colours will be taken next; then the occasional services will be dealt with, the Divine service, the Litany or Procession, and the Celebration of the Eucharist."

I fear that there is nothing to be expected from the new

Alcuin Club likely in any way to benefit the cause of Protestantism. It is an organization which will need careful watching, nor is it at all pleasant to find that the Bishops of Oxford, Salisbury, and Edinburgh, the Principal of one of our Theological Colleges, and the Professor in another Theological College, have joined it. English Churchmen will be glad to hear the good news of their having withdrawn from its ranks.

There are many extremely Ritualistic Societies or Guilds of a merely local character scattered throughout the country, whose objects and operations are well worthy of consideration. It would, however, require a volume to deal with them thoroughly, and I fear that when produced it would not be very interesting. All I can do, therefore, with regard to these local Societies is to call attention to a few of them. The "Laymen's Ritual Institute for Norwich," which existed for several years, and, for anything I know to the contrary, may be still in existence, required its members to take an "*oath*" of fidelity, which probably included the shielding of its secrets. I have two secret "Reports" of this Institute before me, viz., those for 1873 and 1875. In the former it is announced that—

"There has been an accession of members; and the test of membership has been remodelled, *by the requirement of an* OATH *from each candidate*, as a bond of fidelity and adherence."

"The Institute, in conjunction with other Catholic societies, has no other work than steady perseverance in its course, against every obstacle opposing the spread of Catholicism and its Ritual, until such time as it and they shall have *succeeded in banishing for ever from the Church of England* THE BASTARD FAITH *of Protestantism*."[49]

The Report further added that the Institute had circulated papers entitled, *Devout Acts in Honour of Our Blessed Lady*.[50] In the following year an effort was made by some of the members to substitute a "Declaration" for the "Oath" hitherto taken by new members, but on a

[49] *Report of Norwich Laymen's Institute* for 1873, pp. 4, 7.   [50] *Ibid.*, p. 5.

division the proposition was "lost by a large majority."[51] The Institute had a very great hatred for the Reformation, and, in its Report for 1875, expressed its hatred in very vigorous language :—

"Perhaps," it says, "not intentionally, but in fact, the so-called Reformation *is a dark and, in some sense, damnable spot* in our Church's history."[52]

It may be said that the work of an Institute like this is a very small affair, not worthy of notice here. But it is a good old proverb which exhorts us never to "despise the day of small things," whether for good or evil. That this teaching was given a quarter of a century ago only proves how widely the evil had spread even so far back as then. At the present time the evil has grown immensely.

To come closer to our own day. What are we to think of the parochial Guilds connected with the Church of St. Alphege, Southwark? Somehow or other, I know not how, the Roman Catholic priest who edited the *St. George's Magazine*—that is, for St. George's Roman Catholic Cathedral, Southwark, which is close to St. Alphege—got hold of a few books belonging to them, and exposed them in its columns.

"A little book," wrote the Editor, "has lately come into our possession, which we think deserves a few words of notice in our local Magazine. It is issued, in connection with one of the many Protestant [53] places of worship with which we are surrounded, by a clergyman of the Established Church.

"It is called the '*Manual of Tertiaries of the Order of Reparation to Jesus in the Blessed Sacrament.*' It contains the Rules of the 'Order,' a 'Litany of Reparation,' the *Office of Benediction*, a Litany of the Blessed Sacrament, the *Litany of Our Lady*, a Litany of the Incarnation (mainly addressed to the Blessed Virgin), and fourteen hymns—*half of them addressed to Our Lady*, and half to the Blessed Sacrament. The Seven Sacraments are accepted; life vows (for 'Sisters'—perhaps the 'Founder and Father Superior' has some

---

[51] *Report for* 1875, p. 5. [52] *Ibid.*, p. 7.
[53] Roman Catholics always call the Ritualists and their Churches "Protestant," though it is very well known that the Ritualists repudiate the term.

special reason for saying 'the Brothers cannot take solemn vows') are recognized; 'Sacramental Confession' is enjoined, as well as fasting, 'unless dispensation be obtained from the Superior'; 'medals and crosses are *blessed and sprinkled with Holy Water*'; the 'Hail Mary' is prescribed; certain prayers are given to be 'said at Mass after the Canon.' ... Mr. Goulden's Tertiaries sing:—

"'Queen of Heaven, Queen of earth,
Mistress of the Church of Christ,
Mother of our second birth—
Pray for us, O Mother dear,'

" or invoke her in words more familiar and dear to us, as 'Virgin most powerful,' 'Virgin most merciful,' 'Cause of our Joy,' and 'Gate of Heaven.'" [54]

I possess two other Guild books used at St. Alphege, Southwark. One of them is the *Manual of the Church Confraternity*. When I was last in that Church I saw a notice posted up, in very large letters, inside the building, announcing that no person would be considered as a member of the congregation, who had not joined the "Church Confraternity." Of course in this way a kind of moral compulsion is put upon the parishioners to join the Confraternity. On opening the *Manual* I find that all members "must observe the rule of the Church [what Church?] and Communicate every Sunday fasting." [55] Before being admitted into the Confraternity it is required that "every member shall make an open profession of belief in the Catholic and Apostolic Religion" [56] in the presence of the Vicar of the parish. He must profess that he believes "that there are truly and properly Seven Sacraments *instituted by Christ*" [57], though Article XXV. declares that five of these seven "are not to be counted for Sacraments of the Gospel." The members must also profess that in "the Great Eucharistic Sacrifice" we "obtain His Grace for ourselves and the whole world, pardon for all our sins, and that the faithful departed may rest in peace safe in the

---

[54] *St. George's Magazine*, June, 1890, pp. 145, 146.
[55] *Church Confraternity*, p. 5.
[56] *Ibid.*, p. 5. [57] *Ibid.*, p. 6.

arms of Jesus"; [58] and they also declare that "in that most Holy Sacrament of the Eucharist there is verily and indeed the true Body and Blood of Christ, and that under either kind alone Jesus is received whole and entire." [59] I wonder does the Bishop of Rochester know all that is going on in St. Alphege, Southwark? He went down recently to consecrate the church, and spoke in the highest terms of the work being carried on there. I wonder did he look into the special hymn book, copies of which are placed in every seat in the church? He would have found a large number of them addressed to the Virgin and the Saints. Ought not this Popish book to have been swept out of the Church for ever, as an essential condition of consecration? Are the Bishops to be the last persons in their dioceses to find out what their clergy are doing?

Another Guild in the parish of St. Alphege, Southwark, is "The Guild of the Sacred Heart of Jesus." Its annual commemoration is kept "on the Sunday after the Feast of the Sacred Heart of Jesus." [60] This is, as is well known, a Feast in honour of a practice introduced by the Jesuits, for the purpose of worshipping the material heart of our Lord. This Guild is for "boys of good character under twenty years of age," who are expected "To receive the most Holy Sacrament (fasting) every Sunday, and *to go to Confession once a month*." [61] They have given to them a "List of Things to be Remembered," which is as follows:—

"The sign of the Cross should be made before and after prayers, at absolutions and blessings.

"In passing an Altar a bow should be made.

"Boys, when they communicate, must genuflect before going up to the Altar to communicate.

"At the Consecration, immediately the Sanctus Bell rings, everybody should bow down and worship Jesus, Who is then *present on the Altar*, under the Form of Bread and Wine." [62]

---

[58] *Ibid.*, p. 7. [59] *Ibid.*, p. 7.
[60] *S. Alphege, Southwark, the Guild of the Sacred Heart of Jesus*, p. 4.
[61] *Ibid.*, p. 5. [62] *Ibid.*, p. 9.

In the "Form of Reception" used for the "Guild of St. John the Evangelist," in the parish of St. Alban's, Holborn, and "Privately Printed for the Guild," it is ordered that, after certain prayers have been offered :—

"The Priest then sprinkles the Collars, Crosses, and Candles with Holy Water, and incenses them. Those who are about to be admitted then come up to the Altar." [63]

Another Guild at St. Alban's, Holborn, is known simply as "The Perseverance." One of the Rules is "To be present at the Holy Sacrifice every Sunday." [64] As a temptation to join the Guild it is stated that—

"At the death of any Member a *special Funeral Mass* will be said for the repose of his soul." [65]

The members of "The Confraternity of All Saints," Margaret Street, London, are "girls and young women only." In their *Manual* they are instructed that "Special Confession of our sins is also a very blessed help and privilege to many Christians really trying to lead a holy life." [66] One of the privileges which the members enjoy is thus described :—"In case of the marriage (*if approved by the Sister Superior*), to help her in her settlement." [67] I am afraid the Sister Superior would not give her approval if one of the members wished to marry a Protestant Churchman. A Guild like this must necessarily have a powerful influence over the girls who belong to it.

"The Railway Guild of the Holy Cross" is for men employed on Railways. It has a body of "Clerical Associates" attached to it, mostly extreme Ritualists. It has also Women Associates; but it is a rule that their "names are not for publication." [68] There is a slight leaven of Popery in this Guild, for I find in its *Manual* that "The Crosses, with

---

[63] *Guild of St. John the Evangelist*, p. 18. Across the top of the title page, in ordinary type, is printed the words, "Not to be taken away."
[64] *Manual of the Perseverance*, p. 9. "Privately Printed." [65] *Ibid.*, p. 10.
[66] *Manual of the Confraternity of All Saints*, p. 10.   [67] *Ibid.*, p. 4.
[68] *Manual of the Railway Guild of the Holy Cross*, p. 24.

their Cords, being placed upon the Altar, or held by one of the Brethren, *shall be blessed by the Priest*,"[69] though what good that will do the Crosses and Cords the *Manual* does not reveal. The priest is to bless them by saying :—" Ble✠ss, O Lord, we beseech Thee, and sanc✠tify these Crosses, which we bless in love and honour of Thy Glorious Cro✠ss."[70]

These are but a few specimens out of an innumerable body of Guilds scattered all over the country, where the parish is in Ritualistic hands. All these are not equally advanced in a Romeward direction; but what I have quoted may serve to show my readers one of the most powerful means by which the country is being leavened with Ritualism. All Guilds are not secret; but in all cases they enable the local clergy to impart privately to the members, in confidence and safety, High Church notions of the Church, her Sacraments, Orders, and Doctrine. Church of England parents should keep a watchful eye over their young sons and daughters, lest they should join any Guild which does not work on lines that are loyal to the Church of England. The Guild Movement of the present day helps greatly the so-called " Catholicising " of the Church of England, which is essential as a preliminary work, in preparing the way for Corporate Reunion with Rome.

[69] *Ibid.*, p. 15.   [70] *Ibid.*, p. 15.

CHAPTER IX.

THE ROMEWARD MOVEMENT.

Corporate Reunion with Rome desired—Not individual Secession—The reason for this policy—How to "Catholicise" the Church of England—Protestantism a hindrance to Reunion—Reunion with Rome the ultimate object of the Oxford Movement—Newman and Froude visit Wiseman at Rome—They inquire for terms of admission to the Church of Rome—Secret Receptions into the Church of Rome—Growth of Newman's love for Rome—Newman wants "more Vestments and decorations in worship"—William George Ward: "The Jesuits were his favourite reading"—Publication of Tract XC.—Mr. Dalgairns' letter to the *Univers*—Secret negotiations with Dr. Wiseman—"Only through the English Church can you (Rome) act on the English nation"—Keble hopes that yearning after Rome "will be allowed to gain strength"—Mr. Gladstone on the Romeward Movement—He hopes those "excellent persons" who love all Roman doctrine will "abide in the Church"—"The Ideal of a Christian Church"—Dr. Pusey's eulogy of the Jesuits censured by Dr. Hook—Mr. Gladstone's article in the *Quarterly Review*—Pusey hopes "Rome and England will be united in one"—Pusey asks for "more love for Rome"—He praises the "superiority" of Roman teaching—Pusey believes in Purgatory and Invocation of Saints—He "forbids" his penitents to invoke the Saints—Manning's remarkable letter to Pusey—Manning's visit to Rome in 1848—Kneels in the street before the Pope—His double dealing in the Church of England—The Roman Catholic *Rambler* on the Oxford Movement.

THE great object of the Ritualistic Movement from its very birth, in 1833, was that of *Corporate* Reunion with the Church of Rome. The wirepullers have always been opposed to *individual* secession, not so much on the ground that it was a thing evil in itself, but because its tendency was to prevent the realization of their larger schemes. As far back as 1867 a leading quarterly of the advanced Ritualists declared that, instead of seceding to Rome, "it would be much better for us to remain working where we are—for what would become of England if we

[Ritualists] were to leave her Church? She would be simply lost to Catholicism... Depend upon it, it is only through the English Church itself that England can be Catholicised."[1] The same article, referring to this corporate and visible unity with the Church of Rome, declared:—

"Here you have *the real heart and soul of* the present Movement; *this is the centre from which its pulsations vibrate*, and from which its life-blood flows."[2]

As far back as June 13th, 1882, at the annual meeting of the English Church Union, Lord Halifax, its President, declared that corporate reunion "is the crown and completion of that great Movement which has transformed the Church of England";[3] and he has repeated the assertion many times since. But in order to the realization of such a reunion it is first of all necessary to make the Church of England look as much like the Church of Rome as possible. "A Colonial Priest" of the Ritualistic party, writing to the *Church Review*, of September 21st, 1888, remarked:—

"It seems to me utterly premature to consider reunion, especially with the great Patriarchal See of the West [Rome] as within even distant probability, until the Anglican Communion as a whole is Catholicised. *There lies our work* ... Therefore, let every one, while praying daily for reunion, remember that the surest way to accomplish it is by working towards *the purification of our own branch of the Catholic Church.*"

According to the opinion of some of these gentlemen the Reformed Church of England is not sufficiently respectable, at present, for the Pope to have her, even as a present. She first needs "purification" from Protestantism. In a volume, with an Introductory Essay by Dr. Pusey, one of the writers very frankly declared that—

"The first great hindrance that is before us arises from the Protestantism of England. Till this is removed, the Reunion of our

---

[1] *Union Review*, Volume for 1867, p. 410.   [2] *Ibid.*, p. 398.
[3] See official report of this speech, published by the E. C. U., p. 13.

Church, as the Church of England, with either the Greek, or *Latin* Churches, is absolutely hopeless."[4]

May God grant that this "great hindrance" may ever remain to repel the machinations of the traitors to our spiritual liberties!

The reunion schemes of the Tractarians were at first kept a profound secret from all but the initiated. In this, as in so many other matters, the leaders cleverly practised their doctrine of "Reserve." So well was the secret kept that for several years their proceedings were a great puzzle even to many Roman priests. The Hon. and Rev. George Spencer, a prominent priest, and son of an English peer, was one of these puzzled ones for a time; but at last he became enlightened. In a letter to the Roman Catholic *Univers*, of Paris, in 1841, he wrote:—

"Indeed, quite lately I still held to the idea, that, in a short time, we should see them [the Tractarians] prepared to quit their Church in considerable numbers, and unite with us in labouring to effect the conversion of their brethren; but the nearer the approaches they make to Catholic sentiments, the more resolved they appear to be to rectify their position—not by quitting the vessel [the Church of England], as if they despaired of its safety, *but by guiding it together with themselves into the harbour of safety*" [that is, into the Church of Rome].[5]

This leavening of the Church of England with so-called "Catholic" principles and practices—in other words, the infusion into her system of more or less of Popery—commenced with the Tractarian Movement, in 1833, and has been going on ever since. Yet, even now, it appears that we are not, as a Church, decent enough for the Pope to accept us as a present. At the Norwich Church Congress, October, 1895, a Ritualistic clergyman said:—"The Church of England is *not fit* for communion with either the Eastern Church or the Church of Rome. *We are not good enough for them.*"[6] In

---

[4] *Essay on Reunion*, p. 89.

[5] Quoted in Bricknell's *Judgment of the Bishops upon Tractarian Theology*, p. 681.

[6] *English Churchman*, October 17th, 1895, p. 706.

this leavening process, as well as in the carrying out of the ultimate object of the Movement, great " Reserve in communicating Religious Knowledge " was observed.

Much of that which in the early history of Tractarianism was kept a profound secret, has since been made public through the biographies of some of the principal actors. In the " Lives " of these men are now to be read their most confidential communications one with the other, in which their love of Popish doctrines, and their desire for Corporate Reunion with Rome, appear in the clearest possible light. By the aid of this light it may be useful to trace the gradual progress of this Romeward Movement.

The late Cardinal Newman stated that he ever considered the 14th of July " as the start of the religious Movement of 1833." A few months before that date, Newman, in company with his friend, Richard Hurrell Froude, while travelling on the Continent, had visited Monsignor (subsequently Cardinal) Wiseman at Rome. " We got introduced to him," wrote Froude, " to find out whether they would take us in [*i.e.*, to the Church of Rome] on any terms to which we could twist our consciences, and we found to our dismay that not one step could be gained without swallowing the Council of Trent as a whole."[7] While on this journey Newman fell seriously ill with a fever. On his recovery he decided to return at once to England. While in a weak condition, and before starting, he tells us: " I sat down on my bed, and began to sob violently. My servant, who had acted as my nurse, asked what ailed me. I could only answer him :—'*I have a work to do in England.*'"[8] What that work was we now know full well. It was that of Romanizing the Church of England.

With reference to this remarkable visit to Rome, the Rev. William Palmer, who for ten years was one of the foremost leaders of the Tractarian Movement (but subsequently

---

[7] *Froude's Remains*, Vol. I., p. 306.

[8] Newman's *Apologia Pro Vita Sua*, p. 35. Edition, 1889.

retired from it on account of its Romanizing tendencies), and who was the intimate friend of Newman and Hurrell Froude, tells us that " Froude had with Newman been anxious to ascertain the terms upon which they could be admitted to Communion by the Roman Church, *supposing that some dispensation might be granted which would enable them to communicate with Rome without violation of conscience*." [9] Mr. Palmer adds that this visit to Rome was unknown to the friends of Newman, and that if he (Mr. Palmer) had known about these circumstances, it is a question "whether he should have been able to co-operate cordially with him." " Nay," writes Mr. Palmer, " if I had supposed him willing to forsake the Church of England, I should have said that I could in that case have held no communion with him." [10] It must be admitted that there was something very suspicious in thus keeping secret from even their most intimate friends such a very important visit.

Mr. Palmer further states that " Newman and Froude had consulted at Rome (with Dr. Wiseman) upon the feasibility of being received as English Churchmen into the Papal Communion, retaining their doctrines." [11] This statement, however, was denied by Cardinal Newman, in a note dated October 11th, 1883, attached to his *Via Media*, Vol. II., p. 433. Edition 1891. Newman therein says that :—" If this means that Hurrell Froude and I thought of being received into the Catholic Church while we still remained outwardly professing the doctrine and the communion of the Church of England, I utterly deny and protest against so calumnious a statement. Such an idea never entered into our heads. I can speak for myself, and, as far as one man can speak for another, I can answer for my dear friend also." Now this statement of Newman's in the case of any ordinary man of position would be considered as conclusive, but in his case it is not so, and for this reason :—In his note on " Lying

[9] Palmer's *Narrative of Events Connected with the Tracts for the Times*, p. 40. Edition, 1883.   [10] *Ibid*., p. 40.   [11] *Ibid*., p. 73.

and Equivocation," attached to his *Apologia Pro Vita Sua*, Newman writes:—"For myself, I can fancy myself thinking it was allowable in extreme cases for me to lie, but never to equivocate." [12] And again he writes in the same note:—"A secret is a more difficult case. Supposing something has been confided to me *in the strictest secrecy*, which could not be revealed without great disadvantage to another, what am I to do? If I am a lawyer, I am protected by my profession. I have a right to treat with extreme indignation any question which trenches on the inviolability of my position; *but, supposing I was driven up into a corner* [as Newman certainly was by Palmer's statement], *I think I should have a right to say an untruth.*" [13] If such a thing happened as that which Mr. Palmer relates, then it would certainly be "a great disadvantage" to the memory of Hurrell Froude, as well as to himself, if Newman "revealed" the truth about such an underhand proceeding; and therefore, in such a case (assuming it only to exist), Newman would feel that he had "a right to say an untruth" when "driven into a corner." It is evident, therefore, that Newman's denial does *not* settle this important question.

Lord Teignmouth, in his *Reminiscences*, mentions a remarkable case of a dispensation, given with Episcopal sanction, to a pervert to Popery. He says:—

"*I saw the conditions* on which a lady, nearly related to an intimate friend of mine, a Scotch Baronet, had been received into the Romish allegiance by a priest of Amiens, whom she had consulted, *as sanctionedly the Bishop of the Diocese*. They were as follows:—that she should not be required to censure the Church of England, to forego the use of the authorized version of the Holy Scriptures, to abstain from the domestic worship of Protestants, or to acquiesce in any form of Mariolatry." [14]

Fa Di Bruno's *Catholic Belief* has had a very large circu-

---

[12] *Apologia Pro Vita Sua*, p. 360. Edition, 1889.   [13] *Ibid.*, p. 361.
[14] *Reminiscences of Many Years*, by Lord Teignmouth, Vol. II., p. 291. Edinburgh: David Douglas, 1878.

lation in England. In a published letter to the author, dated May 2nd, 1884, Cardinal Manning terms it "one of the most complete and useful Manuals of Doctrine, Devotion, and Elementary information for the instruction of those who are seeking the truth." In this book is contained the following question and answer, which seem to me to have a very direct bearing on the possibility of a secret reception of Dr. Newman into the Church of Rome, in 1833:—

"*Question.*—Nicodemus was a disciple of Christ, though secretly; cannot I in like manner be *a Catholic* in heart and *in secret?*"

"*Answer.*—Nicodemus was a disciple of Jesus Christ in secret; but he presented himself to our Lord. Begin therefore by presenting yourself to the Catholic priest, to be instructed and received into the Church. After being received into the Church *privately*, if weighty reasons in the judgment of your spiritual director justify it, such as loss of home, or property, or employment, *and so long as those weighty reasons last, you need not make your Catholicity public*, but may attend to your Catholic duties privately." [15]

The Tractarian Movement had only been in existence a very short time when people began to suspect it as being in reality a Romeward Movement. Within a month or two after its birth some were calling Newman a "Papist" to his face. On December 22nd, 1833, he wrote to Miss Giberne:— "Mr. Terrington called on me yesterday. He was very kind, and said he intended to sign the Address to the Archbishop, and *did not call me a Papist to my face, as some other persons have.*" [16] As early as May, 1834, Keble asserted privately that "Protestantism, though allowable three centuries since, is dangerous now." [17] As is well known, the publication of *Tracts for the Times* was one of the earliest works undertaken by the party. Directly after their birth they were denounced as containing Popish doctrines. On December 7th, 1833, a clergyman wrote lamenting the

---

[15] *Catholic Belief*, by the Very Rev. Joseph Faà Di Bruno, D.D., p. 230. Fifth edition.

[16] Newman's *Letters*, Vol. II., p. 10.   [17] *Ibid.*, p. 41.

insertion in one of the Tracts of such expressions as "conveying the sacrifice to the people," "intrusted with the keys of heaven and hell," and "intrusted with the awful and mysterious gift of making the bread and wine Christ's body and blood"; and, in view of such expressions, he closed his letter with the wise and much-needed, but sadly neglected warning:—"We must take care how we aid the cause of Popery."[18] On June 5th, 1834, Newman complained to his friend Froude:—"My Tracts were abused as Popish, as for other things, so especially for expressions about the Eucharist."[19] The Tracts, as they continued to appear, from time to time, until the last, in 1841, grew more and more Romish in their character; and they were supplemented by a flood of other publications written by various members of the party, of even a more Romanizing character. The work of "Catholicising" the Church of England was, by these means, pushed rapidly forward. In July, 1834, Newman repudiated the word "Protestant";[20] and even six months before that time Hurrell Froude had the audacity to declare:—"I am every day becoming a less and less loyal son of the Reformation. It appears to me plain that in all matters that seem to us indifferent or even doubtful, we should conform our practices to those of the Church which has preserved its traditionary practices unbroken. We cannot know about any seemingly indifferent practice of the Church of Rome that it is not a development of the Apostolic *ethos*."[21] Already Rome was the model for the Tractarians to follow. On November 5th of this year Newman did a kind act for Popery, which he has recorded in his Journal:—"November 5th.—Did not read the special Gunpowder Plot service." The celebrated M. Bunsen, 1835, declared that, in his opinion, the Tractarians were "introducing Popery without authority."[22] In 1836 people asserted that the Tractarians

---

[18] Palmer's *Narrative*, p. 226.
[19] Newman's *Letters*, Vol. II., p. 47.   [20] *Ibid.*, p. 59.
[21] Froude's *Remains*, Vol. I., p. 336.   [22] Newman's *Letters*, Vol. II., p. 143.

were secretly Romanists. Newman wrote on this subject to Keble, and told him that people were under "the impression that we are Crypto-Papists." [23]

In this year Newman began to use the "Breviary" of the Church of Rome. Of course the Thirty-nine Articles were in the way of the success of the conspirator's plans. "I am no great friend of them," wrote Newman to Perceval, January 11th, 1836, "and should *rejoice* to be able to substitute the Creeds for them." [24] It is, indeed, something to be thankful for that even down to the present time the Ritualists have laboured in vain to remove these "forty stripes save one"—as they have been termed—from off their backs.

It was at about this time that Newman discovered, very much to his astonishment, that the early Fathers of the Church looked upon the Bible as the only Rule of Faith, as all good Protestants do in this nineteenth century. There are several allusions to this unwelcome discovery in Newman's *Letters*. On August 9th, 1835, he wrote to Froude:—"By the bye, I am surprised more and more to see how the Fathers insist on the Scriptures as the Rule of Faith, even in proving the most subtle parts of the doctrine of the Incarnation." [25] Again, on August 23rd, 1835, he wrote:—"The more I read of Athanasius, Theodoret, &c., the more I see that the ancients *did make the Scriptures the basis of their belief.* . . . I believe it would be extremely difficult to show that Tradition is *ever* considered by them (in matters of faith) more than interpretative of Scripture. . . . Again, when they met together in Council they brought the witness of Tradition as a matter of fact, but when they discussed the matter in Council, cleared their views, &c., proved their power, they always went *to Scripture alone.*" [26] Two years later Newman wrote to Mr. Rogers:— "The Fathers do appeal in all their controversies to Scriptures as *a final authority*. When this occurs once only it

[23] Newman's *Letters*, p. 153.   [24] *Life of Dr. Pusey*, Vol. I., p. 301.
[25] Newman's *Letters*, Vol. II., p. 124.   [26] *Ibid.*, p. 126.

may be an accident. When it occurs again and again uniformly, it does invest Scripture with the character of an *exclusive* Rule of Faith." It is, indeed, a pity that Newman and his followers did not imitate the excellent example of the Fathers. We have to thank him, however, for his very candid acknowledgments on this gravely important subject. They prove that the Fathers were thorough Protestants on the question of the Rule of Faith.

Dr. Pusey's biographer states that in September, 1836, Newman informed Pusey that he believed in the Sacrifice of the Mass, as taught by the Council of Trent. "As to the sacrificial view of the Eucharist," he wrote, "I do not see that you can find fault with the formal wording of the Tridentine Decree,"[27] which, as every student knows, teaches the Sacrifice of the Mass. At this time, says his biographer, "Pusey also acquiesced in the formal wording of the Council of Trent on the subject, except so far as its words were modified by the doctrines of Transubstantiation and Purgatory."[28]

For three years Newman and the band of followers who had gathered round him, including Dr. Pusey and the Rev. J. Keble, had been diligently sowing Popish tares in the Church of England, and the harvest was about to commence. By this time Newman had "learned to have tender *feelings*" towards the Church of Rome, as he tells us; but his "*Judgment* was against her." It "went against my feelings," he says, "to protest against the Church of Rome."[29] He had become an adept in the art of mystifying people. "I used irony in conversation," he wrote, "when matter-of-fact men would not see what I meant. This kind of behaviour was *a sort of habit with me.*"[30] "Irony" is defined in our dictionaries as "a mode of speech in which the meaning is contrary to the words," and as "dissimula-

---

[27] *Life of Dr. Pusey*, Vol. II., p. 33.
[29] *Apologia Pro Vita Sua*, pp. 127, 128. First edition.
[28] *Ibid.*
[30] *Ibid.*, p. 115.

tion" for the purposes of ridicule. But surely, when those to whom this irony was addressed, as in this instance, did "not see" the irony, but took the falsehood for truth, they were nothing better than wilfully and shamefully deceived by Newman! Of course, for a few years, the ultimate object of the Movement was not much talked about. Its chief promoter had, as he tells us, come back from Rome, early in 1833, fully convinced that Protestant "Reformation principles were powerless to rescue" the Church of England from her existing condition; and that "there was need of a second Reformation."[31] Three years of that "second Reformation" had now passed by, and its results were highly satisfactory to Newman.

"It was," he wrote, "through friends, younger, for the most part, than myself, that my principles were spreading. They heard what I said in conversation, and told it to others. Undergraduates in due time took their degree, and became private tutors themselves. In this new *status*, in turn, they preached the opinions which they had already learned themselves. Others went down to the country, and became curates of parishes. Then they had down from London parcels of the Tracts, and other publications. They placed them in the shops of local booksellers, got them into newspapers, introduced them to clerical meetings, and converted more or less their Rectors and their brother curates."[32]

From 1836 the Tractarian march to Rome was much more rapid than before, and that under cover of an attack upon Popery. In 1839 it was proposed to erect the Protestant Martyrs' Memorial at Oxford. Pusey did not like it at all. He spoke strongly against it, "as unkind to the Church of Rome," towards which his sympathies were already being drawn out. The erection of a Monastery was contemplated, and plans were being laid for the establishment of Sisterhoods. The Rev. John Keble, another of the leaders, had begun to hate the reformers. "Anything," he wrote to Pusey, January 18th, 1839, "which separates the present

[31] *Apologia Pro Vita Sua*, p. 95. First edition. [32] *Ibid.*, p. 133.

Church from the Reformers I should hail as a great good." [33] In Keble's opinion, at this time, the Reformers "were not as a party to be trusted on ecclesiastical and theological questions." [34] Long before this period the news of the work going on at Oxford had reached Rome, and had greatly rejoiced the heart of the Pope. The then Bishop of Oxford (Dr. Bagot) heard about these Papal rejoicings, and became greatly alarmed. He wrote to Pusey about it :—

> "There are now," he said, "friends of mine staying at Rome— sensible men, too, and without *gossip*—and I am assured that the language of the Pope (as I am informed in one instance), and that of all the English Roman Catholics of rank residing there, is that of joy and congratulation at the advances which are being made in Oxford towards a return to the doctrines of the ' true Church.' " [35]

Newman became Editor of the *British Critic*, and soon after regretted that he had allowed in its pages "an article against the Jesuits," of which he " did not like the tone " ; [36] which is certainly not to be wondered at, for a fellow feeling makes us wondrous kind towards those whose tactics we may adopt. The Rev. Isaac Williams, author of two of the *Tracts for the Times*, in his *Autobiography* writes :—" I have lately heard it stated from one of Newman's oldest friends, Dr. Jelf, that *his mind was always essentially Jesuitical.*" [37]

In 1839 the " second Reformation " had proceeded so far that one of its disciples, the Rev. J. B. Morris, preaching before Oxford University, had the audacity to teach the full doctrine of the Sacrifice of the Mass, and to declare that every one was an unbeliever and carnal who did not believe it. [38]

Early in 1840 Newman became afraid of the mischief he

---

[33] *Life of Dr. Pusey*, Vol. II., p. 71.
[34] *John Keble*, by Walter Lock, M.A., p. 96. London, 1893.
[35] *Life of Dr. Pusey*, Vol. II., p. 73.   [36] *Apologia*, p. 135. First edition
[37] *Autobiography of Isaac Williams*, p. 54.
[38] Newman's *Letters*, Vol. II., p. 291.

was working in the Church, though he had no repentance for his wrongdoing. On January 10th he wrote to his friend Bowden:—"Things are progressing steadily; but breakers ahead! The danger of a lapse into Romanism, I think, gets greater daily. I expect to hear of victims. Again, I fear I see more clearly that we are working up to a schism in our Church."[39] The whole tendency of the Movement has been in the direction of schism. It has already effectually broken up the peace of the Church of England, divided her into parties, and may lead to a great schism at any time. Its tendency has also been in the direction of individual secession to Rome on the part of those who have been too impatient to wait for Corporate Reunion. Some of the Ritualistic leaders occasionally boast that they keep men from going over to Rome. It may be that they do keep a few here and there, for a short time, but the general tendency of their work is the other way. Cardinal Manning knew more about secessions to Rome, and their cause, than any man in England, and this is what he said about them in 1867:—

"Every Parish Priest happily knows *how empty and foolish is the boast* they [Ritualists] make of keeping souls from conversion. *The public facts of every day refute it.* . . . Such teachers are, as Fuller quaintly and truly says, like unskilful horsemen. They so open gates as to shut themselves out, but let others through."[40]

Several months later Newman saw clearly enough that the work of the Tractarians was driving men to Rome, and yet neither he nor they ceased their operations on that account. On September 1st, 1839, he wrote to Mr. Manning, the future Cardinal: "I am conscious that we are raising longings and tastes which we are not allowed to supply; and till our Bishops and others give scope to the development of Catholicism externally and wisely, *we do*

---

[39] Newman's *Letters*, Vol. II., p. 299.
[40] *Essays on Religion*, Second Series, edited by Archbishop Manning, pp. 14, 15.

tend to make impatient minds seek it where it has ever been, in Rome."[41] And what remedy, it may be asked, did Newman propose to Manning for the longings for more Popery which they had created in the minds of their disciples? It was simply that of giving them, in the Church of England, the Popery which they would otherwise go to Rome for, instead of teaching them that they were under a delusion in supposing that Popish poison is the pure "milk of the Word." Ritualists supply Popery in the Church of England as some Irishmen supply whisky—without a *license.*

So Newman, in the letter just quoted, wrote to Manning: —"I think that, whenever the time comes that secession to Rome takes place, for which we must not be unprepared, we must boldly say to the Protestant section of our Church— '*You* are the cause of this; you must concede; you must conciliate, you must meet the age; you must make the Church... more equal to the external. Give us more services, *more vestments and decorations in worship; give us Monasteries...* Till then you will have continual secessions to Rome."[42] Did it never, I wonder, occur to Newman that Protestant Churchmen had conscientious objections to granting the Popery which he coveted for himself and his followers? Loyal Churchmen will have nothing to do with Popery, either within or without the Church of England.

But, as we have seen on the authority of Cardinal Manning, the Ritualistic cure for longings for Popery, is, in practice, an utter failure. A few months later Newman's faith in the Church of Rome had greatly increased, for he had come to fear that she was the only body capable of resisting the devil. "I begin," he wrote, "to have serious apprehensions lest any religious body is strong enough to withstand the league of evil but the Roman Church. At the end of the first millenary it withstood the fury of Satan, and now the end of the second is drawing on."[43] By the end of

---

[41] Purcell's *Life of Manning*, Vol. I., p. 233.   [42] *Ibid.*
[43] Newman's *Letters*, Vol. II., p. 300.

the year he thought " Rome the centre of unity "; [44] and yet for another five years he kept away from that centre. At this period he not only "wished for union between the Anglican Church and Rome," but he also went so far as to do what he could "to gain weekly prayers for that object"; and drew up forms of prayer for union to be used by his disciples.[45] At this time a Roman priest, the Hon. and Rev. George Spencer, was also urging the offering of prayers with the same aim. With this object in view, Mr. Spencer paid a visit to Newman, in 1840. With reference to this visit Newman writes:—" So glad in my heart was I to see him [Spencer] when he came to my rooms, whither Mr. Palmer, of Magdalen, brought him, that I could have laughed for joy; I think I did." Newman, however, thought it best to disguise the joy he felt, and therefore, when Mr. Spencer came he was "very rude to him," and "would not meet him at dinner." [46] The Oxford Tractarians frequently visited the Continent, on holiday tours, and while there cultivated the good opinion of foreign Roman Catholics, and in this they were encouraged by their leaders. In the autumn of 1840 Mr. James R. Hope-Scott was travelling thus abroad, when he received a letter from Dr. Pusey, containing the following paragraph:—" I am very glad that you are seeing so much of the R[oman] C[atholics]. One wishes that they knew more of our Church, and we more of ye better among them." [47] At home the Rev. William George Ward, who subsequently succeeded Newman as the leader of the advanced Tractarians, was diligently engaged in the study of Roman Catholic books of theology. He preferred them to the early Fathers. "Both in ascetics and in dogmatics," writes Mr. Ward's son, "the Jesuits were his favourite reading"[48] at this period. We need not wonder

---

[44] Newman's *Letters*, Vol. II., p. 319.
[45] *Apologia*, pp. 222, 224. First edition.   [46] *Ibid.*, p. 224.
[47] *Memoirs of James R. Hope-Scott*, Vol. I., p. 239.
[48] *William George Ward and the Oxford Movement*, p. 146. First edition.

at this now, though at the time it was kept strictly secret. What an excitement it would have caused in 1840, had it been publicly known that the favourite study of one of the leaders of the Tractarians was the writings of the Jesuits! That kind of study is far more common now amongst modern Ritualists than it was fifty-six years since, and the Romeward Movement is now far more under Jesuitical influence than ever it has been hitherto. Mr. James R. Hope-Scott, during the visit to the Continent just mentioned, frequently visited the Jesuits at Rome, and in his now published letters shows how any feeling which he may have entertained against them gradually wore itself away. On March 27th, 1841, he wrote to his brother:—"The General of the Jesuits I continue to visit, and am grown very fond of him." [49]

The most memorable event of the year 1841 was the publication of Newman's celebrated "Tract XC." A large volume might now be written about its contents and its history. It was a plea for the lawfulness of teaching in the Church of England many Roman Catholic doctrines, as taught authoritatively in that Church, on the ground that they were not opposed by the Thirty-nine Articles, and it was at the same time a very daring attempt to "Catholicise" the Church of England in the interests of the great scheme for Corporate Reunion with Rome. The best description of the objects of Tract XC. seems to me to be that given by the four Oxford Tutors, directly after it was published. One of the Tutors was the Rev. A. C. Tait, afterwards Archbishop of Canterbury.

"The Tract has," wrote the Tutors, "in our apprehension, a highly dangerous tendency, from its suggesting that certain very important errors of the Church of Rome are not condemned by the Articles of the Church of England—for instance, that those Articles do not contain any condemnation of the doctrines—

"1. Of Purgatory.
"2. Of Pardons.

[49] *Memoirs of J. R. Hope-Scott*, Vol. I., p. 266.

"3. Of the Worshipping and Adoration of Images and relics.
"4. Of the Invocation of Saints.
"5. Of the Mass.
" as they are taught authoritatively by the Church of Rome, but only of certain absurd practices and opinions which intelligent Romanists repudiate as much as we do. It is intimated, moreover, that the Declaration prefixed to the Articles, as far as it has any weight at all, sanctions this mode of interpreting them, as it is one which takes them in their 'literal and grammatical sense,' and does not 'affix any new sense to them.' The Tract would thus appear to us to have a tendency to mitigate beyond what charity requires, and to the prejudice of the pure truth of the Gospel, the very serious differences which separate the Church of Rome from our own, and to shake the confidence of the less learned members of the Church of England in the Scriptural character of her formularies and her teaching." [50]

Four days after this Protest had been made by the four Tutors, the Hebdomadal Board of Oxford University condemned the Tract, on the ground that "modes of interpretation, such as are suggested in the said Tract, evading rather than explaining the sense of the Thirty-nine Articles, and reconciling subscription to them with the adoption of errors which they were designed to counteract, defeat the object, and are inconsistent with the due observance of the above mentioned Statutes." [51]

Archbishop Tait never regretted the part he took in condemning Tract XC. In 1880, he said:—"Were it all to happen again I think I should, in the same position, do exactly as I did then." [52] Newman's friend, the Rev. Isaac Williams, says:—"Many have naturally supposed that it was the condemnation of the Tract No. XC., by the Heads of Houses, which gave his [Newman's] sensitive mind the decided turn to the Church of Rome. But I remember circumstances which indicated that it was not so. He talked to me of writing a Tract on the Thirty-nine Articles, *and at the same time said things in favour of the Church of Rome*

[50] *Life of Archbishop Tait*, Vol. I., pp. 81, 82. First edition.
[51] *Ibid.*, p. 84.   [52] *Ibid.*, p. 87.

which quite startled and alarmed me."[53] Two pages later on Mr. Williams writes:—"Nothing had as yet impaired our intimacy and friendship, until one evening,[54] when alone in his rooms, he told me *he thought the Church of Rome was right, and we were wrong*, so much so, that *we ought to join it.* To this I said that if our own Church improved, as we hoped, and the Church of Rome also would reform itself, it seemed to hold out the prospect of reunion. And then everything seemed favourably progressing beyond what we could have dared to hope in the awakening of religion, and reformation among ourselves. That mutual repentance must, by God's blessing, tend to mutual restoration and union. 'No,' he said, 'St. Augustine would not allow of this argument, as regarded the Donatists. *You must come out and be separate.*'"[55] This argument from the conduct of the Donatists was not then for the first time adopted by Newman. In connection with it the essentially Jesuitical and double-dealing tactics of Newman are again clearly revealed. In a "private" letter to the Rev. J. B. Mozley, November 24th, 1843, he wrote:—

"Last summer four years (1839) it came *strongly* upon me, from reading first the Monophysite controversy, and then turning to the

[53] *Autobiography of Isaac Williams*, p. 108.

[54] The *editor* of the *Autobiography* says that "this conversation took place *after* the publication of Tract No. XC."; but I venture to assert that, but for this note, no reader of the *Autobiography* would think otherwise than that the speech was made *before* the publication of Tract XC. The editor, writing long after the death of Williams, makes an assertion, but omits to give any proof of it. On the other hand there is clear evidence that Williams's interview with Newman must have taken place somewhere about this date. Tract XC. was published February 27th, 1841; and Newman withdrew to Littlemore in February, 1842. Now Williams states:—"When he [Newman] shut himself up in his Monastery at Littlemore, *and previously during the latter part of his stay at Oxford*, I was able to withdraw myself from him." The interview referred to must have therefore taken place some time before Newman left Oxford, and therefore in the year 1841. In either case it makes little, or no difference in Newman's essentially dishonest and dishonourable position at that time. An honest man, holding the opinions Newman then expressed to Williams, would at once have seceded to Rome, and not wait till 1845.

[55] *Ibid.*, pp. 110, 111.

Donatist, *that we were external to the Catholic Church. I have never got over this.* I did not, however, yield to it at all, but wrote an article in the *British Critic* on the Catholicity of the English Church, which had the effect of quieting me for two years. Since this time two years the feeling has revived and gradually strengthened. I have all along gone against it, and think I ought to do so still. I am now publishing sermons, *which speak more confidently about our position than I inwardly feel;* but I think it right, and do not care for seeming inconsistent." [56]

This "inconsistency," or double-dealing, or Jesuitism, or whatever it may be called, was only a part and parcel of his ordinary conduct at this time. His friend Isaac Williams says that "the feelings and thoughts he [Newman] would express to one person or at one time, differed very much in consequence from what he might express to another or on another occasion"; and he adds that it "was long before it was publicly known what Newman's thoughts really were, and he was for some time accused by some of dishonesty and duplicity." [57] He was working in the dark, yet actively carrying on the secret underground conspiracy to bring back the Church of England to Rome. In his pamphlet entitled a *Letter to the Bishop of Oxford on Occasion of Tract XC.*, dated March 29th, 1841, Newman wrote of:—" The inestimable privileges I feel in being a member of that Church over which your lordship, with others, presides" (p. 33); "the Church which your lordship rules is a *Divinely ordained* channel of supernatural grace to the souls of her members" (p. 34); and "I consider the Church over which your lordship presides to be the Catholic Church in this country" (p. 34). And yet, for two years before writing this he had come, as we have just seen, to hold the opinion that those who were inside the Church of England "were external to the Catholic Church"! In this same *Letter to the Bishop of Oxford,* Newman further asserted that "it is very plain that the English Church is at present on God's

---

[56] Newman's *Letters,* Vol. II., p. 430.
[57] Williams's *Autobiography,* pp. 112, 113.

side" (p. 39); and that, "Did God visit us with large measures of His grace, and the Roman Catholics also, they would be drawn to us, and would acknowledge our Church as the Catholic Church in this country" (p. 44). It is hard, yea, impossible, I venture to submit, to reconcile such statements as these, with those Newman had already made in writing to his confidential friends. Soon after the publication of the pamphlet just cited, the Rev. W. G. Ward wrote to Dr. Pusey as follows:—"I have heard Newman say that it is, to say the least, doubtful whether there can be said to be a valid Sacrament administered unless the priest adds mentally what our Eucharistic Service omits." [58] On reading this, I cannot help asking myself whether we have in it a key to the fact that in almost all our advanced Ritualistic Churches private prayers are said, by the officiating clergyman, during the Communion Service, which are not required by the Book of Common Prayer. Are they intended to make a doubtful consecration certainly valid, by adding "mentally what our Eucharistic Service omits"?

Very advanced Romanizing doctrines were at this time secretly held by many of the Tractarians, who, it may be remarked in passing, were then becoming known as Puseyites. Even as early as July, 1841, Mr. Ward, writing to Dr. Pusey, stated that:—

"There are *many* persons who, on the one hand, do not accuse the Reformers of disingenuousness, and yet, on the other, consider the following doctrines and practices allowed by the Articles:— (1) Invocation of Saints; (2) Veneration of Images and Relics; (3) An intermediate state of purification with pain;[59] (4) The Reservation of the Host; (5) The Elevation of the Host; (6) The Infallibility of some General Councils; (7) The doctrine of desert by congruity, in the received Roman sense; (8) The doctrine that the Church ought to enforce Celibacy on the clergy."[60]

[58] *William George Ward and the Oxford Movement*, p. 177.
[59] That is, a Purgatory.
[60] *William George Ward and the Oxford Movemet*, p. 176.

If only the majority of the Church of England could have been induced to accept the views of these advanced Romanizers, she would soon have been sufficiently "Catholicised" for reunion with the Papacy. Nothing would have delighted Ward more than such a result. "Restoration of active communion with the Roman Church is," he wrote to a friend, in 1841, "the most enchanting earthly prospect on which my imagination can dwell."[61] The Romanizers evidently thought they were, even then, within a measurable distance of the realization of their hopes. So full of expectation were they that they could not keep the good news to themselves. Their Roman Catholic brethren on the continent must be let into the secret. So an anonymous letter was sent soon after Tract XC. appeared, for publication to the Roman Catholic *Univers* of Paris. The author's name was suppressed for obvious reasons, but it is now known that the author was the Rev. W. G. Ward, and that it was translated for him into French by Mr. J. D. Dalgairns, of Exeter College, Oxford. From this very remarkable and thoroughly Jesuitical letter, I give the following extracts:—

"You see, then, sir, that humility, the first condition of every sound reform, is not wanting in us. *We are little satisfied with our position.* We groan at the sins committed by our ancestors in separating from the Catholic world. We experience a burning desire to be reunited to our brethren. *We love with unfeigned affection the Apostolic See, which we acknowledge to be the head of Christendom;* and the more so because the Church of Rome is our mother, which sent from her bosom the blessed St. Augustine, to bring us her immovable faith. We admit also, that it is not our formularies, nor even the Council of Trent, which prevent our union. After all these concessions, you may ask me, why, then, do you not rejoin us? What is it that prevents you? . . .

"'There are at this moment, in the Anglican Church, a crowd of persons who balance between Protestantism and Catholicism, and who, nevertheless, would reject with horror the very idea of a union with Rome. The Protestant prejudices, which, for three hundred

[61] *William George Ward and the Oxford Movement*, p. 142.

years, have infected our Church, are unhappily too deeply rooted there to be extirpated *without a great deal of address.* [Did he not really mean *sly cunning?*] We must, then, offer in sacrifice to God this ardent desire which devours us of seeing once more the perfect unity of the Church of Christ. We must still bear the terrible void which the isolation of our Church creates in our hearts, and remain still till it pleases God to convert the hearts of our Anglican *confrères,* especially of our holy fathers, the bishops. *We are destined, I am persuaded, to bring back many wandering sheep to the knowledge of the truth.* In fact, the progress of Catholic opinions in England, for the last seven years, is so inconceivable that no hope should appear extravagant. *Let us, then, remain quiet for some years,* TILL, BY GOD'S BLESSING, THE EARS OF ENGLISHMEN ARE BECOME ACCUSTOMED TO HEAR THE NAME OF ROME PRONOUNCED WITH REVERENCE. At the end of this term you will soon see the fruits of our patience."[62]

The publication of this traitorous letter very naturally created a great deal of public excitement. It was translated into German and Italian, and widely circulated on the continent, where it produced great joy in the Roman camp. A Mr. Hamilton Gray of Magdalene College, Oxford, wrote to the *Univers* to say that the letter was not written by any member of the Tractarian party, but by either a Low Churchman or a Romanist. Its authorship is now, however, placed beyond question by the publication of Mr. Ward's life by his son, who tells us that "the fact remained that its sentiments were not disclaimed by the representatives of the 'extreme' party, and a programme far more bold and outspoken than anything in Tract XC. was thus practically known to be in contemplation for moving the Anglican Church in a Romeward direction.[63]

Secret negotiations were entered into with Dr. Wiseman, and the conditions of Corporate Reunion with Rome were discussed with him, at Oscott College. One of the plans then discussed was a secret affiliation of the advanced Tractarians with the Roman Catholic Fathers of Charity,

[62] *Catholic Magazine,* March, 1841, as quoted in Bricknell's *Judgment of the Bishops,* pp. 678-80.   [63] *W. G. Ward and the Oxford Movement,* p. 190.

supplemented by the following extracts from his letters to friends. On September 1st, 1843, he wrote to the Rev. J. B. Mozley:—"The truth then is, I am not a good son enough of the Church of England to feel I can in conscience hold preferment under her. *I love the Church of Rome too well.*"[91] On the 22nd of the same month he wrote to Mrs. J. Mozley:—"You cannot estimate what so many, alas! feel at present, the strange effect produced on the mind when the *conviction* flashes, or rather pours, in upon it that *Rome is the true Church.*"[92] He was here evidently speaking for himself, and of his own "convictions." The claims of Rome seem to have occupied his mind very much at this time. Seven days later he again referred to the subject in a letter to Mrs. Thomas Mozley:—

"I do so despair of the Church of England," wrote Newman, "and am so evidently cast off by her, and, on the other hand, I am so drawn to the Church of Rome, that I think it *safer*, as a matter of honesty, *not* to keep my living. This is a very different thing from having any intention of joining the Church of Rome. *However, to avow generally as much as I have said, would be wrong for ten thousand reasons.*"[93]

So he kept his longings for Rome as a secret within his own breast, and those of a few relatives and near friends whom he could trust. The consequence of this was that he appeared to the public in a character different from that which was really his. A month later he had come to the opinion that the Church of England was "not part of the Catholic Church." He wrote to Dr. Manning, on October 25th, 1843:—

"I must tell you then frankly (but I combat arguments which to me, alas, are shadows) that it is not from disappointment, irritation, or impatience, that I have, whether rightly or wrongly, resigned St. Mary's; but because *I think the Church of Rome the Catholic Church, and ours no part of the Catholic Church, because not in com-*

---

[91] Newman's *Letters*, Vol. II., p. 423.
[92] *Ibid.*, p. 424.   [93] *Ibid.*, p. 425.

munion with Rome; and because I feel that I could not honestly be a teacher in it any longer." [94]

The arguments which thus induced Newman to resign the living of St. Mary's, ought to have induced him at once to resign his membership in the Church of England. He had no moral right to remain in a Communion which he was convinced formed "no part of the Catholic Church." Indeed he ought, on his own showing, to have resigned his living several years before he resigned St. Mary's, since, in his letter to Mrs. J. Mozley, on November 24th, 1844, he wrote :—"A *clear conviction* of the substantial identity of Christianity and the Roman system has now been on my mind *for a full three years*" [95]—that is, from 1841. He did not, however, secede to Rome for another year after writing this letter, so that at least for full four years he had acted a double part—*outwardly* a member of the Church of England; *inwardly* a member of the Church of Rome.[96] On November 16th, 1844, Newman wrote to Dr. Manning :—" As far as I know myself, my one paramount reason for contemplating a change is my deep, unvarying conviction that our Church is in schism, and my salvation depends on my joining the Church of Rome." [97]

From his resignation of St. Mary's until his reception into the Church of Rome, Newman made Pusey his confidant. The correspondence which passed between them is painfully interesting, and shows that Pusey wished for more or less of Popery, but would not submit to the Pope until the Church of England had done so in her corporate

[94] Newman's *Apologia*, p. 221. Edition, 1889.
[95] Newman's *Letters*, Vol. II., p. 445.
[96] From a letter to Dr. Pusey, dated February 19th, 1844, we learn that the date of the birth of Newman's conviction that the Church of England was no part of the Catholic Church was the year 1839. "I must say," Newman then wrote, " that *for four years and a half* [that is, from the year 1839] I have had a conviction, weaker or stronger, but on the whole constantly growing, and at present very strong, that we are not part of the Catholic Church." (*Life of Dr. Pusey*, Vol. II., p. 381.)
[97] Purcell's *Life of Cardinal Manning*, Vol. I., p. 258.

capacity; while Newman had become impatient to depart, and was willing to accept both Pope and Popery, without waiting for the Church of England to set him the example. Pusey wrote that he looked to "a Reunion of the Church as the end" of the Tractarian Movement; and, meanwhile, his anxiety was to ascertain " on what terms and in what way" the Church of England could "be reunited with the rest of the Western Church." [98] Many persons will be surprised to learn that although, on August 28th, 1844, Newman had written to Pusey boldly declaring his conviction that the Church of England was "not part of the Church," yet on the 14th of the following November Pusey thus wrote to the Rev. Prebendary Henderson:—
"You are quite right in thinking that Newman has no feelings drawing him away from us: all his feelings and sympathies have been for our Church." [99] It is difficult to acquit Dr. Pusey of a charge of wilful deception, or at least of equivocation, in writing like this. On October 8th, 1845, Newman was received into the Church of Rome at Littlemore; and on October 16th a letter from Pusey, on his secession, appeared in the *English Churchman*, in which he remarked:—" He [Newman] seems then to me not so much gone from us, as transplanted into another part of the Vineyard." [100]

Many since then have mourned over the loss of Newman to the Church of England. For my part I conceive it to be a blessing that he went. His heart's affection was with the great enemy of the Church of England; his place was therefore no longer within her fold. Already he had infected many of his disciples with a love for Romanism.

The month which witnessed the secession of Newman beheld also the appointment of the Rev. Samuel Wilberforce as Bishop of Oxford. The new Bishop, even before his arrival in his Diocese, had fears as to his approaching

[98] *Life of Dr. Pusey*, Vol. II., p 404.
[99] *Ibid.*, pp. 406, 445. [100] *Ibid.*, p. 461.

relations to the Regius Professor of Hebrew, which he made known in a letter to Miss L. Noel. To her Dr. Wilberforce expressed the opinion that Pusey was "a very holy man"; but he added:—

"He [Dr. Pusey] has greatly helped, and is helping, to make a party of semi-Romanizers in the Church, to lead some to Rome. . . . He says, for instance, that he does not think himself as an English Churchman at liberty to hold all Roman doctrine; but he does '*not censure any Roman doctrine*,' whilst he holds his Canonry at Christ Church, and his position amongst *us*, on condition of signing Articles, one half of which are taken up in declaring different figments of Rome to be dangerous deceits and blasphemous fables." [101]

Pusey wrote to Dr. Wilberforce on the day of his election to the Oxford Bishopric, and received a reply which seems to have surprised him very much. It was a somewhat severe criticism of his teaching. In his rejoinder to the Bishop-Elect, Pusey once more revealed his love for much that was distinctly Roman:—

"I did not mean," wrote Pusey, "to state anything definitely as to myself, but only to maintain, in the abstract, the tenability of a certain position, *in which very many are*, of not holding themselves obliged to renounce any doctrine *formally* decreed by the Roman Church."

Pusey proceeded to inform his future Diocesan that he could no longer refuse his "belief to an intermediate state of cleansing, in some cases through pain"; or, in other words, of his belief in the existence of Purgatory. The effect of his acceptance of this belief was, he said, that ever since he had "been wholly silent about Purgatory." He had also come to believe in Invocation of Saints. On this latter point he acted most inconsistently. He told the Bishop-Elect:— "Practically then I dissuade or *forbid* (where I have authority) Invocation of Saints; abstractedly, I see no reason why our Church might not eventually allow it, in the sense of asking for their prayers"; and towards the conclusion of his letter

---

[101] *Life of Bishop Wilberforce*, Vol. I., p. 311.

he added:—"I cannot but think that Rome and we are not irreconcilably at variance."[102]

It is here seen how rapidly Pusey was marching on the road to Rome, though he seems to have never expected to arrive at the end of the journey. It added much to the difficulties of his position that he had now, in Dr. Wilberforce, a bishop carefully watching his movements, and ready to censure him when necessary. Time went on, and the Romeward Movement with it. By the year 1847, even Archdeacon Manning had discovered its tendency towards Rome, and its illogical position in the Church of England. He wrote to Pusey, on January 23rd of that year:—

"You know how long I have to you openly expressed my conviction that a false position has been taken up in the Church of England. The direct and certain tendency, I believe, of what remains of the original Movement is to the Roman Church. You know the minds of men about us better than I do, and will, therefore, know how strong an impression the claims of Rome have made on them; and how feeble and fragmentary are the reasons on which they have made a sudden stand or halt in the line on which they have been, perhaps insensibly, moving for years. It is also clear that they are 'revising the Reformation'—that the doctrine, ritual, and practice of the Church of England, taken at its best, does not suffice them."[103]

At about the same time Dr. Hook, Tractarian though he was, grew more and more alarmed at the conduct of the Romanizing party. In great trouble he wrote to Manning from his Leeds Vicarage:—

"Those whom I took for Church of England men, and who as such hated Popery, who once, as in the *Tracts for the Times*, openly assailed Popery, I find now to be enamoured of her. I find young men thinking it orthodox to read and study Popish books of devotion, and to imitate Popish priests in their attire; I find Justification by Faith, the doctrine of our Articles, the test of a standing or falling Church, repudiated, and consequently a set of works of supererogation and a feeling in favour of the intercession of those who are supposed to have been more than profitable servants."[104]

[102] *Life of Dr. Pusey*, Vol. III., pp. 43-45. [103] *Ibid.*, p. 135.
[104] *Life of Cardinal Manning*, Vol. I., p. 328.

At this very period the views of Dr. Manning were in a state of transition—his face was turned Romeward. During the summer of 1847, he travelled abroad on the Continent. At Liege he fell in love with the Sacrifice of the Mass, and wrote in his diary:—"I cannot but feel that the practise of Elevation, Exposition, Adoration of the Blessed Eucharist has a powerful effect in sustaining and realizing the doctrine of the Incarnation."[105] In 1848 Archdeacon Manning visited Rome. While there strange things happened, of which the world knew nothing until after his death. One day, while in the Piazza di Spagna, he saw the Papal carriage approaching towards him. As it passed he knelt down in the street before the Pope—and he all the time an Archdeacon in the Reformed Church of England![106] Mr. Purcell, the future Cardinal's biographer, tells us in the chapter which he devotes to this visit to Rome that—

"In his Diary Archdeacon Manning nowhere says in so many words, that he took a personal part in the veneration of relics which he so often witnessed and described with touching fidelity. Yet from the tone and spirit of his testimony I have no doubt that at St. Philip Neri's Oratory at Florence, for instance, the relics of the Saint were laid on the forehead and pressed to the lips of the Archdeacon of Chichester."[107]

The history of Manning's change of views in favour of the Church of Rome, as related by Mr. Purcell, greatly surprised the English public, when it was first published. It revealed an absence of straightforward conduct on Manning's part for which no really valid excuse has yet been offered. His double dealing is frankly admitted by his Roman Catholic biographer, who writes:—

"What, I grant, is a curious difficulty, almost startling at first, is to find Manning speaking concurrently for years *with a double voice.* One voice proclaims in public, in sermons, charges, and tracts, and, in a tone still more absolute, to those who sought his advice in Confession, his profound and unwavering belief in the Church of England as

[105] *Ibid.*, p. 352. [106] *Ibid.*, Vol. II., p 456. [107] *Ibid.*, Vol. I., p. 407, *note.*

the Divine witness to the Truth, appointed by Christ and guided by the Holy Spirit. The other voice, as the following confessions and documents under his own handwriting bear ample witness, speaks in almost heartbroken accents of despair at being no longer able in conscience to defend the teaching and position of the Church of England; whilst acknowledging at the same time, if not in his confession to Laprimaudaye, at any rate in his letters to Robert Wilberforce, the drawing he felt towards the infallible teaching of the Church of Rome."[108]

It was while in this transition state that Manning published several volumes of his Anglican sermons. In 1865, just before he was consecrated titular "Archbishop of Westminster," Manning consulted a friend as to the wisdom of having them republished. The friend gave as his opinion, that, as a Roman Catholic, Dr. Manning could not conscientiously republish them. Yet in the letter conveying this opinion, his friend (Dr. Bernard Smith) bore testimony to the services rendered to the Church of Rome by these Anglican sermons.

"I confess," wrote Dr. B. Smith, "I was greatly surprised to see how close [that is, in these sermons] you bring the Anglican Confession to the Church of Rome. But what I admired most in the perusal of these volumes was not the many strong Catholic truths I met with, but that almost Catholic unction of a St. Francis of Sales, or of a St. Teresa, that breathes through them all. That the reading of these works must have great influence over the Protestant mind I have no doubt. I also believe that no sincere Protestant can read over these volumes, who sooner or later will not take refuge in the ark"[109] [by which, of course, Dr. Smith meant the Church of Rome].

What is here said of Manning's Anglican Sermons may, with equal truth, be said of many scores of volumes written by Ritualistic clergymen. These works teach principles which must logically lead to the Church of Rome, even when, as is sometimes the case, they are accompanied with criticisms on some portions of the Roman system. Doubts as to the Church of England entered Manning's mind as early as 1846.

---

[108] *Life of Cardinal Manning*, Vol. I., p. 463.
[109] *Ibid.*, Vol. II., p. 722, *note*.

In his Diary for the August of that year he wrote that, in his opinion, the Church of England was "diseased organically" by its "separation from Church *toto orbe diffusa* and from *Cathedra Petri*"; by its "abolition of penance," and by its "extinction of daily sacrifice."[110] On July 5th, 1846, he wrote in his Diary:—"Something keeps rising and saying, 'you will end in the Roman Church.'" "If the Church of England were away there is nothing in Rome that would repel me with sufficient repulsion to keep me separate, and there is nothing in Protestantism that would attract me... I am conscious that I am further from the English Church and nearer Rome than I ever was... Yet I have no positive doubts about the Church of England. I have difficulties—but the chief thing is the *drawing* of Rome. It satisfies the *whole* of my intellect, sympathy, sentiment, and nature, in a way proper, and solely belonging to itself."[111] Mr. Purcell adds to the above extracts from Manning's Diary the following significant comments:—

"It is curious to note from these entries that the breakdown of Manning's belief in the English Church took place so early as 1846, two years before Hampden's appointment, and four years before the Gorham Judgment. *In his sermons and charges* there are not the slightest indications of such a misgiving. In his correspondence with Mr. Gladstone at this period, *not a hint or suggestion was conveyed*—not that the Church of England was organically and functionally diseased—but that it had fallen from the high ideal of perfection, which Manning had so fervently and eloquently attributed to it in his public utterances. From the evidence of his own Diary, from his letters to Laprimaudaye and Robert Wilberforce, it seems as clear as daylight that, intellectually Manning had, years before the Gorham Judgment, lost faith in the Church of England."[112]

Notwithstanding his "loss of faith in the Church of England," Manning continued to outwardly profess what in his heart he had ceased to believe in. On February 12th, 1848—three years before he left the Church of England—he wrote from Rome to his intimate friend, Robert Wilberforce:

[110] *Ibid.*, Vol. I., p. 483. [111] *Ibid.*, pp. 485, 486. [112] *Ibid.*, pp. 487, 488.

—"I cannot rest the Church of England and its living witness on anything higher than an intellectual basis. I trust it, because I *think* it to be right, not because I believe it to be right. It is a subject of my reason, and not an object of my faith."[113] The following year he wrote, "under the seal," more strongly:—

"Protestantism is not so much a rival system, which I reject, but no system, a chaos, a wreck of fragments, without idea, principle, or life. It is to me flesh, blood, unbelief, and the will of man. *Anglicanism seems to me to be in essence the same*, only elevated, constructed, and adorned by intellect, social and political order, and the fascinations of a national and domestic history. As a theology, still more as the Church or the faith, it has so faded out of my mind that I cannot say I reject it, but I know it no more. I simply do not believe it. I can form no basis, outline, or defence for it."[114]

And yet he continued to receive the emoluments of a Church in which he had ceased to have any real faith! Was this honest? Was it not, rather, double dealing, such as looked very much like a case of receiving money under false pretences? In any case it reminds us of those of whom it is recorded that they possessed "a conscience seared with a hot iron"—past any conscientious feeling. For more than a year after this Manning wrote letters to his penitents, having for their object the strengthening of *their* faith in the Church of England. One such letter, dated May 6th, 1850, is printed by his biographer, in which occurs the following assertion:—"Judging by the evidence of the Primitive Church there are many, and they very grave and vital, points on which the Church of England seems more in harmony with Holy Scripture than the Church of Rome."[115] One wonders whether Manning at the time really believed what he thus wrote. I very much doubt it. It seems that this letter was the means of preventing Manning's penitent from going over to Rome. Manning's real views at this time were known only to four or five other persons, his intimate friends,

---

[113] *Life of Cardinal Manning*, Vol. I., p. 509. [114] *Ibid.*, p. 515. [115] *Ibid.*, p. 473.

all of whom, like himself, eventually joined the Church of Rome. They were Robert Wilberforce, James Hope, William Dodsworth, Henry Wilberforce, and, perhaps, Laprimaudaye. Mr. Gladstone was an intimate friend, but the secret of his (Manning's) views was carefully kept from that statesman.

"On learning in January last [1895]," writes Mr. Purcell, "the substance of Manning's letters to Robert Wilberforce, Mr. Gladstone was surprised beyond measure. Speaking with evident pain, he said, —'To me this is most startling information, for which I am quite unprepared. In all our correspondence and conversations, during an intimacy which extended over many years, Manning never led me to believe that he had doubts as to the position or Divine authority of the English Church, far less that he had lost faith altogether in Anglicanism. That is to say, up to the Gorham Judgment [in 1850]. The Gorham Judgment, I knew, shook his faith in the Church of England. It was then that Manning expressed to me—and for the first time—his doubts and misgivings.' After a few moments' reflection, Mr. Gladstone added:—'I won't say Manning was insincere, God forbid! *But he was not simple and straightforward.*'" [116]

I venture to submit that the majority of Englishmen will see, in such conduct, clear evidence of insincerity, as well as of a want of "straightforward" conduct. The clearest proof of Manning's ecclesiastical dishonesty—I cannot here use a milder term—is obtained by a comparison of a letter which he wrote to Robert Wilberforce, on June 25th, 1850, with a published letter, which he addressed to the Bishop of Chichester, dated July 2nd, 1850—only a week later. The two letters afford a striking instance of that "double voice" in which he then frequently spoke. In the first of these letters, which was strictly private, Manning wrote:—

"I have not seen Churton's Charge; but the course he and others have taken has helped more than most things to *convince me that the Church of England has no real basis*. . . . Logically, I am convinced that the One, Holy, Visible, Infallible Church is that which has its circuit in all the world, and its centre accidentally at Rome. But I mistrust my conclusion. . . . I have made a first draft on the Oath of Supremacy, in a letter to my Bishop. But I have written myself fairly over the border—or Tiber rather." [117]

[116] *Ibid.*, p. 569. [117] *Ibid.*, p. 558.

In the other letter, to his Bishop, Manning does not write anything which would lead his Diocesan, or the public, to suppose that he had written himself over "the Tiber," or into the Church of Rome. On the contrary, while criticising sharply the relations to the State of the Church of England, and her connection with the Court of Law which had just acquitted Mr. Gorham, he informed his lordship that he had still left a strong faith in the Church of England—though, as a matter of fact, as we have already seen, he had long since ceased to have any faith in her at all.

"We believe," wrote Archdeacon Manning, "*the Church in England*, as a member or province of this Divine Kingdom [the Church], *possesses, 'in solidum,'* by inheritance and participation in the whole Church, the inheritance of the Divine Tradition of Faith, with a share in this full and supreme custody of doctrine and power of discipline, partaking for support and perpetuity, in its measure and sphere, *the same guidance as the whole Church at large*, of which, by our Baptism, we have been made members.

"The Church in England, then, being thus an integral whole, possesses within itself the fountain of doctrine and discipline, *and has no need to go beyond itself for succession, orders, mission, jurisdiction.* . . . But we trust that as, in the period of the great Western schism, the Churches of Spain, France, Germany, and many others, were compelled to fall back within their own limits and to rest upon the full and integral power which, by succession, they possessed for their own internal government, *so the Church in England has continued to be a* PERFECT *member of this Divine Kingdom, endowed with all that is of necessity to the valid ministry of the Faith and Sacraments of Christ.*"[118]

Who, at that time, would have thought that the writer of this strong eulogy of the Church of England actually considered that in writing it he was "fairly writing himself over the border—or *Tiber*"? If the Church of England was all that Manning asserted, possessed of valid Orders and Sacraments, without going "beyond itself" to outside communions, why had he made up his mind to leave a

---

[118] *Appellate Jurisdiction of the Crown in Matters Spiritual:* A Letter to the Bishop of Chichester, by Henry Edward Manning, Archdeacon of Chichester, pp. 4, 5.

Church, which he declared was "a PERFECT member of this Divine Kingdom"? In the history of the Romeward Movement in the Church of England there are but few, if any, incidents more deplorable than the double dealing of Dr. Manning during his last years in that Church.

Down to the year 1851, the Romeward Movement in the Church of England had led to the secession to Rome of a large number of prominent clergymen and laymen. The list of distinguished seceders given in Browne's *Annals of the Tractarian Movement* affords ample proof of the services rendered to the Church of Rome by the Oxford Movement. No wonder that Cardinal Wiseman rejoiced at what he saw going on around him, and looked forward with an almost boyish glee to the good time coming, when, as he hoped, England would once more accept Papal supremacy. But the services rendered to Rome by the Movement were by no means confined to supplying her with some of the ablest of her children. A prominent Roman Catholic magazine, the *Rambler*, during the year 1851, devoted several articles to the subject of "The Rise, Progress, and Results of Puseyism," as it was then commonly termed. The tone of these articles was, throughout, one of deep thankfulness for what had been already accomplished.

"From the moment that the Oxford Tracts commenced," said the *Rambler*, "the Catholic Church assumed a position in the country which she had never before attained since the schism of the sixteenth century. With what a depth of indescribable horror of Catholicism the whole mind of England was formerly saturated, few can comprehend who have not personally experienced it. . . . The sons and daughters of Anglicanism were brought up to regard the Catholic Church as the devil's masterpiece. . . . No one read Catholic books, no one entered Catholic churches; no one ever saw Catholic priests; few people even knew that there were any Catholic bishops resident in England. Except in connection with Ireland, the Catholic Church was forgotten.

"*See now the change which has come over the English people as a nation.* Violently Protestant still, its attitude towards the Catholic

Church is extraordinarily changed. It dislikes her, but it no longer despises her. . . . Crowds attend the services of Catholic and of Puseyite churches; but while in the latter there is hissing and groaning, in the former a stillness the most profound pays strange homage to the elevation of the most Holy Sacrament. None but fools and fanatics deny some merits to the Church of Rome and her clergy. *Everywhere the change appears.* . . . And whatever other causes may have combined to work this wonderful result, *to the Movement of 1833 it surely must chiefly be attributed.*" [119]

[119] *The Rambler*, March 1851, pp. 246, 247.

CHAPTER X.

THE ROMEWARD MOVEMENT.

The Association for the Promotion of the Unity of Christendom—Sermons and Essays on Reunion—Denunciation of Protestantism—Treasonable letter in the Union Review—The A. P. U. C. denounced by the Inquisition—Degrading Reply of 198 Church of England Dignitaries and Clergy—Archbishop Manning's opinion of the Romeward Movement—The Society of the Holy Cross Petition for Reunion with Rome—Signed by 1212 clergymen—The English Church Union—Its work for Union with Rome—Approves Dr. Pusey's Eirenicon—Pusey writes that there is nothing in the Pope's "Supremacy" in itself to which he would object—The Catholic Union for Prayer—A Colonial Priest on Reunion with Rome—The "levelling up" process—The real Objects of the English Church Union—The Lord's Day and the Holy Eucharist—Lord Halifax wants Benediction of the Blessed Sacrament—E. C. U. members find fault with the Book of Common Prayer—E. C. U. Petitions the Lambeth Conference for Reunion—Reunion asked for under "The Bishop of Old Rome"—Lord Halifax prefers Leo XIII. to the Privy Council—Dean Hook in favour of the Privy Council—Mr. Mackonochie's Evidence before the Ecclesiastical Courts' Commission—Asserts there has been no "Ecclesiastical Court" since the Reformation—A Ritualistic Curate supplies the "Kernel" to Roman Ritual—He preaches the Immaculate Conception of the Virgin Mary—Lord Halifax and "Explanations" of the Pope's Infallibility—The Homilies on the Church of Rome—Rome has already reaped a harvest from Ritualistic labours—Secession as well as Union a Scriptural duty—Objections to Reunion with Rome.

THE time at length arrived when it was thought desirable by those who longed for the Corporate Reunion of the Church of England with the Eastern Church and the Church of Rome, to band themselves into societies to promote the object they had at heart. Some of these societies made the Reunion question a part only of their programme; but from the commencement of its existence the Association for the Promotion of the Unity of Christendom laboured for this one object alone. This

Association was founded at a private meeting held in the parish of St. Clement Danes, Strand, London, on September 8th, 1857, on the motion of a Roman Catholic layman, seconded by a Church of England clergyman, and supported by members of the Greek Church. At that meeting thirty-four persons joined the infant Association.[1] In a statement issued by one of its chief officers (the Rev. F. G. Lee) in 1864, it was mentioned that in that year it had grown into a membership of 7099, of whom "nearly a thousand" were Roman Catholics, and about three hundred were "members of the Eastern Church." Mr. Lee also affirmed that, "The Association has been approved in the highest ecclesiastical quarters, both amongst Latins, Anglicans, and Greeks. The Holy Father gave his blessing to the scheme when first started, and repeated that blessing with a direct and kindly commendation to one of the English secretaries, who was more recently granted the honour of a special interview."[2] In an appendix to the volume of sermons from which I have just quoted, and which was "Printed for certain members of the Association for the Promotion of the Unity of Christendom," an official prospectus of the Association is printed, in which it is mentioned that "*the names of members will be kept strictly private.*"[3] On the occasion of its seventh anniversary Masses were said for the success of its work not merely by ordinary clergymen, but even by Archbishops, Bishops, and Monks, and these were offered in England, Scotland, Ireland, France, Austria, Prussia, Denmark, Italy, Belgium, Switzerland, Malta, North America, South America, and South Africa.[4]

The Association still exists, and at the present time numbers upwards of ten thousand members, but from its birth until now it has never, so far as I can ascertain,

---

[1] *Sermons on the Reunion of Christendom*, Vol. I., pp. x., xi.
[2] *Ibid.*, p. xii.   [3] *Ibid.*, p. 329
[4] *The Church and the World*, Vol. I., p. 201.

printed a list of its members, not even for its own private use, so afraid are they lest their names should be found out. In the prospectus just referred to there is printed a short list of Diocesan Secretaries, and of persons to whom applications for information could be made, but as to the rank and file of the Association nobody knows who they are, excepting the head officials. In January, 1863, the *Union Review* was founded by members of the Association, and was subsequently conducted by them, though the Association as such was not held responsible for its contents. But inasmuch as it expressed the views held by those who guided the Association, it may not be considered as inappropriate if I give here a few extracts from it, which show its thoroughly Romanizing character.

"It is a shocking scandal that one of the Homilies of the Established Church should even contain *heretical* reasoning against the belief in a state of connection [*Sic*. Probably *correction* is meant] hereafter, and the benefit of prayers for the departed."[5]

"The English Church is in a state of penance; her daily Sacrifice taken away, and the perpetual Presence on her Altars withdrawn, except in a few favoured places where both have lately been restored."[6]

"The hair shirt, and the spiked cross or belt, sacrificing bodily ease altogether, with the sharper but less wearing means by which the various Acts of the Passion may be followed and sympathized with step by step, *are all valuable* in their several degrees, but require adaptation to particular cases."[7]

"We venture to say, heresy has been practically triumphant for three hundred years together, through the Prayer Book."[8]

"We will not tamely accept the illogical and incomplete system which the Reformers have left us in the Prayer Book as it is."[9]

Perhaps the most remarkable document ever printed in the *Union Review* was a lengthy letter written by a member of the Association to a Roman Catholic priest in Germany. The thoroughly Jesuitical and traitorous character of the Ritualistic Movement is therein very candidly revealed by

[5] *Union Review*, Vol. III., p. 147. Ibid., p. 395. [7] Ibid., p. 397, *note*.
[8] Ibid., p. 621. Ibid., p. 626.

one of its warmest friends. He announced that for the previous twenty-five years—*i.e.*, from 1842—the leaders of the party had been preaching "the Catholic faith," and that their doctrines had "*secretly* yet surely been working, like the leaven," during that period.[10] From this noteworthy letter I give the subjoined additional extracts:—

"Our belief is that the Church of which we are members is Catholic in her Faith, and Catholic in her usages, and that *Protestantism in any shape and form has no legal place within her.*"[11]

"Day and night—in the Church, and in the closets—there ascend in England from thousands of mourning hearts, smitten with a sense of their bereavement, the fervent expressions of an intense longing of a burning desire for the restoration to our unhappy country of this most glorious privilege of Visible Unity [with the Church of Rome]. *Here you have the real heart and soul of the present Movement; this is the centre from which its pulsations vibrate, and from which its life blood flows.*"[12]

"At the outset of this Union Movement our eyes turned Eastward, rather than rest on the spot on which now they so love to dwell. For now, at last, is God mercifully removing the scales from our eyes. Every year we begin to understand you [the Church of Rome] better, and, therefore, to love you more."[13]

"Here, in a sense of the danger of the common foe, and of the identity of that Faith which is to overcome him, we hope to find one strong force of attraction to draw not only the Protestant to us, but both together to you [Rome]. But when? ah! when? The time cannot be so very far off. The strides which have been made during the last ten years are enormous; and, as I say, we are all, however opposed, moving on together."[14]

"I hope I have now said enough to justify any convictions that there is no reason for discouragement, on either of these two heads, but that it is reasonable to hope that at the end of this third period, say twenty years hence, Catholicism will have so leavened our Church, that she herself in her corporal capacity, and not a mere small section of her, like ourselves, will be able to come to you [the Church of Rome] and say:—'Let the hands which political force, not spiritual choice, have parted these three hundred years, be once more joined. *We are one with you in Faith,* and we have a common foe to fight.

[10] *Union Review*, Vol. V., p. 379.   [11] *Ibid.*, p. 380.   [12] *Ibid.*, p. 398.
[13] *Ibid.*, p. 400.   [14] *Ibid.*, p. 408.

There may be a few divergencies of practice on our side. *We seek to make no terms;* we come only in the spirit of love and of humility; but at the same time we feel sure that the Chief Shepherd of the Flock of Christ [the Pope] will deal tenderly with us, and place no yoke upon us which we are not able to bear.'" [15]

"With such hopes, then, and with such a position, it is surely, I say, much better for us to remain working where we are, for what would become of England, if we were to leave her Church? She would be simply lost to Catholicism, and won to Rationalism.... *Depend upon it, it is only through the English Church itself that England can be Catholicised.*" [16]

"The work now going on in England is an earnest and carefully organized attempt, on the part of a rapidly increasing body of priests and laymen, to bring our Church and country up to the full standard of Catholic Faith and practice, and eventually to plead for her union with you [the Church of Rome]." [17]

The object of the Oxford Movement is very truthfully revealed in the last of these extracts from the *Union Review*. Corporate Reunion with the Church of Rome has ever been the great aim of the wire-pullers of the Oxford Movement. This necessarily involves the death of the Reformation Movement of the sixteenth century, at least within the Church of England, and implies that the Reformation was a sin, if not a crime. Here and there some uninfluential Ritualist is now heard to declare that he wants nothing of the kind, but it is well to remember, when we hear such statements, that the movements of an army are not guided by the views of the rank and file, but by the wills of the commanding officers. The language of this article in the *Union Review* is clearly that of a traitor, who remains within the camp of the Church of England for the sole purpose of doing his best to deprive her of her independence and liberty, and hand her over to the tyranny of her greatest enemy. And the strange thing is that this writer's traitorous article was never repudiated by the leaders of the Ritualistic party. There is reason to believe that it only

[15] *Ibid.*, pp. 408, 409. [16] *Ibid.*, p. 410. [17] *Ibid.*, p. 412.

too accurately represented their views of the situation. Before parting with the *Union Review* I may be permitted to give two more quotations from subsequent volumes:—

"We have grown wiser than some of our forefathers; on questions of doctrine, of ritual, and of religious practice, such for instance as the Confessional, *we are separated but a hair's breadth from Rome;* we no longer consider ourselves involved in the guilt and peril of idolatry, if, when we are abroad, we frequent the service of the Mass; we prefer Notre Dame to the Little Bethels of French Protestantism, *and claim affinity with Rome* or the Orientals rather than with Luther or Calvin." [18]

"By way of suggesting something practical ourselves, we will in this paper recommend, as a first and *essential* preliminary towards the Reunion of Christendom, the total abolition of the Thirty-nine Articles." [19]

The members of the Association for the Promotion of the Unity of Christendom were very zealous in furthering the work they had on hand. The papers of the Association were translated into several Continental languages, and the members, while travelling abroad, scattered these papers broadcast throughout Europe. In England its work was brought before the public chiefly in connection with special services in churches, on which occasions the Ritual adopted was of the most advanced type. The cause of the Association was also advocated through the press by means of letters in Ritualistic and other newspapers, warmly advocating Reunion with Rome and the East. Nor was their zeal confined to the periodical press. Two volumes of *Sermons on the Reunion of Christendom* were issued by the members, several of them from the pens of Roman Catholic and Greek clergymen. These were followed, in 1867, by a remarkable volume of *Essays on the Reunion of Christendom,* which, at the time of its publication, attracted a great deal of public attention. The Association, as such, disclaimed any official responsibility for the opinions expressed either in the *Essays* or in the *Sermons,* each member of the

[18] *Union Review,* Volume for 1869. p. 373. [19] *Ibid.,* Volume for 1870, p. 289.

Association who contributed to the volumes being held responsible only for his own utterances. Probably the *Essays* would not have been so widely read were it not that the "Introductory Essay" was written by the Rev. Dr. Pusey, who, as my readers are already aware, had for many years been labouring zealously to promote Corporate Reunion with Rome, and had written two or three volumes on the subject. In his "Introductory Essay" Dr. Pusey wrote:—

"The idea itself, that the Council of Trent might be legitimately explained, so that it could be received by Anglo-Catholics, and that our Articles contain nothing which is, in its grammatical sense, adverse to the Council of Trent, remains untouched and unrepudiated. And this is the intellectual basis of a future union, when God shall have disposed men's hearts on both sides to look the difficulties in the face, and the presence of the common foe, unbelief, shall have driven them together." [20]

There are other articles in this collection of *Essays on Reunion* which call for attention here. The writers are more outspoken than Dr. Pusey, on some points, though on all important matters they seem to agree. Canon Humble, a member of the Scottish Episcopal Church, who wrote on "The Exigency of Truth," evidently believed in the doctrine of "Reserve in Communicating Religious Knowledge," for, in a spirit which I must term Jesuitical, he declared that—

"There are many who are quite willing to admit the Primacy, *or even more*, of the Bishop of Rome, who do not therefore see that they are in anywise bound to proclaim their belief to all the world by immediately joining the Roman Communion." [21]

"Had men listened to the voice of God, in place of giving reins to their violent tempers, we can scarcely doubt that Rome would have become a Monarchy by assent of the whole Church." [22]

"The Primacy of Rome was given to her, certainly not by the Church, but by the great Head Himself. . . . Rome was allowed to have the first place under the Patriarchal system, but she had that which no General Council could either give or take away. She was

[20] *Essays on Reunion*, p. xxviii.   [21] *Ibid.*, p. 9.   [22] *Ibid.*, p. 26.

constituted to be the strength and support of all other Churches—*the centre round which all others should gather.*"²³

The marvel is how a man who could write like this did not consistently act upon his principles, and go over to Rome at once. Only on principles which are commonly termed Jesuitical could he remain as a Minister of a Church which refuses to acknowledge either the Primacy or Supremacy of the Pope. What he terms "the Exigency of Truth" alone compelled him to remain where he was, with a view to Corporate Reunion with Rome. The Rev. George Nugee, then Vicar of Wymering, wrote, in these *Essays on Reunion*, an article on "A Conference of Theologians," in which he, as a clergyman of the Church of England, affirmed that "the Supremacy need not be an abiding hindrance to Reunion."²⁴ If this be so, it follows that the Protestant Reformation was nothing less than a grave error, and the sooner it is undone the better. Loyal Churchmen, however, are of a different opinion. They believe that the Reformation was one of the greatest blessings God has given to England, and that it would be a sin and a disgrace to undo its glorious work. Papal Supremacy, in any shape or form, is an insuperable barrier to Reunion with Rome. There is nothing good to be obtained by it; but it is certain that we should obtain much that is evil, and lose our civil and religious liberties. The Protestantism of England is also, on the other hand, as long as it remains, an insuperable barrier to the Reunion schemes of these Romanizers. They realize this fact to the full, and consequently they do everything in their power to give Protestantism a bad name, as a preliminary to its final removal. This was very candidly admitted by the Rev. W. Percival Ward, Rector of Compton Valence, in his paper on "The Difficulties of Reunion," which I have already quoted (see p. 261), but which will bear repetition here:—

²³ *Essays on Reunion*, pp. 27, 28. ²⁴ *Ibid.*, p. 83

"The first great hindrance," he wrote, "that is before us arises from *the Protestantism of England*. Till this is removed, the Reunion of our Church, as the Church of England, with either the Greek, or Latin Churches, *is absolutely hopeless*."[25]

Here we find a strong reason for maintaining, and even increasing, the Protestantism of the Established Church. So long as it exists Reunion with Rome is "hopeless." It is Protestantism which, by God's help, has been the cause of England's prosperity, and of that of all other Protestant countries. While Roman Catholic countries, which acknowledge Papal Supremacy, are everywhere going down in the scale of nations, Protestant countries are everywhere growing in prosperity, and extending their borders on every hand. The Protestant nations are at the head of the world, in everything which make nations truly great and glorious. We have therefore no reason to be ashamed of the word Protestantism, though we have just cause for being ashamed of the men in the Church of England who are trying to destroy that religion which gives them their daily bread. The man who bites the hand which feeds him is justly held in contempt.

Another of the articles in the *Essays on Reunion*, which was written anonymously, very candidly, and in the most brazen-faced fashion, unblushingly boasted that the Ritualists were doing the work of the Church of Rome within the Church of England. Any honest man of business would say that if they were doing Rome's work they ought to receive Rome's pay, and not that of the Church of England. But it is to be feared that large numbers of Ritualists possess what the Apostle terms a "conscience seared with a hot iron" (1 Tim. iv. 2)—hardened, and past feeling. What I have just said may, at first sight, seem to some of my readers, almost incredible, and therefore I give below the actual words of this Ritualistic writer—

"The marvel is, that Roman Catholics whatever their views may

---

[25] *Ibid.*, p. 89.

be, do not see the wisdom of aiding us to the utmost. Admitting that we are but a lay body with no pretensions to the name of a Church, we yet, in our belief (however mistaken) that we are one, are doing for England that which they cannot do. We are teaching men to believe that God is to be worshipped under the form of Bread, and they are learning the lesson from us which they have refused to learn from the Roman teachers, who have been among us for the last three hundred years. We are teaching men to endure willingly the pain of Confession, which is an intense trial to the reserved Anglo-Saxon nature, and to believe that a man's 'I absolve thee' is the voice of God. How many English Protestants have Roman priests brought to Confession, compared with the Anglican clergy? Could they have overcome the English dislike to 'mummery' as we are overcoming it? ON ANY HYPOTHESIS, WE ARE DOING THEIR WORK." [26]

These traitors within the camp knew very well that the Church of Rome would not care to have the Church of England even as a present, unless she had first of all repented of her Protestantism, and adopted Romish doctrines and practices. Consequently their great efforts, for the time being, centred round the "Catholicising" work described in the above statement.

"Let us be assured," wrote the Rev. T. W. Mossman, Rector of West Torrington, "that the Roman and Greek Churches cannot, if they would, hold out the right hand of fellowship to us, *so long as we are uncatholic in our practice*. . . . We see then most clearly, as the conclusion of the whole matter, that by adopting and promoting really Catholic Ritual observances, we are, as far as in us lies, promoting in the most effectual way possible the accomplishment of Visible Unity and intercommunion amongst all parts of the Church; and that by neglecting or opposing Catholic Ritual we are doing our best, or our worst, to hinder the glorious consummation of the visible, corporate Reunion of the whole Christian family." [27]

For several years after the formation of the Association for the Promotion of the Unity of Christendom, Roman Catholics were permitted to join it. As we have already seen, large numbers of them became members, and Masses for its object were offered in several Romish countries.

---

[26] *Essays on Reunion*, p. 180. [27] *Ibid.*, pp. 288, 289.

But in April, 1864, the Roman Catholic Bishops in England seem to have become alarmed as to possible dangers to their people, through being joined together with non-Romanists in religious work. They, accordingly, addressed a letter to the Inquisition on the subject, asking for an authoritative decision on the question. On September 16th, 1864, the Inquisition sent its official reply, signed by Cardinal Patrizi, to the Bishops, condemning the A. P. U. C., and ordering all Roman Catholics to withdraw from it. From this document I give the subjoined extracts:—

"It has been notified to the Apostolic See that some Catholics and even ecclesiastics, have given their names to a Society established in London in the year 1857, 'for promoting' (as it is called) 'the Unity of Christendom'; and that several articles have been published in the public papers signed with the names of Catholics, in approval of this Society, or supposed to have been written by ecclesiastics in its favour. Now, the real character and aim of the Society are plain, not only from the articles in the Journal called the *Union Review*, but from the very prospectus in which persons are invited to join it, and are enrolled as members. Organized and conducted by Protestants,[28] it has resulted from a view, put forth by it in express terms, that the three Christian Communions, the Roman Catholic, the schismatic Greek, and the Anglican, though separated and divided one from another, have yet an equal claim to the title of Catholic. Hence its doors are open to all men whencesoever—Catholics, schismatic Greeks, or Anglicans—but so that none shall moot the question of the several points of doctrine in which they differ, and each may follow undisturbed the opinions of his own religious profession. . . .

"The Supreme Congregation of the Holy Office, to whose scrutiny the matter has been referred as usual, has judged, after mature consideration, that the faithful should be warned with all care against being led by heretics to join with them and with schismatics in entering this Association. The most Eminent Fathers the Cardinals, placed with myself over the Sacred Inquisition, entertain, indeed, no doubt that the Bishops of those parts address themselves already with diligence, according to the charity and learning which distinguish

---

[28] Roman Catholic controversialists persist in calling Ritualists "Protestants," though they repudiate the name. I need hardly add that no true Protestant would ever join a Society to pray for Reunion with Rome.

the Tractarians, apparently, to remain all the while in communion with the Church of England Mr. Wilfrid Ward tells us that "Mr. Phillipps [a prominent Roman Catholic] had urged that the Fathers of Charity, the Order of the great Italian Reformer Antonio Rosmini, then represented in England by the excellent and pious Father Gentili, *should open their Order* AT ONCE *to the Oxford school*, and adapt its rules to their position and antecedents."[64] The scheme came to nothing, so far as the public are aware, and it is asserted by Mr. Wilfrid Ward that it "met with no encouragement from Newman or from any responsible members of the party." But that it should be seriously discussed at all is in itself sufficiently startling, and proves how far gone in deception those were who desired such a secret affiliation with a Roman Catholic Order.

Dr. Pusey's Romeward tendencies were rapidly developing. In this year he visited several Roman Catholic Convents in Ireland, with a view to starting Anglican Convents in England. One of his disciples, the Rev. E. Churton, sent him an indignant letter of protest on his attitude towards the advanced Romanizers. "Instead of controlling the ebullitions of the young wrong-heads, you have suffered yourselves to be inoculated with their frenzies. . . . You have let them get ahead of you and drag you after them. Hence your proposal of reviving Monastic Life, and your very unfortunate appearance at Dublin [to visit Romish Convents], which has so deeply perplexed our best allies there. . . . As for yourselves, that which has compelled me, most unwillingly, to forsake that entire union with you in which I found so much comfort, has been that you have seemed to treat these excesses as if they were providential indications for your guidance, and thought it a kind of 'quenching the Spirit' to keep them within rule and order."[65] In reply to this

---

[64] *W. G. Ward and the Oxford Movement*, p. 190.
[65] *Life of Dr. Pusey*, Vol. II., p. 269.

very outspoken communication, Dr. Pusey sent a letter to Mr. Churton which must now be considered as far from satisfactory. He mentioned what he termed "the *unnaturalness* of our present insulated state, separated from the rest of the East and West"; but he declared that "there is no wish for a *premature* union; it is only wished and longed and prayed for that we may both become such, that we may safely be united." "As to Monasticism," he continued, "I have *long* [how "long" I wonder] strongly thought that we needed something of this sort; it is not Romanish but primitive. . . . I think it would be a great blessing to our Church to have some such institutions."[66] Dr. Pusey's judgment was directly opposed to that of the Church of England as to Monastic Orders, as anyone can see for himself who reads her "Homily On Good Works," Part Third, in which she terms them, in no complimentary language, "superstitious and pharisaical sects, by Antichrist invented." Early in 1842, the Bishop of Salisbury (Dr. E. Denison), High Churchman though he was, became alarmed at the spread of Romanizing principles in the Church of England, and indignant at the conduct of Dr. Pusey, to whom he wrote on March 9th, 1842:—"Will you also allow me to say how much I regret that you either have not felt disposed or not at liberty to express any strong disapproval of the language about our own Church and that of Rome which has been used in various publications, and has naturally excited a very strong and general sensation."[67] While labouring for Corporate Reunion with Rome, Pusey bitterly opposed any union between the Church of England and the Lutheran Church.

Newman's love for Popery was also growing rapidly. He tells us that:—"In spite of my ingrained fears of Rome, and the decision of my reason and conscience against her usages [he does not say her *doctrines*], in spite of my affection for Oxford and Oriel, *yet I had a secret longing love of Rome*, the

[66] *Ibid.*, p. 271.   [67] *Ibid.*, p. 281.

Mother of English Christianity, and I had a true devotion to the Virgin Mary." [68] He considered that the Anglican Church "must have a ceremonial, a ritual, and a fulness of doctrine and devotion, which it had not at present, if it were to compete with the Roman Church with any prospect of success. . . . Such, for instance, would be Confraternities, particular devotions, reverence for the Blessed Virgin, prayers for the dead, beautiful churches, munificent offerings to them and in them, Monastic Houses, *and many other observances* and Institutions, which I used to say belonged to us as much as to Rome." [69] This was a very extensive Ritualistic "Plan of Campaign"; but I fear that I cannot—judging by the evidence which I have already produced—give Newman credit for any very warm desire that the Church of England should "compete with the Roman Church with any prospect of success." He wanted, not competition, but peace and union between the Churches. It is true that he made some efforts to keep people from going over to Rome; but what was his object in doing so? To a Roman Catholic correspondent he wrote, on April 8th, 1841:—"It is my trust, though I must not be too sanguine, that we shall not have individual members of our communion going over to yours." [70] A month later he explained the reason for this opposition to individual secession, in another letter to a Roman Catholic :—" We are keeping people from you," he wrote, "*by supplying their wants in our own Church.* We are keeping persons from you : *do you wish us to keep them from you for a time or for ever?* It rests with you to determine. I do not fear that you will succeed among us; you will not supplant our Church in the affections of the English nation; ONLY THROUGH THE ENGLISH CHURCH CAN YOU ACT UPON THE ENGLISH NATION. I wish, of course, our Church should be consolidated, *with and through and in your communion,* for its sake, and your sake, and for the sake of unity." [71]

---

[68] *Apologia Pro Vita Sua*, p. 165. Edition, 1889.
[69] *Ibid.*, p. 166   [70] *Ibid.*, p. 188.   [71] *Ibid.*, p. 191.

So that, after all, Newman did not wish to keep the English people from Rome "for ever," but only "for a time," during which Rome should have a chance to "act upon the English nation" in her own interests! Are not these the sly tactics carried on by the majority of the Ritualists in our own day? In 1843, Newman, as we have already stated, publicly withdrew the denunciations of Rome which during the previous ten years he had uttered, as so many "dirty words." In the same year many of the early friends of the Tractarian Movement began to be alarmed at the rapid progress which their followers were making towards Rome, and some of them withdrew from the party on that account: of these, the most prominent was the Rev. William Palmer, who had worked for the Movement since its commencement in 1833. He published the reasons for his withdrawal in a pamphlet entitled, *A Narrative of Events connected with the Publication of the Tracts for the Times, with Reflections on the Existing Tendencies to Romanism.* This pamphlet, with additions, was re-issued by its author, in 1883. In the course of it Mr. Palmer gives ample proof of the Romish tendency of the Movement, as it then existed, by a series of extracts from the writings of its leaders, whose principles, he affirmed, "tend to the restoration of Romanism in its fullest extent, and the total subversion of the Reformation."[72] From these extracts I select the following:—

"We talk of the blessings of 'emancipation from the Papal yoke,' and use other phrases of a like *bold and undutiful tenour*. We trust, of course, that active and visible union with the See of Rome is not of the essence of the Church; at the same time we are deeply conscious that in lacking it, far from asserting a right, *we forego a great privilege.*"[73]

"[The Pope is] the earthly representative of her [the Church's] Divine Head."

---

[72] Palmer's *Narrative*, p. 165. Edition, 1883.   [73] *Ibid.*, p. 161.

"The Holy See [is] the proper medium of communion with the Catholic Church." [74]

This tendency to Romanism does not appear to have given any alarm to such well-known members of the party as the Rev. John Keble and Mr. Gladstone. The former, on May 14th, 1843, wrote to Newman:—" Certainly there is a great yearning even after Rome in many parts of the Church, which seems to be accompanied *with so much good that one hopes, if it be right, it will be allowed to gain strength.*" [75] If Keble were at that time a truly loyal son of the Reformed Church of England, would he have rejoiced at this " great yearning even after Rome," and have hoped that it would gain strength "? Of course this was written in confidence, and Keble never could have anticipated that it would ever have been made public, or there can be no doubt he would have written with greater caution. In the *Foreign and Colonial Quarterly Review* for October, 1843, Mr. Gladstone wrote an article on " The Present State of the Church," in which he admitted that there were at that period, within the Church of England—

" Propagators of Catholic tenets and usages, who do not scruple to denounce Protestantism as a principle of unmixed evil; in whom the attraction of the Church's essential Catholicity is sufficient, but only just sufficient, to overcome the repulsive force of the Protestant elements admitted into her institutions; and who do not dissemble that, in their view, Rome, if not a true normal pattern of Christianity, is yet the best existing standard, and one to which we ought to seek to conform. Rome, who is always at our gates as a foe, though in her legitimate sphere she be also an elder sister. With this foe they parley, and in the hearing of the people on the wall. At the same time they relentlessly pursue, with rebuke and invective, the Protestant name." [76]

One would have supposed that Mr. Gladstone would have recommended that such a set of traitors should at once have been turned out of the Church in disgrace. That is what

---

[74] Palmer's *Narrative*, p. 163.   [75] Lock's *John Keble*, p. 120.
[76] Gladstone's *Gleanings of Past Years*, Vol. V., p. 66.

they richly deserved. But, unfortunately, he heaped up praise on the traitors, and hoped they would not go over to Rome, but remain in the Church of England, and "enlighten it" by their "holy example."

"Although," wrote Mr. Gladstone, "we carefully distinguish this section from the legitimate Catholic development, of which we believe it to be an exaggeration, *we rejoice that these excellent persons abide in the Church, to enlighten it by the holy example of their lives.* We rejoice that they feel the awful responsibility of that condemnation, which they would undertake to pronounce against her, by the act of quitting her communion." [77]

And what was "the holy example" which these men were showing to the Church? A few weeks after Mr. Gladstone thus held them up for admiration, they were described by Mr. Newman, who knew them better than any man living, as men "who feel they can with a safe conscience remain with us [*i.e.*, in the Church of England], while they are allowed to testify in behalf of Catholicism, and to promote its interests, *i.e.*, as if by such acts they were putting our Church, or at least a portion of it, in which they are included, in the position of Catechumens. *They think they may stay, while they are moving themselves, others, nay, say the whole Church, towards Rome.*" [78]

The publication of Mr. Palmer's pamphlet led to the Rev. William George Ward writing his notorious and Romanizing work entitled, the *Ideal of a Christian Church*, which was avowedly a reply to Mr. Palmer. Mr. Ward, shortly before the time when he wrote the *Ideal*, having heard that the Rev. R. W. Sibthorp had left the Church of Rome, and returned to the Church of England, of which he had at one time been an ordained Minister, was greatly annoyed, and vented his indignation in a letter to Mr. Phillipps, a Roman Catholic, in these terms:—"By this time you have doubtless heard of Mr. Sibthorp's step.

---

[77] *Ibid.*, p. 70.
[78] *Memoirs of James R. Hope-Scott*, Vol. II, p. 25.

How unspeakably dreadful: it makes one sick to think of it. . . . His reception among us [Tractarians] will be, I fully expect, of the most repulsive character; I for one shall decline any intercourse with him whatever."[79]

That Romanizing tendencies existed in the Church of England Mr. Ward candidly acknowledged, and even expressed his joy at the fact. In his *Ideal* he quotes, as accurate, the statement of the *Christian Remembrancer*, for November, 1843 (the quarterly organ of the Tractarians), which affirmed that the "tendencies to Rome" were "deeply seated and widely spreading"; and that members of the party were "by hundreds straggling towards Rome."[80] In this same *Ideal* Mr. Ward, referring to the Twelfth of the Thirty-nine Articles, declared:—"I subscribe it myself in a non-natural sense." At page 565 he wrote:—"We find, oh most joyful, most wonderful, most unexpected sight! *we find the whole cycle of Roman doctrine* gradually possessing numbers of English Churchmen." At page 567 he wrote:—"Three years have passed, since I said plainly, that in subscribing the Articles, *I renounce no one Roman doctrine.*"

It is not to be wondered at that disloyal utterances such as these raised a hurricane of indignant opposition in the Church. It would have been a lasting disgrace to her had such statements been allowed to pass unchallenged. On November 10th, 1844, Mr. Ward was summoned to appear before the Vice-Chancellor of the University of Oxford. When he appeared he was asked whether he denied the authorship of the *Ideal of a Christian Church*; and whether he disavowed certain passages in the book? Mr. Ward replied, asking for more time before he answered these questions. This was granted to him. He again appeared before the Vice-Chancellor on December 3rd, when, acting under legal advice, he refused to answer the

---

[79] *W. G. Ward and the Oxford Movement*, pp. 201, 202.
[80] Ward's *Ideal of a Christian Church*, p. 566. Second edition.

questions. On December 13th, notice was given that at a Convocation to be held on February 13th, 1845, certain propositions would be placed before Convocation, two of which were as follows:—

(1) "That the passages now read from a book entitled the *Ideal of a Christian Church Considered*, are utterly inconsistent with the Articles of Religion of the Church of England, and with the declaration in respect of those Articles made and subscribed by William George Ward previously and in order to his being admitted to the degrees of B.A. and M.A. respectively, and with the good faith of him, the said William George Ward, in respect of such declaration and subscription."

(2) "That the said William George Ward has disentitled himself to the rights and privileges conveyed by the said degrees, and is hereby degraded from the said degrees of B.A. and M.A. respectively."

The announcement of this proposed action in Convocation created intense excitement throughout the Church of England, and raised the anger of the advanced Tractarians —including Dr. Pusey and Mr. Gladstone—to a boiling state. The attitude of Dr. Hook towards the book was very remarkable. First of all, he declared that Ward had " maligned the English Church for the purpose of eulogizing that of Rome."[81] Dr. Pusey informed him that although he "did not agree with the book," yet that—

"Ward is really very greatly benefiting the Church by his practical suggestions and opening people's eyes to amend things. It is shocking to think of 'degrading' one by whom we are benefiting."[82]

At first Hook decided not to vote at all on the question to be brought before Convocation. Dr. Pusey's publications, more especially his praise of Ignatius Loyola, the founder of the Jesuits, had greatly displeased him.

"I do honestly confess," he wrote to Pusey, "that the publication of Romish Methodism by yourself, and your eulogy of the founder of the Jesuits, had some influence upon my mind, and makes me pause as a strong, decided, vehement Anti-Romanist. These publications and the legendary Lives of the Saints will have the

---

[81] *Life of Dr. Pusey*, Vol. II., p. 415.   [82] *Ibid.*, p. 421.

same effect in England as the fanatical movement in France; they will make men decided Infidels."[83]

On February 13th Ward appeared before the Convocation, and made a defence of his book, after which it was condemned by a majority of 391 votes; his degradation was affirmed by a majority of 58 only. At the same meeting of the Convocation a proposal was made to censure Tract XC., and there can be no doubt that it would have been carried were it not that the Proctors rose and vetoed the motion, which consequently had to be abandoned. One of the Proctors afterwards was promoted to the Deanery of St. Paul's (Dr. Church), and even received the offer of the Archbishopric of Canterbury on the death of Dr. Tait.

Dr. Hook and Mr. Gladstone both voted against the condemnation of Mr. Ward's book, and against his degradation. Mr. Gladstone's vote was given after a careful study of the *Ideal of a Christian Church*. In the December, 1844, issue of the *Quarterly Review* he had written a lengthy review of the book, in which, while he criticised many of Mr. Ward's statements, and expressed his dissent from them, he at the same time gave expression to his own views of Mr. Ward's attitude towards Rome in terms which gave great offence to loyal Churchmen.

"We are prepared to contend," wrote Mr. Gladstone, "that even those who may be influenced more or less by the sympathies which Mr. Ward has avowed for Romish opinions, and by his antipathy to the proceedings taken at the Reformation, are in no degree thereby released from their obligation to continue in the communion of the Church. If their private judgment *prefers the religious system of the Church of Rome to their own*, and even holds the union of the English Church with Rome to be necessary to her perfection as a Church, yet, so long as they cannot deny that she is their spiritual parent and guide ordained of God, they owe to her not merely adhesion, but allegiance. . . . The doctrine that such persons ought to quit the pale of the Church,

[83] *Life of Dr. Pusey*, Vol. II., p. 431.

in our view both drives them upon sin, and likewise constitutes an unwarrantable invasion of the liberty which the Church herself has intended for them." [84]

I venture to submit that Mr. Gladstone's argument would not be accepted in the Army. If, in a time of warfare, it were discovered that some of the officers in a citadel preferred the rule of the enemy to that of their own sovereign, and at the same time were actively at work for the purpose of handing over the whole citadel to the enemy, the authorities would soon deal with the traitors in a very different manner from that suggested by Mr. Gladstone for the traitor officers of the Church Militant. It would not be thought "an unwarrantable invasion of the liberty" of those officers to treat them as they deserved; indeed, it would be considered a bounden duty to deprive them at once of their commissions in the army, and turn them out of it in disgrace.

It must not be supposed that Dr. Hook's vote in defence of Ward was the result of any wish on his part to aid in the reunion of the Church of England with the Papacy. Individual or corporate reunion with Rome was ever an abomination to Hook, who, in his later years, fought most vigorously against the more advanced Romanizers. At the close of the year 1844 he viewed with horror the thought that Newman might secede, and rejoiced when he heard a rumour that he would not go over. In this cheerful frame of mind he wrote to Dr. Pusey:—

"I am so glad and thankful that Newman has been saved from this downfall: may he be still preserved from the fangs of Satan. Although I am quite convinced that the number of Romanizers is very small, yet there are several persons who would follow Newman, and I should myself fear that any person going from light to darkness would endanger his salvation. I should fear that it would be scarcely possible for anyone who should apostatize from the only true Church of God in this country to the Popish sect, to escape perdition; having

[84] Gladstone's *Gleanings*, Vol. V., pp. 152, 153.

yielded to Satan in one temptation he will go on sinking deeper and deeper into the bottomless pit." [85]

In this letter Dr. Hook further asserted that Rome is identical with Antichrist, and that "Romanism is preparing the way for infidelity." Dr. Pusey was not at all pleased with this letter. It annoyed him very much to hear from his friend such plain denunciations of the Papal Communion; and therefore he wrote back a letter of protest against Hook's strong language:—

"I am," wrote Pusey, "frightened at your calling Rome Antichrist, or a forerunner of it. I believe Antichrist will be infidel, and arise out of what calls itself Protestantism, *and then Rome and England will be united in one* to oppose it. Protestantism is infidel, or verging towards it, as a whole." [86]

Pusey's hatred of Protestantism here comes out in the strongest light; and his hatred of it was shared by the other leaders of his party. But he could not bear to hear any of his disciples or friends say anything against Rome. Soon after he had written the above letter to Dr. Hook, he was very disappointed with the new Charge of Archdeacon Manning, because of its severe criticism of the Papacy. So he wrote to Manning:—

"Thank you for your Charge. While it is in a cheering tone, *is there quite love enough for the Roman Church? . . . I only desiderate more love for Rome.*" [87]

In the light of Manning's subsequent history it does indeed seem strange to find him thus censured at this period for not loving Rome enough. Manning did not agree with Pusey on this subject. There was more manliness in his reply than could be found in the letter of his leader:—

"One powerful obstruction," he wrote to Pusey, "to the very work in which you are spending yourself arises, I believe, out of the tone you have adopted towards the Church of Rome. Will you forgive me if I say that it seems to me to breathe, not charity, but want of

---

[85] *Life of Dr. Pusey*, Vol. II., p. 446.   [86] *Ibid.*, p. 447.   [87] *Ibid.*, p. 454.

decision? ... Now what are the facts but these? The Church of Rome for three hundred years has desired our extinction. It is now undermining us. Suppose your own brother to believe that he was divinely inspired to destroy you. The highest duties would bind you to decisive, firm, and circumspect precaution. Now a tone of love such as you speak of seems to me to bind you also to speak plainly of the broad and glaring evils of the Roman system. Are you prepared to do this? If not, it seems to me that the most powerful warnings of charity forbid you to use a tone which cannot but lay asleep the consciences of many for whom, by writing and publishing, you make yourself responsible."[88]

Dr. Pusey's biographer acknowledges that his "attitude at this juncture created perplexity in still higher quarters."[89] It seems to have perplexed the Archbishop of Canterbury, whose Chaplain, the Rev. B. Harrison, wrote to Pusey a letter on the subject. Pusey's biographer does not print this letter, but he does print the reply to it, in which Pusey's dislike for unity with Protestants, and his love for much that is Roman, is candidly acknowledged.

"I cannot," wrote Pusey, "any more take the negative ground against Rome; I can only remain neutral. I have indeed for some time left off alleging grounds against Rome, and whether you think it right or wrong, I am sure it is of no use to persons who are really in any risk of leaving us... From much reading of Roman books, I am so much impressed with *the superiority of their teaching;* and again, in some respects, I see things in Antiquity which I did not (especially I cannot deny some purifying system in the Intermediate State, nor the lawfulness of some Invocation of Saints) that I dare not speak against things."[90]

Dr. Hook's hopefulness as to the state of Newman was without solid foundation. No one can read Newman's *Letters,* or the *Life of Dr. Pusey,* without finding abundant evidence to prove that Newman's heart had been for many years in Rome, and that, to be consistent, he ought to have seceded several years before he actually did leave the Church of England. Some evidence of Newman's love for Rome has already been given above. This may now be

[88] *Ibid.,* p. 455.   [89] *Ibid.,* p. 455.   [90] *Ibid.,* pp. 456, 457.

them, to point out the evils which that Association diffuses, and to repel the dangers it is bringing on. Yet they would seem wanting to their office, did they not, in a matter of such moment, further enkindle the said Bishops' pastoral zeal; this novelty being all the more perilous as it bears a semblance of religion, and of being much concerned for the unity of the Christian society.

"The principle on which it rests is one that overthrows the Divine constitution of the Church. For it is pervaded by the idea that the true Church of Jesus Christ consists partly of the Roman Church spread abroad and propagated throughout the world, partly of the Photian schism and the Anglican heresy, as having equally with the Roman Church, one Lord, one faith, and one baptism. . . . The Catholic Church offers prayers to Almighty God, and urges the faithful in Christ to pray, that all who have left the Holy Roman Church, out of which is no salvation, may abjure their errors and be brought to the true faith, and the peace of that Church, nay, that all men may, by God's merciful aid, attain to a knowledge of the truth. But that the faithful in Christ, and that ecclesiastics, should pray for Christian unity under the direction of heretics, and, worse still, according to an intention stained and infected by heresy in a high degree, can no way be tolerated. . . .

"Hence, no proof is needed that Catholics who join this Society are giving both to Catholics and non-Catholics an occasion of spiritual ruin : more especially, because the Society, by holding out a vain expectation of those three communions, each in its integrity, and keeping each to its own persuasion, coalescing in one, lead the minds of non-Catholics away from conversion to the faith, and, by the Journals it publishes, endeavours to prevent it.

"The most anxious care, then, is to be exercised, that no Catholics may be deluded, either by appearance of piety or by unsound opinions, to join or in any way favour the Society in question, or any similar one; that they may not be carried away by a delusive yearning for such new-fangled Christian unity, into a fall from that perfect unity which by a wonderful gift of Divine Grace stands on the firm foundation of Peter.

"C. CARD. PATRIZI."

"ROME, *this 16th day of September*, 1864." [29]

The issuing of this document was, indeed, a terrible blow to the promoters of the A. P. U. C. It not merely proclaimed

---

[29] I quote from the official Roman Catholic translation, in *Synodi Dioeceseos Suthwarcensis, Londini*, 1868, pp. 186-190.

war against the Association, but treated it with unmitigated contempt. Its members are termed "heretics"; and the Association is declared to be engaged in the task of "diffusing evils," and producing "dangers" in the Church. Its chief "principle" is even said to "overthrow the Divine constitution of the Church"; and its "intention" is declared to be "stained and infected with heresy in a high degree." But some of the Ritualists seem to take a special delight in humbly kissing the Papal toe which has just kicked them. No fewer than 198 clergymen of the Church of England, members of the A. P. U. C., answered the document issued by the Inquisition of cruel and evil memory, with an address of contemptible humiliation and explanation. The one thing they seemed to dread was to offend the Pope. Not a thought of the effect of their traitorous conduct on the Protestants of England ever seems to have entered their heads. They put their names to their address, but, no doubt, with the knowledge that none of the public would ever know who they were. The secret has been kept ever since. What a storm of indignation would have swept over them, had their identity been known at the time to the people amongst whom they ministered! It will be observed that some of them held high office in the Church of England, describing themselves as "Deans" and "Canons." Their address to what they termed "the *Sacred* Office" of the Inquisition is not generally known, and therefore I print it in full :—

"*To the Most Eminent and Most Reverend Father in Christ and Lord C. Cardinal Patrizi, Prefect of the Sacred Office.*

"We, the undersigned Deans, Canons, Parish Priests, and other Priests of the Anglo-Catholic Church, earnestly desiring the visible reunion, according to the will of our Lord, of the several parts of the Christian family, have read with great regret your Eminence's letter 'to all the English Bishops.'

"In that letter, our Society, instituted to promote the Reunion of all Christendom, is charged with affirming in its prospectus that 'the three Communions, the Roman Catholic, the Eastern, and the Anglican, have an equal claim to call themselves Catholic.'

"On that question our prospectus gave no opinion whatever. What we said, treated of the question of *fact*, not of *right*. We merely affirmed that the Anglican Church claimed the name of Catholic; as is abundantly plain to all, both from the Liturgy and the Articles of Religion.

"Moreover, as to the intention of our Society, that letter asserts our especial aim to be, 'that the three Communions named, each in its integrity and each maintaining still its own opinions, may coalesce into one.'

"Far from us and from our Society be such an aim as this; from which must be anticipated, not ecclesiastical unity, but merely a discord of brethren in personal conflict under one roof. What we beseech Almighty God to grant, and desire with all our hearts, is simply that œcumenical intercommunion which existed before the separation of East and West, founded and consolidated on the profession of one and the same Catholic faith.

"Moreover, the Society aforesaid should all the less excite your jealousy that it abstains from action, and simply prays, in the words of Christ our Lord, 'May there be one Fold and one Shepherd.' This alone finds place in our hearts' desire, and this is the principle and the yearning we express to your Eminence with the utmost earnestness, with sincere heart and voice unfeigned.

"As to the Journal entitled the *Union Review*, the connection between it and the Society is purely accidental, and we are, therefore, in no way pledged to its *dicta*. In that little work, various writers put forth indeed their own opinions, but only to the further elucidation of the truth of the Catholic faith by developing them. That such a mode of contributing papers should not be in use in Rome, where the controversies of the day are seldom under discussion, is hardly to be wondered at; but in England, where almost every question becomes public property, none results in successful conviction without free discussion.

"To hasten this event, we have now laboured during many years. We have effected improvements beyond what could be hoped for, where the faith of the flock, or Divine worship, or clerical discipline, may have been imperfect; and, not to be forgetful of others, WE HAVE CULTIVATED A FEELING OF GOODWILL TOWARDS THE VENERABLE CHURCH OF ROME, that has for a long time caused some to mistrust us.

"We humbly profess ourselves your Eminence's servants, devoted to Catholic unity."[30]

On this document, and the reply given to it by the Inquisition, Cardinal Manning addressed a pastoral letter to the clergy, entitled the *Reunion of Christendom*. In this document, while firmly upholding the decision of the Inquisition forbidding Roman Catholics to join the A. P. U. C., Dr. Manning showed how much he rejoiced in his heart at the work of that Society. Of the address to the Inquisition, by 198 Church of England clergymen, he wrote :—

"We do not regard this as a merely intellectual or natural event. We gladly recognize in it an influence and an impulse of supernatural grace. It is a wonderful reaction from the days within living memory when fidelity to the Church of England was measured by repulsion from the Church of Rome. It is as wonderful an evidence of the flow in the stream which has carried the minds of men onwards for these thirty years nearer and nearer to the frontiers of the Catholic faith. It is a movement against the wind and tide of English tradition and of English prejudice; a supernatural movement like the attraction which drew those who were once farthest from the Kingdom of Heaven to the side of our Lord. A change has visibly passed over England. Thirty years ago its attitude towards the Catholic Church was either intense hostility or stagnant ignorance. It is not so now."[31]

At this period Dr. Manning seems to have devoted a great deal of his attention to the Romeward Movement in the Church of England. He thankfully acknowledged the services rendered by the Ritualists to the Church of Rome, and simply laughed to scorn their boast that they kept their followers from joining the Church of Rome by giving to them Popery within the Church of England, in order that it might be unnecessary for them to go to Rome for it. In the course of his inaugural address to the Roman Catholic Academia, in 1866, Archbishop Manning entered at considerable length

---

[30] Purcell's *Life of Cardinal Manning*, Vol. II., pp. 279, 280.
[31] *Ibid.*, p. 286.

into the effects of Ritualism on the prosperity of the Church of Rome in England. He said:—

"In the last thirty years there has sprung up in the Anglican Establishment an extensive rejection of Protestantism, and a sincere desire and claim to be Catholic. Ever since the Reformation, indeed, the writers of the Anglican Church have claimed to be Catholic; but none that I know disclaimed to be Protestant. They assumed that a Protesting Christian was *ipso facto* a primitive Catholic. Not so now. Protestantism is recognized as a thing intrinsically untenable and irreconcilable with the Catholic faith. The school of which I speak claim to be Catholic because they reject Protestantism with all its heterodoxies. In this school are to be found many Catholic doctrines, not exactly or fully expressed or believed—for such are not to be found either full or exact outside of the Catholic Church—but more or less near to truth. For instance, the Church of England forbids the use of the term Transubstantiation, by declaring the doctrine to be an error. The doctrine of the Real Presence, less Transubstantiation, is like the doctrine of one God in three Persons, less the doctrine of the Trinity. Not only is the term rejected, but the conception is correspondingly inaccurate. This runs through all the Catholic doctrines which are professed out of the unity of the Church, and apart from the traditions of its sacred terminology. It is under this limitation that I go on to say that at this time the doctrine of the Sacraments, their nature, number, and grace; the intercession and invocation of saints, the power of the priesthood in sacrifice and absolution, the excellence and obligations of the religious life, are all held and taught by clergymen of the Church of England. Add to this, the practice of Confession, and of works of temporal and spiritual mercy in form and by rule borrowed from the Catholic Church, are all to be found among those who are still within the Anglican communion. I must also add the latest and strangest phenomenon of this movement, the adoption of an elaborate ritual with its vestments borrowed from the Catholic Church.

"On all these things I trust a blessing may descend. I see in them many things: First, they are a testimony in favour of the Catholic Church, which has always unchangeably taught and practised these things; secondly, a testimony against the Anglican Reformation, which has always rejected and cast them out."[33]

"Every parish priest happily knows how empty and foolish is the

---

[22] *Essays on Religion and Literature*, pp. 12, 13. Second series.

boast they [Ritualists] make of keeping souls from conversion [to the Church of Rome]. The public facts of every day refute it. They may keep back the handful who surround them, and hide the truth from their own hearts, but the steady current of return to the Catholic and Roman Church throughout the whole of England is no more to be affected by them than the rising of the tide by the palms of their hands. Against their will, certainly, and perhaps without their knowledge, they are sending on numberless souls into the truth which they probably will never enter. But the number of those [Ritualists] whose good faith is doubtful is not great. The multitude of those who are drawn by a simple and natural reverence to clothe what they sincerely believe with a becoming ritual, and who worship piously and humbly in Churches which might almost be mistaken for ours . . . is very great, and is perhaps continually increasing. They are coming up to the very threshold of the Church. They have learned to look upon it as the centre of Christendom, from which they sprang, and upon which their own Church is supposed to rest. They use our devotions, our books, our pictures of piety; they are taught to believe the whole Catholic doctrine, and to receive the whole Council of Trent, not indeed in its own true meaning, but in a meaning invented by their teachers. This cannot last long. Such teachers are, as Fuller quaintly and truly says, like unskilful horsemen. They so open gates as to shut themselves out, but let others through." [33]

Since the year 1867 the Association for the Promotion of the Unity of Christendom has not come very prominently before the public. But it has worked in private ever since, in ways with which the outer world is not generally acquainted. It is advertised in several of the Ritualistic annuals, and twice a year "Celebrations" for the "intention" of the Society are offered in English, Scottish, and Colonial Churches. The Church of Rome no longer gives the Association any help; she only reaps the fruit of its labours.

Amongst the Ritualistic societies which, as a portion only of their operations, advocate and labour for the Corporate Reunion of the Church of England with the Church of Rome, is the secret Society of the Holy Cross. In the year 1867, at the Wolverhampton Church Congress, this Society

[33] *Ibid.*, p. 14.

issued an *Address to Catholics*, in which its deep, heartfelt longings for Reunion with Rome found expression.

"It may well be," says this *Address*, "nay, it is, *a very grievous drawback* to the Church of England that she is not now in visible communion with the Western Patriarchate." [34]

By the "Western Patriarchate" is, of course, meant that of the Church of Rome. I venture to assert that the majority of loyal Churchmen are quite certain that the absence, during the past three centuries, of "visible communion" with Rome, instead of being "a very grievous drawback to the Church of England," is, in reality, a great blessing for which England cannot be too thankful to Almighty God. It is no "drawback" to either individuals, nations, or Churches, to be spiritually free from Papal bondage. Should the S. S. C. gain its objects, then farewell for ever to our religious liberty!

During the few months immediately preceding the Wolverhampton Church Congress, of 1867, the authorities of the Society of the Holy Cross were busily engaged in securing signatures, from both clergy and laity, to an Address to the Bishops assembled that year, at the first Lambeth Conference. The Romeward leanings of the Society, which was described at that time, by a Ritualistic newspaper, as "a shy and retiring organization," [35] are still more clearly seen in this Address, which was publicly advertised at the time as emanating from the S. S. C. The following extract from this document will be read with disapprobation by all who love the freedom of the Church of England, and believe that it would be a sin to join the Roman communion, whether individually or corporately:—

"We are mindful of efforts made in former time by English and foreign Bishops and theologians *to effect*, by mutual explanations on either side, *a reconciliation between the Roman and Anglican Communions.* And, considering the intimate and visible union which existed between

[34] *S. S. C. Address to Catholics*, p. 13.
[35] *Church News*, August 21, 1867, p. 372.

the Church of England and the rest of Western Christendom, we earnestly entreat your lordships seriously to consider the best means of renewing like endeavours; and to adopt such measures as may, under the guidance of God's Holy Spirit, be effectual in REMOVING THE BARRIERS which now divide the Western Branch of the Catholic Church."[36]

I do not know any expression which more clearly and accurately describes the work of the Ritualists than that of "removing the barriers" between the Church of England and the Church of Rome. Those "barriers" were set up by our Reformers, nearly 350 years ago, and for good and sufficient reasons. They are as much needed now as ever, for Rome has not improved, but has rather grown worse, since the Reformation. It is, therefore, the bounden duty of all who love the Reformation, whatever may be their ecclesiastical or social position, however exalted, or however humble, to resist all attempts at removing them, whether those attempts are made by the secret Society of the Holy Cross, or by any other Ritualistic society or individual. This S. S. C. Address to the Lambeth Conference was signed by no fewer than 1212 clergymen in the Church of England, and by 4453 of the laity, of whom 1995 were women.[37] It will no doubt surprise many of my readers to learn that so far back as the year 1867 such a large number of clergymen were found anxious for "a reconciliation between the Roman and Anglican Communions." If so many could be found then, is there not good reason for fearing that the number has multiplied since, and that the dangers to our Church from this Romeward Movement have multiplied also? A few names only of those who signed this Address were published in the papers—the great majority of them are unknown until this day. Amongst others, it was signed by the Rev. Dr. Pusey; the late Canon H. P. Liddon; Canon T. T. Carter, of Clewer; the Rev. W. Butler, late Dean of Lincoln; the Rev. F. H. Murray, then and now Rector of

---

[36] *Ibid.*, September 11th, 1867, p. 426. [37] *Ibid.*, September 25th, 1867, p. 455.

Chislehurst; the Rev. R. M. Benson, then head of the Cowley Fathers; the Hon. and Rev. H. Douglas, now Vicar of St. Paul's, Worcester; the Rev. A. Wagner, Vicar of St. Paul's, Brighton; Rev. P. G. Medd, now Rector of North Cerney, Cirencester; the Rev. G. R. Prynne, Vicar of St. Peter's, Plymouth; the Hon. Colin Lindsay, then President of the English Church Union, and subsequently a seceder to Rome; and the Hon. C. L. Wood, now Lord Halifax, and the present President of the English Church Union.

The secrecy which surrounds the work of the Society of the Holy Cross has prevented me from learning much as to its operations in furtherance of Reunion with Rome since 1867, but I have heard nothing which would lead me to suppose that it has withdrawn from the position which it then adopted. There can be no doubt that during that period it has laboured zealously in Romanizing the services of the Church of England, and it even went so far as to make the adoption of "Roman Ritual" the rule for the Brethren to follow. And it has certainly laboured hard ever since 1867 in teaching Romish doctrine. The Master of the Society, in his Address to the September, 1876, Synod, went so far as to declare that "no Brother [of the S. S. C.] should be considered disloyal to the Society who agrees in opinion with the rest of Western Christendom, except in one article, or its immediate consequences, which denies that the Brother himself is a Catholic."[38] The "one article" here referred to, there can be no question, was that of Papal Infallibility. A man can therefore agree with every other doctrine of "the rest of Western Christendom," that is, with the Church of Rome, without being in any way "disloyal" to the Society of the Holy Cross. That, no doubt, is the case; but here the important question comes in, Is not such a man "disloyal" to the Church of England? At the September, 1878, Synod of the S. S. C. the following resolution proposed

[38] The *Master's Address*. Festival of the Exaltation of the Holy Cross, 1876, p. 5.

by Brother Lowder, and seconded by Brother Goldie, was carried *nem. con.*:—" That this Synod regards with much interest the attempts to revive the life and action of the A. P. U. C. [Association for Promoting the Unity of Christendom], and holds that the time is now come for its adopting some more practical measures for the promotion of the Unity of Christendom, and in particular that the S. S. C. would desire to co-operate with the A. P. U. C. in obtaining the sanction of the Catholic Patriarchs of Western and Eastern Christendom for freedom to English Catholics to communicate at Catholic altars in foreign countries." [39] In the course of the discussion which took place on this resolution, Brother Mossman informed the Brethren that the Order of Corporate Reunion "had arisen out of the yearning of many hearts for visible unity and communion with the See of Peter. He gave an account of an interview he had had with Cardinal Manning, to whom he had mentioned four points which, he believed, would be urged by the Catholic party in any negotiations with the Holy See. (1) The recognition of Anglican Orders; (2) the marriage of priests; (3) the giving of the chalice to the laity; (4) the Liturgy in the vernacular. The answers of his Eminence had been satisfactory, though he would not commit himself to speak authoritatively on the matter." [40] At this same Synod the Society of the Holy Cross considered its attitude towards the Order of Corporate Reunion, and a Committee was appointed to consider the subject. Subsequently the Society adopted and published the Report of this Committee. It was decidedly against the O. C. R. The conclusion arrived at is contained in the following paragraph :—" We therefore hold that the assumed jurisdiction of the Order of Corporate Reunion is without any lawful foundation, that its claims cannot be substantiated, and that Catholics should therefore be warned against joining the Association, as involving

[39] *S. S. C. Analysis of Proceedings*, September Synod, 1878, pp. 9-11.
[40] *Ibid.*, p. 10.

themselves thereby in the guilt of schism, and probably of sacrilege."[41]

One of the members of the Society of the Holy Cross, the Rev. N. Y. Birkmyre, Vicar of St. Simon's, Bristol, gave expression, in 1888, to his wishes for Reunion in a very candid manner indeed. He was preaching for the Church of England Working Men's Society on that occasion, and, speaking for himself and the Society, he declared :—

"We must never be content to settle down till the Church of England can say boldly, not by the mouth of two or three individuals, but by the mouths of the Archbishops and Bishops of the Church, to the Sister Churches :—' See, *here we have cast out from ourselves Protestantism*, we now every one of us believe and use the Sacraments, and now we say, receive us again into inter-communion, *let us all be one again.*' . . . And the second great danger is the idea of building up a modified, but still practically a National religion. People say that the Church of Greece *and the Church of Rome* teach one thing, and the Church of England something else, *but if the Church of England teaches anything about the Blessed Sacrament different from the others she teaches a lie.* No, we must understand that the teaching is one."[42]

Another Ritualistic Society, which has make Corporate Reunion with Rome one of the planks in its platform, is the English Church Union. In its earlier years this subject was kept somewhat in the background, and when mentioned in public was generally referred to as "the Corporate Reunion of Christendom," a convenient expression which may mean more or less according to the intention of the person who uses it. The attitude of the Union was to a large extent that which it adopted, in its earlier years towards Ritual. Its rules did not fully reveal their plans to the public. One of the most prominent members of the Union, the Rev. T. W. Perry, at an ordinary meeting of that Society on February 16th, 1869, very candidly explained

---

[41] *Statement of the Society of the Holy Cross Concerning the Order of Corporate Reunion*, p. 10. Revised edition.
[42] *Church Times*, August 14th, 1885, p. 623.

the tactics of the Union in the following terms:—"It is quite clear," he said, "it would never do for the President and Council, any more than it would do for a general and his officers, to explain all their tactics. They must be as candid as they can, but they must observe such reticence as is necessary."[43] The English Church Union had been many years in existence before it became officially pledged to Corporate Reunion with Rome. Previous to that period its work consisted largely in educating its followers as to the alleged duty and necessity of such a union. The subject was frequently discussed at meetings of its branches throughout the country, and these branches occasionally passed resolutions on the question, which, while they were not binding on the Central Council, yet served to show the direction in which the tide was flowing Romeward. To sooth the minds of the more timid of their followers the Unionists were heard, from time to time, talking against some of the practical abuses of the Church of Rome, and finding fault with a few of the doctrines taught in Continental books of devotion. What Bishop Robert Abbot said of Laud and his followers, might with equal justice be said of those wily Ritualists who, while denouncing Rome, are labouring zealously for Reunion with her.

"If they do at any time," said Dr. Abbot, "speak against the Papists, they do but beat a little about the bush, and that but softly too, for fear of waking and disquieting the birds that are in it; they speak nothing but that wherein one Papist will speak against another, as against equivocation, and the Pope's temporal authority, and the like; and perhaps some of their blasphemous speeches. But in the points of Free Will, Justification, Concupiscence being a sin after Baptism, Inherent Righteousness, and certainty of Salvation; the Papists beyond the seas can say they are wholly theirs; and the Recusants [Romanists] at home make their brags of them. And in all things they keep themselves so near the brink, that upon any occasion they may step over to them."[44]

---

[43] *English Church Union Monthly Circular*, Volume for 1869 p. 99.
[44] Heylin's *Lif of Laud*, p. 42. Dublin, 1719.

At the Annual Meeting of the English Church Union, June 12th, 1861, the President of the Union, the Hon. Colin Lindsay (who subsequently seceded to Rome) congratulated the members that on that morning they had offered up to the Throne of Heaven their "united prayers for the Reunion of Christendom." Though he does not appear to have mentioned it by name, there can be no doubt that he included Reunion with Rome in that expression.

In 1865 Dr. Pusey startled the ecclesiastical world by the publication of the first volume of his *Eirenicon*, the object of which, as the title-page states, was to prove that the Church of England, as "a portion of Christ's one Holy Catholic Church," might become "a means of restoring visible unity" to the whole of the Church throughout the world. A more detailed, and also an accurate summary of its object was that given by the *Union Review*, which remarked that :—"The object of the book is to prove that in all essentials for Unity, the Churches of England and Rome are one, and that, as a Catholic interpretation can most readily and truly be given both to the Decrees of Trent and the Thirty-nine Articles, nothing need hinder their mutual acceptance. He holds it to be a mistake to suppose that any of the Articles were levelled against the doctrines of the Roman Communion as set forth by the Council of Trent, or that the Decrees of Trent were levelled against anything upheld by the English Church, or that they really maintain anything which the English Church has condemned.[45] Dr. Pusey considers that those parts of the Roman system which are popularly spoken of as Romanism are but excrescences like the many heresies among ourselves."[46] In other words, his attitude towards Rome was very much like that of Laud and his followers, as

---

[45] Those who wish to read an able and conclusive refutation of the position adopted by Dr. Pusey, should read Dean Goode's *Tract XC. Historically Refuted*. Second edition, 1866. London: Hatchards.

[46] *Union Review*, Volume for 1866, p. 2.

described by Bishop Robert Abbot, in the sermon quoted above. The only differences between the two are that Dr. Pusey went much further in a Romeward direction than Laud ever dreamt of, and that he wrote far more gently of Papal error than Laud would ever have sanctioned. The Roman Catholic newspaper, the *Weekly Register*, reviewed the *Eirenicon* at considerable length, and this drew from Dr. Pusey himself a letter, dated November 22nd, 1865, addressed to the Editor of that paper, in the course of which he made the following remarkable statements:—

"I have long been convinced that there is nothing in the Council of Trent which could not be explained satisfactorily to us, if it were explained *authoritatively*, i.e., by the Roman Church itself, not by individual theologians only. This involves the conviction on my side, that there is nothing in our Articles which cannot be explained rightly, as not contradicting anything held to be *de fide* in the Roman Church. . . . As it is of moment, that I should not be misunderstood by my own people, let me add, that I have not intended to express any opinion about a visible head of the Church. *We readily recognize the Primacy of the Bishop of Rome;* the bearings of that Primacy upon other local Churches, we believe to be matter of ecclesiastical, not of Divine law; *but neither is there anything in the Supremacy in itself to which we should object.*"

No doubt Dr. Pusey would wish the "Supremacy" of the Pope to be exercised over the Church of England—in case of Reunion—in the gentlest possible manner, but to be willing to accept it in any shape or form, with the lessons of the past for our guidance, is an act which must be abhorred by every liberty loving Englishman. This country knows, from bitter experience, what Papal supremacy means. The lessons of the Martyr fires lit in Mary's reign are not yet forgotten in England.

Dr. Pusey's book speedily attracted the attention of the English Church Union. At its next annual meeting a resolution was unanimously carried, expressing the rejoicing of the Union at its publication, together with an earnest hope for the Reunion of Christendom. The resolution was proposed by the Rev. W. Gresley, Vice-President of the Union, in the following terms:—

"That this Union rejoices in the publication of Dr. Pusey's letter (the *Eirenicon*) to the author of the *Christian Year*, and earnestly hopes and prays that God, in His own time and in His own way, will so dispose the hearts and minds of His people, that the sad divisions which now rend the seamless robe of Christ may be healed; and that the whole of Christendom may be re-united into one holy communion and fellowship, to the glory of our Lord God, and the salvation of the human race." [47]

Mr. Gresley, in moving this resolution, informed the members of the Union that he had brought the subject forward at the request of the Council. He said that their scheme for Reunion included not only the Roman and Greek Churches, but the Dissenters also. "It would not," he declared, "be a truly Christian scheme which did not embrace them also"; but he did not stop to explain that the only condition on which Dissenters will ever be admitted into the Church of England—by Ritualists—is that of absolute surrender, and that is a condition which they can never be expected to accept. So that Reunion with Dissenters, on Ritualistic principles, is quite "out of the range of practical politics." Individual Dissenters may come over to the Church of England on this condition, but to expect that any Nonconformist Church will do so, as a body, is simply the dream of sacerdotal fanatics. The discussion on Mr. Gresley's resolution was enlivened by the appearance of the Rev. Archer Gurney—a member of the Union—who stood up to propose an amendment. His remarks were received, however, with hisses and uproar, and constant interruption, and he could only find three persons to vote for him. Yet he told the Union some plain and wholesome truths, which it would have done well to lay to heart. He declared that there were members of the Union (though, as it turned out, there were only three in the meeting) "who are

---

[47] *English Church Union Monthly Circular*, Volume for 1866, p. 191.

not prepared to assent to Reunion with Rome on any basis whatsoever, constituted as Rome now is, and maintaining the claims she now maintains." While Mr. Gurney was speaking Dr. Pusey was present at the meeting, which had just elected him a Vice-President of the English Church Union. When, therefore, Mr. Gurney attacked him by name, he at once roused the anger of the Romanizers. Yet, nothing daunted, Mr. Gurney went on with his indictment. "I am," he continued, "heartily persuaded that the *Eirenicon*—recognizing, as I do, the purity of motive of the writer—is, nevertheless, most dangerous in its effects, and, in addition, calculated to deprive us of the truth as it is in Christ Jesus. . . . These are the principles which I come before you to uphold this day —the independence of the Catholic Episcopate of any Pope, of any single Bishop claiming to exercise Universal Primacy and Supremacy. And he [Dr. Pusey] whom you so much delight to honour has expressed his conviction that there is nothing objectionable in such a Supremacy. I hold his own words in my hand, and he has distinctly said, not only that 'we readily recognize the supremacy [48] of the Bishop of Rome,' but that 'there is nothing in that Supremacy in itself to which we should object.' I say, as a Catholic, he is not Catholic who uses such language as this; . . . and mark this, one of the chief Bishops of the American Church has told us, that the man whom you delight to honour is a Gallican on the wrong side of the water." At this point there was great confusion in the meeting, and angry shouts from the Romanizers were heard all over the room. When Mr. Gurney sat down, Dr. Pusey rose to reply to him, and was received with long-continued cheering. As to the question of Papal Supremacy, he said that he did "not know where it is defined in what Supremacy consists." "It matters not," he continued, "under whom

---

[48] The word actually used by Dr. Pusey was "Primacy" not "Supremacy."

we live,[49] so that by living under that authority it does not touch our conscience."

At the next annual meeting of the English Church Union, June 19th, 1867, the President announced the formation of a new Society ("The Catholic Union for Prayer") which had been promoted by the Union, for the purpose of praying for the whole Church, and more especially for the restoration of its unity.

"There is," said the President, "one powerful weapon we can all use; that is, Prayer. The Council, feeling this so strongly, have promoted the establishment of a new Union, called the 'Catholic Union for Prayer.' The object of this Union is to combine all who love God and His Church in an Holy Confraternity to pray for the Holy Catholic Church, and for our portion of it in particular. If we all unite in saying the Lord's Prayer once every day for this great object, we may, relying upon the Divine promise to grant all petitions offered in Christ's name, look forward with confidence to the speedy deliverance of the Church of England, *and her Reunion with East and West. Let us labour hard for this glorious end.*"[50]

A prospectus of this "Catholic Union for Prayer," which I possess, states that its Warden was Dr. Pusey, the Hon. Colin Lindsay its secretary, and that fourteen well-known members of the Ritualistic party—seven clerical and seven lay—constituted its Council. "All Churchmen," it states, "being communicants of the Catholic Church, are earnestly nvited to join this bond of prayer, *this Holy Confederation, for the Reunion of Christendom*"; and, no doubt with a view to promote secrecy, it is added that "the names of the Associates shall not be published." The "Catholic Union for Prayer" is mentioned in every volume of the monthly magazine of the English Church Union for several years after its formation, after which I can find no record of its

---

[49] Most Churchmen believe that it *does* matter very much "under whom they live"; but it is evident that with Dr. Pusey to live under Papal Supremacy, "would *not* touch our [*his?*] conscience." With loyal Churchmen it would be otherwise.

[50] The *Liberties of the Church*, an Address by the Hon. Colin Lindsay, p. 22, English Church Union Office.

existence. Probably we shall know more about it when the last volume of the *Life of Dr. Pusey* is published.

The subject of the Reunion of Christendom was kept prominently before the public by the English Church Union, after the publication of Dr. Pusey's *Eirenicon*. It was discussed at the meetings of many of its branches, and occasionally resolutions on the subject were passed. When the Lambeth Conference met, in 1878, at the annual meeting of the Union that year, a resolution was carried unanimously, affirming that the Union viewed the Conference with the deepest interest, "in the hope that their united counsels may tend to the peace and well-being of the Church, the reunion of those separated from her fold at home, and the restoration of visible communion between the various Apostolic Churches of Eastern and Western Christendom."[51] In the annual report of the President and Council adopted at the same meeting, a paragraph appeared which was almost word for word the same as the resolution I have just quoted.[52]

No one can doubt, who has studied the operations of the English Church Union, that the prime mover in all its Corporate Reunion work has been its President, Lord Halifax. He was elected to that office, April 21st, 1868, on the resignation of the first President, the Hon. Colin Lindsay. That gentleman, in his letter of resignation, assigned reasons for ceasing to be President which were only ostensible. He pleaded his state of health.[53] No doubt he was in ill-health at the time, but that which brought on the crisis was his determination to secede to the Church of Rome, an event which took place not long after his resignation. At that time the new President had not been called to the House of Lords, and was known as the Hon. Charles L. Wood. Since he became President of the English Church Union his whole heart and soul have been thrown into the work of healing the breach that took place between

---

[51] *Church Union Gazette*, Volume for 1878, p. 179. [52] *Ibid.*, p. 154.
[53] *History of the English Church Union*, p. 99.

England and Rome in the sixteenth century, and he has done all that in him lay to assist that "levelling up" process within the Church of England which seems to have been thought necessary, as a preparation for the expected reconciliation. It seems to have been generally accepted as a principle by the advanced section of the Ritualists that the Church of England is not in a sufficiently Catholic condition —at least in practice—to make her respectable enough to keep company with the truly holy and Catholic Church of Rome! Hence the necessity for "levelling up." This idea of the relative position and purity of the Churches of England and Rome found expression in a letter written by "a Colonial Priest," which appeared in the *Church Review* of September 21st, 1888. A brief extract from this letter I have already given, but it may be well to give its statements at greater length.

"It seems to me," wrote this Ritualistic priest, "utterly premature to consider Reunion, especially with the great Patriarchal See of the West [*i.e.*, with Rome], as within even distant probability, until the Anglican Communion, as a whole, is Catholicised. *There lies our work;* for every priest and every faithful lay person to live, each in his or her little sphere, the Catholic life. When as yet the Holy Sacrifice of the Mass is offered daily in only two hundred churches; while the Holy Sacrament of Unction is ignored by every member (so far as I know: I shall be delighted to find that I am wrong) of the Anglican Episcopate; while multitudes of laity never dream of purging their souls of deadly sin by Sacramental Confession, and multitudes of priests never teach them that such is their bounden duty; while fasting reception of the Body and Blood of our Lord is still the exception; while almost every kind of heresy can be taught unchecked from our pulpits; while Bishops can still deny the very existence of sacrifice or priesthood in the Christian Church; while it is still possible for a Bishop to be threatened with legal penalties for celebrating the Divine Mysteries with bare decency, and for the head of the Anglican Communion, the successor of St. Augustine and St. Thomas of Canterbury, to decline taking proceedings on merely legal grounds; *while these scandals, and a thousand like them, still daily take place, is it not premature to think of asking the Apostolic See* [Rome] *to reconsider its position towards us,* for which it has had only too much justification? And yet English Catholics, *knowing the fearful corruption yet disgracing the English Church*,[54] can find it in their hearts to accuse the Latin communion of Mariolatry, and such like. We, to accuse Continental Catholics of excess of devotion to blessed Mary, when with us the most holy Mother of God has, at the best, but a mere grudging honour paid to her, as if every offering of love at the feet of Mary could be anything but a most real worship of her Incarnate Son! *Let us cleanse our own house of heresy.* Let us get rid of that Pharisaic self-righteousness which imagines all perfection to be contained within the four corners of the Prayer Book, and despises everything 'un-English.'

" Before any communication with either East or West can be even thought of, the following *reforms* [?] must be accomplished:—

" 1. A daily celebration of Mass by every priest to become the rule, according to the long-standing Western custom.

" 2. The restoration to our Altars generally of the sweet perpetual presence of Jesu in the most Holy Sacrament.

" 3. The full recognition and use of Extreme Unction.

" 4. Sacramental Confession of mortal sins to be recognized as the Church's rule.

" 5. Restoration to our formularies of definite and distinct Prayers for the Faithful Departed, and of Invocations of our Lady and the Sain

" 6. Universal belief throughout our communion in (*a*) the Real and Substantial Presence of our Lord, under the form of bread and wine, in the Sacrament of the Altar; (*b*) that in the Mass a true, real, and propitiatory Sacrifice, as well for the living as the departed, is offered to God the Father, even the Immaculate Lamb; (*c*) that there are seven Sacraments of the New Law, though the two 'Sacraments of the Gospel' are of pre-eminent dignity and necessity. . . .

" I firmly believe that the day will come when such a *Reformation* [?] will have penetrated throughout the length and breadth of the English Communion, from the Primate of All England to the peasant at the plough. God has wrought such great things for us during the last fifty years, that it would be faithless to doubt that, in His own time, *every vestige of Protestant heresy will be purged out from us.* But the time is not yet. Therefore let everyone, while praying daily for Reunion, remember that *the surest way to accomplish it is by working towards the* PURIFICATION *of our own branch of the Catholic Church.*"

I do not in any way hold the English Church Union

---

[54] Not a word does this Ritualistic writer say about the "fearful corruption" which actually *does* exist in the Roman Communion.

responsible for this letter of "A Colonial Priest"; but I do assert that the *principles* which he lays down are those which have guided the Union. I am not aware that it has, like this correspondent of the *Church Review*, advocated the Invocation of Saints, but it has certainly, by means of the literature on sale at its central office, advocated the Mass for the living and the dead. It now holds a "Requiem Service" for its deceased members every year. It has, as we have seen, advocated the Confessional, and many of its branches even defended the Society of the Holy Cross, when attacked for its indecent confessional book, the *Priest in Absolution*. This policy of "levelling up," which has made the English Church Union such a thoroughly "Preparatory School for Rome," was boldly advocated by the Rev. V. S. S. Coles, now the head of the Pusey House, Oxford, in a sermon which he preached on "The Place of E. C. U. Objects in a Churchman's Life." The sermon was printed *verbatim* in the *Church Union Gazette*, for September, 1891.

"We must," said Mr. Coles, speaking for himself and his brethren of the E. C. U., "pray that we may all recognize the true unity of the great portions of the Church, *Roman*, Greek, Anglican, now, through our sins and those of our fathers, outwardly divided, and that these outward divisions may pass away in a day of blessed Reunion. *Meanwhile*, that the . . . unspeakable mystery of the Altar may be recognized as a Divine Communion, *a true Sacrifice, a Real Presence demanding a special adoration;* that Holy Communion may be rightly prepared for, and to this end that there may be wider opportunities, and more frequent use of *Private Confession;* that the ancient Catholic rule of *Fasting Communion* may be better observed; . . . that the *Anointing of the Sick* may be rightly and dutifully restored; that all *rites and ceremonies* which witness to our union with the rest of the Catholic Church, and to the doctrines which we hold in common, may be protected and restored. . . *These are the objects with which our Society is chiefly concerned."*

It must be admitted that this is going a long way towards carrying out the Plan of Campaign laid down by "A Colonial Priest" three years before, while it is entirely founded on the principles which guided his very discreditable letter. The English Church Union is clearly responsible for what Mr. Coles said, since they published his sermon, without finding any fault with it, in their official organ. And what made Mr. Coles' statement of E. C. U. policy so gravely important was, that it represented the policy of a Society which at that time numbered nearly four thousand clergymen, and twenty-four bishops, in its ranks.

All through this modern agitation for Corporate Reunion there has but little been said against the corruptions of the Church of Rome. Some of the practical abuses found in her fold have been censured, but it has been in the gentlest possible manner, and with many apologies to Rome for taking such a liberty; and it has been carefully explained that fault has not been found so much with the *authorized* religion of Rome, as with that "*unauthorized*" teaching given by some of her children, especially on such a subject as the extravagant devotion to the Virgin Mary. To quote again the words of Bishop Abbot, "If they do at any time speak against the Papists, they do but beat a little about the bush, and that but softly too, for fear of waking and disturbing the birds that are in it." The "levelling up" process, the work of preparing the way for Reunion with Rome has not yet, in the estimation of Lord Halifax, and some of his brethren on the Council of the English Church Union, been fully accomplished, even in the most advanced of Ritualistic Churches. The Ritualistic party no longer declare that they are satisfied with the Book of Common Prayer. They wish to add largely to it from Roman sources. For many years they resisted Revision of the Book of Common Prayer, on *Protestant* lines: now, influential members of the party are now advocating it on Romanizing lines. A remarkable volume of Essays was published in 1892, entitled the *Lord's Day and the Holy Eucharist*. Of the eight gentlemen who contributed to it, seven were members of the English Church Union, and of these four were members of its Council, including Lord Halifax, President of the Union. I look upon this volume as, *indirectly*, a manifesto of the English Church Union, or at least as an indicator of what its policy is likely to be, though officially the Union has not given it its approval. But we can best judge of what the future policy of a Society will be by ascertaining the views of those who rule it. The first essay in this volume was from the pen of Lord Halifax himself. His lordship affirms that some of the "changes in the Liturgy" made by the Reformers in the sixteenth century were "mistaken," and that we should not decline to do our "very best to get them remedied."[55] In other words, we should pull down a part of the work of the Reformation. He goes on to affirm that there are "shortcomings" in the English Church; and that the "arrangements of our present Liturgy, with the dislocation of the Canon which those arrangements involve, is *a most serious blot* on the Eucharistic Service of the English Church," which "urgently calls for reform."[56] In other words, Lord Halifax is thoroughly dissatisfied with the Prayer Book, and is determined to go in for its Revision, but, to save appearances, he will not use that word, but expresses what he wants by the term "reform." The result of seeing services conducted on strictly Church of England lines, even under High Church auspices, seems to fill him with disgust. He sighs for what he has seen on the Continent.

"In this connection," writes the President of the English Church Union, p. 38, "let me say it, though I say it with shame, that of all the sad and discouraging sights which it is possible to see, none appears to me so sad and so discouraging as the sight of an English Cathedral, even the best, after being any time on the Continent. Contrast Westminster Abbey with the Cathedral at Cologne, or any French Cathedral, and you will almost wish never to enter it again till a radical change has been effected in all its arrangements."

Lord Halifax evidently wishes English Cathedrals to be

[55] *The Lord's Day and the Holy Eucharist*, p. 27. [56] *Ibid.*, p. 28.

modelled after the Roman Catholic Cathedrals of the Continent. There are, it is well known, several English Cathedrals where the services are conducted on High Church lines, but even of these, Lord Halifax is ashamed: the sight of them makes his heart sad, and discourages the Romanizing hopes that fill his breast. We may well ask, had the Reformers of the sixteenth century been men of the views of Lord Halifax, would England ever have escaped from the degrading slavery and cruel intolerance of Papal bondage? We cannot doubt that if those who guide the policy of the English Church Union could have their own way, the iron heel of the Papacy would once more crush the independence and liberty of the Reformed Church of England. In his essay Lord Halifax asks, "Why should not the recitation of the Commandments be omitted at the choral celebration of Holy Communion on Sundays, just as is now often done at early celebrations of Holy Communion"?[57] We may well answer this question by asking him another—What do you want them left out for? Are the Commandments of God "grievous" (1 John v. 3) unto you? Or is the reason of your wish to omit them to be found in the manifest fact that the Second of them forbids the use of pictures and images in Divine worship? It is, no doubt, most inconvenient for a Ritualistic priest to read aloud that Second Commandment before the congregation, when they can see the skirts of his dress touching one of the forbidden things? Every lover of the Word of God will—Lord Halifax notwithstanding—plead that the Commandments of God may remain, whatever else it may be necessary to remove from the Communion Service.

The fact that the President of the English Church Union pleads so earnestly for additions to the Communion Service is a clear proof that he, and his followers, are longing for many things which the Church of England, in her wisdom, has thought it best not to provide for her children. He

[57] *Ibid.*, p. 29.

wants additional Gospels, Epistles, and Collects to be provided for the Black Letter Days, and for "Services for the Dead."[58] He also "pleads" for the "restoration where it is possible of the practice of Reserving the Blessed Sacrament in our Churches."[59] The ostensible reason for restoring the Reserved Sacrament is that it is then always ready to be given to the sick in cases of emergency; but the real reason is for purposes of adoration. The Ritualists do not plead for the Reservation of the wine; but only for *half* a Sacrament—the consecrated wafer. Why not both? Loyal Churchmen are aware that there is no provision in the Book of Common Prayer for giving the sick the Communion in one kind, according to the modern Roman Catholic fashion, first made obligatory in the fifteenth century. The English Communion for the Sick requires the clergyman to consecrate both wine and bread in the sick room. Suppose, then, the Church were to give permission to Reserve the *bread*, how much time would the Minister gain by such a permission, were he still to be required to consecrate the wine in the sick room? None whatever. The real reason then why the Reserved Sacrament is so earnestly longed for is adoration, and this is shown in Lord Halifax's essay, in which he makes it plain that he is most anxious for the restoration of the service known as the "Benediction of the Blessed Sacrament," which cannot be performed unless a Reserved wafer is kept until evening for this service.

"It will be said," writes Lord Halifax, "by some that it [the Reserved Sacrament] will be a step to *Benediction* and other practices which are of comparatively modern origin; by others, that in the imperfectly instructed condition of our people it might lead to irreverence. Now, in regard to *both* these objections may not this be asked—and it is a remark which, I think, applies to many other matters of a not dissimilar nature—why should we object to certain practices which have grown up round the Blessed Sacrament, and *which experience has proved to be useful for encouraging the devotion of the Faithful?*"[60]

[58] *The Lord's Day and the Holy Eucharist*, p. 29. [59] *Ibid.*, p. 35. [60] *Ibid.*, p. 35.

The answer to all this is that the service of the Benediction of the Blessed Sacrament, and the Reservation of the Sacrament, would both certainly lead to that which the Black Rubric terms "idolatry to be abhorred of all faithful Christians."

Another contributor to this volume of essays, who is also a member of the English Church Union, the Rev. E. W. Sergeant, seems anxious for the *entire* omission of the Ten Commandments from the Communion Service. "It is," he writes, "no part of the priest's office in the ritual of the Eucharist, like another Moses from Mount Sinai, to convey God's laws to the people."[61] Another supposed defect in the Book of Common Prayer, which is nothing less than gall and wormwood to the whole Romanizing party, is termed by Mr. Sergeant "one of the most mischievous innovations in our Eucharistic Office." It is that, "whereas in the rubrics alone of the Ordinary and Canon of the Mass in the Sarum Missal the word altar occurs *thirty* times, *it does not occur once in any part of our Prayer Book.*"[62] This gentleman is also sorely grieved because "such marked prominence" is given in the Prayer Book to the title, "The Lord's Supper"; and he asks with burning indignation, "Why change the title? Why reject the old and certainly inoffensive term 'the Mass'?"[63]

It is, therefore, quite clear that these gentlemen are not satisfied with the Prayer Book *as it is*. They are not content, however, with introducing all these Romanizing novelties on their own responsibility, and without any sanction from the law. What they now want is that they shall be incorporated into the Book of Common Prayer, and thus made part and parcel of the law of the Reformed Church of England. If it is asked, why do Prayer Book Churchmen object to these changes and additions, the answer is that the result of adopting them would be a gigantic schism in the Church of England. The Church

[61] *Ibid.*, p. 125.   [62] *Ibid.*, p. 124.   [63] *Ibid.*, p. 121.

which for nearly four centuries, excepting during the brief interval of the Commonwealth, has stood firmly against all the storms and oppositions through which it has passed, would at once fall to the ground, rent asunder by traitors within her fold. Can statesmen view such a possibility with pleasure? A Prayer Book Romanized on the lines of the English Church Union could not be accepted by any honest Protestant Churchman, and the whole Protestant power of Protestant England would be behind those who would then once more fight again, for dear life, the battle of the Reformation. Yet nothing less than this will satisfy the wire-pullers of the Ritualistic party. It is useless to talk of a possible compromise between the Lord's supper and the Sacrifice of the Mass. They are as opposed to each other as light and darkness, as the Word of God and the corrupt Traditions of men. This preparatory work for Corporate Reunion with Rome must be resisted by all in whose hearts the memory of the Protestant Martyrs is not dead; by all who love civil freedom and religious liberty.

As time went on the English Church Union became more and more energetic in labouring for Reunion. As I have said, the volume of essays on *The Lord's Day and the Holy Eucharist*, which appeared in 1892, was not issued by the Union, though it certainly does clearly indicate what its policy is. Going back four years from that date, we find the Council of the E. C. U. bringing the Reunion Question once more before the Lambeth Conference, which again met in that year. At the annual meeting of the Union, June 14th, 1888, an Address to the Conference was unanimously adopted, which concluded with the following paragraph :—

"We would conclude with our most earnest prayers that the counsels of this great gathering of the Episcopate round the chair of St. Augustine may be so guided and inspired by God the Holy Ghost, as to quicken the life of the Church of England throughout all its branches, to win back those who have separated themselves from its fold, and, *above all*, to prepare the way for *the restoration of visible unity between the Anglican Communion and the rest of the Western*

Church, and the Reunion of East and West, and to hasten the dawn of that blessed day of restored peace and goodwill among all Christian people, when there shall be One Flock and One Shepherd." [64]

In moving the adoption of this Address, Lord Halifax said that Corporate Reunion was "that hope which is nearest and dearest" to the hearts of the members of the Union, and that they longed for the time "when the schisms and divisions which divide the West shall have been healed, when East and West shall be again one, and all shall be again united in the bonds of a visible unity as in the days of old." The views of the Council of the E. C. U. were echoed by its branches. At a meeting of the Cheltenham Branch, December 17th, 1889, the Chairman, the Rev. G. Bayfield Roberts, who was subsequently selected to write the official *History of the English Church Union*, said that—

"Unhappily, as a Protestant, Canon Bell looked to Reunion with Dissenters, and to an utter and irremediable breach with the Churches of the East and West. They, as Catholics, looked to Reunion with those Churches of the East and West which, in their fine ancient Patriarchates, possessed the historical Episcopate, *to Reunion under the Primacy of him to whom the Fathers gave the Primacy . . . the Bishop of 'old Rome.'* Was this a rash statement? At any rate, it was historically true, and was substantially the same as that to which *Lord Halifax* gave utterance at the Annual Meeting [of the E. C. U.] in London, in 1885:—'Peace among yourselves, peace with our separated brethren at home, the restoration of visible unity with the members of the Church abroad, East and West alike, *but, above all, with the great Apostolic See of the West*, which has done so much to guard *the true faith* in the Incarnation of our Lord Jesus Christ and the reality of His life-giving Sacraments. These things surely should be our object—*the object nearest our hearts.*' " [65]

Lord Halifax's speech, in 1885, in favour of Reunion with Rome, quoted by Mr. Roberts, led to a correspondence between his lordship and Canon Hole, now Dean of Rochester, in which the President of the English Church Union declared that although he did " most earnestly desire

[64] *Church Union Gazette*, Volume for 1888, pp. 168, 216-220.
[65] *Ibid.*, Volume for 1890, p. 45.

the restoration of visible communion between ourselves and the members of the Roman Church," yet he did not wish for such a union " by a sacrifice of the truth, but through the truth."[66] But here of course comes in the question, What *is* " the truth " which his lordship is unable to sacrifice ? I have no doubt that he would be willing to " sacrifice " a great deal of that which Protestant Churchmen consider as Scriptural truth. The really practical question is, how much of that which the Pope considers as the " truth" would Lord Halifax require him to surrender as the price of Reunion ? Would he require him to give up either his Primacy or Supremacy, or any one of the doctrines of the Council of Trent? I very much doubt it. Lord Halifax would be very glad to " sacrifice " Protestantism, but there is very little, if anything at all, in the official doctrines of Rome which he would wish a re-united Church to lose. The speech which Mr. Roberts quoted was referred to by Lord Halifax himself the year after it was delivered. At the annual meeting of the E. C. U. in 1886, Lord Halifax said :—

"I ventured to say something on this subject at our last annual meeting, and though fault has been found in some quarters with what I then said, I have nothing to retract. On the contrary, I desire to emphasize what I said last year. The crown and completion of the Catholic Revival which has transformed the Church of England within the last fifty years is the Reunion of Christendom. We desire union with those from whom we are separate, not by a sacrifice of truth, but through the truth, and among our brethren with whom we long to be at one, *none come before those who are in communion with the Roman See.* . . Our own instincts—nay our own experience as Anglicans—point out *the practical need of a central authority.* What has been the history of the South African Church ? Has it not been on one side a willingness to recognize in the Archbishop of Canterbury the authority of an Anglican Patriarch ; on the other an attempt to claim the fulness of Papal authority for the Privy Council ? After all, if a central authority is good for the Anglican Communion, *a central authority must be good for the Church at large.* . . . Certainly those who are willing to recognize an appeal from the Archbishop of

[66] *Church Union Gazette,* Volume for 1890, p. 50.

Canterbury to the Judicial Committee need not scruple to an *appeal to a Christian Bishop*. IS THERE A SINGLE INSTRUCTED CHRISTIAN WHO WOULD NOT PREFER LEO XIII. TO THE PRIVY COUNCIL ?"[67]

The answer to Lord Halifax's question is that there is a very large number of very well "instructed Christians" who would prefer the Privy Council to the Pope. There is a great deal of misconception as to what the functions of the Judicial Committee really are. I suppose that most High Churchmen will admit that the late High Church and learned Dean Hook was an "instructed Christian." Yet this is what he wrote on the subject :—

"I see no objection to the Committee of Privy Council being our Final Court of Appeal: they do not form a Synod, and here is the mistake so often made. In an ancient Synod the members were legislators as well as judges. If they decided that such or such a thing was contrary to law, they might say, 'The law is a bad one, therefore we will make a new law.' The Committee of Privy Council does nothing of the kind. I wish to obey the law. You say that the law says one thing, I say it means another—and who shall decide ? It is a question, not of opinion, but of fact ; and who can deal with such a subject so well as lawyers ? *Who could be worse judges than ecclesiastics*, who would endeavour to bend the law to their opinions ?

"The old High Churchman was wont to say, 'I will do what the Church orders me to do.' 'I like,' he might say, 'lights upon the altar ; but if *you* dislike it, let us ask what the law says. To ascertain that fact I go, not to parsons but to lawyers, who are not to make the law, but to discuss what it was made by ecclesiastics."[68]

It is here most important to point out that Lord Halifax and the English Church Union are manifestly bent on pulling down the authority of Her Majesty's Judicial Committee of Privy Council, for the sole purpose of setting up that of the Pope of Rome in its room. "Who would not," asks Lord Halifax, "prefer Leo XIII. to the Privy Council" ? There is, he says, "a practical need for a central authority"; and such an authority would, he thinks,

---

[67] *Ibid.*, Volume for 1886, p. 242.
[68] *Life and Letters of Dean Hook*, p. 588. Sixth edition.

"be good for the Church at large"—the authority, of course, being that of the Pope. It may be well to remind my readers that the Reformers of the sixteenth century were of a different opinion. It was their glory and their boast that they cut themselves off from all communication with such a "central authority" as the Pope, and inserted in the *Reformed Prayer Book* the petition:—"From the Bishop of Rome, and all his detestable enormities, Good Lord, deliver us." The fact is that there is no *existing* authority within the Church of England to which the Ritualists will give their full obedience, when its decisions come into conflict with what they, in their superior wisdom, assert to be the law of the Church. Reasonable men would say that it is better to have some authority within the Church of England, however imperfect it may or may not be, than to have no binding authority at all. It is better to have unsatisfactory Ecclesiastical Courts than to have no Ecclesiastical Courts at all. It is better to have the Privy Council as the Final Court of Appeal than to have no Court of Appeal at all. One result of the labours of the English Church Union is the spread of Anarchy in the Church. That well-known Ritualist, the late Rev. A. H. Mackonochie, Vicar of St. Alban's, Holborn, who was for many years supported by the English Church Union—of which he was a leading member—in his rebellion against the decisions of the Courts of Law, gave evidence, on March 2nd, 1882, before the Royal Commission on Ecclesiastical Courts. From the official Report of that Commission I take the following extracts of Mr. Mackonochie's evidence bearing on the subject before us:—

"6089. Then is there no Ecclesiastical Court?—Not as far as I can see.

"6090. So that every man can do what is right in his own eyes?—That is not our fault.

"6091. Of course not. That is the state of things?—Yes.

"6092. Has there never been an Ecclesiastical Court?—*Not since the Reformation.*"

"6171. Then why do you think that the Bishops have no authority now ?—Because they have got bound up in the State Courts."

"6178. But does it not strike you that that is *fatal to the idea of any society existing*, that he must judge entirely for himself?— Yes; then I cannot help it."

Anarchy and lawlessness in the Church, a state of things in which every clergyman does that which is right in his own eyes, and in which he will submit to no authority which opposes his own opinions, is certainly one calculated to create alarm. I do not assert that it exists amongst the whole of the clergy of the Church of England. Far from it. We may be thankful that there are yet thousands of clergymen who love law and order; but, on the other hand, it cannot be denied that the lawless spirit is very widespread indeed amongst the Romanizing clergy. Nor should it be forgotten that the spirit of lawlessness and anarchy is a contagious disease. It will not stop within the Church. The people of England will argue that what is good for the clergy is good also for them. If the Ministers of the Gospel will not obey the laws of the Church, why should they obey the laws of the State? This is an aspect of the Ritualistic question which is deserving of the serious attention of statesmen. But the unfortunate thing is that those in authority in the State, in only too many instances, smile upon rebellion, give the rebels words of encouragement, and present them to many of the high places in the Church which are in their patronage, while those who show respect to law and order are frequently frowned upon, and left out in the cold. The time has come when the people of England should, through Parliament, bring both the Government for the time being— both Conservative and Liberal Governments are equally guilty —to account. No law-breaker should ever receive promotion at the hands of the Crown through its accredited advisers.

I might easily multiply quotations from the utterances of members of the English Church Union advocating Corporate Reunion with the Church of Rome, but I should only weary my readers by doing so. As illustrating the kind of Romish teaching frequently given to the branches of the Union, I may, however, be permitted to add here the following extract from a speech delivered at the annual meeting of the Devon Branch, on July 30th, 1889. On that occasion the Rev. Ernest Square, then Vicar of St. Mary Steps, Exeter, but now Rector of Wheatacre, Suffolk, said :—

" He did not know where they were to go for their Ritual if it was not to the Church of Rome, which seemed to be the living Church, and in whose Ritual he could see nothing harmful. She was the greatest Church in Christendom—there could be no doubt about it— and he did not think they could go to a better pattern than the Church of Rome for their Ritual. She had kept up her Ritual, which the Church of England had not done, through all the ages. We had been most slovenly, and with us it had been a kind of domestic Ritual, no more than they would have in their own homes or at their own tables —and not so good. The Church of Rome had always kept her own Ritual, and, therefore, he did not see why the English Church should not go to her for help in this matter." [69]

The adoption of the full Roman Ritual has now become very common in Ritualistic churches; but some of the party go even further than Mr. Square, for they teach all the *doctrines* of Rome which the Ritual is intended to symbolize. Three years before Mr. Square's Exeter speech, the Rev. William Stathers, Curate of St. Matthias', Earl's Court, and now Curate of St. Benet and All Saints', Kentish Town, was dismissed from his curacy by his Vicar, on the charge of Romanizing. The charge seemed an extraordinary one, coming from a Vicar who himself adopted, in the services of his Church, the full Ritual of the Church of Rome. In self-defence Mr. Stathers, who was then, and still is, a member of the English Church Union, published a *Letter of Explanation* to the members of the congregation, in the form of a pamphlet of sixteen pages. He pleaded that while Mr. Luke, his Vicar, had given his congregation the *shell*, he (Mr. Stathers) had given them the *kernel*, and he evidently

[69] *Western Times*, July 31st, 1889.

thought the kernel a much better thing than the shell. The shell was Roman *Ritual;* the kernel was Roman *doctrine.*

"The teaching," wrote Mr. Stathers, "which I have regularly given from the pulpit of S. Matthias's is in perfect harmony with the Ritual of that Church. There are only three kinds of Ritual possible in our churches:—The Ritual of self-pleasing, invented out of the Incumbent's own head; the old English Ritual, very elaborate and now lost, but which some are fruitlessly trying to bring back; and *the Modern Roman*, very simple, *regulated by the Sacred Congregation of Rites at Rome*, and possessing present authority. It is the *latter* Ritual, I am happy to say, which is followed at S. Matthias's, and I am bound to say that while the accuracy of it would be a lesson to many Roman congregations, they could never hope to approach its dignity. To many it will not seem surprising that finding St. Matthias's possessed of a particular kind of shell, I did my best to provide the corresponding kernel, or that finding myself face to face with a skeleton, I did my best to clothe it with flesh and make it instinct with life.

"Some persons may perhaps be of opinion that in *preaching the doctrine of the Immaculate Conception of our Lady* I have gone beyond Tridentine limits, and have thus far been inconsistent. I have never, however, insisted on the doctrine as of necessity for faith, but have simply given the reasons for it, and have left objectors free to hold the Immaculate Birth instead. Moreover, the doctrine, though outside the Tridentine definitions, can hardly be said to be outside Prayer Book limits." [70]

I am not aware that Mr. Stathers has ever publicly repudiated his teaching, as expressed in this pamphlet, though he still holds a curacy in the same Diocese of London. In his *Protest* he further informed his readers that—

"Mr. Luke having desired to be informed more precisely as to the exact meaning which I attached to the phrase 'general teaching Tridentine' [contained in Mr. Stathers' advertisement for a curacy in the *Church Times*],[71] I explained to him at a private interview, and, if

---

[70] *A Protest and Explanation*, by the Rev. William Stathers, p. 12.

[71] Mr. Stathers' advertisement, which he truly described as "most unmistakable," was as follows:—"Town Curacy or Sole Charge (in the South) desired at once, by a priest of considerable experience; 35, musical, unmarried, fond of children. Extempore and written sermons. Ritual (not necessarily advanced) *on Roman lines preferred. General teaching Tridentine.*—W. S., 85, Marton Road, Middlesbro."—*Church Times*, December 21st, 1883, p. 959.

I remember rightly, by letter, that I meant the general teaching of the Western Church, the most satisfactory summary of which teaching, and at the same time an authoritative summary, *is to be found in the Catechism of the Council of Trent*, points having reference to the Papal Supremacy being excluded by the necessity of the case." (⁷²)

I must now hasten on to the time when, on February 14th, 1895, Lord Halifax delivered at Bristol his now notorious speech on Reunion with Rome. It was, I may here remark, delivered at a meeting of the Bristol branch of the E. C. U., and was subsequently printed and circulated by the Council, thus giving to it an official sanction and approval. It was a very long speech, and its delivery created a great deal of excitement and controversy in Church of England circles. Its influence went further and extended to Rome, where the Pope himself greatly rejoiced at the welcome news which it contained. In this speech the President of the E. C. U. went further towards Rome than ever he went before. Even some of his own friends were surprised, though they did not repudiate his utterances. His lordship laid down what he considered as reasonable conditions on which Reunion between England and Rome could take place; but it was noticed that he did not require the Church of Rome to give up any one of her peculiar doctrines, not even the doctrine of the Pope's personal Infallibility, as taught by the Vatican Council of 1870! As to the latter truly monstrous doctrine all that he seemed to require, to enable English Churchmen to accept it, was that it should be sugar-coated to suit the English palate!

"Even in regard to the Vatican Council," said Lord Halifax, "it appears not impossible that mistakes and exaggerations as to its scope and consequences may have been made, and that as time goes on *explanations will emerge* which may make the difficulties [ought he not to have said falsehoods?] it seems to involve less than they have sometimes appeared? . . . If by Papal Infallibility it is only meant that the Pope is Infallible when acting as the Head of the whole Church, and expressing the mind of the Church, and after taking all the

---

⁷² *A Protest and Explanation*, p. 3.

legitimate and usual means for ascertaining that mind, in determining which the authority and witness of the Bishops, as representing their respective Churches, must be paramount, and then only in regard to the substance of the deposit handed down from Christ and His Apostles, *it would seem that the difficulty of a possible agreement is not so insuperable* as it has been sometimes represented. Certainly, it is not such as to preclude all endeavours to find possible terms of peace on other matters. In any case, till it is proved to the contrary, let us nourish the hope that such explanations are possible." [73]

But here it may well be asked, would not the acceptance of the Pope's Infallibility, in any shape or form, or with any "explanation," be in a reality a "sacrifice of the truth"? How could a Union based on such a falsehood be a Union "through the truth"? "Do not let us be afraid," said Lord Halifax, in his Bristol speech, "to speak plainly of the possibility, of the desirability of a union with Rome. Let us say boldly *we desire peace with Rome with all our hearts.*" [74] Language like this is very different from that of the old-fashioned High Churchman, the Rev. John Moultrie, of Rugby :—

> "Your Pope may be a learned priest, and a prince of high degree,
> But God and Jesus Christ are more Infallible than he;
> And I in God, through Jesus Christ, rest all my faith and hope,
> And indeed I cannot part with these for Prelate or for Pope.
> I still must keep my simple creed, and tread the path I've trod
> By the help of my Redeemer—by the guidance of my God." [75]

> "No peace, but deadly warfare still, between those twain must be,
> While the one would bind both heart and mind, and the other set them free;
> No peace for Rome and England, but a stern, relentless strife;
> Till Light shall vanquish Darkness, Death be swallowed up of Life." [76]

If there is one man of the sixteenth century who, more than any other, is honoured by Protestants all over the

---

[73] *Reunion of Christendom.* Speech by Lord Halifax, p. 24. (English Church Union Office.)
[74] *Ibid.*, p. 35.
[75] Moultrie's *Altars, Hearths, and Graves,* p. 79. Edition, 1854.
[76] *Ibid.*, p. 63.

world, it is Martin Luther. But he was God's instrument for freeing the nations from Papal bondage, and for this amongst other reasons, he is hated and reviled by modern Ritualists, who are not worthy to unloose his shoe strings. In his Bristol speech Lord Halifax went out of his way to insult his honoured memory by declaring that although he began his career as "a harmless and necessary Reformer," he eventually became "a needless and noxious rebel."[77] Luther certainly was, very much to his credit be it recorded, a "rebel" against the usurped Supremacy of the Pope; but in the opinion of the majority of the ablest men who have lived since his times, his rebellion was a very necessary one, and by no means "needless." It was the only way in which the world could get rid of an intolerable spiritual slavery. Luther's rebellion against the Pope was obedience to Almighty God, and therefore it makes us justly indignant to find such a brave and holy deed stigmatized as a "noxious" crime. It will, I trust, never come to pass that the children of this great "rebel" against tyranny and corruption will come to terms of peace with that system against which he waged an unrelenting warfare, not even at the invitation of Lord Halifax. "Who," asked his lordship, "can endure the sense of being separated from those [Roman Catholics] with whom in all essentials of belief and sentiment we are one?"[78] The answer to such a question is that there is no need whatever for the Ritualists to "endure" such a melancholy state of things for even one day longer. Why need they be "separated" any more? The Papal door is wide open to receive them, and the sooner they go over the better it will be for the Reformed Church of England. When traitors are discovered within the citadel zealously pleading with its rulers to surrender to an enemy whose yoke is too heavy to bear, the best thing to do is to turn them out of the citadel at

---

[77] *Reunion of Christendom.* Speech by Lord Halifax, p. 8.
[78] *Ibid.,* p. 18.

THE HOMILIES ON THE CHURCH OF ROME. 355

once, if they refuse to go voluntarily. There is no safety for the citadel while traitors are within its walls. It cannot, I think, be seriously pleaded that there are any doctrines officially taught by the Church of Rome to which gentlemen of Lord Halifax's stamp can have any conscientious objections. "We are convinced," he says, "on the one hand that there is nothing whatever in the authoritative documents of the English Church which, apart from the traditional glosses of a practical Protestantism, contains anything essentially irreconcilable with the doctrines of the Church of Rome."[79] Certainly, the majority of loyal Churchmen think otherwise. They still retain the opinion that the Thirty-nine Articles contain a great deal which *is* "irreconcilable with the doctrines of the Church of Rome," and that is also the opinion of Roman Catholic divines who may be allowed to know what the real doctrines of their Church are much better than any member of the English Church Union. One of the "documents of the English Church" is the Book of Homilies. Every clergyman of the Church of England has solemnly subscribed to the Thirty-nine Articles. Every curate must subscribe them, and every new incumbent of a living is bound to *read* them through to his new congregation. In one of those Articles —the 35th—it is declared that the Homilies "contain a godly and wholesome Doctrine, *and necessary for these times*," that is, for this year of our Lord, 1897. We know very well that the clergy are not bound to accept every historical statement in the Homilies, but they are bound to the "doctrine" taught in them. I would therefore ask Lord Halifax whether *he* can reconcile the following extract from the "document" known as the *Homily of the Peril of Idolatry, Part Third*, "with the doctrines of the Church of Rome"? The language is somewhat rough, but, as it is "appointed to be read *in Churches*," there can be nothing wrong in reading it in *this book* of mine.

[79] *Ibid.*, p. 30.

"Which the idolatrous Church [of Rome] understandeth well enough. For she being indeed not only an harlot (as the Scripture calleth her), but also a foul, filthy, old withered harlot (for she is indeed of ancient years) and understanding her lack of natural and true beauty, and great loathsomeness which of herself she hath, doth (after the custom of such harlots) paint herself, and deck and tire herself with gold, pearl, stone, and all kind of precious jewels,[80] that she, shining with the outward beauty and glory of them, may please the foolish phantasy of fond lovers, and so entice them to spiritual fornication with her; who, if they saw her (I will not say naked) but in simple apparel, would abhor her, as the foulest and filthiest harlot that ever was seen: according as appeareth by the description of the garnishing of the great strumpet of all strumpets, 'the mother of whoredom,' set forth by St. John in his Revelation."

Soon after his Bristol speech, Lord Halifax went to Rome, where he had several interviews with the Pope, with a view to the success of his Reunion schemes. In his speech at Bristol he had not, as I have said, asked Rome to give up one of her doctrines as a condition of her Reunion with England, not even the Papal Infallibility. But he did insist on the Pope's recognition of the validity of Anglican Orders. There went with Lord Halifax to Rome two members of the English Church Union, whose travelling expenses were paid for by the Union. A *verbatim* report of their interviews with the Pope would be interesting reading. One of the party, the Rev. T. A. Lacey, a member of its Council, and also a member of the secret Society of the Holy Cross, wrote a document for the private use of the Roman Cardinals, to whom the question of the validity of Anglican Orders had been remitted for consideration. Probably Mr. Lacey never dreamt that such a document would ever see the light of day in England; but, somehow or other, the *Tablet* got hold of a copy, and published it in full—translated from the original Latin—in its issue for November 7th, 1896. In this document Mr. Lacey made some very candid admissions, and some inaccurate assertions, such as the following :—

---

[80] Just like our modern Ritualistic priests, who "deck and tire" themselves and their Churches in a similar fashion.

"The Reformation," wrote Mr. Lacey, "begun under Henry VIII., effected nothing contrary to Catholic faith. There took place, I admit, certain things which were *criminal*, and certain things which are still to be *deplored; the withdrawal from the Communion of the Roman Church*, the extirpation of the Religious Life."

"The English Church, delivered from so many dangers, *has differed in nothing* from the other national Churches included in the Catholic unity, save that she has lacked communion *in Sacris* with the Holy See."

"Many have turned their eyes with great desire to the Holy Roman Church as to the Mother from whom the light of the Gospel was first shed upon us."

"In the year 1865, he [Dr. Pusey] published his *Eirenicon*, in which he dealt with the question of visible unity to be brought about by means of the Anglican Church. He added much concerning the differences of worship and doctrine; *that such things did not relate to faith;* the discord between the Anglican and Roman formularies to be more apparent than real; *the power of the Roman Pontiff to be a not insuperable obstacle;* and the like. This letter of so celebrated a man created incredible enthusiasm."

The hopes of Lord Halifax and his followers were doomed to disappointment. Instead of recognizing the validity of Anglican Orders the Pope issued his now famous Bull declaring them to be, in his estimation, invalid. This Bull came as an unexpected thunderstorm in the Ritualistic camp. The Romanizers had flattered, cringed to, and prostrated themselves before the Church of Rome in a state of abject humiliation, in the hope that the Pope would do them the honour of recognizing them as real sacrificing priests. Instead, however, of being honoured by him, they were treated with the most unmitigated and well-deserved contempt. Instead of receiving a Papal blessing, they were spurned from the throne of the Vatican with a Papal kick. For a time, in bitter rage and dissatisfaction, the Ritualists turned their faces towards the Eastern Church, and declared that they would go in for Union with that corrupt communion, and leave Rome to her fate. A few Churchmen were deceived by these professions, and declared that the English

Church Union would now cease to labour for Reunion with Rome. But they little realized the depths of spiritual degradation of which the Ritualists are capable. The tide has already turned, and once more we see the Ritualists crawling along to kiss the Papal toe that kicked them only the other day. In his speech at the annual meeting of the English Church Union, June 1st, 1897, Lord Halifax bitterly complained that the present dominant authority in the Church of Rome in England threw "every obstacle in the way of any step that may be taken towards bringing about a better understanding, and the eventual Corporate Reunion of the Anglican Communion with the Roman Church." "We have indeed," said his lordship, "honestly desired—*we desire still*—to see the relations which existed between St. Cyprian and the Church of Carthage on the one side, and St. Stephen and the Roman Church on the other, as insisted on in the Encyclical *Satis Cognitum*, restored between Canterbury and Rome." [81]

It is a noteworthy fact that while the leaders of the Ritualistic party have advocated Corporate Reunion with Rome, and have opposed individual secession, yet the overwhelming majority of individual perversions to Rome in this country have been from the ranks of the Tractarians, Puseyites, and Ritualists. The Tractarians prepared the ground, the Puseyites planted, the Ritualists watered, and the Pope has reaped the harvest. As far back as 1850 Bishop Samuel Wilberforce wrote to Dr. Pusey:—"I firmly believe that the influence of your personal ministry does more than the labours of an open enemy to wean from the pure faith and simple Ritual of our Church the affections of many of those amongst her children." [82] To the Rev. C. Marriott, the Bishop wrote, November 23rd, 1850:—"He (Dr. Pusey) tries to retain these souls to the Church of England, but in vain. He has given the impetus, and he cannot stop

---

[81] *Church Times*, June 4th, 1897, p. 668.
[82] *Life of Bishop Wilberforce*, Vol. II., p. 80.

them. He has no deep horror of the Popish system; none has been infused into the early beginnings of their awakened spiritual consciousness; *they have practically been set by him on a Romish course.*"[83] Even Dr. Pusey's Father Confessor, the Rev. J. Keble, acknowledged that "a larger number, possibly, has seceded to Rome from under his (Dr. Pusey's) special teaching than from that of any other individual now among us."[84] It has been more or less the same with all the Ritualistic teachers. A correspondent of the Roman Catholic paper called the *Ransomer*, who was in an excellent position for obtaining accurate information on the subject, wrote as follows :—

"But has this development of Ritualism in the Establishment satisfied souls, won the working classes, or last, but not least, *stayed the stream of secessions to Rome? Not one whit.* I have never met a high Anglican who was contented with the condition of his Church. The vast multitudes of the poor, and the labouring men and women are more conspicuous than ever by their absence from the functions of Ritualism. *As to conversions* [to Rome] it is *well known that nine out of every dozen are the direct result of Ritualistic training.*"[85]

In the year after this testimony was written, the Rev. Mr. Whelan, a Roman Catholic priest, preaching at St. Wilfrid's, York, said :—

"I am bold enough to say here that *Ritualism is one of our consolations,* for I think it to be the *Preparatory School* for the training of English Catholics. By Ritualism our great dogmas are taught to thousands who would not listen to us. In Ritualism we have a powerful solvent for melting the frost-bound traditions of three centuries. Many, perhaps, may be hindered from finding the real home of truth, but *a larger number* are helped by this approximation in externals, and become obedient children of the faith."[86]

The *Irish Ecclesiastical Record*, the official organ of the Roman Catholic priesthood of Ireland, in its issue for July, 1891, published a remarkable article on "The Conversion of

---

[83] *Ibid.*, p. 85. [84] *Ibid.*, p. 95.
[85] *Ransomer*, July 22nd, 1893.
[86] *Catholic Standard*, June 23rd, 1894.

England," written by a priest residing in Manchester. It says :—

"There are two forces at work regarding the Catholicism of the country... One is inside the Church, and the other outside it; one Catholic, the other Protestant, though Catholicising. *The Ritualists, and the Ritualists alone, are doing all that is being done among Protestants.* How many parsons from Newman to Rivington have been converted by priests? True, all have been *received* by priests. But how many have confessed their obligations to our sermons or our writings that we Catholic priests were in any degree answerable for their conversion? The Catholicising movement in the Establishment has not been the result of the missionary activity of the Catholic Church in England. It is true to say that convert priests receive more converts than others, but that is mainly on account of personal influence in certain non-Catholic quarters where we have no access, as well as having a keener grasp of difficulties which we never feel. Men who pass through the fire themselves are good guides. This external movement is of vast importance. At this hour *five thousand Church of England clergymen are preaching from as many Protestant pulpits the Catholic faith* (not, indeed, as faith) to Catholicising congregations, much more effectively, *with less suspicion and more acceptance than we can ever hope to do.* Protestant sisterhoods are doing, we feel sure, the best they can under the circumstances to familiarize the Philistine with Nuns—and that is much. Protestant societies, like St. Margaret's, Westminster, furnish poor country missions (there *are* poor country Protestant missions, and city ones too) with Black Vestments for Requiems on All Souls'. This is, indeed, a matter for devout thankfulness. *We could desire no better preparation for joining the Catholic Church than the Ritualists' Preparatory School; and the fact that from them we have secured the majority of our converts*, strengthens us in our view of it." [87]

The *Month*, the organ of the English Jesuits, in its issue for November, 1890, published an article on "The Newest Fashions in Ritualism," in which it declared that—

"At any rate the Ritualists are doing a good work, which in the present state of the country, Catholics cannot do in the same proportion; they are preparing the soil and sowing the seed for a rich harvest, *which the Catholic Church will reap sooner or later."* [88]

[87] *Irish Ecclesiastical Record*, July, 1891, p. 644.
[88] *The Month*, November, 1890, p. 333.

There remains one great question to be considered. Many will ask, Why should there not be a movement for the Corporate Reunion of the Church of England with the Church of Rome? What harm can it do? Is not Christian unity a Christian duty? To this I answer, that Protestants, in objecting to Reunion with Rome, do not forget that Christian unity is a Christian duty, but it is to be feared that modern Ritualists do forget that *separation* is just as much a Christian duty as unity. It was by God's command that, in Old Testament times, the Jews were separated from the Gentile nations. This separation was considered by Moses as a special result of God's favour, when he addressed the Lord in these words:—" For wherein shall it be known here that I and Thy people have found grace in Thy sight? Is it not in that Thou goest with us? so shall we be *separated*, I and Thy people, from all the people that are upon the face of the earth" (Exodus xxxiii. 16). It would have been a grievous offence against Almighty God, had the Israelites sought unity with the Gentiles, though it was always open to the latter to seek unity with the former. And in the Christian Church this duty of separation is clearly set forth in the New Testament. How else are we to explain such texts as " Wherefore come out from among them, and be ye *separate*, saith the Lord, and touch not the unclean thing; and I will receive you" (2 Cor. vi. 17); and, " I heard another voice from heaven saying, Come out of her my people, that ye be not partakers of her sins, and that ye receive not of her plagues" (Rev. xviii. 4)? It is wisdom for Churches, as well as individuals to keep out of bad company. We must be united only with that which is good, and separate from all that is evil. The written Word of God, and the traditions of man can never unite together. Protestantism and Popery must evermore remain separated.

There are many other grave and weighty reasons against Reunion with Rome, but it would require a volume to exhaust the subject. I may, however, point out, that from a merely worldly point of view there are strong and sufficient reasons for trying to defeat the schemes of the English Church Union and kindred societies. *Popery is an enemy to National Prosperity.* Looking abroad throughout the whole world, we find that Popery degrades the nations, instead of raising them to a higher level. The Ritualists cannot point to a single Roman Catholic country which is even on a level with, much less superior to, Protestant countries. On the contrary, Popery has dragged down Spain from her proud eminence, to be the most degraded and poverty-stricken nation in Europe, excepting Turkey. It has kept the South American republics and nations in a state of degradation, immorality, and ignorance deplorable to behold. Would any Englishman wish this Protestant country to become what the Papal States were under the temporal rule of Pope Pius IX.? Would English working men wish to exchange wages with their brethren in any Roman Catholic country in the world? Every part of Ireland is under the same government. Why, then, is it that the Roman Catholic portions of that unhappy land are those in which more poverty, dirt, disloyalty, and ignorance are to be found, than in the Protestant portions? The answer to this question must be that the religion of Popery is at the bottom of this marked difference. Before we listen with pleasure to the Reunion with Rome plans of the Ritualists, let us calmly consider the facts, not only of history, but of the everyday life around us. When we contrast Popish countries with Protestant lands, can we doubt any longer which religion most promotes *National Prosperity?* Is there any valid reason for supposing that England will become more prosperous if she forsakes her civil and religious liberties, and goes back to Papal bondage, at the request of Lord Halifax and the English Church Union? Common sense can answer these questions in only one way. Protestantism and *National Prosperity* go together, like Siamese twins. They cannot be separated. And let it not be said that this is an argument which

Christians should ignore, for has not the Word of God taught us that true "Godliness is profitable unto all things, having promise of the life that now is, and of that which is to come" (1 Timothy iv. 8)?

We also object to Reunion with Rome *because we have nothing good to gain by it.* As Protestants we already possess the *whole* of the Christian religion, in that we possess the Bible. What more do we need? Ours is the religion of St. Matthew, St. Mark, St. Luke, St. John, St. Peter, St. Paul, and the Blessed Virgin Mary. They taught nothing but Protestantism, and never taught even one of the peculiar doctrines of Rome. Open the New Testament, and if you consult either the Authorized Version or the Roman Catholic version in English, the result will be the same. You will not discover one word in either version about the Supremacy of the Pope, or of Papal Infallibility, of Purgatory, Auricular Confession, the Sacrifice of the Mass, the Invocation of Saints, Prayers for the Dead, Indulgences, Holy Water, Holy Scapulars, Holy Wells, Holy Breads, Holy Beads, or any one of the false doctrines and superstitions of Romanism, which have now become dear to the hearts of our modern Romanisers. What will England gain if she takes all these things back again? She will gain what we should gain were we to throw away the good gold sovereigns supplied to us from Her Majesty's Mint, and instead apply to the makers of bad money for a supply of sovereigns, made from a slight quantity of real gold, and a large quantity of base metal. To act like this in worldly matters would be accounted folly; but is it not even greater folly to act so in spiritual things? Yet this is what the Ritualists are anxious for us to do. And our answer to their solicitations must be a stern resolve to allow of *no adulteration* of the Christian religion which, thank God, we possess. Popery is the great adulterator of the Christian religion. She has *nothing* to give us that is good for the souls of men. What she is anxious to do in Protestant England is well described in the Bible as "making the Word of God of none effect through your tradition" (Mark vii. 13); and "teaching for doctrines the commandments of men" (Matt. xv. 9). The question before us is, Shall Protestant England submit to be fed with the chaff which comes from the Pope's table, when she is already fed with the good grain of the Gospel, as contained in the Bible? Our answer is, that, by God's grace, this thing shall never be. Shame, double shame, on the Ritualistic traitors who are trying to bring us back to Papal bondage!

We object further, to the Reunion schemes of the Ritualists because they are *opposed to our National Independence, and to our civil and religious liberties.* Should the Ritualists succeed, we should have again a Roman Catholic King of England, and the unhappy days of James II. would be repeated. By means of his spiritual weapons, the Pope of Rome, through the Confessors of the King and his Statesmen, would rule the British Empire in temporals as well as spirituals. Rome has, during the past half century, put forth her claims to temporal power with a haughtiness which was never exceeded by a Hildebrand or an Innocent III. The throne itself would be at the mercy of the Pope. I know some of my readers will smile at this, as the utterance of a visionary and an alarmist. Yet, for all this, Mr. Gladstone's statement is literally true:—"Rome has refurbished, and paraded anew, every rusty tool she was fondly thought to have disused."[69] The late Rev. Thomas Francis Knox, of the Brompton Oratory, tells us, in a book published as recently as 1882, and compiled at the request of Cardinal Manning, that the following decree, passed at the Fourth Council of Lateran, is still a "part of the ordinary statute law of the Church":—

"If a temporal lord, after having been required and admonished by the Church, shall neglect to cleanse his land from heretical

[69] *Rome and the Newest Fashions in Religion,* by the Right Hon. W. E. Gladstone, p. xxvii.

defilement, let him be excommunicated by the metropolitan and the other Bishops of the province. And if he shall through contempt fail to give satisfaction within a year, let this be signified to the *Sovereign Pontiff, that he may thereupon declare his vassals absolved from allegiance to him,* and offer his land for seizure by Catholics that they may, *after expelling the heretics,* possess it by an incontestable title and keep it in the purity of the faith." [90]

Is it wise to bring about a state of things in which this law may stand a chance of being enforced? Is a system which still retains such a law to be trusted by liberty-loving Englishmen? In a volume of essays, edited by Cardinal Manning, a similar claim is put forward, in which we read that—

"To depose Kings and Emperors is as much a right as to excommunicate individuals and to lay Kingdoms under an interdict. These are no derived or delegated rights; but are of the essence of that Royal authority of Christ with which His Vicegerents on earth are vested." [91]

How can National Independence exist when such a law as this is enforced? The real ruler would be, not the nominal sovereign, but a foreign potentate called the Pope. Mr. Gladstone's assertion on this point, supported as it was by abundant proofs, should not be forgotten. "No one," he wrote, "can now become her [Rome's] convert without renouncing his moral and mental freedom, *and placing his civil loyalty and duty at the mercy of* another," [92] that is, the Pope. Mr. Gladstone made this statement in 1874, and has never withdrawn it. But has Rome improved since Mr. Gladstone wrote? On the contrary, these disloyal utterances have been re-asserted again and again by her theologians. In the fourth edition of the *Catholic Dictionary*, published in 1893, with the *Imprimatur* of Cardinal Vaughan, we are told what is the opinion on the subject of the Deposing Power *now* held by Roman theologians. It is stated that this power is at present fallen "into abeyance." But that

[90] *Records of English Catholics*, by Thomas Francis Knox, D.D. Vol. II., p. xxvii.
[91] *Essays on Religion and Literature*, edited by Archbishop Manning, p. 417. Second series.
[92] *Rome and the Newer Fashions in Religion*, p. xxiv.

is not the fault of the Pope and his party. It is the result of the strong arm of Protestantism. Anyhow the statement of the *Catholic Dictionary* affords a strong confirmation of Mr. Gladstone's assertion that "Rome has refurbished and paraded anew every rusty tool she was fondly thought to have disused."

"*The ordinary opinion of Roman theologians* may be seen stated in full in the pages of Ferraris. 'The common opinion teaches that the Pope holds the power of both swords, the spiritual and the temporal, which jurisdiction Christ Himself committed to Peter and his successors. . . . The contrary opinion is held to savour of the heretical belief condemned by Boniface VIII. in the Constitution *Unam Sanctam.*' 'Accordingly, *unbelieving kings and princes can be deprived by the sentence of the Pope*, in certain cases, of the dominion which they have over believers; for instance, if they have forcibly seized upon Christian countries, or are endeavouring to turn their believing subjects from the faith, and the like.' Barbosa and other Canonists hold that '*a King who has become a heretic can be removed from his Kingdom by the Pope*, to whom the right of electing a successor passes, if his sons and kindred are also heretics.' 'There is nothing strange in attributing to the Roman Pontiff, as the Vicar of Him Whose is the earth and the fulness thereof, the world and all that dwell therein, the fullest authority and power to lay bare, a just cause moving him, not only the spiritual but also the material sword, *and so to transfer sovereignties, break sceptres, and remove crowns.*' The Canonists produce numerous instances where this has been actually done, as when Gregory II. deposed the Byzantine Emperor Leo III.; Gregory VII. deposed the Emperor Henry IV.; Innocent IV., in the Council of Lyons, deposed the Emperor Frederick II., &c.

"The celebrated Constitution *Unam Sanctam* (1303) teaches that 'both swords, the spiritual and the material, are in the power of the Church, but the latter is to be wielded for the Church, the former by the Church; one by the hand of the priest, the other by the hand of Kings and magistrates, but at the pleasure and sufferance of the priest. One sword must be under the other, and the temporal authority must be subject to the spiritual power.'" [93]

The *political* aspect of the question of Corporate Reunion, set before us in the above extracts, is one which seems to be

---

[93] *Catholic Dictionary*, p. 280. Fourth edition.

almost entirely ignored; yet it is one which every patriotic Englishman would do well to consider. The Church of Rome is not only a religious body, she is also a political power as well; and, therefore, her twofold character must be taken into view. A proposal, which should involve the bestowal on the Emperor of Russia of the right to depose our Queen from her throne, would at once be reprobated by all loyal Englishmen. Why should a proposal, such as that of the Ritualists, which involves the right of the Pope to depose the Queen, be thought of more highly? All true friends of our *National Independence* will, therefore, oppose the Ritualistic plans for Corporate Reunion with Rome.

We are also opposed to Corporate Reunion with Rome because it would certainly lead to the *death of our Religious Liberty*. The "woman drunken with the blood of the saints" (Rev. xvii. 6) has not lost her cruel nature. She has slain the saints of God with the sword and fire, and has never repented of her crimes and wickedness. Has she ever expressed sorrow for burning to death our Protestant Martyrs? The history of many centuries is red with the blood she has shed. Is there no feeling of shame left in those Ritualists who plead for Corporate Reunion with *her?* If Rome had ceased to be what she once was, we would not bring her past crimes and murders to her remembrance. But in this point, alas! more than in any other, she is indeed *semper eadem*. Her persecuting laws are still the same as when in the Dark Ages her infernal Inquisition performed, unhindered, its bloodthirsty work. The modern authorities of the Church of Rome still glory in the intolerant work of their Church in those days. The leading quarterly journal of that Communion in this country, as recently as 1877, said :—

"It would have been a kind of ingratitude and treachery to Jesus Christ Himself—we may almost say it would have exhibited the implicit spirit of apostasy—had the hideousness of sectarianism been permitted [in the Dark Ages] to sully the fair form of Catholic unity, had heresy been permitted to poison the pure air of Catholic truth. ... *So far is any apology from being needed for the then existent intolerance of heretics that, on the contrary, an apology would be now needed for the Mediæval Church*—and would indeed not very easily be forthcoming—*had she tolerated the neglect of such intolerance*. ... And we need hardly add—though we will not dwell on this—that *the same principle, which applied to Mediæval Europe, applies in its measure to any contemporary country*, such as Spain, in which Catholicity has still entire possession of the national mind."[94]

This is a fair warning, which might well set Ritualistic Reunionists thinking. It is confirmed by the testimony of a modern Jesuit Professor, whom Cardinal Newman termed "a great authority" and "one of the first theologians of the day," the late Rev. Edmund J. O'Reilly, s.j., who had been a Professor at Maynooth College, and at St. Bruno's College, North Wales. Professor O'Reilly declared that—

"The principle [of "liberty of conscience"] is one which is not, and never has been, *and never will be*, approved by the Church of Christ."[95]

Another late Professor of Maynooth College, the Rev. T. Gilmartin, is equally strong in his denunciations of liberty of conscience.

"The State," he writes, "can punish heresy as an evil in itself and as an offence against the Church, *and the Church can require the assistance of the State in suppressing heresy*, if its interference be deemed necessary for the good of society."[96]

Another contemporary priest, who has been made a Monsignor by the present Pope (Leo XIII.), argues strongly against allowing "political Liberty of Conscience" in Roman Catholic countries. "How," he asks, "could the Catholic State allow this so-called Liberty of Conscience? As well might you ask a person to allow poison to be introduced in

---

[94] *Dublin Review*, January, 1877, p. 39.

[95] *The Relations of the Church to Society*, by Edmund J. Reilly, s.j., pp. iii., 273. London, 1892.

[96] *Manual of Church History*, by the Rev. T. Gilmartin. Vol. II., p. 228. Dublin, 1892.

his body. Do you say, what a cruel and bigoted thing for the Catholic Church and State to put down heresy? We only ask you to allow the Catholic State the right no man will deny himself or his neighbour, to reject poison from his system."[97] I need hardly add here that the *State* can only "put down heresy" by physical force. Again, this Monsignor remarks: "If to-morrow the Spanish Government, *as advised by the Catholic Church*, were to see that a greater evil would ensue from *granting* religious liberty than from *refusing* it, *then it would have a perfect right to refuse it.* Of course the Protestant Press would teem with charges of intolerance; and we should reply: TOLERATION TO PROTESTANTS IS INTOLERANCE TO CATHOLICS."[98]

Now, the Ritualists know all this very well, just as much as you or I do; yet, strange to relate, their dearest ambition is to place English Churchmen under the rule of this cruel and intolerant Church. Are they not, in this, real foes of our religious liberties? The faithful and eloquent warning of the late Canon Melville may well be quoted here:—

"Make peace, if you will, with Popery; receive it into your Senate; shrine it in your churches; plant it in your hearts. But be ye certain, as certain as that there is a heaven above you, and a God over you, that the Popery thus honoured and embraced is the very Popery that was loathed and degraded by the holiest of your fathers: the same in haughtiness, the same in intolerance, which lorded it over Kings, assumed the prerogative of Deity, crushed human liberty, and slew the Saints of God."

And now, in bringing this volume to a close, I would name one last and crowning reason against adopting the Reunion Plan of Campaign of the Ritualists. They wish our Church and nation to be joined once more, in a Corporate capacity, with the Church of Rome. They do

---

[97] *Liberty of Conscience*, by the Rev. Walter Croke Robinson, p. 22. London: The Catholic Truth Society.
[98] *Ibid.*, p. 24.

not, as a preliminary condition, require the Church of Rome to purge herself of a single one of her false doctrines. They do not seek—though that would be a vain task—to raise her to the higher level of the Reformed Church of England; but they seek to drag down the Church of England to the level of the Church of Rome. It is an unholy task which they have undertaken, on which the smile and blessing of Almighty God cannot be expected to rest. In common with most of the learned Divines of the Church of England since the Reformation and—as we have seen—in accordance with the teaching of her Homilies, we object to Reunion with the Papacy because *the Church of Rome is the Babylon of the Revelation.* This has been most clearly and conclusively proved in that brief, able, unanswered, and unanswerable treatise of the late Bishop Christopher Wordsworth, of Lincoln, entitled:—*Union with Rome: Is not the Church of Rome the Babylon of the Apocalypse?*" I cannot too urgently press upon my readers the great advantage of reading this shilling book. It was not written by an Evangelical Churchman, but by one of the old-fashioned High Church School, one whose great learning is acknowledged by all scholars. He proves that to expect the Reformation of the Church of Rome is to go contrary to the spirit of the Revelation. Her hopeless doom is to be " burnt with fire." She will be Babylon even unto the end.

"Nearly eighteen centuries," writes Bishop Wordsworth, "have passed away since the Holy Spirit prophesied, by the mouth of St. John, that this Mystery would be revealed in that city which was then the Queen of the Earth, the City on Seven Hills—*the City of Rome.*

"The Mystery was then dark, dark as midnight. Man's eye could not pierce the gloom. The fulfilment of the prophecy seemed improbable—almost impossible. Age after age rolled away. By degrees the mists which hung over it became less thick. The clouds began to break. Some features of the dark Mystery began to appear, dimly at first, then more clearly, like Mountains at daybreak. Then the form of the Mystery became more and more distinct. The Seven Hills, and the Woman sitting upon them, become more and more visible. Her voice was heard. Strange sounds of blasphemy were muttered by her. Then they became louder and louder. And the golden chalice in her hand, her scarlet attire, her pearls and jewels were seen glittering in the sun. Kings and Nations were displayed prostrate at her feet, and drinking her cup. Saints were slain by her sword, and she exulted over them. And now the prophecy became clear, clear as noon-day; and we tremble at the sight, while we read the inscription, emblazoned in large letters, 'MYSTERY, BABYLON THE GREAT,' written by the hand of St. John, guided by the Holy Spirit of God, on the forehead of the CHURCH OF ROME." [99]

And now we know, in a nutshell, what the Ritualistic Conspiracy really means. What the future may bring forth God only knows. But what the duty of all loyal Churchmen is, is clear and evident. We must raise once more the good old war cry, "NO PEACE WITH ROME." While Lord Halifax and his followers would lead us astray from the good old ways of our forefathers, into open rebellion against the revealed will of God, let us hearken to God rather than to man. And His cry to one and all is not to join the Church of Rome, but to separate ourselves as far as possible from her. The command of God the Holy Ghost is, "COME OUT OF HER, MY PEOPLE, THAT YE BE NOT PARTAKERS OF HER SINS, AND THAT YE RECEIVE NOT OF HER PLAGUES. FOR HER SINS HAVE REACHED UNTO HEAVEN, AND GOD HATH REMEMBERED HER INIQUITIES" (Rev. xviii. 4, 5).

For the Church of England let our prayer be :—

" God send her swift deliverance from the plagues which vex her now,
God heal the discord in her heart, and chase the trouble from her brow !
And when her penal hour hath past, and purged her from her sin,
Restore her prosperous state without, and her peace and joy within.

---

[99] Wordsworth's *Union with Rome*, p. 62. Eleventh edition. London: Longmans, 1893.

" God give her wavering clergy back that honest heart and true,
  Which once was theirs, ere Popish fraud its spells around them
    threw ;
  Nor let them barter wife and child, bright hearth and happy home,
  For the drunken bliss of the strumpet kiss of the Jezebel of Rome.

" And God console all holy hearts, now yearning for the day,
  When this black cloud shall pass at length from England's skies
    away !
  God help us all to struggle still, with patience and with might,
  Against darkness, lies, and bondage, for Freedom, Truth, and
    Light !

" And God forgive the fallen ones—by their own weak hearts
    betrayed,
  And convert the misbeliever, and reclaim the renegade
  And God unite the good and true, the faithful and the wise,
  Till the Dayspring come on the night of Rome, and the Sun of
    Truth arise " ! [100]

---

[100] Moultrie's *Altars, Hearths, and Graves*, p. 65. Edition, 1854.

APPENDIX.

WHAT THE RITUALISTS TEACH.

I HAVE been requested to give, as an appendix, a series of classified quotations showing " What the Ritualists Teach" in their published writings. For this purpose I have taken nothing at second hand. I have examined the original of every authority cited, and have carefully examined the context of each quotation. Unlike the quotations in the body of this book, those given in this appendix are free from any italics inserted by myself. Where italics occur they are those of the author cited. It is hoped that this collection of quotations may be useful for reference, and for this purpose it has been made intentionally lengthy.

THE BIBLE.

"The recollection of these events should suffice to prove the mistake of supposing that the Sacred Scriptures, without note or comment, in the hands of all, are a sufficient guide to truth; the Bible thus used is not useless only, but dangerous to morality and truth."—*Golden Gate,* by the Rev. S. Baring-Gould, Rector of Lew Trenchard, Part I., p. 177. Edition, 1875.

"Whether a dogmatic creed or belief in the infallibility of a book [the Bible], furnish the best grounds of religion may be doubted, but what is certain is, that the former is the toughest, if only because least easily proved false. A may man believe in God, because he feels that the world is an enigma without that key, and it is impossible to demonstrate the non-existence of a God. But if a man's faith is pinned to a document, and that document be proved to have flaws in it, away goes his faith."—*Germany Past and Present,* by Rev. S. Baring-Gould, Vol. I., p. 193. Edition 1879.

"The Crucifix should be the first lesson book for their [English Home Missionaries] disciples, and the Holy Scriptures must never be put into the hands of unbelievers."—*Union Review* for 1867, p. 13.

"Gradually it had come to be taken for granted that the Holy Scriptures were sufficient for our guidance without the Church's teaching, and that Christian men were justified in drawing their religious faith directly if not exclusively from that source. Hence an endless variety of sects."—*Union Review* for 1865, p. 148.

"The Church is not the ambassador only, but the plenipotentiary of God in the world: the credentials of a plenipotentiary may serve to identify him, and even to map out for him his policy, but his name implies an authority unlimited by any instruction or credentials; and it must be borne in mind that the credentials of an ambassador serve for his introduction only, not for future use; and his instructions, if he has any, are for his own private and secret perusal, not for the inspection of those with whom he treats. Whether the advocates of Biblical supremacy as against Church authority are willing to accept a metaphor which so inadequately suits their purpose is a matter about which there cannot be much doubt."—*Union Review* for 1870, p. 298.

"To hear the Church was to hear the Bible in its truest and only true sense. Was it not an abuse of the Bible to send shiploads of copies across the seas to convert the nations?"—*Speech of the Rev. R. Rhodes Bristow, Vicar of St. Stephen's, Lewisham*, at a meeting of the English Church Union, January 22nd, 1890. Reported in the *Church Union Gazette*, March, 1890, p. 99.

"The Bible is not the *sole* and *only* Rule of Faith."—*Paper read by Mr. H. W. Hill*, at a meeting of the Chiswick Branch of the English Church Union, February 3rd, 1890. Reported in *Church Union Gazette*, May, 1890, p. 153.

"Nor is it any infringement of the reverence due to the Bible, as God's Word, to declare openly and distinctly that 'Bible Christianity' is an invention of the Devil, having for its object to obstruct and defeat God's Word under the hypocritical pretence of love and zeal for His Word."—*Church Review*, July 12th, 1862, p. 427.

"The Catholic Church is always in time (as well as in degree) before the Bible."—*Church Review*, October 8th, 1864, p. 989.

"A faith appealing to the Bible only can find no firm resting place."—*On the Use and Abuse of the Bible*, by the Rev. Thomas Robinson, M.A., p. 27. London: Church Printing Co.

"The Church did not give us the Bible that we might *each take his own religion from it*. We *take* our religion from the Church, which is living; then we *prove* it, if we will, from the Holy Bible."—*St. Andrew, Worthing, Parish Magazine*, December, 1893, p. 3.

"Our Blessed Lord did not intend any written document to be the basis of the Faith He founded."—*Christ Church, Doncaster, Parish Magazine*, March, 1895.

THE BOOK OF COMMON PRAYER.

"I would only urge that we should not on this account ignore the serious character of the actual changes made [in the Liturgy by the Reformers in the sixteenth century], or decline to do our very best to get them remedied. The more really secure we feel as to the position of the English Church, the more willing we should be to acknowledge its shortcomings."—*Lord Halifax*, in the *Lord's Day and the Holy Eucharist*, p. 27. London, 1892.

"How has it been possible that Catholics—not ultra-Catholics, but Catholics teaching the doctrines and observing the ritual of the Universal Church—have been, and to some extent still are, subject to suspicion and ill-treatment in a National Church professing to be Catholic, and acknowledging the authority of 'the Church,' and referring, as to a standard, to the usages of the Primitive Church? The answer, it is feared, to these questions must be, that these troubles have their origin in the defects of the English Service Book; in the fact that our Reformers, with a clear duty marked out, went beyond the line which the finger of duty marked out, and thus entailed upon the Reformed Church a heritage of weakness and indecision."—*The Rev. E. W. Sergeant*, in the *Lord's Day and the Holy Eucharist*, p. 120.

"Why bring into such marked prominence [in the Communion Service] the title 'The Lord's Supper,' a name for the Eucharist of comparatively infrequent use and of doubtful applicability to the actual rite? . . . Laudable as the motive may have been, the effect has been disastrous, more disastrous perhaps than any of the other Liturgical changes, since it has given occasion to ignorant and heretical writers to represent our 'Communion Service' as something generically different from the 'Mass,' whereas it is nothing less than the same thing in another form."—*Ibid.*, pp. 121, 122.

" What a contrast between the careful instructions and the beautiful preparatory office for the priest provided in all the old English Service Books, in the Roman and most of the Greek, and the utter absence of any such provision in the Book of Common Prayer! Not a word about vesting, or about the reverent and careful preparation of the elements: not a syllable to correspond to the minute and exhaustive *Cautelæ Missæ* of the old books."—*Ibid.*, p. 122.

" Besides these numerous admissions, our [Communion] Office has, it must be said, other faults. The chief and most obvious is, that it sadly obscures the oblation."—*Ibid.*, p. 127.

" Is it possible, with every allowance for their difficult position, to acquit our Reformers of causing needless offence (to say the very least) when, not contenting themselves with a liberty which they exercised to the very verge of license in the way of expurgation and modification, they cut up and reset with not too skilful hands the splendid mosaic of the ancient service, so that the very outlines of the old pattern are barely recognisable?"—*Ibid.*, p. 131.

" Good men cannot understand that we should not be perfectly satisfied with things as they are, 'apostolic order and evangelic truth,' according to the favourite formulary, and be willing to fight a tremendous fight for the retention of all the Rubrics, *totidem verbis*. We are not to be scandalized, it seems, by such extraordinary directions as we are almost ashamed to quote, but where is the use of closing our eyes wilfully to facts? 'And there shall be no celebration of the Lord's Supper, except there be a sufficient number to communicate with the Priest, *according to his discretion*. And if *there be not above twenty persons in the Parish* of discretion to receive the Communion, there shall *be no Communion, except four, or three at the least, communicate with the Priest*.' There can be no mistaking the meaning of that—the intention. It was to take away, to extirpate as as far as might be, the notion of the Sacrifice! And this setting at nought by authority of the primary act of Catholic worship from the days of the Apostles downwards, is to be mildly acquiesced in, or even bravely battled for. No, that is asking rather too much. How can Catholics be supposed to support this? How can they hide their light under a bushel, for the sake of conciliating sound Anglicans who do not believe in the Presence and the Sacrifice? Are they not obliged to protest against a rule which is not a dead letter, but still takes away the Daily Sacrifice from almost all our altars, which renders the offering at least uncertain in most of our churches, which strips the country priest of his right to communicate in his village church, with the whole Church throughout the world, unless three Protestant clodhoppers happen to be of his way of thinking! . . . Yet the rule in question is simply odious in itself, and we cannot fight for its retention in order to gratify moderates. We believe the Blessed Sacrament to be the daily Food of the priest of God, and by this obnoxious Rubric he is stripped of his heritage."—*Union Review* for 1865, pp. 619, 620.

"We venture to say, heresy has been practically triumphant for three hundred years together, through the Prayer Book. It was designed to be so, and it has been so."—*Ibid.*, p. 621.

"We cannot allow it to be thought that we are satisfied with the Prayer Book as it is. It would not be honest not to say that we aim at nothing short of Catholic Restoration, and as one step to this, at the excision of these grievous Rubrics, and, a little later, at the modification of these ambiguous Articles, if they are to be retained at all."—*Ibid.*, p. 622.

"We cannot and we will not tamely accept the illogical and incomplete system which the Reformers have left us in the Prayer Book as it is. It has been tried for three hundred years and found wanting."—*Ibid.*, p. 626.

"And when we remember that this essential service [Sacrifice of Mass] was taken away by the unhappy, the presumptuous Rubrics we have cited, we lack words to express our sense of moral indignation at the daring of the men who framed them. But peace be with them! They knew no better. May God be merciful to their souls!"—*Ibid.*, p. 630.

THE THIRTY-NINE ARTICLES.

"The half-abrogated Articles 'cracked and strained by three centuries of evasive ingenuity,' are rather a trashy foundation for anything."—*Rev. H. H. Henson, Vicar of Barking*, in *Guardian*, August 24th, 1892, p. 1251.

"Of course, there has been a large party who swear by them [the Thirty-nine Articles], and the existence of whose forms of belief in the Church of England is guaranteed by their being retained; but it is impossible to deny that they contain statements, or implications that are verbally false, and others that are very difficult to reconcile with truth. In the times that are coming over the Church of England, the question will arise, What service have the Articles of the Church of England ever done? . . . Before union with Rome can be effected, the Thirty-nine Articles must be wholly withdrawn."—*Christian Remembrancer*, No. 131, p. 188.

"By way of suggesting something practical ourselves, we will in this paper recommend, as a first and *essential* preliminary towards the Reunion of Christendom, the total abolition of the Thirty-nine Articles."—*Union Review*, for 1870, p. 289.

"Some [of the Thirty-nine Articles] contain statements which are unintelligible; in the case of others, one is tempted to wish that the statements were unintelligible or nonsensical in order to escape the disagreeable impression of their being—well, truly Protestant; others contain contradictions, or qualifications which eviscerate or destroy what has gone before: there are statements of facts which are not wholly indisputable; there are trivial points of Christian discipline or of every-day life, which derogate from the importance and value of a confession of faith. Meanwhile, with all these defects and blemishes, the Thirty-nine Articles continue to be paraded as *the* authoritative standard of Anglican doctrine, and they are imposed as a heavy yoke upon the consciences of all who would serve in the ministry of the Church. And we venture to assert that one of the most imperative reforms in the Church of England is the total abolition of these Thirty-nine Articles."—*Ibid.*, p. 294.

"We maintain that so long as this Article [Article VI.] remains among the formularies of the Church of England, so long will there be an insuperable bar to any union or fusion of the Church of England with the rest of the Catholic family. The Article distinctly ignores Tradition, and it positively affirms private judgment."—*Ibid.*, p. 295.

"Of all the obstacles and hindrances to reunion with Rome, probably the greatest is that rather unwieldy compilation known as the Thirty-nine Articles, somewhat facetiously called the 'Forty Stripes save one.'"—*Church Review*, November 12th, 1864, p. 1127.

"How strange it seems that in our Prayer Book we should pray that all Christians 'may agree in the truth of God's Holy Word, and live in unity and godly love,' when in the very same book—in the Articles—the Roman Church is charged with '*superstitions*' and '*vain inventions contrary to the Word of God*' (see Articles XXII., XXVIII., &c.). We need not wonder at such incongruity in 1572—but how long?"—*Olive Leaf*, by Rev. W. Wyndham Malet, Vicar of Ardeley, p. 50.

"Doubtless they [Thirty-nine Articles] are Articles of Peace, and have always been intended to be construed largely and charitably, so as to square with 'The Faith once delivered to the Saints'; but the *primâ facie* aspect of more than one of them is nothing less than most erroneous. To turn at once to perhaps the most obnoxious, the Twenty-fifth. We are there told, to the horror of that valuable periodical, the *Union Chrétiennes*, that the five great Sacramental Ordinances—Confirmation, Penance, Orders, Matrimony, and Extreme Unction—have grown 'partly of the corrupt following of the Apostles.' What a singular assertion, only to be understood in any sense of one out of the five (*Extreme* Unction), and in that case surely a very bold and uncalled-for denunciation of a foreign practice. Then there is the Thirty-first, which seems to come very near denying the Eucharistic Sacrifice. . . The fact is, then, I must conclude that the sooner we are rid of the Thirty-nine Articles the better. We can, and we must, and do put a Catholic interpretation on them as they are, but this is only making the best of a bad matter."—*Letter of the Rev. Archer Gurney, Curate in Charge of Rhayader*, in *Church Review*, January 3rd, 1863, pp. 9, 10.

"Almost all sincere Reunionists would allow that whatever temporary advantages accrued from the setting forth of the Thirty-nine Articles three centuries ago, very great permanent disadvantages have followed from their continued retention in the English Church since. They have done little good at home and untold mischief abroad. For there are some Articles which, unless their language is duly weighed and carefully explained, sound very startling in the ears of foreign Catholics, whether Greeks or Latins: and do more to render the idea of corporate Reunion impracticable than anything else. Of late years, however, so many contradictory explanations of them have been given—Sharpe, and Tomline, Hey, Newman, and Harold Browne, have so greatly shattered people's *belief* in them—that at the present time, as the *Christian Remembrancer* has more than once declared, they might be quietly set aside, to the great advantage of religion and morality in the Church of England."—*Church News*, August 21st, 1867, p. 367.

REUNION WITH ROME.

"We have no wish to revile the faith of Roman Catholics, for it is the same faith as our own; we have no wish to insult their worship, for we worship God in the same Eucharist; and as for those practical evils which disfigure their faith and worship, we believe that intelligent Roman Catholics, in their inmost hearts, think much the same about these things as we do ourselves. The real difference in matters of faith between a sincere and intelligent Roman Catholic and a Catholic-minded member of the Church of England is the merest shadow of a shade. Each refers to Holy Scripture, each refers to the history of the Church through its eighteen centuries of existence, as the real test of the truth of its doctrines, and the difference between them cannot therefore be great. The spirit of schism would lead each to magnify difference to the greatest possible extent, but the spirit of Christian faith and love will lead to a different conclusion. Two things we know for certain, viz., *first*, that Catholic Unity is a plain Christian duty; and, *secondly*, that there can be no such thing as Catholic Unity without the Bishop of Rome as the lawful Primate and President of Christendom. Let us maintain and declare these truths frankly and fearlessly."—*Catholic Unity*, by the Rev. Edward Stuart, Perpetual Curate of St. Mary Magdalene, Munster Square, London, p. 79. London, 1867.

"Of course to those whose cry is 'No peace with Rome,' and whose glory is in the shame of divided Christendom, it [*i.e.*, Corporate Reunion] is a thing as incredible as hateful, the wish that it may ever be so is father to the thought; but to others I would say, do remember that even now there *is* union, although unhappily not visible and corporate. . . . What we have to strive and pray for, is the restoration of the outward, visible, corporate manifestation of that unity. Do, brethren, consider seriously these things, and be not led away by blind

prejudice, and by that insensate outcry against Rome and Popery."—
Disunion and Reunion, p. 14. A Sermon by the Rev. C. J. Le Geyt, Incumbent of St. Mathias', Stoke Newington.

"The Council of Trent is not an insurmountable obstacle to Reunion [with the Church of Rome], but that it may be so explained that we could receive it."—*Dr. Pusey in his Letter addressed to the Editor of John Bull*, and dated December 7th, 1865.

"But they [Anglicans] should know well, and never forget, that for the English Church Corporate Reunion without Reunion with Rome is, if not an impossibility, a step not to be desired."—*Reunion Magazine*, No. 1, p. 5.

"I still feel, that as matter of doctrine, that is of belief, the difference between what is held by English Churchmen and what is held by Roman Catholics, is infinitesimal."—*Reminiscences of the Oxford Movement*, by Rev. T. Mozley, formerly Rector of Plymtree, Vol. II., p. 386. Second edition.

"It is most refreshing to find that the doctrinal differences which separate the Roman and Anglican Communions disappear when viewed in the light of unimpassioned inquiry."—*Union Review*, for 1868, p. 363.

THE POPE'S INFALLIBILITY, PRIMACY AND SUPREMACY.

"I used to be as opposed to the doctrine of Papal Infallibility as it was possible for anyone to be. Deeper reflection has, however, convinced me that there is really nothing in it to which exception need be taken. Granting an administrative head of the whole Catholic Church, granting a Primate of Christendom, by the same right even that the Archbishops of Canterbury profess to be Primates of the English Church—namely, 'by Divine Providence,' it is surely only reasonable to believe that, if this head of the Universal Church were to teach *ex cathedra*, or authoritatively, anything pertaining to faith or morals, to the whole flock of God, of which he is the chief shepherd upon earth, he would most surely be guided by the Holy Ghost in such a way as not to teach Satan's lie instead of the truth of God. This is the way in which I should feel disposed to understand the Vatican decree. And so far from seeing anything inconsistent with reason, or history, or Holy Scripture, or the Catholic Faith, in that decree, thus understood, it appears to me that natural piety itself, and a belief in God's providential guidance of His Church, would lead us to accept it."—*Rev. Thomas W. Mossman, Rector of Torrington*, in *Church Review*, November 3rd, 1882, p. 531.

"It is quite true that we do not assume an attitude of independence towards the Holy See. We frankly acknowledge that, in the Providence of God, the Roman Pontiff is the first Bishop in the Church, and, therefore, its visible head on earth. We do not believe that either the Emperor of Russia or the Queen of England is the head of the Church. As the Church must have some executive head, and as there is no other competitor, we believe the Pope to be that head. But he is more to us than this, for he is our Patriarch as well. So that we admit his claim to the veneration and loyalty of all baptized men, and in a special degree of all Western Christians."—*Letter of a Bishop of the Order of Corporate Reunion*, in *Reunion Magazine*, No. 2, p. 242.

"We in England look upon the Patriarch of Rome as the First Bishop, the President of the General Council of the Church of Christ."—*Olive Leaf*, by Rev. William Wyndham Malet, Rector of Ardeley, p. 12.

"England has her holy orders and ordinances of worship from Rome. She recognizes His Holiness as the chief bishop of all."—*Ibid.*, p. 38.

"In the Church of England, likewise, the Bishop of Rome has no authority. But in the Church of God, a universal spiritual body, all, of course, belongs to St. Peter's successor, which was originally given to St. Peter by our Lord. Whatever the Divine donation was originally, man did not bestow it, and man cannot take it away. Moreover, the government of the Catholic Church by Bishops, Primates, Metropolitans, and Patriarchs, with One Visible Head, is so exactly of that practical nature, that no wholly independent and isolated religious body can possibly participate either in its government or in the blessing of being rightly governed, so long as it remains independent. . . . The Visible Head of that One Christian Family, as Christendom has universally allowed, is the Bishop of the See of St. Peter. Unlike all other Bishops, he has no superior either in rank or jurisdiction. Now, when any part of a family, by misunderstanding and perverseness, becomes disobedient to, or out of harmony with, its Visible Head, weakness and confusion as regards its oneness is certain to supervene." *Order out of Chaos*, by Rev. F. G. Lee, Vicar of All Saints', Lambeth, pp. 60-62.

THE REFORMERS AND THE REFORMATION.

"I have to own that, in spite of the telling illustrations of Mrs. Trimmer's *History of England*, I never yet succeeded in getting up an atom of affection or respect for the three gentlemen canonized in the 'Martyrs' Memorial' at Oxford. As Lord Blachford once observed to me, 'Cranmer burnt well,' and that is all the good I know about him."—*Reminiscences of the Oxford Movement*, by Rev. T. Mozley, Rector of Plymtree, Vol. II., p. 230.

"To protest altogether against the wickedness of the Reformation by ENTIRELY IGNORING its pretended claims upon English Christians, the Monks of Llanthony have set up 'the Shrine of the Perpetual Adoration of the Most Holy Sacrament.' "—*Little Manual of Devotions*, by Rev. J. L. Lyne, *alias* "Father Ignatius," p. 4.

"Don't beat about the bush to try and deceive, to try and make people believe you [Ritualists] are what you are not. You know you have no respect for the Reformation; you know you believe it has wronged our dear old Church of England; you know you believe that it was a cruel, cowardly piece of tyranny of a wicked, murderous despot; and although after centuries have painted over and gilded over the diabolical acts of Henry VIII., yet you cannot point to one single Scriptural or ecclesiastical authority that can be quoted for the manner in which the work was carried out, or the work itself."—*The Present Position of the Ritualists*, by "Father Ignatius," p. 25.

"For ourselves we do not scruple to say that we regard the death of Edward and the accession of Mary as the most fortunate circumstance for the Church of England."—*Union Review* for 1871, p. 358.

"In Germany the Church was utterly rooted out, and a new religion, called Protestantism, invented by Luther and Calvin and other malcontents, was substituted in its place. But in England this was not the case. The Church remained, but remained in fetters. In character it was identical with the Church of old, holding the same essential truths, sacraments, and orders; but it was infected with Protestantism, which poisoned its blood, and diseased the whole body, yet without destroying its vitality. Thank God, the Church of England is rapidly recovering her health, and though heresy may still linger on in her members, she has sufficient strength in time to expel every trace of the disease and recover her ancient vigour. In England the Church was corrupted by Protestantism."—*Golden Gate*, by Rev. S. Baring-Gould, Rector of Lew Trenchard, Part I., p. 146. Edition, 1875.

"The English Reformation, as carried out, was, from every sound Churchman's standing-point, an unjustifiable and wicked act—heartily reprobated and condemned by many."—*Reunion Magazine*, No. 1, p. 6.

SOME RITUALISTIC "ORNAMENTS OF THE CHURCH."*

An Altar with Super Altar.
An Altar Cross or Crucifix.
A Super-Frontal.
Corporal.
Burse.
Chalice Veil.
A Canister for Wafers.
A Spoon.
A Perforated Spoon.
A Chalice Cover and Lace for Veiling the Blessed Sacrament.
Ciborium.
Maniples.
Ampulla.
An Aumbrye.
A Triptych.
Pede Cloth.
Houselling Cloth.
Corona.
Rood Screen.
A Scallop Shell.
A Baptismal Shell.
A Water Bucket.
A Baptismal Cruet.
Paintings and Images of Our Lord, Our Lady, and Saints.
A Portable Altar.
Altar Bread Cutters.
Altar Bread Irons.
Altar Canister.

Two Standard Candlesticks.
Flower Vases.
Processional Candlesticks.
Torches.
Lanthorns.
Cantoral Staves.
Amice (for an Archbishop or Bishop).
Alb.
Maniple.
Stole.
Dalmatic.
Girdle.
Tunicle.
Zucchetto.
Biretta.
Chasuble.
Cope.
Grey Amyss.
Buskins.
Sandals.
Subcingulum.
Pectoral Cross.
Tunic.
Mitre.
Crozier.
Gremial.
The Cappa Magna.
The Pall.

* From the *Directorium Anglicanum*, pp. 336-341. Fourth edition.

THE REAL PRESENCE.

"Thou, God and Man, art in our midst,
　The Altar is Thy Throne;
We bow before Thy Mercy Seat,
　And Thee, our Maker, own.
My soul, fall prostrate to adore,
　In lowliest worship bent;
Each day I live I love Thee more,
　Sweet Sacrament! Sweet Sacrament!"

—*St. Agatha's, Landport, Sunday Scholars' Book*, Appendix, Hymn 474.

"You will go [to the Altar] with this one solemn thought ever present to your mind, namely, that your body is about to become a tabernacle for the most sacred Flesh and Blood of Jesus, God Incarnate!"—The *Parish Tracts*, by Rev. J. H. Buchanan, First Series, No. X., "Confirmation."

"Let every one who hears you speak, or sees you worship, feel quite sure that the object of your devotion is not an idea or a sentiment, or a theory, or a make-believe, but a real personal King and Master and Lord: present at all times everywhere in the omnipresence of His *Divine* Nature, present by His own promise, and His own supernatural power in His *Human* Nature too upon His Altar-Throne, there to be worshipped in the Blessed Sacrament as really, and literally, and actually, as you will necessarily worship Him when you see Him in His beauty in Heaven."—*St. John the Baptist*. A Sermon by the Rev. H. D. Nihill, Vicar of St. Michael's, Shoreditch, p. 8.

"Yes, in that piece of consecrated Bread he knew our Lord had come—had changed that very Bread into His own Body, and that wine in the chalice into His most precious Blood. Little child as he was, the Holy Spirit had taught him all the great mystery of that Sacrament, and when he saw his father kneel to receive what appeared to his eyes but a piece of bread, he knew his father had really eaten the Body of His Saviour."—*Stories Told to the Choir*, No. 2, p. 19. Oxford: Mowbray, 1874.

"Kenneth understood now, and he would understand more some day, how that Jesus comes at the bidding of His priest upon the Altar, and passes Himself into the little Pieces of Bread and into the Wine in the Chalice, and so is 'verily and indeed taken and received by the faithful in the Lord's Supper.'"—*Ibid.*, p. 22.

"And then to think that Jesus comes His Own very Self to offer Himself in Sacrifice to God, and to listen to all our prayers. That's the sign He's come, when the big bell tolls three, just as the priest says the words of consecration 'This is my Body—This is my Blood.'"—*Ibid.*, No. 5, p. 20.

"Think of Jesus on the Cross dying for you. Think of His coming down upon our Altars under the forms of Bread and Wine! Every crumb on the paten, every drop in the chalice has now become the whole Body, Blood, Soul, Spirit, and Divinity of Jesus! Now is the time for you to worship Him!"—The *Server's Mass Book*, by the Rev. G. P. Grantham, p. 21. London: Masters.

"The following is a beautiful method of manifesting devotion to the Most Holy Sacrament:—When the Hymn, 'Hail, Jesus, Hail!' is sung, let the Ceremoniarius, or his Assistant, carry a hand-bell, and as often as the words, "Sweet Sacrament we Thee adore,' occur, let him sound it. The procession will pause, and all, excepting the sacred Ministers, turning round, will sink humbly on their knees, and adore the Blessed Sacrament."—*Oratory Worship*, p. 32. London: Church Press Company, 1869.

"Far worse than any kind of idolatry is the Christian religion, if the Host on the Altar is not Very God."—The *Sacrament of the Holy Eucharist*. A Lecture by Rev. J. L. Lyne, *alias* "Father Ignatius," p. 16.

"Other Sacraments contain the Grace of God, but the Holy Eucharist is God Himself."—*Practical Thoughts for Sisters of Charity*, p. 137. London: Hodges, 1871.

"As surely as the Boy Carpenter was the great Eternal God, so also surely the Bread and Wine which you have seen and handled, and received into yourself this day is the great and Eternal God too: the God who hideth Himself. Adore in silence and in trembling awe."—*Ibid.*, p. 300.

"Hidden God and Saviour, Have mercy upon us. Most High and adorable Sacrament, Have mercy upon us. Tremendous and life-giving Sacrament, Have mercy upon us."—The *English Catholic's Vade Mecum*, pp. 71, 72. Third edition.

"As you walk to Church, say:—

> "I rise from dreams of time
> And an Angel guides my feet,
> To the Sacred Altar Throne
> Where Jesus' Heart doth beat."

—*Private Prayers*, edited by the Rev. W. H. Hutchings (now Archdeacon of Cleveland), p. 43. Windsor: privately printed.

"Lord Jesus, I have this day received on my tongue, Thy most holy Flesh and Blood."—*Ibid.*, p. 52.

"Again, as to our conversation. How jealous should Communicants be over the words that pass through the door of those lips, wetted with the Holy Blood, spoken by the tongue that has tasted the Sacred Body of the Lord."—*Instructions on the Holy Eucharist*, edited by Canon T. T. Carter, p. 124. Second edition. London: Parker.

THE POWER AND DIGNITY OF SACRIFICING PRIESTS.

"They [priests] are peacemakers under Him who carry on this work for Him, applying the precious Blood to the souls of men by the Sacraments for the remission of sin."—The *Evangelist Library: Exposition of the Beatitudes*, edited by the Cowley Fathers, p. 31.

"The priest is permitted to share certain sorrows of Christ in which the layman has no part."—*Ibid.*, p. 32.

"But those priests who worthily fulfil their office shall be more specially called the sons of God, because they shall have an especial likeness to Him, having been made partakers in a chosen way of the priesthood of His only begotten Son."—*Ibid.*, p. 33.

"You are not, then, to look upon him [the Confessor-Priest] as a friend only, or a constant sympathizer, but as one who is over you in the Lord—one who should sometimes reprove, and you to accept it without feeling as though the rebuke was given by an equal, who may sometimes encourage you, but rather as a guide than a friend; one with whom you are to be on terms of intimacy different to your relation to all other persons on earth; with whom you are not to talk as you would to others, as on an equal footing, but as speaking to one to whom respect and obedience is due. He is neither to be spoken to nor of, in any manner approaching to familiarity."—*Hints to Penitents*, p. 128. Third edition.

"The priest, as far as his priesthood is concerned, is Christ Himself the Sovereign and Eternal Priest."—*A Brief Answer to Objections Brought Against Confession*, Translated by the Feltham Nuns, p. 23.

"The priest perpetuates Jesus Christ in our midst to endless ages, that is why we should go to him as Jesus Christ, and to Christ by him."—*Ibid.*, p. 21.

"Learn to perceive Almighty God concealed for you in His priests."—*Ibid.*, p. 23.

"A penitent, prostrate at the feet of the priest, is a man raised, and elevated, and supremely honourable."—*Ibid.*, p. 24.

"Fear the eye and the voice of the priest."—*Ibid.*, p. 24.

"The priests are, on earth, the spiritual police of Almighty God; they must hunt out, track, pursue, and arraign sinners, as the police pursue and apprehend thieves and rascals."—*Ibid.*, p. 26.

"The lay element already too greatly preponderated [in the Church of England], and no more of it was needed. It was not that he undervalued the office of the laity, whose high and noble prerogative it was to listen and obey, but it was for the Ministers of the Church with all their responsibilities to magnify their office, if so be that others would intrude upon it."—*Extract from a Speech by the Rev. Luke Rivington*, at an Ordinary Meeting of the English Church Union, January 14th, 1868. *English Church Union Monthly Circular*, for 1868, p. 65.

> "They may call me a Papist, and laugh at my Creed,
> 'Tis the Faith that will save in the hour of need;
> Let them talk, let them laugh, but when death is at hand
> The priest is the only true friend in the land."
> *Hensal-cum-Heck Church Monthly*, November, 1895.

THE SACRIFICE OF THE MASS.

"*Q.* Have we not already named another way in which we are to be mindful of the Departed?

"*A.* Yes; we offer the Holy Sacrifice for them.

"*Q.* Why so?

"*A.* As being propitiatory. The Sacrifice of the Cross was

propitiatory for all, for the Living and the Faithful departed. The Sacrifice of the Eucharist, which is one with the Sacrifice of the Cross, is alike propitiatory for all."—*A Catechism on the Church*, by Rev. C. S. Grueber, Vicar of St. James's, Hambridge, p. 158. Edition 1874.

"If you speak about the Mass, do not beat about for some one or other of the names which mean the same thing, but under cover of which men are accustomed to allow that is in their idea not the same thing. Men hate the little word, because they think it means the same thing that they see done abroad in other portions of the same One Holy Catholic Church : and is not that, if we belive in *One* Holy Catholic Church, precisely the truth that we ought to be labouring in every way to teach them ?"—*St. John the Baptist.* A Sermon by the Rev. H. D. Nihill, p. 2.

"An attempt to approach nearer to the Roman Catholics in the manner of celebrating High Mass would be of immense service to our Church ; and if we could introduce such a little office as is often seen at the Brompton Oratory and other places, where the people seem to have everything their own way, except that a young priest gives out the hymns, and recites a few Aves and Paternosters, the whole being followed by a good extempore sermon, and the Benediction of the Blessed Sacrament, we should have little cause to complain of the inroads of the Methodists."—*Union Review*, for 1868, p. 22.

"The Sacrifices of the Golden Altar and the Earthly Altar are as much Sacrifices of Praise, of Thanksgiving, of Prayer, and of Propitiation for Sin, as was the Sacrifice of the Cross."—*Union Review*, for 1866, p. 260.

"Teach men to deny the Sacrifice of the Mass, and they are on the high road to the denial of all Sacrifice whatever."—*Church News*, February 17th, 1869, p. 99.

"It is the glory of the Eucharist that, through the instrumentality of that Body and Blood which He gave for the life of the world upon the Cross, and which He still gives to us under the veils of bread and wine in the Sacrament of the Altar, Jesus Christ perpetuates on our behalf, here below in the visible sanctuaries of His Church, the functions of His Eternal Priesthood : it is our dignity, and the glory of our consecration as a royal priesthood, that He has entrusted the offering of the Sacrifice made on Calvary to human agencies, and that He permits it to depend upon us whether He, the great High Priest of our profession, shall be allowed to exercise His priestly functions at our altars or no. By His gracious condescension, the free will of the Blessed Virgin was permitted to co-operate with God in determining the time of the Incarnation : by a condescension no less gracious He leaves Himself in our power in the Eucharist, which is the extension of the Incarnation."—*Eighteenth Annual Report of the C. B. S.*, paper by Hon. C. L. Wood, now Lord Halifax, p. x.

'The Sacrifice of the Altar is one and the same Sacrifice with that offered on Calvary. It is not a different Sacrifice, nor a repetition : it is the same."—*Golden Gate*, by the Rev. S. Baring-Gould, Rector of Lew Trenchard, Part III., p. 163. Edition, 1875.

"By virtue of this life-giving Sacrament, have mercy, O most kind Lord Jesus Christ, on the holy universal Church. . . . Give, by this holy Sacrament, true charity to our enemies and to ourselves, and to all Thy faithful people succour, help, and consolation; bestowing Thy grace upon those still in the flesh, and granting eternal rest to all the faithful departed."—The *Communicant's Manual*, by the Bishop of Lincoln (Dr. King), pp. 55, 57. Sixth edition. London : Mozley and Smith, 1877.

"The mode in which High Mass should be sung in the Oratory of the Society of the Holy Cross on Festivals, should be of the highest type known to Catholic Christendom, by which the Holy Sacrifice may be offered according to the use of the Church of England. It should possess every element in ritual, and music, and other accessories, which the tradition of the Church sanctions. . . . But the founders of the Oratory would not feel satisfied until they restored to the Church of England a rendering of the sacred Mass which was fully Mediæval in the correctness of its use, and more than Mediæval in the richness, costliness, taste, and perfection of its details. Thus we should desiderate these elements at the least :—The Asperges ; the 'Censing of persons and things,' or the use of incense in a ritual manner; the correct Introits, Graduals, Offertories, Communions; Gospel Lights ; Consecration Lights on the Altar and Consecration Candles in front of the Altar, in addition to the Six Altar Candles and two Sacramental Lights; the use of the Altar Bell; the Lavabo ; and, of course, the Eucharistic Vestments, for Celebrant, Ministers, Servers, and Acolytes."—The *Four Cardinal Virtues*, by the Rev. Orby Shipley, pp. 246, 247. London : Longmans, 1871.

"And under the Christian covenant of grace, and in the Church which is the Body of Christ, the Christian Priest may daily stand before the altar offering up the great commemorative Sacrifice of Christ, for his own sins, and for the sins of the people. . . . Daily, therefore, in the 'Church's Prayer Meeting' held when the Celebrant, representing the congregation, and assisted by, and in union with them, makes effectual intercession for the people, pleading the tremendous Sacrifice for sin before God, and standing, like Aaron, between the living and the dead, to make atonement for them."—*St. Philip's, Sydenham, Church Magazine*, March, 1896, p. 1.

"So then, be sure, whatever else you do, that you go to Mass on this great day. A Christian child who is able to go to Mass on Christmas Day, and who does not go is not good. He does not deserve to have any Christmas treats, and he ought not to enjoy them if he has them."—*Hosanna: A Mass Book for Children*, with Preface by the Rev. R. A. J. Suckling, Vicar of St. Alban's, Holborn, p. 44. London: W. Knott, 1891.

"And Thurifer first, with his censer bright,
And then Sub-deacon the cross who bears,
Lifted on high
That all may descry;
And on either side is an Acolyte,
With other Clerics together in pairs,
Walking to West and back to East,
With vested Deacon and vested Priest,
All of them bearing the taper Light.

"Then to the Altar returned, they say
The Holy Mass; and the people all
Hold up their lighted tapers high,
While Gospel and blessed Canon are sung,
And *Gloria* shouted by every tongue,
—God grant that all
Who on Jesus call
May one day mingle that throng among,
Who ever shall keep in the yonder sky,
With happy rapture and bliss for aye,
The gladness and joy of a Candlemas day!"

—*The Mysteries of Holy Church*, by the Rev. G. P. Grantham, p. 99. London: Masters.

"Father, gentle, full of love,
   Hear us while we humbly pray !
Look Thou from Thy throne above
   On the Sacrifice to-day.

"Which at Christ, our Lord's command
   We, redeemed from sin's control,
Offer for our Church and land,
   And for every faithful soul.

   .   .   .   .   .   .

"Mindful of Our Lady dear,
   Saints and all the ransomed quire,
Who in rest for ever blest
   Serve Thee with love's fond desire.

"Hear this prayer ; and by the power
   Of this holy Sacrifice
Grant us grace to see Thy face
   In the halls of Paradise ! "

Ibid., pp. xviii, xix.

"THE CATHOLIC FAITH IN DONCASTER, AT LAST.
Oh dear! We want such a lot of things for our poor District Church (St. John's): Vestments, Cope, Processional Crucifix, Tabernacle (for use), Sanctus Bells. Pictures, and Everything. The thorough cleaning of the Church (first time for thirty years) is exhausting our means. Do send something, PLEASE.—Address, Priest-in-charge, 2, Pavilion-street, Doncaster."

"100 LITTLE MARYS WANTED.—Is *your* name Mary? Then do send me a shilling, there's a dear child, towards a shrine for Our Lady in our poor Church of St. John. Tell me your little troubles and I will remember you at Mass.—Address, Priest-in-Charge, 2, Pavilion-street, Doncaster."—*Advertisements in the Church Review*, June 14th, 1894.

"The Mass is not one Sacrifice and Calvary another. It is the same Sacrifice."—*A Book for the Children of God!* p. 119. London: W. Knott, 1891.

"The one Sacrifice for sin for ever, the same at the altar and at the Cross, the 'Eucharistic Sacrifice,' or 'Sacrifice of the Mass.' "— The *Rights of the English Churchmen*, a Sermon preached before the " Church of England Working Men's Society," by Rev. H. D. Nihill, p. 21. Published by the Society.

THE CEREMONIES OF LOW MASS.

"In celebrating Mass some portions have to be said *secretly*, so that the Celebrant hears himself, but is not heard by others."— *Ceremonial Guide to Low Mass,** by two Clergymen of the Church of England, p. 5.

"There are three occasions only when the elbows are placed on the Altar—(1) At the consecration of the Host. (2) At the consecration of the Chalice. (3) While receiving the Host."—*Ibid.*, p. 7.

"The head is bowed towards the Book whenever the names occur of the Blessed Virgin Mary, or of the Saint of whom the Mass is said."—*Ibid.*, p. 18.

"The Hands [of the Consecrating priest] are to be joined palm to palm; and before the Consecration the fingers are to be extended one opposite the other, and the right thumb placed over the left in the form of a cross."—*Ibid.*, p. 27.

"As is remarked by St. Liguori, it is a mistake, on making a genuflection, to raise the tips of the fingers upwards."—*Ibid.*, p. 30.

"On saying 'The holy Gospel is written,' the Celebrant separates his hands, and placing the left upon the Book, he makes a small Sign of the Cross with the tip of the thumb of the right hand on the Book, in the place of the opening words of the Gospel that is to be read. Then, placing his left hand on the lower part of his breast, he makes similar Signs of the Cross with the right thumb on his forehead, and breast."—*Ibid.*, p. 36.

"When the Wine has been consecrated and the inclination made, the Chalice is raised in a straight line, in order that it may be seen and adored by the people; but the foot must not be lifted higher than the eyes of the Celebrant."—*Ibid.*, p. 41.

"When the priest is to bless any person or any thing he turns the little finger of the right hand towards the object which he is to bless."—*Ibid.*, p. 43.

---

* In the Preface of this disloyal book, occurs the following significant passage:—" The original of this book is *Low Mass* (London : Burns and Oates), which is an English translation of the fourth book of Cesari's *Ceremonie della Messa*. . . . The thanks of the Editors are offered to the courteous translator and editor of the English edition, a clergyman of the Society of Jesus, who kindly gave them leave to adapt the book to the use of the English Church " (p. vi.).

"The breast is struck with the right hand ten times.—During the *Confiteor*, at the words 'my fault,' the breast is struck with the fingers of the right hand united and slightly curved."—*Ibid.*, p. 46.

"If, on his way to the Altar, he [the priest] passes the place where the Blessed Sacrament is reserved, or where a relic of the Holy Cross is exposed, he genuflects on one knee."—*Ibid.*, p. 60.

"The priest then says the *Confiteor*. . . . 'I confess to God, to Blessed Mary, to all Saints, and to you; that I have sinned exceedingly in thought, word, and deed, by my fault. I beseech holy Mary, all Saints of God, and you, to pray for me."—*Ibid.*, p. 64.

"He [the priest] must bow his head to the Cross when passing the middle of the Altar."—*Ibid.*, p. 78.

"On saying [at the Creed] 'in one God,' the priest joins his hands and bows his head to the Cross. . . . At 'Jesus Christ' he bows his head to the Cross. . . . At 'together is worshipped' he bows his head to the Cross."—*Ibid.*, p. 82.

"He [the priest] raises his eyes to God and immediately lowers them, saying meanwhile secretly:—'Receive, O Holy Trinity, this oblation which I, a miserable and unworthy sinner, offer in honour of Thee and of Blessed Mary and of all Thy Saints for my sins and offences; for the salvation of the living and the repose of all the faithful departed. In the name of the Father and of the Son, and of the Holy Ghost. Amen.'"—*Ibid.*, p. 86.

"The priest holds the newly consecrated Host over the Altar in his thumbs and forefingers, the other fingers being held together and extended: he raises his body, withdrawing his elbows from the Altar, but leaving on it his hands as far as the wrists, and at once inclines and adores the Host. Then raising himself, he elevates the Host as far as he conveniently can, that It may be seen and adored by the people."—*Ibid.*, p. 103.

"After the Consecration he replaces the Chalice upon the Corporal, and inclining reverently, adores the Sacred Blood."—*Ibid.*, p. 106.

"Having signed himself, he brings the Chalice to his mouth, holding the Paten under it, and raising it to about the level of his chin. Then, standing upright, he reverently receives the Precious Blood."—*Ibid.*, p. 121.

"He [the priest] makes a profound Reverence to the principal Image in the Sacristy."—*Ibid.*, p. 132.

"If any Particle [of the Consecrated Wine] fall on any of the Altar Linen, or on the ground, the priest is to place a clean cloth on the spot, choosing a more convenient time for doing what is requisite. He must afterwards wash the linen or the ground, scraping it somewhat on the place where the Particle fell: the water and whatever may have been scraped off are to be thrown into the Sacrarium."—*Ibid.*, p. 177.

"Palls having the upper side of silk, are prohibited by the Sacred Congregation of Rites."—*Ibid.*, p. 187.

"When once employed in the Sacrifice of the Mass, it [the "Purificator"] should not be used for other purposes, nor be handled by Laics (not having the required permission), until after having been washed by a Clerk in Holy Orders."—*Ibid.*, p. 187.

"The Sacred Vessels are the Chalice, Paten, Ciborium, and Pyx, none of which may be handled by those not in Holy Orders, unless with special permission."—*Ibid.*, p. 189.

"By a decree of the Council of Bishops (October 25th, 1575), the exterior of the Tabernacle is to be gilt, and the interior lined throughout with white silk. . . . The Tabernacle is exclusively reserved for the preservation of the most Holy Sacrament. . . . The Sacred Congregation of Rites [the Pope's own Congregation at Rome] forbids Relics of the Passion, or of the Saints, or the Holy Oils, to be placed within the Tabernacle."—*Ibid.*, p. 195.

"According to the Constitution of Benedict XIV., July 16th, 1746, the Cross is to be placed between the Candlesticks."—*Ibid.*, p. 196.

"Statuettes of the Saints, in gold or silver, are, in Rome, often placed upon the Altars during the great festivals."—*Ibid.*, p. 198.

SOME CAUTIONS FOR MASS PRIESTS.

"The seventh Cautel [Caution] is: that before Mass the priest do not wash his mouth or teeth, but only his lips from without with his mouth closed as he has need, lest perchance he should intermingle the taste of water with his saliva. After Mass also he should beware of expectorations as much as possible, until he shall have eaten and drunken, lest by chance anything shall have remained between his teeth or in his *fauces*; which by expectorating he might eject."—The *Directorium Anglicanum*, by the Rev. F. G. Lee, p. 110. Fourth edition.

"The question arises, if after having communicated of the Body he [the priest] shall have the water already in his mouth, and shall then for the first time perceive that it is water—whether he ought to swallow it or to eject it. . . . It is, however, safer to swallow than to eject it; and for this reason, that no particle of the Body [of Christ] may be ejected with the water."—*Ibid.*, p. 113.

"If a fly or spider or any such thing should fall into the Chalice before consecration, or even if he [the priest] shall apprehend that poison hath been put in, the wine which is in the chalice ought to be poured out, and the chalice ought to be washed, and other wine and water put therein to be consecrated. But, if any of these contingencies befall after the consecration, the fly or spider or such-like thing should be warily taken, oftentimes diligently washed between the fingers, and should then be burnt, and the ablution together with the burnt ashes must be put in the piscina. But the poison ought, by no means, to be taken, but such Blood, with which poison has been mingled, should be reserved in a comely vessel, together with the relics."—*Ibid.*, pp. 113, 114.

"If the Eucharist hath fallen to the ground, the place where it lay must be scraped, and fire kindled thereon, and the ashes reserved beside the Altar. Also, if by negligence any of the Blood be spilled, upon a table fixed to the floor, the priest must take up the drop with his tongue, and the place of the table must be scraped, and the shavings burnt with fire, and the ashes reserved with the relics beside the altar, and he to whom this has befallen must do penance forty days."—*Ibid.*, pp. 115, 116.

"If anyone by any accident of the throat vomit up the Eucharist, the vomit ought to be burned, and the ashes ought to be reserved near the altar. And if it shall be a cleric, monk, or presbyter, or deacon, he must do penance for forty days."—*Ibid.*, p. 116.

PURGATORY.

"The preacher then enlarged upon the thought of the penal aspect of Death, and drew a distinction between the temporal and the eternal punishment of sin, pointing out that, while to venial sin there is a temporal punishment annexed, mortal sin involves both an eternal and a temporal punishment: and next proceeded to insist that upon this doctrine is really based the solemnities of the dead, in which that congregation were then engaged. The Church had not given us them to gratify our feelings. They were assembled there to do a great act of charity towards the dead, to fulfil a great duty towards them and not merely for the sake of keeping their memory green, as the world does. We had much more to do than that: we had an intercession to make for the dead, and that was founded upon this distinction which he had tried to draw between the temporal and eternal punishment for sin. For while God remitted the eternal punishment for repented sin, He did not necessarily remit the temporal punishment, part of which is the penalty of death. For the vast majority of Christians the temporal punishment must be paid in the world to come, and the souls in Paradise, because they had not taken up their cross here, and not been mindful of the example of our Lord, are offering the homage of their spiritual sufferings in the realms of Purgatory, and were helped by our prayers and Eucharists, offered in their behalf."—*Sermon by the Rev. E. G. Wood, Vicar of St. Clement's, Cambridge*, preached at the Solemn Requiem of the Confraternity of the Blessed Sacrament, November 10th, 1890, and reported in the *Church Times*, November 14th, 1890, p. 1117.

"From the power of evil spirits, good Lord, deliver them [the faithful dead]. From the gnawing worm of conscience, good Lord, deliver them. From cruel flames, good Lord, deliver them. From intolerable cold, good Lord, deliver them."—The *Priest's Prayer Book*, p. 188. Fourth edition.

"From the shades of death, where they sit desiring the light of Thy countenance, good Lord, deliver them ['the faithful departed ']." "From the pains, which are the just penalty of their sins, good Lord, deliver them ['the faithful departed ']."—*Manual of the Guild of all Souls*, p. 20. Fourth edition. London, 1880.

"Were it not for the prevailing looseness and inaccuracy of thought and expression upon theological questions, which is one of the characteristics of the present age, it would be a matter for surprise that the extreme moderation of the Roman Church upon the doctrine of Purgatory should be so little known and recognized."—*St. Catherine of Genoa on Purgatory*, with Introductory Essay by a Priest Associate of the Guild of All Souls, p. 11. London, 1878.

"How great a thing is Purgatory! For myself, I can neither say nor conceive anything that approaches to it. I have a glimpse only, that those pains, being as sensible as the pains of hell, the soul, nevertheless, which has in it the least stain, or the least imperfection receives them as a particular witness of God's goodness to her."—*Ibid.*, p. 40.

"At the death of any Member a special Funeral Mass will be said for the repose of his soul, when all members are, if possible, to attend."—*Manual of the Perseverance*, St. Alban's, Holborn, p. 10.

"Q. Is there a Purgatory of any sort?

"A. Purgatory means a condition or state of purgation. All who are perfected can only be 'made perfect through suffering,' either in this world, or that which is to come, or in both. We may, therefore, rightly speak of this process as Purgatorial, and of the sphere of its operations as Purgatory."—*A Catechism on Some Great Truths*, by the Rev. J. B. Johnson, M.A., p. 36. Second Edition. London: Masters, 1893.

> "And when the altar is decked with care,
>   The Clergy to celebrate Mass prepare.
>   They enter the Chancel-gate within,
>   As the Choir solemn Introit begin :
>   'Grant them, O Lord, Thy rest divine,
>   'And light perpetual o'er them shine'!
>
> "The Deacon the corpse hath censed ; the Priest
>   Hath sung the Collects ; and humbly prayed
>   That she who now on her bier is laid,
>   Partake maybe in the heavenly Feast.
>
> "And when Epistle and Tract are o'er,
>   Again is the smoking censer swung
>   About the body which lies before,
>   Ere is the Holy Gospel sung.
>
> "The Priest hath finished ; the Mass is said ;
>   The living in holy brotherhood,
>   In blest commune with the saintly dead,
>   Have feasted on the all-precious Food.
>   And while his cope doth the Priest resume
>   And rigid biretta, the Choir alone
>   The *Dies Iræ*, the *Day of Doom*,
>   Solemnly chanteth in mournful tone."

—*The Mysteries of Holy Church*, by the Rev. G. P. Grantham, p. 121. London: Masters.

"The Church in the Middle state is called the Suffering Church. It is Purgatory, the place where holy souls are made perfect."—*A Book for the Children of God*, p. 83. London: W. Knott, 1891.

AURICULAR CONFESSION AND PRIESTLY ABSOLUTION.

" Be assured that this is one of the gravest faults of our day in the administration of the Sacrament of Penance, that it is the road by which a number of Christians go down to hell."—Dr. Pusey's *Manual for Confessors,* p. 315.

" Telling his penitents that they must explain the motives which led to their faults, and that they must not confess carelessly, but lay bare all the sources and movements of their sins to their Confessor, as, without so doing, they could not be purified."—*Ibid.,* p. 26.

" It is a sad sight to see Confessors giving their whole morning to young women-devotees, while they dismiss men and married women . . . with ' I am busy, go to some one else.' "—*Ibid.,* p. 108.

" Be sure you [Confessor] impress upon those who have hidden their sins [from the priest in Confession] the enormity of the crime they have committed in trampling under foot their Saviour's blood."—*Ibid.,* p. 128.

" Those [scrupulous persons] who do not live under a Rule must voluntarily submit themselves to a learned and wise Confessor, obeying him as God Himself, laying all their concerns freely and simply before him, and never coming to any determination without his advice. Such an one, S. Philip said, need not fear being called to account by God."—*Ibid.,* p. 180.

" No Confessor should ever give the slightest suspicion that he is alluding to what he has heard in the tribunal, but he should remember the Canonical warning: ' What I know through Confession, I know less than what I do not know.' Pope Eugenius says that whatever a Confessor knows in this way, he knows it ' ut Deus '; while out of Confession he is only speaking ' ut homo': so that, 'as man,' he can say that he does not know that which he has learned as God's representative. I go further still: As man, he may swear with a clear conscience that he knows not, what he knows only as God ! ! ! "—*Ibid.,* p. 402.

" That Confession is ordinarily—*i.e.,* where it may be had, and where the soul is capable of grasping the fact that it is so—necessary in case of mortal, *i.e.,* conscious, wilful, deliberate sin, which destroys the grace of Baptism and the union of the soul with God; and that it is not necessary in any other case."—*The Rev. A. H. Mackonochie in the Priest in Absolution and the Society of the Holy Cross: A Correspondence,* p. 23.

"Since it [the *Priest in Absolution*] has been so prominently before the public, I have been trying to make acquaintance with it, and find that its principles are those which govern, I believe, all Confessors among ourselves."—*Ibid.*, p. 16.

"Jesus the sinless One bore all their sins this day [Good Friday]; even Judas went to the priests this day, and said, 'I have sinned.'"— *Mission Tract: Good Friday*, p. 4. London: Church Printing Co.

> "Yes, I am going to God's priest,
>   To tell him all my sin,
> And from this very hour I'll strive
>   A new life to begin.
>
> "When I confess with contrite heart
>   My sins unto the priest,
> I do believe from all their guilt
>   That moment I'm released.
>
> "I go then with a humble heart,
>   To have my sins forgiven!
> And angels, while I kneel, will sing
>   A hymn of joy in heaven."

—*Manual of the Children of the Church*, p. 40. Third edition. London: Church Sunday-school Union, which is a Branch of the Kilburn Sisterhood.

"If you are tempted to hide a sin in Confession, say, 'O God, help me to tell my sins, because the devil is tempting me not to tell them.'"—*Ibid.*, p. 41.

"The labourer is worthy of his hire, and those who minister to us in spiritual things should reap the benefit of our carnal things, *i.e.*, our worldly substance, our *money*. As there is no fee for hearing Confessions, gratitude requires that we should at least contribute either to the Offertory or to the Alms-box whenever we make use of the Sacrament of Penance; especially we should make a point of this when we Confess at a Church which is not our own Parish Church." —*How to Make a Good Confession*, p. 14. Seventh thousand. London: W. Knott.

"Nor should you [in Confession] make any mention of feelings of any kind, unless they are wilfully indulged feelings of hatred or lust."—*Ibid.*, p. 9.

"I must again repeat that Confession and Absolution form God's regular channel for conveying His forgiveness, and that if we will net take pardon in His way, we are not likely to get it in our own."— *Why Don't You Go to Confession?* p. 7. Thirteenth thousand. London: C. J. Palmer.

Ask pardon for your impious defiance of His love. Turn and throw yourself at His feet, like the Prodigal Son. He waits for you in the Confessional, hidden in His priest."—*Brief Answers to Objections Brought Against Confession*, p. 40. London: E. Longhurst.

" Confession is the toilet of the conscience. The priest washes and cleanses the soul, soiled with sin; he restores it to health, pure and white. Those children who will not be attended to by their mothers, remain all day dirty and disgusting. The souls who will *purposely* neglect the cleansing of Confession are unclean souls, vile and base souls."—*Ibid.*, p. 29.

"God alone is the giver of all spiritual life and grace and favour, and yet we are not bid to go *direct to God* for these gifts (for that right we forfeited at the fall); but we are to go to the Church which stands between us and God in its appointed sphere."—The *Mediation of the Church*, by the Rev. Edward Stuart, M.A., p. 9. Second edition. London: C. J. Palmer.

" When a penitent, perfectly contrite, cannot Confess, either through physical inability, or impossibility of obtaining a Confessor, mortal sin is remitted by the mercy of God, anticipatorily. . . . Imperfect contrition or attrition is sorrow arising from mingled or lower motives, and requires the application of the Sacrament. . . . Mortal sin cannot ordinarily be forgiven, without absolution. But the priest cannot loose what he has no knowledge of. Therefore, mortal sin must be enumerated. Confession must be entire, true, simple. Entire : No mortal sin consciously omitted. Mention modifying circumstances. . . . Name the number or the duration of each kind of sin— sins of thought as well as deed. Nothing hidden which may show the state of the soul. Nothing hidden through proud shame."— *Catechetical Notes*, by the Rev. Dr. Neale, of East Grinstead, pp. 138, 139.

" Cases of Sacrilege: 1. A false confession consciously made: it invalidates every succeeding confession until this sin be acknowledged." —*Ibid*, p. 140.

" Our Church puts no kind of restriction either upon the disclosures of the penitent, or the inquiries of the Confessor; and this throws open a door to all that minuteness of detail which is sometimes thought to constitute the especial evil of the Roman Confessional."—*British Critic.* Volume for 1843, p. 326.

"We know that he [the Confessor] is bound by every tie, moral, divine, and ecclesiastical, to keep our secrets. For these and other reasons, we ought to put away shame, and readily confess all our sins to him without reserve."—The *Destruction of Sin*, by the Rev. J. C. Chambers, Editor of the *Priest in Absolution*, p. 15.

"The power of the remission of sins is ordained in the hands of the priesthood, and no other channel whatsoever is appointed for our assured forgiveness."—The *Ministry of Consolation*, p. 26. Edition 1854.

"Our Church, moreover, howsoever men may mistake her meaning, does indeed enjoin the absolute completeness and unreservedness of our confession."—*Ibid.*, p. 36.

"The obedience which alone befits the human soul in spiritual relations must be free and unquestioning, preventing with a settled purpose of submission, every command which the judgment of the priest may see fit to lay upon us."—*Ibid.*, p. 76.

"There are, therefore, generally more sins to be found under this commandment [seventh] than under any other—and remember, we pray thee, that it were a false shame utterly misplaced at the tribunal of Penitence, even as of necessity, if thou wert to shrink from confessing, openly and honestly, all sins against purity and modesty."—*Ibid.*, p. 154.

"Perfect absolution is only promised to those who make special confession of their sins. I mean a confession of all the sins on their conscience, confessed to Almighty God in the hearing of His priest, mentioning every sin."—*Simple Lessons*, edited by the Rev. T. T. Carter, Part III., p. 106. Edition 1876.

"Those who have never heard of Confession to God through his priest, or having heard of it, are really and honestly unable to believe that it is of any use, we are bound charitably to hope and pray that it [Confession to God] may be enough. Those who have died without confessing, and there are millions such, must be left to the 'uncovenanted mercies of God.' . . But, just as God has appointed

Holy Baptism for our regeneration, and the forgiveness (in the case of adults) of all sins committed up to that time; just as He has ordained the Holy Communion for 'the strengthening and refreshing of our souls, by the Body and Blood of Christ'; so has He most mercifully appointed a way—one way and only one—for the certain forgiveness of sins committed after Baptism, by applying to our souls, for this special purpose, 'the Precious Blood of Christ,' once shed for us upon the Cross of suffering. That way, and I repeat that there is no other, is Sacramental Confession. Confession to a Priest."—*Plain Speaking on Confession*, p. 6. London, 1869.

"Thy garments, spotless, white and pure,
   From the baptismal sea,
 Need daily cleansing to restore
   The first 'Absolvo Te.'

"Take not a conscience to thy God
   Stained with impurity;
 The fountain flows for thee to wash,
   Its name 'Absolvo Te.'

"There is no other cleansing now,
   Our Saviour left the Key
 Which opens rivers of His Blood,
   In the 'Absolvo Te.'"

—*Stories Told to the Choir*, No. VIII., "Sprinkled with Blood," p. 12. London: Mowbray.

"And then my eyes were opened, and there knelt in the distance little Gerald Deane; and I thought I saw, yet very indistinctly, one self-denying and wearied priest sitting near Gerald's side. And above them I saw the Form of One Crucified, from whose hands, which were raised in benediction fell, drop by drop, the Precious Blood. And as each drop fell on the burden, it dissolved away, and the priest heard the whisper, 'Loose him, and let him go,' and then I heard one priest's voice, in solemn, measured tones, 'By His Authority committed unto me, I absolve thee;' and as Gerald returned and knelt by Philip's side I knew he was at peace, that the heavy burden of sin was laid at the foot of the Cross, that he was marked with the Precious Blood which had fallen so lovingly on his soul. And the priest was ever at his duty, the delegate of the Invisible Presence, and the Form was ever by his side, and ever and ever dropped from the

Hands and Feet and Side the 'Blood which cleanseth from all Sin.'"
—*Ibid.*, pp. 11, 12.

"The words on the lips of a Christian priest in such days are of this nature: 'You are ill of a disease that almost must, to a certainty, kill you eventually. There is no known remedy but this which we hold in our power. This cannot fail, if properly applied. I do not say that your case is hopeless; I do not say that you *cannot* be otherwise healed; but, honestly, I know no other way of curing you! Will you try it?' As has been well and truly said by one not long ago gone to his rest: The man who confesses to God may be forgiven; he who confesses to a priest must be forgiven."—*Six Plain Sermons*, by Richard Wilkins, Priest, pp. 28, 29. London: E. Longhurst.

INVOCATION OF SAINTS.

"Holy Michael, Archangel, defend us in conflict: that we perish not in the dreadful day of Judgment."—The *Grail*, by Rev. G. A. Jones, Vicar of St. Mary's, Cardiff, p. 21.

> "Star of Ocean fairest
> Mother, God who barest,
> Virgin thou immortal,
> Heaven's blissful portal.
>
> "Loose the bonds of terror,
> Lighten blinded error,
> All our ills repressing,
> Pray for every blessing.
>
> "Virgin, all excelling,
> Gentle past our telling,
> Pardoned sinners render,
> Gentle, chaste, and tender."
>
> *Day Office of the Church*, p. xxiii.
>
> "Mother of the King Eternal,
> Virgin, loved by choirs supernal,
> Save us from our foes infernal,
> With thy gentle prayers above."
>
> *Union Review* for 1863, p. 503.

" Dear Spouse of sweet Mary, we ask for thine aid,
Thy patronage crave, and thy prayers;
Saint Joseph, blest guardian of Jesus our Lord,
Oh! soothe all our griefs and our cares."

Oratory Worship, p. 90.

" Next to Mary, what thy power,
Tutor of the God-man!
Oh! shield us in temptation's hour;
Save us from sin's hateful ban.

" Alleluia! glory, Joseph!
Glory, dearest Saint, to thee!
Alleluia! glory, Joseph!
Thankful praise we give to thee."

Ibid., p. 93.

"*When the soul is about to depart from the body, then more than ever ought they who are by to pray earnestly upon their knees around the sick man's bed; and if the dying man be unable to speak, the name of Jesus should be constantly invoked, and such words as the following again and again repeated in his ear:*—

" Into Thy hands, O Lord, I commend my spirit. O Lord Jesus Christ, receive my spirit.

" Holy Mary, pray for me.

" Holy Mary, mother of grace, mother of mercy, do thou defend me from the enemy, and receive me at the hour of death."—The *Golden Gate*, Part III., p. 127, by Rev. S. Baring-Gould, Rector of Lew Trenchard.

" Some very extravagant expressions of St. Alphonsus Liguori, respecting the blessed Virgin Mary, can be easily explained, and placed in a light that the most Protestant Christian must receive if he believes what our Lord says of the power of prayer, *e.g.*, such expressions as 'O Mary save me; When Jesus will have no mercy, I turn to thee; give me thy help; guide me; save me, for in thee do I put my trust.' "—*Popery*, a sermon by " Father Ignatius," p. 3.

" O ye holy Virgins of God, pray for us, that we may obtain pardon of our sins through your prayers."—*Lesser Hours of the Sarum Breviary*, p. 120. London, 1889.

" Remember, O most loving Virgin Mary, that never was it known that any who fled to thy protection, implored thy help, and sought thy intercession, was left unaided. Encouraged with this assurance, I fly unto thee, O Virgin of Virgins, my Mother, to thee I come, before thee I stand sinful and sorrowful. O Mother of the Incarnate Word, despise not my petitions, but mercifully vouchsafe to hear them."—*Catholic Prayers for Church of England People*, by the Rev. A. H. Staunton, Curate of St. Alban's, Holborn, p. 136. Second edition. London: W. Knott, 1893.

"O Thomas [a Becket] Martyr most constant, and invincible Confessor, splendour of the priesthood, the glory of France, the glory of England! Reign, O blessed father, over the Church for which thou didst shed thy blood, and pour forth thy prayers to God for the salvation of us all."—*Devotions in Honour of St. Thomas of Canterbury*, by the Rev. H. G. Worth, late Curate of St. John the Divine, Kennington, p. 138. Second edition. London: W. Knott, 1895.

THE VIRTUES OF HOLY SALT, HOLY WATER, AND HOLY OIL!

"*The Priest shall bless the Salt on this wise.*

"We humbly implore Thee, Almighty and Everlasting God, that of Thy bountiful goodness thou wouldst be pleased to bl✠ess and sanc✠tify this creature of Salt, which Thou hast created for the service of men, that it may profit for the health both of soul and body of them that take it, and that whatsoever is touched or sprinkled therewith may be freed from all uncleanness, and from all attacks of spiritual wickedness; through Jesus Christ our Lord. Amen."—The *Priest's Prayer Book*, p. 221. Seventh edition.

"*He shall then bless the Water on this wise.*

"O God, Who in ordaining divers mysteries for the salvation of mankind, hast been pleased to employ the element of Water in the chiefest of Thy Sacraments: give ear to our prayers, and pour upon this water the might of Thy bless✠ing, that as it serves Thee in those holy mysteries, so by Thy divine grace it may here avail for the casting out of devils, and the driving away of diseases; that whatsoever in the houses or places of the faithful is sprinkled therewith, may be freed from all uncleanness, and delivered from hurt."—*Ibid.*

"The [dead] body is then decently laid out, and a light placed before it. A small Crucifix is put in the hands of the deceased, upon his breast, or the hands are themselves placed crosswise, while the body is sprinkled with Holy Water."—The *Golden Gate*, Part III., p. 128.

"*The Exorcism of the Salt.*

"I exorcise thee, creature of salt, by the living God, ✠ by the true God, ✠ by the holy God, ✠ by the God Who, by the Prophet Eliseus, commanded thee ✠ to be cast into the water that the barrenness of the water might be healed, that thou mightest be salt exorcised for the spiritual health of believers, and be to all who take thee health of soul and body."—The *Directorium Anglicanum*. Edited by the Rev. F. G. Lee, Vicar of All Saints', Lambeth, p. 306. Fourth edition.

"*Exorcism of the Water.*

"I exorcise thee, creature of water, in the name of God the Father Almighty, and in the name of Jesus Christ His Son our Lord, and in the virtue of the Holy Ghost, to become water exorcised to chase away all power of the enemy, and to be able to uproot and overthrow the enemy himself and his apostate angels; by the virtue of the same Lord Jesus Christ."—*Ibid.*, p. 307.

"The priest then sprinkles the Collars, Crosses, and Candles, with Holy Water, and Incenses them. Those who are to be admitted [into the Guild] then come up to the Altar."—*Guild of St. John the Evangelist, St. Alban's, Holborn, London, Form of Reception*, p. 18. Privately printed.

"In the death chamber let a small table be placed at the foot of the bed to serve as a stand for a Cross and two Candles, these latter to be kept burning night and day till the hour of interment arrives, as a sign of the light into which the departed soul has passed."—The *Parish Tracts*, by Rev. J. Harry Buchanan. First Series. No. IV., "The Dying and the Dead."

"*The Exorcism [of Oil].*

"I adjure thee, O creature of Oil, by God the Father ✠ Almighty, Who hath made heaven and earth, the sea and all that therein is. Let all the power of the adversary, all the host of the devil, and all haunting and vain imaginations of Satan be cast out, and flee away from this creature of Oil, that it may be to all them that shall use the same health of mind and body in the Name of God the Father ✠ Almighty, and of Jesus ✠ Christ His Son our Lord, and of the Holy Ghost the Comforter, and for the love of the same Jesus

Christ our Lord, Who is ready to judge both the quick and the dead, and the world by fire. R. Amen."—*Day Office of the Church*, p. lxix.

MONASTIC INSTITUTIONS.

"We long to hear the Divine Office ever going up to God from thousands of Religious Houses, and to see Fountains and Tintern and Kirkstall, and other noble foundations blossoming up again all over the land."—*St. John the Baptist.* A Sermon by the Rev. H. D. Nihill, Vicar of St. Michael's, Shoreditch, p. 14.

"It is a pious custom of devout Christians on seeing a Monk, to kneel and kiss the hem of the Sacred Habit; if done from love to Jesus, and reverence to the Habit of the Consecrated Life, a great blessing will be received."—*Little Manual of Devotions*, by Rev. J. L. Lyne, *alias* " Father Ignatius," p. 6.

" Parents such as these [*i.e.*, those parents who refuse to permit their children to become Monks or Nuns], lose all claim to such privileges as the fourth Commandment of the Decalogue gives to them; they are the enemies of God and their children's souls. Blessed are those children who hearken to God rather than to them." —*Llanthony Monastery Tracts*, No. I.: "Why are you a Monk?" p. 12.

" Some of our Protestant friends tell us that Monkery, as they call it, is, not of Christian origin, but of Pagan origin. My Protestant brethren, I quite agree with you that it is. You are perfectly correct, Monasticism *is* of Pagan origin. The best illustration of the Monastic school among the Philosophic Pagans was Plato."—*An Answer to the Question, Why are you a Monk?* by Father Ignatius, p. 11.

" Brethren, the five hundred million Buddhists, the largest and most influential religion in the world, possess Monasteries to a vast extent. In Banghok, the capital of Siam, in that capital alone, there are over ten thousand monks."—*Ibid.* p. 15.

PROTESTANTISM.

" He forgets what has been humourously pointed out, that the first Protestant of all was the Devil. .... Just as the first Non-Catholic and Anti-Ritualist was Judas."—The *Congregation in Church*, p. 78. New edition. London: Mowbray.

" Heretic means a choice, and it is not always perceived that heretic and a Protestant are much the same thing."—*Ibid.*, p. 187.

" Protestants can be shown to detest Jesus Christ and His teaching, and to prefer immorality, polemics, and cant thereto."—*Brainless, Broadcast Benevolence*, p. 17. Brighton: H. and C. Treacher.

THE IMPORTANCE OF RITUAL.

"The Protestant is quite right in recognizing the simplest attempt at Ritual as the 'thin end of the wedge.' It is so. . . . It is only the child who is not terrified when the first creeping driblet of water and the few light bubbles announce the advance of the tide, and the Protestant is but a child who does not recognize the danger of the trifling symptoms which are slowly and surely contracting the space of ground upon which he stands."—*Church Review*, June 24th, 1865, p. 587.

" The Ritual question is one which, you will agree with me, is of great importance. To abolish Scriptural and Catholic Ritual, and at the same time to hope to maintain *unimpaired* the Catholic Faith, is, in my humble opinion, a great delusion. They both go together; and if one falls, both will fall. . . . With the abolition of the symbolic *ornamenta* of the Church, doctrinal loss will be the result; and the great Movement now going on will become stationary, and will gradually cease."—The *President of the English Church Union—Church Review*, April 25th, 1868, p. 402.

" Nor, again, are we merely contending for the revival among ourselves of certain ceremonies because they are practised by the rest of the Catholic Church; but we contend for our Ritual for the precise reason which is urged for its suppression—because it is the means, the importance of which becomes clearer every day, which the Church has seen fit to employ to express the truth of Christ's Sacramental Presence amongst His people."—The *President of the English Church Union—Church Review*, June 20th, 1868, p. 583.

"Now there are, of course, many Catholic practices that necessarily result from a belief in the Real Presence of our dear Lord upon the Altar. Among the minor ones are bowing and genuflecting. Bowing to the Altar at all times, not because it is so much wood or stone put together in a certain shape, covered with handsome cloths, decked with flowers and lights; not for this, were it all ten times as gorgeous. Not for this, but because the Altar is the Throne of God Incarnate, where *daily* now, thank God, in many a Church in the land He deigns to rest. . . . And genuflecting, not to the Altar, but to the '*Gift that is upon it;*' to the God-Man, Christ Jesus, when He is there."—*Six Plain Sermons*, by Richard Wilkins, Priest, p. 57. London: E. Longhurst.

DISSENT.

"Nevertheless, although not actually schism, it is schismatical to attend Dissenting Meeting Houses, or to subscribe to, or assist the sectarian objects of Dissenters in any way. The same cannot be said of Roman Catholic Churches, and their objects, because the Roman Catholics are a branch of the true Church."—The *Congregation in Church*, p. 202. New Edition. London: Mowbray.

"The Catholic Church is the home of the Holy Ghost. It is His only earthly home. He does not make His home in any Dissenting sect. Sometimes people quarrel with the Church, and break away from her, and make little sham churches of their own. We call these people Dissenters, and their sham churches sects. The Holy Ghost does not abide—does not dwell—with them. He goes and visits them perhaps, but only as a stranger."—*A Book for the Children of God*, p. 77. London: W. Knott, 1891.

"The Bible is the Book which God has given to His Church, and it belongs to the Church alone, and not to any Dissenting sect. No one but a Catholic can safely read the Bible, and no Catholic can read it safely who does not read it in the Church's way."—*Ibid.*, p. 100.

INDEX.

Abbot (Bishop Robert) on timid speaking against the Papists, 329, 339
Aberdeen (Dean of) [Very Rev. William Webster] objects to changes in Statutes of S.S.C., 141
Address to Catholics by the Society of the Holy Cross, 63
Alcuin Club, 253, 254
— its work, 253
— its Episcopal members, 253
Alison (Rev. L.), 138
Allen (Archdeacon) on Immoral Ritualistic Confessors, 117, 119
All Saints', Margaret Street, Sisterhood, Vows in, 174
— how its inmates dispose of their property, 177, 178
All Souls' Day, a Popish Festival observed by the Guild of All Souls, 230
Altar Book for Young Persons, 217
Anglican Sister of Mercy, 169
Anarchy (Ecclesiastical), viii., 348, 349
Archdeacon of Cleveland (Ven. W. H. Hutchings) hopes the S. S. C. will favour Roman Ritual, 77
— Proposes Revision of S.S.C. Statutes, 128
— Member of Committee for Revising Statutes of the S. S. C., 138
Ascot Priory, Private Burial Ground at, 192
Association for the Promotion of the Unity of Christendom, 307-323
— its birth and membership, 308, 309
— its Letter to the Inquisition, 317
— Reply of the Inquisition, 317-319
— and the Society of the Holy Cross, 327
Association of the Friends of the Church, 5
— Mysterious "Suggestions" for, 5
Auricular Confession and Priestly Absolution, What the Ritualists teach about, 399-404
Autobiography of Isaac Williams, 9, 271, 277, 278

Bagot De La Bere (Rev. J.) [formerly Edwards] defends the term "Sacrament of Penance," 142
Bagshawe (Rev. Francis Ll.) on the *Roll of Brethren* of S. S. C., 78
— Secret Letter on the *Priest in Absolution*, 100, 101
— Letter to the Bishop of London, 104
— the *Priest in Absolution* in his care, 104, 139
— Resigns the office of Master of the S. S. C., 137
— Remarkable Speech to Brethren of S. S. C., 139
Banbury Guardian, 208
Baring-Gould (Rev. Sabine) recommends Holy Water, 62
Barnet Times, Jesuitical Letter to, 235
Barrett (Rev. T. S) appeals for S. S. C. Oratory at Carlisle, 67
Bath and Wells (Bishop of) [Lord A. C. Harvey)] Speech on the *Priest in Absolution*, 116
Bathe (Rev. Anthony) on the Master of S.S.C., 127
Beckett (Rev. H. F.) on Wives, Husbands, and the Confessional, 81, 82
Benediction of the Blessed Sacrament in a Ritualistic Convent Chapel, 193, 194
— Lord Halifax on, 342
Benson (Rev. R. M.) on a Nun's Vow of Obedience, 169
Beveridge (Bishop) on the Real Presence and Eucharistic Sacrifice, 222
Bible (The) What the Ritualists teach about, 373-375
Binney (Rev. John Erskine) glories in being a Member of S. S. C., 146
Biography of Father Lockhart, 26
Birkmyre (Rev. N. Y.) on Reunion with Rome, 328
Bishop of Oxford (Dr. Bagot) writes to Newman about Littlemore Monastery, 22

INDEX.

Bishops (The) smile on and favour law breakers, ix.
— their neglect of duty, 42
— their opinion of the *Priest in Absolution*, and Society of the Holy Cross, 110-117
— on the Confessional, 111-116
— five or six wish well to S. S. C., 133
— and Ritualistic Sisters of Mercy, 194-196
Blachford (Lord)—see Rogers (Mr. F.)
Blessing the Paschal Candle, 246
Bloemfontein (Bishop of) [Dr. J. W. Hicks] presented with a set of Low Mass Vestments, 240
— a Vice-President of the Society of St. Osmund, 240
Bodington (Canon Charles) on Confession, 75
— on the circulation of the *Priest in Absolution*, 109
— Member of Committee for Revising Statutes of the S. S. C., 138
— Speech in Secret Synod of S. S. C., 142
Body (Canon George), his reasons for remaining in the S. S. C., 132
— Member of Committee for Revising Statutes of the S. S. C., 138
— on the Eucharistic Sacrifice, 219
Book of Common Prayer, not complete, 71
— Proposed additions to, 71, 72
— Revision of, on Ritualistic lines, 339-344
— What the Ritualists teach about the, 375-377
Books for the Young. No. I., Confession, 54, 56, 111, 112, 115
— termed "A wretched little book," 113
Bowden (Mr. J. W.) 4, 5, 6, 16, 17, 42, 272
Bowden's *Life of Father Faber*, 28, 30, 31, 32, 34, 35, 41, 42
Bricknell's *Judgment of the Bishops*, 7, 9, 262, 281
Brinckman's *Controversial Methods of Romanism*, 155
British Critic, 271
Bristol Branch of English Church Union sympathises with S. S. C., 137
Bristow (Canon Rhodes) on the " Sacrament of Penance," 75
— hopes " the Roman Use would still prevail," 77
— on Convocation, 78
— on the *Priest in Absolution*, 136

Bristow (Rev. Canon Rhodes) Member of Committee for Revising Statutes of the S. S. C., 138
— Speech on Revision of Statutes of S. S. C., 141
Brotherhood of the Holy Cross, 233
— the inner circle of the O. H. R., 233
— its " very existence to be kept in strict secrecy," 233
— its secret *Intercession Paper*, 233
Browne (Rev. E. G. K.) on Tractarians going secretly to Mass, 29
— *Annals of the Tractarian Movement*, 30, 89
Bruno's *Catholic Belief*, 265
Bunsen (M.) on the Work of the Tractarians, 267
Burgon (Dean), v.
— *Lives of Twelve Good Men*, 215
Butler (Dean William J.) on Husbands, Wives, and the Confessional, 91
Byron (Miss H. B.) Mother Superior of All Saints', Margaret Street, Sisterhood, 177
Cairo (Bishop of) a Vice-President of the Society of St. Osmund, 240
Cardinal Newman: a Monograph, 26, 27
Carlisle (Bishop of) [Dr. Harvey Goodwin] severely censures S. S. C., 146
Carlisle, Oratory of the Society of the Holy Cross at, 66-69
Carter (Canon T. T.) on "The Sacrament of Penance," 74
— and the *Statement* of S. S. C., 108
— revises the Proof Sheets of the *Priest in Absolution*, 109
— and the circulation of the *Priest in Absolution*, 109, 110
— Speech on the "animus" of the Bishops, 124
— Member of Committee for Revising Statutes of the S. S. C., 138
— *Vows and the Religious State*, 175
— Advice about *Intercession Paper* of C. B. S., 205
— on Eucharistic Adoration, 218
Catholic Dictionary, 366
Catholic Standard on the work of the Order of Corporate Reunion, 161
Catholic Union of Prayer, 334
Cautions for the Times, 200
Celibates of the Society of the Holy Cross, 52, 53
— their secret Oath, 53
Celibacy (Vow of) taken by a girl of eighteen for life, 180
Ceremonies of Low Mass, What the Ritualists teach about the, 393-395
Ceremonial of the Altar, 241-244

INDEX. 413

Chadwick (Rev. J. W.) Member of Committee for Revising Statutes of the S. S. C., 138
Chambers (Rev. J. C.) translates and Edits the *Priest in Absolution*, 93-95, 104, 105
Chaplin (Rev. E. M.) advocates Roman Ritual, 77
Character of Dr. Littledale as a Controversialist, 193, 194, 203
Charles Lowder, 57, 59, 60, 128
Chauntry Priests, 250
Cheltenham Chapter of the Society of the Holy Cross, 108
Chichester (Bishop of) [Dr. Durnford] severely censures the Society of the Holy Cross, 116
Chronicle of Convocation, 111-117
Church of England Working Men's Society present an address of sympathy with the Society of the Holy Cross, 121, 137
Church Review, 91, 153, 157, 208, 261, 336, 337
Church Times, 154, 158, 208, 214, 228, 231, 253, 328, 358
Church Union Gazette, 335, 345, 346, 347
Churton (Rev. E.) protests against Dr. Pusey's conduct, 282
Civilita Cattolica, 158
Clerical Celibacy, 118, 119
Clewer Sisterhood, its Rules of Poverty, Chastity, and Obedience, 174
— how its inmates dispose of their property, 175
Close (Dean) opposes Carlisle Oratory of S. S. C., 67, 68
Cobb's *Kiss of Peace*, 229
Coles (Rev. V. S. S.) on the "levelling up" policy of the English Church Union, 338
"Committee of Clergy," The, 49
Confession, Lord Salisbury on habitual, 70
— Secret discussion on, 74, 75
— Dr. Pusey on the Seal of, 82
Confessions, The secret stealthy way Tractarians heard, 89
— How Archdeacon Manning heard, 90, 91, 92
— How Dr. Pusey heard Ritualistic Sisters', 187
Confessional, Jurisdiction in the, 76
— The Secrecy of the Ritualistic, 80-92
— Indelicate Questions to a Married Woman in the, 81
— Wives, Husbands, and the, 81, 82, 91
— Ritualistic Sisters and the, 83

Confessional, The age Children should be brought to the, 83
— The priest is "in the Confessional a Fox," 92
— The Bishops on the, 111-116
— Ritualistic Priests ruin Women through the, 117
— often the road "down to hell," 121
— and the property of Ritualistic Sisters of Mercy, 172
Confessor, Extraordinary Letter to a Young Lady from a, 70-72
Confessors, Petition for Licensed, 70-72
— Immoral and Wicked, 117-121
— How Ritualistic Sisters should treat their, 167
Confraternity of the Blessed Sacrament, 202-226
— its birth, 204, 210
— its secret *Intercession Paper*, 204, 205
— its medals may be buried with members, 205
— exposed by the *Rock* and *Western Daily Mercury*, 206, 207
— keeps as far as possible out of public notice, 207
— its secret doings in America, 208
— its secret *Roll of Priests-Associate*, 209, 210
— the "daughter" of the Society of the Holy Cross, 210
— its *Manual*, 211
— its objects, 211
— advocates Masses and Prayers for the Dead, 211, 213
— and Fasting Communion, 211, 215, 216
— prays for Corporate Reunion with Rome and the East, 212
— its secret Annual Conference, 213
— and Purgatory, 214
— its *Altar Book for Young Persons*, 217
— prays for the Restoration of the Reserved Sacrament, 217
— agrees with Rome on Eucharistic Adoration, 218
— prays for Restoration of Extreme Unction, 218
— observes Corpus Christi Day, 218
— advocates Sacramental Confession, 218
— advocates the Real Presence and Eucharistic Sacrifice, 219
— advocates the Mass, 222, 223
— teaches Transubstantiation, 223-225
— its Episcopal Members, 225
— Bishop Wilberforce on its Popish character, 225
Convent of S. Mary and S. Scholastica, West Malling, 184

Convents, Shocking Cruelty in Ritualistic, 40, 189
— Private Burial Grounds in, 191, 192
Convocation, Society of the Holy Cross debate on, 78
Convocation (Canterbury House of) Discussion on the *Priest in Absolution* and the Society of the Holy Cross, in, 110-117
— Resolution of Upper House, censuring both Society and book, 113, 117
Cookesley (Rev. W. G.), 168
Corea (Bishop of) [Dr. C. J. Corfe] on the Revision of Statutes of S. S. C., 141
— a Member of the Confraternity of the Blessed Sacrament, 225
Council of Trent, 263, 269, 330
Cross, Adoration of, at St. Cuthbert's, Philbeach Gardens, 245
Crouch (Rev. William), 64
— opposes giving up the *Priest in Absolution*, 109
Cusack (Miss) her experience in Dr. Pusey's Sisterhoods, 186, 187
Dalgairns (Mr. J. D.), 280
D'Aubigne's *History of the Reformation*, 70
Davidson (Rev. J. P. F.) President of the Guild of All Souls, 231
Dawes (Rev. N.) [now Bishop of Rockhampton] becomes a Member of the Society of the Holy Cross, 76
Denison (Archdeacon) joins the Society of the Holy Cross, 127, 139
— Laughs at Synodical condemnation of S. S. C., 134
— opposes the disbanding of S. S. C., 134
— objects to changes in Statutes of S. S. C., 141
Denison (Rev. H. P.) on compulsory Confession, 75
— Letter about the C. B. S. *Roll of Priests-Associate*, 210
Desanctis (Rev. Dr.) on Jesuits disguised as Puseyites, 32
— *Popery and Jesuitism*, 33, 34
Devonport Manual, a secret book of Dr. Pusey's Sisters, 197, 198
" Disciplina Arcani," 1, 2, 3
" Discipline " (The) at Elton, 35
— Dr. Pusey sends for a, 36
— as used by Ritualists described, 38
— Cruelties of, 38
— prescribed for Ritualistic Sisters of Mercy, 39, 185
— used most cruelly on a Ritualistic Nun, 40

Dissent, What the Ritualists teach about, 410
Dunn (Rev. James) on Confession to Young Priests, 75
" Economical " mode of speaking and writing, 2
" Economy " and St. George's Mission, 59
Edinburgh Chapter of the Society of the Holy Cross, 108
Enclosed Nuns in Ritualistic Convents, 183
— in Dr. Pusey's Sisterhood, 183, 184
— at Feltham, 184
— at West Malling, 184
— at Llanthony, 184
— at Slapton, 184
English Churchman, 97, 155, 156, 236, 240, 252, 262, 296
English Church Union (Bristol and Penrith Branches of) sympathises with S. S. C., 137
— its Council do not "explain all their tactics," 329
— offers prayers for the Reunion of Christendom, 330
— approves of Dr. Pusey's *Eirenicon*, 331, 332
— its first President secedes to Rome, 335
— its " levelling up " policy, 338
— Address to Lambeth Conference in favour of Reunion of Christendom, 344
— Speech before the Exeter Branch of, 350
Equivocation, 16
Essays on Reunion, 261, 313-316
Eucharistic Adoration, 218
Eucharistic Sacrifice, 219, 221, 222
Evangelical Party (The) described by Mr. Maskell, 44
Evening Communion, 213, 214
Extreme Unction, 218
— Superstitious service of, 218
Eyton (Canon Robert) Speech on the Society of the Holy Cross, 124
— on the circulation of the *Priest in Absolution*, 144
Faber (Rev. Frederick William) visits the Continent, 28
— not scandalised by Relic Worship, 30
— declares Protestantism a diabolical heresy, 30
— kisses the Pope's foot, 31
— prays at the Shrine of Aloysius the Jesuit, 31
— thinks Heaven " is like Rome," 31
— returns with Rosaries blessed by the Pope, 32

INDEX. 415

Faber (Rev. Frederick William) his work at Elton, 34
— his Secret Society at Elton, 35
— discovers he is " living a dishonest life," 41
— his *Life of St. Wilfrid*, 42
— received into the Church of Rome, 42
Fasting Communion, 211, 215
— Bishop S. Wilberforce on, 215
"Father George" of the O. H. R., his Jesuitical conduct in a Protestant parish, 238
Fathers (The) and the Rule of Faith, 268
Fathers of Charity, 281, 282
Feltham Ritualistic Nuns, 184
Five Years in a Protestant Sisterhood, 85
Fleming (Mr. Robert) how he discovered the *Priest in Absolution*, 97
Foote (Rev. John Andrewes) and the *Priest in Absolution*, 95
— Member of Committee for Revising Statutes of S. S. C., 138
Frere (Rev. William John) Speech on the *Priest in Absolution*, 144
From Oxford to Rome, 89
Froude (Rev. Hurrell) proselytises in an "underhand way," 6
— *Remains*, 6, 46, 267
Gilmartin's *Manual of Church History*, 368
Gladstone (Mr.) on the Romeward Movement, 286, 287, 290
— *Gleanings of Past Years*, 286, 287, 290
— on Archdeacon Manning's want of Straightforwardness, 303
— *Rome and the Newest Fashions in Religion*, 364, 365
Godwin (Rev. Robert Herbert) objects to changes in Statutes of the S. S. C., 141
Goldie (Rev. C. D.) on the action of S. S. C., 108, 132
— Member of Committee for Revising Statutes of S. S. C., 138
— says the *Priest in Absolution* is "needed," 144
Goodman (Miss Margaret) on the serious evils in Ritualistic Sisterhoods, 170, 171
— *Sisterhoods in the Church of England*, 167, 171, 184, 188-191
— Her sad story of a dying Sister of Mercy, 176
Gore (Rev. Canon Charles) on the Real Presence and the Consecrated Elements, 219
Grahamstown (Bishop of) [in 1877], expresses his "goodwill" to the S. S. C., 137

Grant (Mr. William) Letter on the Order of Corporate Reunion, 158
Green-Armytage (Rev. N.) on the Church of Rome, 77
Guild of St. Alban's, London and Wolverhampton Provinces of, sympathise with the S. S. C., 137
Guild of All Souls, 227-232
— its Objects, 227
— its secret *Intercession Paper*, 228
— its *Office for the Dead According to the Roman and Sarum Uses*, 228
— its semi-secrecy, 228
— teaches Transubstantiation, 229
— its *Manual*, 229, 230
— observes "All Souls' Day," 230
— its President promoted by Bishop Temple, 231
Guild of the Sacred Heart of Jesus, 257
Guilds, their work, 259
Gurney (Rev. Archer), his courageous attack on Dr. Pusey, 332, 333
Halifax (Lord) on the use of the Ten Commandments, 341
— on Benediction of the Blessed Sacrament, 342
— most earnestly desire visible communion with Rome, 346
— prefers Leo XIII. to the Judicial Committee of the Privy Council, 347
— his Speech at Bristol, 352, 353
— on Papal Infallibility, 352, 353
— terms Luther "a needless and noxious Rebel," 354
Hammond (Rev. Canon C. E.), 77
Heylin's *Life of Laud*, 329
Hislop's *Two Babylons*, 165
Hoare (Rev. R. Whitehead), 137
Hodgson (Rev. James) Letter on the C. B. S., 208
Holy Water used by Ritualists, 62, 247
— dead bodies to be sprinkled with, 62
— its supposed virtues, 63
Homily Concerning Prayer, 213
Homily on Repentance, 218
Homily on Good Works, 283
Homily on Peril of Idolatry, 356
Honorarium for a Mass, 250, 251
Hook (Rev. Dr.) anxious to establish a Sisterhood at Leeds, 163
— his remarkable letter to Dr. Pusey on Sisters of Charity, 164
— on Pusey's eulogy of the Jesuits, 289
— on Secession to Rome, 291
— on the Judicial Committee of Privy Council, 347
Hooker's *Works*, 220
Hope-Scott (Mr. James R.), 14, 25
— Visits the Jesuits at Rome, 275

INDEX.

Hornby (Bishop) a member of the Confraternity of the Blessed Sacrament, 225
Hoskins (Rev. Edgar) and the *Priest in Absolution*, 122
— favours revision of the Statutes of S. S. C., 128
— opposes disbanding S. S. C., 129
— Member of Committee for Revising Statutes of S. S. C., 138
Hughes (Miss Marian) takes a Vow of Celibacy, 165
— visits Roman Catholic Convents on the Continent, 165, 166
Hutchings (Rev. W. H.)—see Archdeacon of Cleveland
Hymns, Ancient and Modern, 245
Immaculate Conception of the Virgin, 351
Incense, Driving the Devil out of, 246
Inquisition (The) Letter to, from the A. P. U. C., 317
— Reply of the, 317-319
— Memorial to, from English clergy, 319-322
Instructions for Retreats, 58
Intercession Paper of the Confraternity of the Blessed Sacrament, 204, 205, 206, 213, 214, 215, 217, 218
— ordered to be destroyed when used, 205
— exposed in the *Rock*
— exposed in the *Western Daily Mercury*, 206
— how the first copy was found by a Protestant, 207
— its secret character admitted, 208
Intercession Paper of the Guild of All Souls, 228
Intercession Paper of the B. H. C., 233, 235, 236
— recommends Liguori's *Glories of Mary*, 233
Invocation of Saints, Dr. Pusey believes in, 297
— what the Ritualists teach about, 404-406
Irish Ecclesiastical Record, 359
Jenner (Bishop), on the Ritual of the Society of the Holy Cross, 77
— 132, 142
Jesuits in Disguise, 32
Jesuit Order, 131
Jesuits (The), Newman dislikes an article against, 271
— their works the "favourite reading" of Rev. W. G. Ward, 274
— Mr. J. R. Hope-Scott's visits to, 275
— Dr. Pusey eulogises the Founder of, 289

Johnson (Rev. John Barnes) on the Fire of Purgatory, 230
Judicial Committee of Privy Council, 347
— Lord Halifax and Dean Hook on the, 347
Jurisdiction in the Confessional, 76
Kane's *Notes on the Roman Ritual*, 211
Keble (Rev. John) on "Yearning after Rome," 286
— would allow, but not enjoin the "Discipline," 37
— on Protestantism, 266
— on the Reformers, 270
Kempe (Rev. John William) praises the term "Mass," 142
Kensit (Mr. John) exhibits Ritualistic Instruments of Torture, 38
Kilburn Sisterhood, 83
King (Rev. Bryan), 59, 60
King (Rev. Owen C. H.), what he saw in a Ritualistic Convent Chapel, 193, 194, 203
Kirkpatrick (Rev. R. C.) on hearing Confessions, 75
Lacey (Rev. T. A.) his secret Mission to Rome, 356
— his Paper for the private use of Roman Cardinals, 357
Latimer (Bishop) *Sermons*, 203
— *Remains*, 203, 226
— on forged Sacrifices, 226
— on "Purgatory Pick Purse," 251
Laymen's Ritual Institute for Norwich, 254, 255
— its secret Oath, 254
Lea's *History of Sacerdotal Celibacy*, 118
Lebombo (Bishop of) [Dr. W. E. Smythe] a Member of the Society of the Holy Cross, 61
— His work in Zululand, 61, 62
— a Member of the Confraternity of the Blessed Sacrament, 225
Lee (Rev. F. G.) and the Order of Corporate Reunion, 153-155
— on the "rank and authority" of the Pope, 156
Lewington (Rev. A. L.) Teaches Transubstantiation, 223
"Levelling Up," how it is done, 336, 338
Liberty of Conscience denounced, 368, 369
Licensed Confessors (Petition for), its secret history, 70-72
Lichfield (Bishop of) [Dr. Selwyn] Speech on the Society of the Holy Cross, 114
Life of Archbishop Tait, 97, 98, 102, 180, 181, 276

Life of Bishop Wilberforce, 60, 181, 182, 297, 358
Life of Dr. Pusey, 10, 19, 20, 36, 37, 85, 163-166, 271, 282, 283, 289, 290, 292, 293, 296, 298
Linklater (Rev.) on the Ritual of the S. S. C., 77
Litany of Our Lady, 255
Litany of the Saints, 246
Little (Canon Knox) his sermon on the *Priest in Absolution*, 126
— his connection with the Society of the Holy Cross, 126
— on revision of the Statutes of the S. S. C., 129
Little (Rev. C. Hardy) and the *Priest in Absolution*, 97
Littledale (Rev. Dr.), 108
— on how to prevent secessions to Rome, 147
— *Defence of Church Principles*, 148
— Chaplain of a Ritualistic Sisterhood, 193
— officiates at Benediction of the Blessed Sacrament, 194
Littlemore Monastery, 16-28
Liturgy of the Church of Sarum, 249, 250
Llandaff (Bishop of) [Dr. Ollivant] Speech on the Society of the Holy Cross, 113
Llanthony, Enclosed Nuns at, 184
London (Bishop of) [Dr. Jackson] censures the *Priest in Absolution*, 104, 112, 113
Longley (Archbishop Charles T.) Letter on Confessing a Married Woman, 81
Lord's Day and the Holy Eucharist, 339-344
Lowder (Rev. Charles) describes the first Ritualistic Retreat, 57, 58
— and St. George's Mission, 59-61
— on Auricular Confession, 75
— on Convocation, 78
— recommends withdrawal of *Priest in Absolution* from circulation, 108
— Speech on the action of Bishop Mackarness, 123
Luke (Rev. W. H. Colbeck) on disbanding the S. S. C., 133
Luther (Martin) Speech at Diet of Worms, 69
Macfarlane (Rev. Brother) on the " Sacrament of Penance," 74
Mackonochie (Rev. A. H.) on the "caution" of the S. S. C., 47
— Letter on Carlisle Oratory of S. S. C., 66
— on the principles of the *Priest in Absolution*, 99

Mackonochie (Rev. A. H.) opposes S. S. C. deputation to the Bishops, 108
— Speech on the action of the Bishops, 123
— on compulsory Confession, 126
— opposes disbanding S. S. C., 133
— thinks the *Priest in Absolution* "a most useful book for young priests," 136
— his evidence before the Royal Commission on Ecclesiastical Courts, 348
Manners (Lord John) [now Duke of Rutland] secures Rules of Romish Sisterhoods, 164
Manning (Archdeacon), how he heard Confessions, 90, 91, 92
— his double-dealing, 299-305
— kneels before the Pope's carriage, 299
— Mr. Gladstone on his want of straightforwardness, 303
Manning (Cardinal) on Secessions to Rome, 272, 321-323
— *Essays on Religion*, 272, 321-323, 365
Manual of Confession for Children, 84
Marshall (Rev. T. Outram) secret Speeches on the Bishops, 124, 133
— opposes destruction or publication of the *Priest in Absolution*, 136
Maskell (Rev. William) describes the crooked ways of Tractarians, 44
— *Second Letter*, 44, 45
— *Letter to Dr. Pusey*, 86, 87
Mass, The, Bishop Latimer on, 202
— preached before the University of Oxford, 271
— Rev. E. W. Sergeant on, 343
"Mass Penny," 252
Melville (Canon) his warning against Popery, 369, 371, 372
Memoirs of J. R. Hope-Scott, 14, 25, 36, 274, 275, 287
Monastic Institutions, What the Ritualists teach about, 408
Monastic Orders, 283, 284
Monastic Times, 185
Monks and Nuns. Pagan origin of, 165
Morris (Rev. J. B.) preaches the Sacrifice of the Mass before Oxford University, 271
Mossman (Rev. T. W.) and the Order of Corporate Reunion, 154, 155, 159-161
— professes faith in the Pope's Infallibility, 157
— his secret Letter on the Order of Corporate Reunion, 160
— his Report on the O. C. R. to the S. S. C., 159

Mozley (Rev. Professor James B.), 3, 17, 18, 277, 294
Mozley (Rev. Thomas), his description of Littlemore Monastery, 20, 25
Nassau (Bishop of) [Dr. E. T. Churton] a Member of the Confraternity of the Blessed Sacrament, 225
Neale (Rev. Dr.) advice to Ritualistic Sisters, 83, 172, 173
Newman (Rev. J. H.) on secret doctrines, 1-3
— on truthfulness, 2
— does not wish the names of his party known, 4
— expects to be called a Papist, 6
— writes strongly against Popery, 10-13
— eats his "dirty words," 14, 285
— establishes a Monastery, 17, 21
— Bishop of Oxford's Letter to, 22-24
— life in Newman's Monastery, 26-28
— his interview with Wiseman at Rome, 263, 264
— has "a work to do in England,' 263
— on uttering an untruth, 265
— called a Papist to his face, 266
— begins to use the Breviary, 268
— believes in the Sacrifice of the Mass, 268
— his use of "irony," 269
— his mind "essentially Jesuitical," 271
— dislikes an article against the Jesuits, 271
— thinks "Rome the centre of unity," 274
— "thought the Church of Rome was right," 277
— has "a secret longing love of Rome," 283
— writes :—" I love the Church of Rome too well," 294
— his secession to Rome, 296
— *Letters*, 4, 5, 6, 10, 15, 16, 17, 19, 20, 266, 267, 268, 271, 272, 273, 274, 294, 295
— *Via Media*, 264
— *Apologia Pro Vita Sua*, 13, 21, 22-24, 25, 263, 265, 270, 271, 274, 284, 295
— *Letter to the Bishop of Oxford*, 278
Nicholas (Rev. G. Davenport) and the *Statement* of S. S. C., 108
— on the secret nature of S. S. C., 122
Night Hours of the Church, 200
Nihill (Rev. H. D.) on the "Sacrament of Penance," 74
— is "not ashamed of the *Priest in Absolution*," 144

Nineteenth Century, article on the Order of Corporate Reunion in the, 161
Nunnery Life in the Church of England, 40, 41, 185
Oakeley (Rev. Frederick) on life in Littlemore Monastery, 21
— describes Tractarian conduct on the Continent, 29
Offices from the Breviary, 200
"One of our Consolations," 359
Order of Corporate Reunion, 147-161
— its Objects, 148
— its Birth, 148
— First Pastoral of the, 149-151
— "Thomas, Rector" of the, 149
— "Joseph, Provincial of York," 149
— "Laurence, Provincial of Caerleon," 149
— opposes School Boards, 150
— doubts the validity of the Orders of the Church of England, 151
— professes "loyalty" to the Pope, 152
— acknowledges the Pope as "visible head" of the whole Church, 152
— Who are the secretly consecrated Bishops of the, 153-155
— Mr. William Grant's letter on, 158
— The *Civilita Cattolica* on the, 158
— The Society of the Holy Cross and the, 159-161, 327, 328
— said to have reordained eight hundred clergy of the Church of England, 161
— accepts the dogmas of the Council of Trent, 251
Order of the Holy Redeemer, 233-239
— its mysterious inner circle, 233
— its *Monthly Leaflet*, 233
— its Popish profession of Faith, 234
— acknowledges the Pope as "Teacher" of the whole Church, 234
— treasonable Letter of "John O. H. R." 235
— afraid of the light, 235
— opens a Convent at Stamford Hill, 236
— its object the subjection of England to Rome, 236
— "Rev. Father Square's" address to, 237
Order of St. John the Divine, a secret Society in East London, 239
Oscott College, Reunion with Rome discussed at, 281
Our National Independence in peril, 365, 366

INDEX. 419

Oxenham (Rev. Frank N.) censures the *Priest in Absolution* 102, 109, 110, 122
Oxford (Bishop of) [Dr. S. Wilberforce] on Dr. Pusey as a Roman Confessor, 88
— [Dr. Mackarness] Speech on the Society of the Holy Cross, 115
— [Dr. Mackarness] tries to save the S. S. C. from censure, 123
Oxford Martyrs' Memorial, Pusey dislikes it as "unkind to the Church of Rome," 270
Parker (Rev. James Benjamin) and the *Roll* of the S. S. C., 110
Palmer's *Narrative of Events*, 4, 264, 267, 285, 286
Papal Infallibility, 157, 352
— What the Ritualists teach about, 381, 382
Parnell (Rev. Charles) on the Roman Ritual, 77
— opposes publication of *Priest in Absolution*, 136
Pattison (Rev. Mark), his experience in Littlemore Monastery, 27
— goes once to Dr. Pusey to Confession, 187
"Peace with Rome with all our hearts," 353
Penitentiary Committee of the Society of the Holy Cross, 55
Penrith Branch of English Church Union sympathises with the S. S. C., 137
Perjury and Lying, 82, 83
Perry (Rev. T. W.) and the Society of the Holy Cross, 108
Phillimore (Sir Walter) and the Society of the Holy Cross, 108
Pixell (Rev. C. H. V.), 67
Plymouth Ritualistic Sisterhood, "a hell upon earth," 186
Pope (The) (The Order of Corporate Reunion recognises) as "Visible Head" of the Church, 152
— Prayed for as "*our Pope*," 242
— recognised as Governor of the Church, 248, 250
— rejoices at the work of the Tractarians, 271
— the "Representative" of the Divine Head of the Church, 285
— Dr. Pusey on the Supremacy and Primacy of, 331
— Rev. G. B. Roberts on the Primacy of, 345
Protestantism a "Bastard Faith," 254
— "a dark and damnable spot in the Church's History," 255

Protestantism, the great hindrance to Union with Rome, 261
— " is dangerous now," 266
— Dr. Pusey's opinion of, 292
— What the Ritualists teach about, 409
Popery, an enemy to National Prosperity, 362
Powell (Rev. J. B.) on the Ritual of the Society of the Holy Cross, 77
Priest in Absolution, vii.
— its original price, 56
— Secret History of, 93-147
— translated and edited by Rev. J. C. Chambers, 93-95
— said to be a "golden treatise," 94
— praised by the *Church Review*, 94
— curious letter about the, 95
— supplied only to High Church priests, 95
— its copyright purchased by the Society of the Holy Cross, 95, 96
— secret documents concerning, quoted, 95, 96, 100-110, 121-144
— its sale, 96, 103
— how Mr. Robert Fleming discovered the, 97
— exposed in the House of Lords, 97, 98
— Lord Redesdale on the, 98
— Archbishop Tait terms it "a disgrace to the community," 98
— peers protest against the, 99
— its "principles" said to guide all Ritualistic Confessors, 99
— secret Letter on, from Rev. Francis Ll. Bagshawe, 100, 101
— debate on, in secret Synod of S. S. C., 134-136
— another debate on, in secret Synod of S. S. C., 142-144
Priest's Prayer Book on Holy Water, 63
— its services for Sisters of Mercy, 194-196
Private Burial Grounds in Ritualistic Convents, 191, 192
Prynne (Rev. G. R.) Member of Committee for Revising statutes of S. S. C., 138
Puller (Rev. F. W.) on valid Absolutions, 76
— on Revising the statutes of S. S. C., 132
— Member of Committee for Revising Statutes of S. S. C., 138
— on Evening Communion, 215
Purcell's *Life of Cardinal Manning*, 91, 92, 273, 295, 298-303, 321
Purgatorial Society, A, 227-232
Purgatory and the C. B. S., 214

Purgatory and the Guild of All Souls, 228-231
— What the Ritualists teach about, 396-398
"Purgatory Pick Purse," 251
Purton (Rev. William) defends the Society of the Holy Cross, 129
Pusey (Rev. Dr.) joins the Tractarian Movement, 6
— his subtle scheme for writing against Popery, 10
— approves of Newman's proposed Monastery, 19
— sends for a "Discipline," 36
— wears hair-cloth, 36
— would like to be ordered the "Discipline," 37
— *Manual for Confessors*, 39, 40, 82, 83, 120, 121, 136, 167, 185
— first Retreat held in his rooms, 57, 58
— and St. George's Mission, 59, 60
— on the Seal of Confession, 82, 187
— on bringing children to Confession, 83
— begins to hear Confessions in 1838, 85
— in 1842 writes against Confession, 85, 86
— how Confessions were heard in his Sisterhood, 87
— "doing the work of a Roman Confessor," 88
— *Hints for a First Confession*, 87, 88
— on the fearful evils of the Confessional, 120, 121
— eager to set up Sisters of Mercy, 163
— visits Romish Convents in Ireland, 164
— procures the Rules of Romish Convents, 164
— Enclosed Nuns of "The Sacred Heart" in his Sisterhood, 183, 184
— recommends the "Discipline" for Sisters of Mercy, 185
— charged with breaking the Seal of Confession, 187
— hears Confessions "on the sly," 87
— his Introductory Essay to *Essays on Reunion*, 261
— dislikes the Oxford Martyrs' Memorial, 270
— his eulogy of the Founder of the Jesuits, 289
— his opinion of Protestantism, 292
— desires "more love for Rome," 292
— his conduct censured by Dr. Manning, 292
— praises the "superiority" of Roman books, 293

Pusey (Rev. Dr.) Bishop Wilberforce censures his Romanizing work, 297, 358
— acknowledges his belief in Purgatory and the Invocation of Saints, 297
— *Eirenicon*, 330-332, 357
— on the Primacy and Supremacy of the Pope, 331, 333
— said to have been "a Gallican on the wrong side of the water," 333
Railway Guild of the Holy Cross, 258
Real Presence, What the Ritualists teach about the, 385-387
Records of English Catholics, 365
Reformers and the Reformation, What the Ritualists teach about the, 383, 384
Reilly's *Relations of the Church to Society*, 368
Relics (Shrine with) recommended by the Society of St. Osmund, 248
"Removing the Barriers" between England and Rome, 325
Requiem Masses, 212, 213, 228
Reserve in Communicating Religious Knowledge, 7-9
"Reserve" observed in the St. George's Mission, 59
"Retreat Committee" of the Society of the Holy Cross, 57
Retreats, *Instructions* for, 58
— the first in Dr. Pusey's rooms, 60
Reunion Magazine, 149, 150, 151, 153
Revision of the Prayer Book on Ritualistic lines, 339-344
Riley (Mr. Athelstan) his Connection with the Society of St. Osmund, 240
— translates the *Mirror of Our Lady*, and the *Hours of the Blessed Virgin Mary*, 243
Ritualism, its Object from its birth, 260
— "the Preparatory School for Rome," 359, 360
— one of the "consolations" of Rome, 359
Ritualists (The), their Objects and work, 261
— doing Rome's work, 316
— the results of their teaching, 359, 360
— preparing a harvest for Rome, 360
Ritualistic Sisterhoods, 162-201
Reunion with Rome, 261
— Rev. W. G. Ward on, 280
— *Union Review* on, 311, 312
— *Essays on Reunion* on, 313, 315, 316
— Protestantism the "great hinderance" to, 315

INDEX. 421

Reunion with Rome, Work of the Society of the Holy Cross for, 323-327
— Rev. N. Y. Birkmyre on, 328
— How to promote, 336-338
— E. C. U. Address to Lambeth Conference on, 344
— Lord Halifax most earnestly desires, 346
— Objections to, 362-372
— What the Ritualists teach about, 380, 381
Roberts (Rev. G. Bayfield) *History of the English Church Union*, 335, 345
— on the Primacy of the "Bishop of Old Rome," 345
Robinson (Rev. George Croke) on the Revision of the Statutes of S. S. C., 141
Rock, 67, 72, 78, 95, 206, 207, 209
— publishes the *Roll of Brethren* of S. S. C., 101
Rockhampton (Bishop of) becomes a Member of the Society of the Holy Cross, 76
— on the Secrecy of the Society of the Holy Cross, 125
Rogers (Mr. F.) 4, 16, 19
Roman Ritual (Discussion on) in S. S. C. Synod, 77
Rome (Church of) Reunion with, 261
— we are "Not good enough for" the, 262
— Secret Receptions into the, 265, 266
— Rev. W. G. Ward on Reunion with the, 280
— How Reunion with, is to be accomplished, 280
— Conditions of union with, discussed at Oscott College, 281
— "Yearning after" the, 286
— Work of the A. P. U. C. for Reunion with the, 307-323
— "A friendly feeling towards" the, 320
— Speech in favour of the Ritual of the, 350
— What the Church of England says about the, 356
— The duty of separation from, 361
— Objections to Reunion with, 362-372
— the Babylon of the Book of the Revelation, 370, 371
Rome (The name of) "pronounced with reverence," 281
Romeward Movement (The), 260-372
Russell (Rev. H. Lloyd) on Punishment in Purgatory, 230
"Sacrament of Penance," Secret discussion on the, 74, 75

Sacrifice of the Mass, What the Ritualists teach about the, 388-392
Salisbury (Bishop of) [Dr. Moberly] on Habitual Confession, 116
Salisbury (Bishop of) [Dr. E. Denison] alarmed at the Romeward Movement, 283
Salisbury (Lord) denounces Habitual Confession, 70
Secessions to Rome, How Ritualists try to prevent, 147
— Cardinal Manning on, 272
— Newman's plan for preventing, 284
— Dr. Hook on, 291
— the *Rambler* on, 305
— mainly from the ranks of the Ritualists, 359
Secret teaching of the Tractarians, 1-3
Secret doctrines not learnt from Scripture, 1-3
Secret Societies, Church of England honeycombed with, vi.
Sellon (Miss), Mother Superior of Dr. Pusey's Convent, 166
— her "disgusting insult" to a Sister of Mercy, 168
— a warning against, 186
— and the Confessions of her Sisters of Mercy, 187
— Miss Margaret Goodman's estimate of, 188-190
Sergeant (Rev. E. W.), his suggested Revision of the Book of Common Prayer, 343
Separation, The Duty of, 361
Shipley (Rev. Orby) on the Doctrine of Reserve, 9
— proposes an Oratory of the S. S. C., 65
— on Convocation, 78
Sibthorp (Rev. R. W.), 287
Sisterhood of the Holy Cross, 179 *note*
Sisterhoods, Ritualistic, 162-201
— formed on Roman models, 163-166
— are really secret societies, 163
— the "Vow of Obedience" in Dr. Pusey's, 167
— the "Vow of Poverty" in Dr. Pusey's, 169
— evils of the Vow of Obedience in, 169
— Miss Goodman on the serious evils in, 170, 171
— it is difficult to leave, 171
— are their accounts audited ? 173
— Miss Cusack's experience in Dr. Pusey's, 186, 187
— and Romanizing doctrines and practices, 192-201
— service for Clothing Novices in, 194, 195

Sisterhood at Llanthony, 40, 185
— at Kilburn, 83, 199
— at St. Margaret's, East Grinstead, 83, 172, 173, 193, 194
— at Clewer, 174, 175
— at All Saints', Margaret Street, 174, 178, 192
— at Slapton, 184
Sister Mary Agnes most cruelly whipped, 40
— O. S. B., 185
Sisters of Mercy, Dr. Pusey on obedience to their Spiritual Father, 40
— Dr. Pusey's advice to, 167
— in the Confessional, 167
— one ordered to lick the floor with her tongue, 168
— Benson's book for their guidance, 169, 174
— sad story of a dying, 176
— ordered the "Discipline," 185
— shocking cruelty to, 189
— hungry, 191
Slapton, enclosed Nuns at, 184
Smith (Rev. Joseph Newton), Founder of the Society of the Holy Cross, 47
— on the "wisdom of the serpent," 125
Smythe (Rev. W. Edmund), 61-62, see also Lebombo, Bishop of
Society of the Holy Cross (The Master of) on "Reserve," 9, 10
— its first members, 47
— its caution and secrecy, 47, 48, 63, 64, 65, 121, 125, 127
— its *Statutes*, 48, 128
— its *Officia*, 48
— its Cross, 48
— founded, 48
— its mysterious "Committee of Clergy," 49, 50
— its secret Synods and Chapters, 50, 51
— its secret Roll of sworn Celibates, 52, 53
— the Celibate Oath, 53
— the Brethren pledged to bring young and old to Confession, 54
— its *Books for the Young*, 54, 55
— its "Penitentiary Committee": their names, 55, 56
— its "Retreat Committee," 57
— starts the Retreat Movement, 57
— starts the St. George's Mission at St. Peter's, London Docks, 58, 59
— the *Master's Address*, 1870, 63
— the *Master's Address*, May, 1876, 64
— the *Master's Address*, May, 1875, 64
— afraid of Post Cards, 64

Society of the Holy Cross, the *Master's Address*, Sept., 1876, 65
— organizes the Petition for Licensed Confessors, 70-72
— its Secret *Roll of Brethren*, 78, 79, 101, 110, 126
— purchases the copyright of the *Priest in Absolution*, 95, 96
— the *Rock* publishes its *Roll of Brethren*, 101
— its interview with the Bishops, 105
— its *Statement* to the Bishops, 105, 106
— Special Chapter of July 5th, 1877, 107-110
— Canterbury Houses of Convocation discuss the, 110-117
— termed "a Conspiracy" by Archbishop Tait, 112
— its secret Chapter, July 10th, 1877, 121-126
— its action towards the Bishops, 123-125
— its secret Chapter, August, 1877, 127
— its secret Synod, September, 1877, 127-137
— proposal to disband it, 130-134
— its secret debate on the *Priest in Absolution*, 134-136
— Committee for Revising Statutes of; Names of its members, 138
— great secession from its ranks, 139
— its secret Synod, May, 1878, 139-144
— — their Report, 140-142
— refuses to destroy the *Priest in Absolution*, 144
— it condemns the Order of Corporate Reunion, 159-161
— its *Address to Catholics*, 324
— its Address to the Lambeth Conference, 324, 325
— by whom it was signed, 325, 326
— approves of the A. P. U. C., 327
— its secret discussion on the Order of Corporate Reunion, 327, 328
Society of St. Osmund, 240-254
— its Episcopal Vice-Presidents, 240
— and London School Board Election, 240
— its Objects, 240, 241
— works for the restoration of the Sarum Ritual, 241
— its puerile ceremonial, 241, 242, 243
— prays for "*our* Pope," 242
— its Confessions to the Virgin and Saints, 242
— its "worship" of the Virgin, 243, 244
— its *Services for Holy Week*, 244-249
— its Adoration of the Cross, 245
— its Litany of the Saints, 246

INDEX. 423

Society of St. Osmund drives the Devil out of Incense and Flowers, 246, 247, 248
— its Service for Palm Sunday, 247
— recommends a "Shrine with Relics," 248
— Recognises the Pope, as Governor of the Church, 249
— its *Ceremonial and Offices of the Dead*, 250-252
— dissolved, and merged into the Alcuin Club, 253, 254
Some Cautions for Mass Priests, 395, 396
Some other Ritualistic Societies, 227-259
Some Ritualistic " Ornaments of the Church," 384
Spencer (Rev. George) Letter on the tactics of the Tractarians, 262
— his visit to Newman, 274
Spirit of the Founder, a secret book for Ritualistic Sisters, 83, 84, 172, 173, 175, 199
Square (Rev. " Father ") address to the secret Order of the Holy Redeemer, 237
Square (Rev. Ernest) Speech in favour of Roman Ritual, 350
St. Albans (Bishop of) [Dr. Claughton] Speech on the Confessional, 114
St. Alban's, Holborn, 258
St. Alphege, Southwark, 255-257
— its *Manual of Tertiaries*, 255
— its *Manual of the Church Confraternity*, 256
— its " Guild of the Sacred Heart," 257
St. Asaph (Bishop of) [Dr. Hughes] Speech on Confession by the, 115
St. Cuthbert's, Philbeach Gardens, 245
St. George's Mission, 58-61
St. Margaret's, East Grinstead, Sisterhood, 172, 173
— Vows of Poverty, Chastity, and Obedience taken for life, 172
— how the Sisters dispose of their income, 172, 173
— Popish service in one of its Convent Chapels, 193, 194
— its *Night Hours of the Church*, 200
St. Matthias', Earl's Court, 231, 350, 351
St. Peter's Parish Magazine, 61, 62
St. Saviour's Hospital, Osnaburgh Street, N.W., 200
Stallard (Rev. Arthur Gordon) on Revision of Statutes of S. S. C., 141
Stanton (Rev. A. H.), 108
Stathers (Rev. William), his remarkable *Protest and Explanation*, 350, 351

Stocks (Rev. J. E.), 77
Synodi Diœceseos Suthwarcensis, 317, 318
Tait (Archbishop) on the *Priest in Absolution*, 98
— on the S. S. C., 102-107
— Speech in Convocation, 111, 112
— Terms the S. S. C. " a Conspiracy," 112
— Opposed to Perpetual Vows in Ritualistic Sisterhoods, 182, 183
— on Tract XC., 275, 276
Teignmouth (Lord), his *Reminiscences*, 265
The Importance of Ritual, What the Ritualists teach about, 409, 410
The Power and Dignity of Sacrificing Priests, What the Ritualists teach about, 387, 388
The " Preparatory School for Rome," 359, 360
The Romeward Movement, 260-372
The Ten Commandments and the Ritualists, 341, 343
The Thirty-Nine Articles, What the Ritualists teach about, 378-380
— Newman "no great friend " of, 268, 330
— the Rev. W. G. Ward on, 279
Thynne (Lord Charles) on the Tractarian Confessional, 89
" Toleration to Protestants is Intolerance to Catholics," 369
Towne (Rev. Lyndhurst B.), 141
Tracts for the Times " abused as Popish," 267
— 298
Tract *On Reserve in Communicating Religious Knowledge*, 7-9
— Condemned by the Bishops, 7, 9
— rightly understood by Evangelicals, 9
Tract XC., 275, 276, 290
Tractarian Movement, Birth of the, 1, 263
— its promoters fear publicity, 4
— Joshua Watson on its ulterior destination, 5
— " Suggestions " for its formation, 5
— Dr. Pusey joins the, 6
— Mr. Gladstone joins the, 6
— attacked by the *Standard* and *Edinburgh Review*, 10
Tractarians go secretly to Mass in disguise, 30
— described by Mr. Maskell, 44
— their real object a profound secret, 263
— " Introducing Popery without authority," 267
— said to be " Crypto-Papists," 268
— greatly rejoice the Pope, 271

424 INDEX.

Tractarians on the Continent, 274, 290
— their Jesuitical tactics described, 280, 281
— their negotiations with Dr. Wiseman, 281, 282
— Moving towards Rome, 287
Transubstantiation taught by the C. B. S., 223-225
— taught by the Guild of All Souls, 229
Treatise of S. Catherine of Genoa on Purgatory, 228, 229
Truro (Bishop of) [Dr. Gott] recommends the *Priest's Prayer Book*, 194
Urquhart (Rev. E. W.) teaches Transubstantiation, 223-225
Union Review, 94, 152, 261, 309-312, 330
Vaux (Rev. J. E.), 148
Virtues of Holy Salt, Holy Water, and Holy Oil, What the Ritualists teach about the, 406-408
Vow of Obedience by Ritualistic Sisters, 167, 168, 169
— of Poverty by Ritualistic Sisters, 169-179
— of Celibacy taken by a girl of eighteen for life, 180
— censured by Bishop S. Wilberforce, 181
Vows in St. Margaret's Sisterhood, East Grinstead, taken for life, 172
— of Ritualistic Sisters censured by Bishop S. Wilberforce, 180
Vows (Perpetual) by Ritualistic Sisters censured by Archbishop Tait, 182, 183
Ward (Rev. A. H.) favours disbanding the Society of the Holy Cross, 133
Ward (Rev. William George), his Jesuitical conduct, 15
— on Equivocation, 16
— the Jesuits his "favourite reading," 274
— on Union with Rome, 280
— *Ideal of a Christian Church*, 287, 288-290
— holds all Roman doctrine, 288
Walker (Rev. Henry Aston) opposes S. S. C. deputation to the Bishops, 108
Wallace (Rev. C. S.), and the Society of the Holy Cross, 127
— thanked by S. S. C. for his conduct, 127
— opposes publication of *Priest in Absolution*, 136
Watson (Mr. Joshua) on the ulterior destination of Tractarianism, 5

West Malling, enclosed Ritualistic Nuns at, 184
What the Ritualists Teach, 373-410
Wilberforce (Bishop Samuel), v.
— on the Vows of Ritualistic Sisters, 180
— Censures Vows of Celibacy in Ritualistic Sisterhoods, 181
— on Fasting Communion, 215
Williams (Rev. Isaac), 7, 8, 9
William G. Ward and the Oxford Movement, 16, 274, 279-282, 288
Willington (Rev. Henry Edward) Member of Committee for Revising Statutes of S. S. C., 138
Wilson (Rev. Robert James) and the *Priest in Absolution*, 100, 122
— Member of Committee for Revising Statutes of S. S. C., 138
Wiseman (Cardinal), 28, 29, 30
— interview with Newman and Froude, 263, 294
— discusses Reunion with Rome with Tractarians, 281
Wolverhampton Province of the Guild of St. Alban's sympathises with the S. S. C., 137
Women and the Confessional, 81, 82, 83, 87, 90, 91, 120
— ruined by Ritualistic Confessors, 117
Wood (Hon. C. L.) (see also under Halifax) advocates Masses for the Dead, 213
— Elected President of the English Church Union, 335
Wood (Rev. E. G.) his resolutions for disbanding S. S. C., 130
— on the Jesuit Order, 131
— on Purgatory, 214, 231
— on Jurisdiction in the Confessional, 76
— his subtle advice to the Society of the Holy Cross, 125
— on compulsory Confession, 126
Wordsworth (Bishop Christopher) on Rome as the Babylon of the Revelation, 370
— *Union with Rome*, 370, 371
Zanzibar (Bishop of) [Dr. Richardson], 76
— a Member of the Society of the Holy Cross, 79
— a Member of the Confraternity of the Blessed Sacrament, 225
Zululand (Bishop of) [Dr. W. M. Carter] a Member of the Confraternity of the Blessed Sacrament, 225

The Secret History of the Oxford Movement.

By WALTER WALSH.

Fourth Edition. 3s 6d net. Post free, 4s.

This is a most startling exposure, and has created a great sensation in the public mind.

It is the duty of every Protestant to obtain a copy, read it, and lend it to others.

NOTICES OF THE PRESS, &c.

"I have no difficulty in saying that I think it the most valuable book on the anti-sacerdotal side that has been published."—LORD GRIMTHORPE.

"Contains one of the most startling revelations ever made to the people of any country."—CANON McCORMICK, *Chaplain-in-Ordinary to the Queen.*

"*Nothing is over-stated or aught set down in malice.* The work is soberly and temperately written. We advise all who wish to have full and accurate knowledge on this sadly important subject to read the book. . . . It is a magazine of information on this important subject. *We can cordially recommend it to the serious perusal of sober-minded Churchmen.*"—*Liverpool Courier.*

"Mr. Walsh has written with studied moderation and fairness, and there is nothing in all the four hundred pages of this book that can offend any independent mind. The work is an important contribution to the literature of the Ritual controversy, which everyone desiring to become acquainted with the inner workings of the Movement should most certainly consult."—*Record.*

"This is a remarkable book, which ought to be read, examined, and pondered by every Englishman who wishes to see his country free and enlightened. . . . We cannot too strongly recommend the purchase and study of this History."—*English Churchman.*

"The volume is one which Churchmen would do well to consult for themselves. Its revelations are extraordinary, its proofs indisputable. . . . The author has done his work well, and deserves the gratitude of Churchmen."—*Western Times.*

"The gravest indictment that has yet been made against the High Church party. . . . It is a book with a purpose. It demanded courage to write it, and is full of information that ought to be circulated broadcast."—*Baptist.*

THE CHURCH ASSOCIATION.

THE Council invite all those who have been convinced by the reading of this book that a serious attempt is being made to Romanize the Church of England, to support the Church Association, the only Church Society that has stood in the forefront of the Anti-Ritualistic Movement for thirty-three years.

A perusal of the following will give some idea of the work in which the Church Association is engaged :—

A correspondent, writing with regard to the Council, refers to them as "Those who have on every occasion exhibited an amount of judgment, discretion and resolution, which it would be hard to match in the transactions of any other deliberative and administrative body."

The Rev. Canon Christopher *writes:*
"I measure the value of the Church Association not so much by its success as by its Scriptural objects, and the faith and courage of its members in seeking to obtain them.

"The success of Cranmer, Latimer, and Ridley in preserving the Reformation they had so well begun, did not seem to be very great when they were being burnt alive within a quarter of a mile of this rectory. Yet we know what great results God ultimately gave to their noble self-sacrifice for the cause of His Truth."

The Rt. Rev. the Lord Bp. of Liverpool (*when the Rev. Canon Ryle*) *spoke of the Church Association as follows:—*

"I know no way of meeting the evil around us except by such a combination as that presented by the Church Association—a combination like the Volunteer movement, whose motto should be 'Defence not Defiance.' The Bishops will not act: they have charged and charged and charged for twenty years, and their Charges have been so much *brutum fulmen*, and have wrought no deliverance. —Convocation can do nothing.—It can growl, and whine, and bark; but it has no teeth, and cannot bite : it is chained, and cannot move.— The House of Commons will do nothing at present. They dislike religious questions in St. Stephen's, unless positively forced to handle them; and they will not handle Ritualism, except under the pressure of public opinion.—There is nothing left but the voluntary union of all Protestant Churchmen in such a Society as the Church Association. By uniting to spread information, awaken sleeping zeal, and enlighten public opinion,—by rallying and getting together the sound members of our Church, and organizing their strength,—by combining to employ every legal and constitutional means to maintain the Protestant character of our Church,—by such work much good may be done, for union is strength. Such work the Church Association has done, is doing, and I trust will continue to do for many a day."

"**Your Association** is at least standing in the gap before the Lord in the land, that He should not destroy it. (*Ezekiel* xxii. 30.) You are doing your best to 'make up the hedge' against the adversaries of our Zion, and it is better to try, and fail, than not to try at all."—Another Correspondent.

The Church Association was instituted in 1865 to Uphold the Doctrines, Principles, and Order of the United Church of England and Ireland, and to counteract the efforts now being made to pervert her teaching on essential points of the Christian faith, or assimilate her Services to those of the Church of Rome, and further to encourage concerted action for the advancement and progress of Spiritual Religion.

It seeks to resist all innovations in the order of the Service as prescribed by the joint authority of Church and State—whether in vestments, ornaments, gestures, or practices borrowed from the Church of Rome, and symbolical of her errors—and especially to prevent the idolatrous adoration of the elements in the Lord's Supper, contrary to the order of our Communion Service and the terms both of the Liturgy and Articles.

It seeks to resist all attempts to restore the use of the Confessional, and every exercise of that Priestly authority which was put down at the Reformation, and also to oppose the introduction of doctrines contrary to the teaching of the Church, as set forth in her Liturgy and Articles.

It seeks to effect these objects by publicity through Lectures, Meetings, and the use of the Press, by the employment of Colporteurs, Lay Evangelists, and Protestant Vans, by Protestant Lay Missions, and by Appeals to Parliament to pass such measures as may be needed to restrain clergymen from violating the order of their Church, and obtruding on their parishioners practices and doctrines repugnant to the Formularies and Articles of our Reformed Church.

The Church Association has at considerable cost obtained the condemnation by the Ecclesiastical Courts of more than SIXTY ceremonies and practices symbolical of Popish Doctries illegally introduced by the Ritualists into the Services of our Reformed Church.

It has circulated literature "wholesome and necessary" for these times—millions of Pamphlets and Tracts against Ritualism—and by these means the country has been awakened to the dangers of the Ritualistic "Conspiracy." The Association is really a Ch. of England Protestant Tract Society.

It has no sympathy with imprisonment of clergymen. It introduced into Parliament a Bill which, if passed, would have substituted Deprivation for Imprisonment.

It introduced a Bill into Parliament to abolish the Bishops' Veto, which at present bars the Laity from their right of appealing to the Ecclesiastical Courts in cases where the Romish Mass is thrust upon them in their Parish Churches.

It has to cope with lawlessness in high places, and to defend the interests of Law, Order, and Truth.

It has to satisfy appeals for advice and help from distressed and oppressed congregations.

It has to aid Protestant Home Mission-work, to assist those involved in controversy, to furnish papers on matters that arise affecting Evangelical religion, and to provide suitable Lectures.

It has to devise how to meet the schemes of Sacerdotalism in the widening arena of Politics.

It has to guard the interests of the Laity in all Church matters, especially in the matter of " Church Reform," as it has done in the matter of the " Benefices " Bill.

It has to check the attempted revival of sacerdotal caste privileges, and " benefit of clergy."

It has to contest the ground inch by inch in fighting the battle of the Reformation and defending the Constitutional Settlement of Church and State.

It has established the National Protestant League, which is not a new Society, but a further development of the Church Association to enable the masses to take a part in opposing the present great conspiracy to Romanize our Church and Nation.

It has appointed Colporteurs and Lay Evangelists for certain counties and it hopes to increase the number. These men are doing splendid work amongst the much neglected rural populations, distributing Protestant literature, explaining the inroads of Ritualism, preaching the simple Gospel, and urging Electors to vote for the most Protestant candidate at the Parliamentary elections.

It has sent forth into the Provinces eleven Travelling Vans, with a Colporteur Evangelist in each. They each carry with them a large stock of Bibles, Prayer Books, and Protestant literature, for sale and free circulation. These Vans travel on each day to a fresh town or village, Protestant Gospel addresses are given each evening and large quantities of literature distributed. Great good to the Protestant Cause has already resulted from this latest development of the work of the Association.

It has established at the head Office regular meetings for Prayer and the study of God's Word.

It has gathered together the finest Protestant library in the Kingdom, consisting of some ten thousand books and pamphlets. The Library is open to Members on Wednesday in each week.

It has induced the Government to publish a facsimile of the " annexed " book which is the statutable authority for our present Prayer Book, and is endeavouring to compel the Queen's Printers to issue printed Prayer Books in conformity with it, and without unauthorized alterations; and in this it has already been partly successful.

PROTESTANT PUBLICATIONS.

The **Church Association** publishes in its monthly organ, the *Church Intelligencer*, exact information as to controverted points in the meaning and structure of the Book of Common Prayer, the Thirty-nine Articles, and the Formularies; calls attention to attacks upon the Protestant principles of the Reformed Church of England, whether in Parliament, in Convocation, or in the Press; analyzes the drift of the movement for increasing sacerdotal privileges and assumptions, and especially the tendency to vest irresponsible power in the hands of the Bishops, and is a channel for the exchange of thought between Churchmen who value these objects. *The Church Intelligencer* costs 1*d* per month, and may be ordered of any bookseller.

It issues five volumes which deal with nearly every point of the Ritualistic Controversy, and shows the practices which have been condemned as unlawful in the Church of England. They form a complete Library on the Ritualistic Controversy, and should be in the hands of every Protestant Churchman throughout the country. Sent free by post, 1*s* 4*d* each vol., or handsomely bound in cloth at 1*s* 10*d* each volume.

It publishes an Almanack and Diary for the pocket, price one penny, which is full of interesting matter. Statistics as to the Ritualistic Conspiracy. Dates of principal events in Reformation. Lists of Archbishops, Bishops, Deans, Chancellors. Table of Lessons for every day in the year. Sunday Notes for Clergy, &c., &c., &c. Price, post free, 1½*d*.

It publishes a Guide to Ecclesiastical Law for the use of Church-wardens and Parishioners, full of hints and suggestions for opposing Ritualism. Price, post free, 1*s* 2½*d*.

It has published the Rev. Dyson Hague's invaluable book, *The Protestantism of the Prayer Book*, the most readable book on this subject. Price, 1*s* 6*d*; post free, 1*s* 10*d*.

It has published a work by Mr. J. T. Tomlinson entitled, *The Prayer Book, Articles and Homilies: some forgotten facts in their History which may decide their interpretation*. Price 5*s* net, post free.

It has published a work by Mr. Walter Walsh entitled, *The Secret History of the Oxford Movement*, the first two editions of which were sold at 10*s* 6*d*, but which is now issued at 3*s* 6*d*.

It has published *An Indictment of the Bishops, shewing how the Church of England is being corrupted and betrayed by them*. Post free, 1*s* 2*d*.

It has just published the sixth edition of *The "Historical" Grounds of the Lambeth Judgment*. Post free, 7½*d*.

PROTESTANT VAN MISSION WORK IN THE VILLAGES OF ENGLAND.

The State of the Villages where the Vans go.

The Rock puts the case of the Villagers somewhat in this way—Picture to yourself Churchman in a **Country Village** in which the Church is **in the hands of a Sacerdotalist.** Try and realise the **deadening effect** on their **spiritual life** week by week, not only never hearing a sermon which does not irritate rather than help them, but unable to attend a service in which they can heartily join, **debarred the Lord's Table** because the ritual adopted symbolises a doctrine they hold to be false, and commits them to a worship which they regard as idolatrous. Picture to yourselves their children being slowly won by sensuous services and the persevering blandishments of priestlings, so that a wall is growing up between them and those they love most dearly—and then let us ask, Who will come to our help to enable us to continue to carry the blessed Gospel to these dark spots in rural England?

Van Work during 1897.

Number of Protestant Publications distributed free . 116,003
Number of Protestant Publications sold . . . 40,721
Number of Villages and Towns visited . . . 1,541
Number of Gospel and Protestant Addresses given . 2,322

The Church Association appeals for support—

1.—Because it is necessary to oppose Ritualism, as helping to thrust upon the unwary the Popery which was cast out at the Reformation, and which made England cringe to a foreign potentate, kept back the Bible from our people, deluged our land with superstition and ignorance, and burned our Protestant Reformers.

2.—Because a powerful organisation is needed to oppose the thoroughly organised efforts of those who are trying to undo the work of the Reformation; and it is the only organisation with the special object of opposing the numerous agencies of Ritualism.

3.—Because the "English Church Union," the "Society of the Holy Cross," the "Confraternity of the Blessed Sacrament," the "Association for the promotion of the Unity of Christendom," and numerous Guilds, Brotherhoods, and Sisterhoods are actively promoting the avowed object of "un-Protestantising" our Church.

4.—Because a large number of the clergy and laity have joined the Church of Rome, and a much larger number have adopted thoroughly Romish doctrines and practices while still continuing in the Church of England; therefore all Protestant clergy and laity should support a Society exclusively devoted to the work of defending the Protestantism of our Church.

5.—Because good Churchmanship, as well as good citizenship, demands that the law now clearly decided should be obeyed.

6.—Because the Ritualists are endeavouring to bring English men, women, and even children within the unhealthy and unhallowed influences of the Confessional, to which the Association is most resolutely opposed.

7.—Because though God alone can defend our Church and country from all dangers, religious or national—and to Him must be all the glory of giving us the victory—He expects His servants as His instruments, to be "workers together with Him," to "earnestly contend for the faith," and when His truth and honour are concerned, to be careful that as a Church we are "*first* pure, *then* peaceable."

The **Church Association** enrols Associates at 5s; Lay Members at 10s; Clerical Members at 5s.

The work is greatly crippled for want of adequate funds. Urgent appeals for help from aggrieved Parishioners are unwillingly rejected on this account. Increased support means increased work. The Council would say with Bishop Barrington "If the Reformation was worth establishing it is worth maintaining, but it can only be maintained by a constant vigilance in support of those principles which effected it in the sixteenth century."

All Special Donations and Subscriptions to carry on the work indicated above should be sent to the Secretary, Mr. HENRY MILLER, 14, Buckingham Street, Strand, London; or may be paid to the account of the Association at the Bank of Messrs. BARCLAY & Co., Limited, 1, Pall Mall East, S.W., and 54, Lombard Street, E.C., London.

Post-Office Orders should be made payable to HENRY MILLER, and drawn upon Charing Cross.

A PROTESTANT ELECTORAL ROLL.

The Council of the National Protestant League is anxious to obtain in every constituency a Roll of 100 Voters who undertake not to pledge themselves to vote for any Candidate at the next Election until after they have been called together to consider, in conjunction with the London Council of the National Protestant League, how their united votes may be best used in the Protestant interest.

Persons willing to undertake the collection of One Hundred Signatures should write to the REGISTRAR, NATIONAL PROTESTANT LEAGUE,

MR. HENRY MILLER,
14, BUCKINGHAM STREET,
STRAND, LONDON.

For some of the Protestant Books, Pamphlets, and Tracts published by the Church Association for present day reading, see next page.

The Prayer Book, Articles and Homilies:

SOME FORGOTTEN FACTS IN THEIR HISTORY WHICH MAY DECIDE THEIR INTERPRETATION.

By J. T. TOMLINSON.

Price 5s net, post free, 320 pp., with Photozincographic Illustrations taken from the "Durham Book."

"A learned and lucid exposition of the Liturgy of the Church of England, its history and meaning."—*Western Times*, June 6th, 1897.

"Mr. Tomlinson is a scholarly and accurate student, who has in all cases carefully collated the documents with the originals at Lambeth, Cambridge, Durham, and the British Museum, and states clearly the grounds of the conclusions at which he has arrived."—*Manchester Guardian*, June 29th, 1897.

"On such still vexed and important points as the Ornaments Rubric, the Injunctions and Advertisements of Elizabeth, the Thirty-first Article, the 'Black Rubric,' and other heads, Mr. Tomlinson has been at pains to collate carefully his documents with the originals in the great public libraries, besides producing here photozincographs of the famous 'Durham Book.'"—*Bookseller*, July 7th, 1897.

"Ought to become a text-book in every bishop's examination for Orders."—*Rock*, July 9th, 1897.

"Mr. Tomlinson writes with learning, candour, good temper, and moderation, and it is hoped that both sides will make themselves masters of his laborious investigations."—*Churchman*, August, 1897.

"Mr. J. T. Tomlinson is well known as an acute and learned controversialist, and his latest volume *The Prayer Book, Articles, and Homilies* (Elliot Stock) is not unworthy of him."—*The National Church*, August 14th, 1897.

---

	s.	d.
A Set of the Tracts (1 to 250) bound in 5 volumes, at 1s per vol., or post free 5s 8d; in cloth at 1s 6d per vol., or post free . . . . . These form a complete Library on the Ritualistic Controversy, and should be in the hands of every Protestant Churchman.	8	4
Collected Tracts on Ritual. Edited or written by J. T. TOMLINSON 2s, or post free	2	4
The Protestantism of the Prayer Book. By the REV. DYSON HAGUE, M.A. Cloth . . . . . . reduced to 1s 6d, or post free For popular reading the best book of its kind.	1	10
A Guide to Ecclesiastical Law, for Churchwardens and Parishioners. Compiled by HENRY MILLER. With Plates illustrating the Vestments, &c. Fifth edition . . . . . . 1s, or post free	1	2½
The Church Intelligencer, the Organ of the Church Association, published monthly, price 1d; Annual Subscription . . . free by post	1	6
Historical Grounds of the Lambeth Judgment. By J. T. TOMLINSON. Sixth edition . . . . 6d, or post free	0	7½
The "Legal History" of Canon Stubbs. By J. T. TOMLINSON 6d, or post free	0	8
The Great Parliamentary Debate in 1548 on the Lord's Supper. By J. T. TOMLINSON . . . . . 6d, or post free	0	7
The Secret Work of the Ritualists. A Startling Exposure 2d, or post free	0	2½
Prayers for the Dead. By the REV. DR. WRIGHT 2d, or post free	0	2½
The Greek Church. Her Doctrines and Principles contrasted with those of the Church of England. Is Union desirable or possible? A Lecture by the REV. JOSEPH BARDSLEY, D.D. . . . 2d, or post free	0	2½
"The Liturgy and the Eastward Position." Illustrated by fifteen of the oldest known representations of the Lord's Supper. By J. T. TOMLINSON . . . . 2d, or post free	0	2½
Union with Oriental Churches. By the REV. H. E. FOX, M.A. post free	0	1
The Reunion Question as it regards Protestant Churches. By the REV. TALBOT A. L. GREAVES . . . . . post free	0	1
The Use of the term "Priest" in the Prayer Book 2d per doz., post free	0	2½
The Modern Confessional. (*Illustrated.*) 2d per doz., post free	0	2½
Modern "Mass" in the Church of England. (*Illustrated*) 2d per doz., post free	0	2½
"Making Plain for all Time," a Pamphlet of 48 pp. post free	0	7
Society of the Holy Cross, with List of Members up to 1897 . . . . 10d per doz., or post free	1	0

CHURCH ASSOCIATION, 14, BUCKINGHAM STREET, STRAND, LONDON.

www.ingramcontent.com/pod-product-compliance
Lightning Source LLC
Chambersburg PA
CBHW020526300426
44111CB00008B/561